For Peace and Justice

For Peace and Justice

PACIFISM IN AMERICA
1914–1941

By Charles Chatfield

KNOXVILLE : THE UNIVERSITY OF TENNESSEE PRESS

LIBRARY OF CONGRESS CATALOG CARD NO. 70–142143
INTERNATIONAL STANDARD BOOK NO. 0–87049–126–1

FOR MY FATHER AND MOTHER
AND MARY

Preface

This book is about the ideas that lifted pacifists into the political struggles of the past half-century, often to fly against the currents of their time. It is also about the roles they played among the many wings of the modern movement for peace and justice.

Who were the pacifists and what was their role in forming American opinion on foreign affairs and in channeling it into policy? They have been characterized both as isolationists and as internationalists; they are believed to be the most obdurate of all peace advocates, men who not only want peace but will not fight. They are said to be dominated by religious or secular ideologies and to stand isolated at the far left of the peace movement. Pacifists attract a public following only at the level of avoiding specific war commitments, it is said; they are essentially irrelevant, and therefore they need not be taken seriously.

There is some truth in each aspect of this image. Some pacifists were dogmatic and obdurate, all of them took an extreme position on warfare, and the public has mostly identified with them on issues rather than on principles. Ultimately, however, the stereotype fails to account for the cooperation and leadership of pacifists in the general peace movement, the controversy and changes within pacifist thought, and the significance of pacifist dissent for the development of foreign policy. These elements constitute the substance of this study.

Quite apart from the objective merits of their cause, I have been deeply touched by the impulses which have motivated many pacifists. Their devotion, which is matched by that of numerous militant patriots, cannot be expressed by abstract words such as *religious, idealistic,* or *altruistic.* The mood of selfless dedication of some pacifist leaders and the personal involvement of others had much to do with the development of their programs and rationale, but the relationship of mood and movement is virtually indefinable. I have pleaded for or criticized pacifists only as far as it seemed necessary in order to clarify their story. I would be both unappreciative and unhistorical, however, if I failed to mention the force of their personalities.

This is a controversial subject, of course. It is treated as a development requiring analysis and description rather than personal commitment, on the assumption that pacifism has historical importance apart from its propositional truth. Much remains to be known, and doubtless much can be explained in other ways. There is no more exacting and exciting discipline than the study of real men and women struggling to know themselves and their world. It is the central drama for many historians because it is prior to the dramatic narrative of men dealing with themselves and one another; but it is prior only in a logical sense, surely, for knowing and being are the warp and woof of human life.

CHARLES CHATFIELD

Springfield, Ohio
January, 1971

viii

Contents

Illustrations

Abbreviations

A.F.C.	America First Committee
A.F.S.C.	American Friends Service Committee
A.U.A.M.	American Union Against Militarism
C.A.I.P.	Catholic Association for International Peace
CARE	Cooperation for American Relief Everywhere
C.M.E.	Committee on Militarism in Education
C.N.V.A.	Committee of Nonviolent Action
C.O.	Conscientious Objector
CORE	Congress of Racial Equality
C.P.S.	Civilian Public Service
E.P.C.	Emergency Peace Campaign
FDR	Franklin Delano Roosevelt (papers)
F.O.R.	Fellowship of Reconciliation
I.C.D.	Interorganization Council on Disarmament
I.F.O.R.	International Fellowship of Reconciliation
I.L.O.	International Labor Organization
K.A.O.W.C.	Keep America Out of War Congress
N.C.P.W.	National Council for Prevention of War
N.P.C.	National Peace Conference
N.S.B.R.O.	National Service Board for Religious Objectors
NYPL	New York Public Library
SANE	Committee for a SANE Nuclear Policy
SCPC	Swarthmore College Peace Collection
S.P.A.	Socialist Party of America
W.I.L.P.F.	Women's International League for Peace and Freedom
W.P.S.	Women's Peace Society
W.P.U.	Women's Peace Union
W.R.L.	War Resisters League
Y.M.C.A.	Young Men's Christian Association
Y.P.S.L.	Young People's Socialist League
Y.W.C.A.	Young Women's Christian Association

For Peace and Justice

"Toppling the Idol"

Adapted from Nelson Harding's 1927 Pulitzer prize-winning cartoon, which first appeared in the Brooklyn *Eagle*.

Introduction

Toward the end of July, 1936, a lanky American, fifty-one years of age, strolled along the left bank of the Seine. He felt relaxed. A summer spent in Europe had dissipated much of the tension he had accumulated in years of feverish labor work, organizing unions and directing strikes. He and his wife had come to Paris as tourists.

He walked away from the river a few blocks and paused before the strangely eclectic Church of St. Sulpice. Its construction had spanned centuries, and successive architects had erected a classical facade beneath tall neo-Gothic towers. Through Grecian-like columns the visitor entered a church reminiscent of the Middle Ages. The American might have found the setting appropriate. He had been ordained into the Presbyterian ministry as a young man. Increasingly disturbed by the conservatism of the church, however, he finally rejected it, became a thorough-going Marxist, and devoted himself to the Trotskyist cause. He came to St. Sulpice fittingly, for this mixture of the medieval and the classical, of reverence and reason, itself had been dedicated to a revolution in 1793 and renamed the Temple of Victory.

The building was cluttered with statues, he noticed. Repairs were being made, and scaffolding partially obscured the front of the church. Nevertheless, the visitor sat on a rude bench and looked at the altar and cross. His mind resolved the confusing elements of the interior into a coherent impression. He felt a sensation of peacefulness, as something inside of him seemed to say, " 'This is where you belong, in the church not outside it.' "[1] He was immediately sure that upon his return to the United States he would break with Trotskyism and rejoin the church. With quickened steps he left St. Sulpice, which in 1802 also had been returned to the uses of Christian worship.

As A. J. Muste reflected upon his Paris experience he was prone to interpret it mystically, as he viewed several previous events in his

3

life. He acknowledged also, however, that on his summer tour he had become disillusioned with radicalism. His practical labor work in America had been frustrated by factional bickering over theoretical questions. He had found violent reactionism, or its portent, everywhere in Europe; and all that radicals seemed to offer in reply was more violence. The hope of revolution was all but extinguished, he noted. Great Socialist parties in Germany and Austria had been stilled by fascists. Russian Communists had created a nationalistic dictatorship. Physical respite freed Muste's mind for reflection. Behind a jerry-built scaffolding of Marxist dogmas he found again his essentially religious social concern. When he returned to America and to the church he did not abandon radicalism, but he reevaluated its strategies. Whatever happened to A. J. Muste in St. Sulpice, his recollection is a dramatic symbol of the dilemmas faced by pacifists in the movement for peace and justice from World War I to Vietnam.

The word *pacifist* changed under the pressure for patriotic conformity in 1917–18. Having had the benign connotation of one advocating international cooperation for peace, it was narrowed malevolently to mean one who would not support even a "war to end war." Pacifists —newspapers virtually snarled their opprobrium—were linked with draft dodgers, Socialists, and Communists, portrayed in hues from yellow to red; and in the lobby of 70 Fifth Avenue, where some of their groups were housed, was rudely inscribed the taunt, "Treason's Twilight Zone."[2] The very word was henceforth plagued with double meaning, and more than one prowar peace advocate hastened to explain that "those who are now called 'pacifists' here do not include all or most of those who were called 'pacifists' before the war."[3] Later, when it was respectable to be against war, the word was broadened again; but it would be used by pacifists themselves as it is used here: to designate those who not only worked for peace but also refused to sanction any given war.* The narrower definition masked a new dimension in the American peace movement, as it developed a wing which combined vigorous social action with absolute rejection of violence.

Pacifism has become important in American life since that time,

* There is a still narrower definition also used by pacifists which includes only those opposed to all war. This is the basis for legal recognition of conscientious objection in the United States, too, and there is considerable merit in its usage. The definition used in this book includes absolute and religious and also selective and political objectors to war at any given time. This definition is philosophically untidy, but it is historically useful since the impact and significance of pacifism varied with its changing constituency, and since pacifists of all persuasions responded to the same historical events.

4

although its influence is hard to delineate, partly because when it has been most widespread it has extended beyond those who absolutely abjure war to those who are encouraged to apply transnational political and religious criteria to the conduct of foreign affairs. Pacifists have exerted specific historical influence, however, on church history, the Socialist Party, the struggle for economic justice, civil rights and black history, and especially on the organized peace lobby and American foreign policy. They were part of a world peace movement in which Americans played an ever more active role. At the same time, experiences shared by most Americans—two world wars, the rise and modification of the social impulse in religion, the depression, the labor and socialist movements, the apprehension of fascism and communism, the drive for racial equality, and the cold war—these things have modified the character of pacifism in the United States. Because it was a movement organized to influence public policy, it was affected by public problems. For this reason the story of pacifism in the past half-century is an integral part of the history of American life and thought.

Pacifists developed organizations with staffs, journals, thousands of members, and factional disputes. They tried to interpret domestic and international affairs from a realistic as well as a moral standpoint. They were forced to take positions on foreign policy, and they developed techniques by which they mobilized public opinion in support of those policies so that they deliberately broadened the political basis of decision-making. Fundamentally internationalists and involved as they were in virtually every effort to stave off war, liberal pacifists supported and often led agencies to coordinate peace work. They lobbied against every evidence of militarism: compulsory military training, arms increases and the munitions interests, strident nationalism, alliances, and nuclear weapons. They tried to create an antiwar public which would be committed to internationalism but convinced that war was futile and that the United States should stand aside from power struggles in Europe and Asia and from the economic exploitation of Latin America. They were especially active in the churches, one after another of which renounced the religious sanction of war and recognized conscientious objection first as an ethical option for Christians and recently as a valid ethical position for anyone.

Pacifists have continually reevaluated their own doctrines and modified them. If in the cases of class and racial struggle and in world and limited wars they have felt compelled to draw arbitrary lines beyond which they would not sanction the use of force, if like A. J. Muste they have sought some coherent impression against which to measure the limits of struggle, then they have groped toward a philosophy of non-violent action. The measure of their development is the extent to which they have departed from the religious nonresistance and traditional peace programs from which modern pacifism emerged.

There had been pacifism in the strict sense of the word before World War I, of course, but it was identified with a religious point of view. There was no substantial body of secular pacifism in America before the twentieth century.[4] The peace societies of the early nineteenth century drew their support from Christian people and their officers largely from the clergy. Not all of these men were absolute pacifists in the sense that they refused to fight, but the outstanding pacifists were Christians. Their thought was represented by the three so-called historic peace churches—the Friends (Quaker), Brethren, and Mennonite.

These groups were larger than other pacifist sects, such as Seventh-day Adventists and the Jehovah's Witnesses. They had longer histories, they persistently had sought exemption from military service for their nonresistant members, and they furnished most of the conscientious objectors in the Civil War and both world wars. Although they were by no means the only or the most absolute objectors to the First World War, they received practically official recognition for their similar doctrinal and historic positions.

With few exceptions, such as reforming Quakers of the first half of the nineteenth century, these people were not disposed to question governmental authority or social polity except as it applied to them in the specific case of military service. They were instead, and Mennonites still make the distinction, *nonresistants* obedient to religious injunctions against killing or complying with the military. The historic peace churches differed with regard to the source of religious authority, the relationship of individual and social ethics, and the importance of social service, but they agreed on their opposition to fighting.

The duty of a nonresistant was sharply defined: The Bible records that Jesus forbade revenge or resistance; that he commanded that evil should not be returned for evil, but that the sword should be put up; and that he taught his disciples to love and pray for their enemies. Beneath its words the scripture breathes the hope that men will be at peace with one another. Theological distinctions fade in the face of such demands put squarely upon the individual. If participation in carnal warfare is a test of allegiance between Christ and the world, and if the promises of the New Testament are taken as seriously as its injunctions, then duty seems plain; one must submit to but not participate in the violence of this world.

6

Put this way, nonresistants were left with the apparent choice of either compromising on the principle of opposition to war or refusing to have anything to do with the worldly state, and so they developed a dualism which allowed different standards of ethical action to redeemed individuals and to the imperfect state. The nation must and will fight wars; true Christians should neither willfully offend nor violently resist force. This dual system of values, one for the Christian community and another for the state, persisted in nonresistant ranks into the twentieth century. It left innumerable nonresistants in mental anguish over where to draw the line at cooperation with the government. It resulted in part from assigning the causes of war to imperfections in the human spirit so that unredeemed men were bound to use means prohibited to Christians. It resulted in part, too, from emphasizing strict obedience to God's will whether revealed scripturally or directly.

An emphasis on obedience would characterize twentieth-century pacifism, not only that of the traditional peace churches, but of other denominations as well. It would be evident in the admonitions of Protestant pacifists after the First World War and in the statements of conscientious objectors to World War II and the Vietnamese action. Devere Allen, himself a prominent pacifist, would write in 1930 that "no Christian pacifist of to-day need flatter himself that he has contributed any substantial originality to the religious case for peace. The special responsibility of Christians for the abolition of war, because of Jesus' teaching, was recognized by all pioneer spokesmen of the cause."[5] Perhaps Allen's contemporaries would quote scripture less than their forefathers, but most of them would continue to urge obedience to the spirit and word of the New Testament.

There was in the nonresistant heritage another element related to obedience to God's law—service to man. It was largely this emphasis on loving service that kept the Quaker's doctrine of direct and continuing revelation from becoming unbridled mysticism. Ultimately, it provided the transition from nonresistance to modern pacifism.

Stressing loving service and human brotherhood led early English Quakers, such as Robert Barclay and William Penn, to appreciate the fact that every facet of life is related to the problem of peace. In America eighteenth-century teacher and author Anthony Benezet opposed both war and slavery. His kind of loving service was the basis of Quaker humanitarianism which embraced so many reforms in his century and the next. Slavery and prisons, alcoholism and pauperism, education and war—these and other areas fell under the merciful purview of Friends. Benezet insisted that slavery abused not only the gospel of

7

Christ and rational justice, but his most human feelings as well; that was to say, it violated the will of God as revealed in his Bible, his mind, and his intuition. Benezet was only one of many Quakers who were repelled by social injustice, sensitive to its relation to violence and war, and convinced that evil could be overcome by love.

However, the religious humanitarians thought in nineteenth-century terms. They were concerned mainly with specific cases of suffering or injustice, and gave little thought to changing the social order, except perhaps in the case of slavery. By the end of the nineteenth century they generally had a complacent faith in progress. Quakers belonged largely to the upper middle class. They were often disconnected from American social problems. Their social spirit had been "chilled and nipped by the early frost of theological controversy and disastrous separations."[6] Their pacifism was often nominal and passive, and with few exceptions, they merged into the broad peace movement of the progressive era.

If sectarian pacifists eschewed social reform before the First World War, few reformers stressed the war question, and even fewer seriously considered conscientious objection to war service. Indeed, the prewar advocates of peace, conservative and progressive alike, hardly sensed the possibility of divided loyalties. They assumed that war was anachronistic, a remnant of the social jungle out of which civilization was evolving. They neglected economic and social causes of warfare, perhaps partly because they assumed that differences of whatever origin could be composed amicably. Reason, embodied in arbitration, and law embodied in treaties and international juridical institutions, such as the Permanent Court of International Justice at The Hague, together would obviate recourse to war. In this respect peace advocates were internationalists, and so they liked to think of themselves. But with few exceptions they were nationalists as well, for they accepted America's virtues as unique and her interests as paramount. If the nation ever should go to war, therefore, its democratic politics and humanitarian traditions would guarantee its cause to be just and necessary. In short, confidence that reason and good will increasingly characterized American life was the counterpart to the faith that they would be ever more important in international relations. Peace advocates found reasons for confidence in the decade before 1914 as their societies acquired unprecedented strength and reputation.

The leaders of these organizations were, for the most part, directors also of established business and educational corporations; or they accepted such men as models. They gave to their peace movement a literary, patriarchal, and elitist quality. They relied on education and discussion rather than political action. They valued their acceptability in the circles of power and believed that it gave them influence. Edwin Ginn, Andrew Carnegie, Nicholas Murray Butler, and even the more liberal David Starr Jordan were established men.* As a matter of course they valued order and distrusted radical challenge to authority. They were successful men, and as a matter of course they aimed at the further perfection of their society. They were confident men, and with others of their generation they tended to assume that the grapes of wrath were withering away.

Violence did not wither. It fermented until it produced the First World War and contradicted the doctrine of social evolution, at least as applied to Europe. In its early months the war was commonly regarded as something shocking but alien and irrelevant; however, it challenged American idealism even as it threatened American neutrality. Far from being a relic of European barbarism, fighting slowly embroiled the United States. American intellectuals were forced to relate the war to their assumption of ethical progress. The established peace movement faltered and fell into disarray, with some of its older figures grief stricken by the war—Andrew Carnegie and Benjamin Trueblood before their deaths in 1916, and the author and lecturer Edwin D. Mead. By April, 1917, most of its leaders had joined the war effort, determined to establish a universal peace along American lines.

Their shift was illustrated by that of the American Peace Society, formed in 1828 by William Ladd. After decades of hesitation, it had come to stand against all war. Benjamin Trueblood, its intrepid secretary since 1892, resigned in 1913 because of ill health; but he edited the *Advocate of Peace* until the spring of 1915. He died the following year. For a few months more his successor, Arthur Deerin Call, held that the "supreme fact of the Christian ethic was then, and ought to be now, that Jesus Christ was a pacifist," a man opposed to the use of force anywhere. When Congress determined on war, however, the American Peace Society seemed to equate *pacifist* with *patriot.* It held that the

---

* Edwin Ginn, a Boston publisher, established the World Peace Foundation; Andrew Carnegie, steel magnate and philanthropist, founded the Carnegie Endowment for International Peace and the Church Peace Union; Nicholas Murray Butler, president of Columbia University, was also head of the Carnegie Endowment. David S. Patterson has calculated that of thirty-nine of the most active prewar peace advocates, thirty-three had college degrees and twenty-six of these had higher degrees in law, religion, and education; those without college education included Carnegie and Lucia Ames Mead, an authority on international law. Patterson, "The Travail of the American Peace Movement, 1887–1914" (Ph.D. dissertation, University of California, Berkeley, 1968).

world had passed beyond any reconciliation except by force of arms. Its paper declared:

> We must help in the bayoneting of a normally decent German soldier in order to free him from a tyranny which he at present accepts as his chosen form of government. We must aid in the starvation and emaciation of a German baby in order that he, or at least his more sturdy little playmate, may grow up to inherit a different sort of government from that for which his father died.[8]

This change of emphasis was representative of the old-line peace movement which almost unanimously hastened to support the new crusade.

Of all the older societies, the Carnegie Endowment for International Peace was most important, since to a considerable extent its grants financed the others (the American Peace Society itself received from the Endowment 70 per cent of its total receipts for the year ending June 30, 1917). Almost from the outset the Carnegie Endowment favored the Allies in their struggle. Upon the American declaration of war, its trustees issued a unanimous resolution that "the most effectual means of promoting a durable international peace is to prosecute the war against the Imperial German Government to a final victory for democracy . . . ."[9] The organization turned over its offices in Washington to the official propaganda arm of the government, the Creel Committee on Public Information, and it headed its own stationery in red ink, "Peace through Victory."[10]

Similarly, the Church Peace Union, endowed by Andrew Carnegie in 1914, supported the official war policy of the government and promoted a league of nations to ensure a just peace. The American School Peace League even changed its name to the American School Citizenship League. The fact-finding World Peace Foundation was rendered ineffective even before American intervention, despite the fact that it had been handsomely endowed in 1910 by Edward Ginn, a Boston publisher who died in 1914. It was run by Edwin D. Mead and was, for a time, outspoken against armament propaganda. After 1914, however, the organization was racked by a conflict between its prowar trustee, President A. Lawrence Lowell of Harvard, and its chief antiwar speaker, Chancellor David Starr Jordan of Stanford. Jordan withdrew from his position as director, but the World Peace Foundation ceased to be a vigorous peace society.

The League to Enforce Peace, founded in Philadelphia, June 17, 1915, seemed by its very title admirably suited to prosecute peace by warfare. The idea of the league was advanced by A. Lawrence Lowell and Hamilton Holt, a New York publicist and editor of the *Indepen-*

dent, among others. The organization sponsored meetings and published literature in order to generate public support for a postwar international association. Presidents William Howard Taft and Woodrow Wilson approved of a League of Nations, which became, in fact, an American war aim. The League to Enforce Peace officially sponsored campaigns for both "peace and preparedness." By holding that peace was thwarted by militant Germany, it was able to reconcile thousands of peace advocates to what Jane Addams, the founder of Hull House, called the "pathetic belief in the regenerative results of war."[11] Accustomed to look for evil on the surface, not in the heart of man, many leaders of the established peace movement identified it with one nation, Germany. Peace was held at bay by Prussianism, they said; victory became the prerequisite of progress.

PART ONE

World War I and Peace

"Building the Nest"

An adaptation of W. J. Enright's *Harper's Weekly* cover for September 18, 1915.

 I

Peace as an Organizing Principle

Large numbers of people . . . vaguely thought of themselves before 1914 as pacifists. "Peace societies" existed in considerable profusion. As a matter of fact, however, the contemporary religious pacifist *movement* consciously and deeply committed to renunciation of all organized violence and to a way of life that taketh away the occasion of all wars, . . . came into being during the last war and the years immediately following.

—A. J. MUSTE[1]

The wartime pacifists were those few individuals with the temerity to reject the war effort and advance alternatives to fighting. They helped to reorganize the American peace movement, giving it much of the structure, leadership, social concern, and assumptions that would characterize it for a generation and ultimately would lead to the so-called new pacifism of the sixties. Where it had been educational and legalistic, the peace movement also became aggressive; where it had been conservatively Brahmin, it also acquired a socialistic base; where it had assumed progress, it would claim only possibility. The movement remained divided—perpetually it seems—between competing points of view and programs, but it acquired vital leadership and broad social concern from the pacifist wing that was first articulated in World War I.

Between 1914 and 1917 the old peace societies were largely supplanted by new ones that embodied a coalition which reconstituted the peace movement: action-oriented peace advocates, feminists, social workers, publicists, and social-gospel clergymen. It was essentially a progressive coalition, to which antiwar Socialists were added. It grew at the same time that national alternatives in foreign policy narrowed to war itself, however, and so it was sifted of those who for one reason or another fell into the line of national march.

15

Even before the established peace societies were converted to pro-war idealism they were supplanted by a new peace coalition of able progressives who viewed the European war as a threat to the values they had fought uphill to implement. It must not come to America, they agreed; and more, its very existence in Europe challenged the open-ended world in which these problem-solvers felt at home. *This war* was no abstraction. It was a compelling social problem, they insisted, and it required concerted social action to solve. This was the response of the man who personified cosmopolitanism to thousands of college students—Louis Lochner.* "I am surprised and amazed at the conservatism of many who profess to stand for peace but are afraid to show their colors when a crisis like the present breaks out," he wrote late in 1914; and he called for a newly "vigorous, prophetic, constructive" peace movement.[2] Lochner's destined vocation was journalism, but for the duration he lent his energetic mind to the task he had defined. Shortly after the outbreak of war he quit the American Peace Society; tried to refashion the Chicago Peace Society; and with Jane Addams and others, launched a National Peace Federation in December. It was one of a series of new organizations designed to federate liberal and peace forces.

Fanny Garrison Villard, the dynamic daughter of William Lloyd Garrison, wife of Henry Villard, and mother of Oswald Garrison Villard, voiced a sharper dissent than Lochner's. This heir of Garrisonian nonresistance had been a member of existing peace societies for many years, and at a meeting in New York, September 21, 1914, she charged,

> They are weak and ineffectual because they compromise. They assert in one breath that war is wrong and wicked, and then with perfect equanimity and amazing inconsistency they say that a recourse to war is sometimes justifiable . . . . The fear of being called peace-at-any-price men makes cowards of them all.[3]

American women should found a new and aggressive peace organization, she urged.

The day after this speech, Lillian Wald and Jane Addams, founders of Henry Street Settlement House in New York and Hull House in Chicago, respectively, called upon twenty-six reformers to consider to-

---

* Lochner, with George Nasmyth and the help of the American Peace Society, had organized the Cosmopolitan Club movement. The organizations in which he played a leading role included besides the Cosmopolitan Club: The Ford Peace Expedition (which he managed, Nov.–Dec., 1915), the First American Conference for Democracy and the Terms of Peace (May 30–31, 1917), and the People's Council of America for Peace and Democracy (June, 1917). He was also active in other peace movements of the period.

16

gether how they might respond to the war. Less than half of those originally invited continued to be active in antiwar work, but they were joined by other social workers and clergymen, educators, and publicists who were conscious of a bond of social concern formed in response to industrialism and urbanism. Their little gatherings involved many of the same people who had met before at Henry Street House to fight child labor or to forge the Industrial Relations Commission: social workers Mary Simkhovitch and Florence Kelley, for example, editors Paul Kellogg of the *Survey* and Oswald Garrison Villard of the *Evening Post* and the *Nation*, and clergymen John Haynes Holmes and Rabbi Stephen Wise.* From the meetings which continued for more than two years there and at other centers of social reform emerged the new peace movement which Mrs. Villard and Louis Lochner envisioned.

Late in 1914, Emmeline Pethic-Lawrence, English feminist and peace advocate, and Rosika Schwimmer, Hungarian feminist and journalist, visited the United States and met women's groups across the land.† The two Europeans pressed the Americans to organize at least a small group which would discuss reasonable peace terms, promulgate a conference of neutrals, and "protest against war as a method of settling international difficulties."[4] Largely in response to their tour and at the request of their fellow suffragette Carrie Chapman Catt, Jane Addams called a convention of representatives of women's groups for January 10, 1915. When from these origins the Woman's Peace Party was formed it was clear that peace advocacy "provided a common ground

---

* Mary Simkhovitch was vice president of the National Federation of Settlements and a lecturer at the New York School of Social Work; Florence Kelley was a pioneer in efforts for federal regulation of child labor and with Miss Wald had written the bill that became law in 1912; John Haynes Holmes, pastor of the Church of the Messiah, New York, had presided over the Unitarian Fellowship for Social Justice, 1908–11; and Rabbi Wise valued his post at the Free Synagog of New York for the opportunity it gave him to defend labor and Negro minorities.

† Emmeline Pethic-Lawrence, author of *My Part in a Changing World*, was the wife of an equally famous feminist, Frederick William Pethic-Lawrence, who was the joint editor of *Votes for Women* and subsequently a member of Parliament and a secretary of state for India and Burma (1945–47). Rosika Schwimmer was the Hungarian delegate to the International Conference of Women at The Hague in 1915 and a moving force in the crusade for a Conference of Neutral Nations for Mediation. She subsequently was appointed Hungarian minister to Switzerland in 1918, but she fled after the government of Count Mihály Károlyi fell; she came to the United States in 1921. In 1927 she applied for citizenship and was denied it because she refused to swear that she would bear arms in defense of the country. The famous case was upheld by the Supreme Court decision of May 27, 1929, Justice Oliver Wendell Holmes and Associate Justices Louis D. Brandeis and Edward T. Sanford dissenting.

upon which could meet American women from almost every section of their organizational life."[5]

The first point in the platform of the new society was "the immediate calling of a convention of neutral nations in the interest of early peace."[6] Madame Schwimmer had presented to President Wilson a petition urging him to call a conference of neutrals, and Miss Julia G. Wales, instructor in English at the University of Wisconsin, had drawn up a detailed plan for "continuous mediation" by an international commission of experts with "scientific but not diplomatic functions," who would make proposals for peace terms. American women joined hands with their counterparts in Europe late in February when they agreed to send a delegation to an International Congress of Women at The Hague, April 28 to May 1. Jane Addams, as a prominent neutral citizen and chairman of the Woman's Peace Party, was asked to preside. The Hague congress organized a Women's International Committee for Permanent Peace, with headquarters at Amsterdam. To neutral and belligerent leaders it sent emissaries with its resolutions, particularly its plan for a conference of neutral nations continuously standing ready to clarify war aims and to negotiate a peace. Jane Addams and Alice Hamilton accompanied three European women to the principal war capitals, while Emily Greene Balch, the first head of Boston's Denison House Settlement and a professor of economics and sociology at Wellesley College, visited major neutral countries with two Europeans.* Cordially received by statesmen everywhere, the women became increasingly convinced that neutral mediation was feasible if the United States would seize or accept leadership, and they tried to induce President Wilson to adopt their program.

Wilson seemed unresponsive, so the women turned to their plan for a mediation commission of private citizens as an alternative to government action. Madame Schwimmer, together with Louis Lochner, made an important convert to the idea when she won the support of Henry Ford. With characteristic enthusiasm, Ford promised substantial funds to the Women's International Committee, chartered the ocean liner *Oscar II* to carry an American peace delegation abroad, tried in vain to sell the project to President Wilson, and then called upon the nation to "get the boys out of the trenches by Christmas." Christmas was only

---

* Alice Hamilton was special investigator of dangerous trades for the U.S. Department of Labor. The European women were Arletta Jacobs of Holland, Rosa Genoni of Italy (until she returned to her country when it entered the war), Frau van Walfften Palthe of The Hague, Chrystal Macmillan of Britain, Rosika Schwimmer of Hungary, and Madame Ramondt-Hirschmann of Holland.

a month away when Ford coined that slogan and, consequently, arrangements were made hastily. The affair became increasingly promotional. The press ridiculed it, and numerous distinguished peace advocates declined to embark.

A wave of derision in the wake of the peace ship obscured the significance of a new nongovernmental organization, the Neutral Conference for Continuous Mediation, which was organized at Stockholm on January 26, 1916. Henry Ford even promised it some $10,000 a month. Its workers prepared formal studies in an effort to reconcile the various national points of view; and as an international commission it began to gain prestige, especially after President Wilson circulated his peace note of December 18, 1916, to the belligerents. Hope was short lived, for after Germany resumed unrestricted submarine warfare in February, Ford announced that he would withdraw his financial support of the commission. Mediation, whether private or official, became an increasingly empty dream.[7] Nonetheless, in their campaign the women peace advocates had forged links with civic and professional groups that would survive the war in the form of the American branch of the Women's International League for Peace and Freedom (W.I.L.P.F.). They had brought new blood into the peace movement, too, and had created a modern pressure group of a kind familiar to progressive reformers.

Earlier in the month that Ford booked passage for the women peace advocates, the peace movement acquired a prophetic note and another constituency from religious pacifists. Newspapers carried lists of Americans killed in the submarine sinking of the *Ancona* as cn November 11–12, 1915, sixty-eight men and women considered together the implications of the injunction, "love your enemies."[8] Theodore Roosevelt was demanding an army of a quarter of a million men and a navy second only to Britain's as those earnest people gathered at Garden City, Long Island, to resolve their dual obligations to their violent world and to their pacific ideals. Their Fellowship of Reconciliation, like the Woman's Peace Party, was initiated largely in response to the visit of a European pacifist.

Henry T. Hodgkin, an English Quaker, had made many American friends as a member of the Edinburgh Continuation Committee, the Student Christian Movement, and the Committee of the World Alliance of the Churches Promoting International Friendship.* He was the

---

* Hodgkin belonged to a distinguished Quaker family and had been educated at King's College, Cambridge. He was traveling secretary for the Student Christian Movement for three years before going to China in 1905 under the Friends Foreign Mission Association. There he helped to found West China

chairman of the British Fellowship of Reconciliation (F.O.R.), an organization of persons dedicated to the Christian principle of love, which, they believed, prohibited participation in war. The British F.O.R. joined in the relief work of the Friends among war refugees and civilians in France and Belgium and among enemy aliens stranded in England and Germany. It published books stressing international good will, and its members met in small groups for fellowship. In America, Hodgkin, and later Richard Roberts and Leyton Richards, two clergymen who also were leaders in the British F.O.R., found many people who were troubled by the conflict between "the principles of Christianity and war and by the contrast between Christian ideals and many aspects of our present social order."[9] Through invitations issued to about 130 Americans active in service and religious organizations, Hodgkin proposed a conference to consider the principles of the British Fellowship of Reconciliation, and how they might be expressed in the United States.

The Fellowship's ideals were presented at Garden City. They were positive and constructive, it was emphasized, not negative and critical. After six long discussions of the complex wartime implications of Christian love, Frederick Lynch, secretary of the Carnegie-endowed Church Peace Union, concluded that he "never wanted to hear the term 'the simple gospel' again."[10] As involved as they recognized the problems were, and as fraught with contradictions, over forty of those present were willing to sign the set of F.O.R. principles, including a promise not to sanction war in any form. They also authorized a committee to proceed with the organization of an American Fellowship of Reconciliation, and elected as the first chairman Gilbert A. Beaver, the son of a Pennsylvania governor and a Y.M.C.A. worker in South America and, subsequently, in this country. Edward W. Evans, a Quaker lawyer from Philadelphia, and Charles J. Rhoades, a banker and the son of the founder of Bryn Mawr College, were elected secretary and treasurer, respectively. The new society was guided by a Fellowship Committee which opened an office in New York City, a modest beginning for the central organization of religious pacifists for over half a century.

The formation of the Fellowship was an integral part of the restructuring of the peace movement to include a broader and more progressive constituency. Its early members were drawn especially from social-gospel clergymen, Quakers, and Y.M.C.A. leaders (including not only Gilbert Beaver but also David Porter, Fletcher Brockman, Charles

---

Union University; he returned to England as secretary of the Association in 1910 and, in 1914, was clerk to the London Society of Friends.

D. Hurrey, and John R. Mott).* It was not intended to be a highly organized or action-oriented group.[11] War would force the central organization to become more active, however, and would elicit a social philosophy that linked it to the Woman's Peace Party, the American Union Against Militarism (A.U.A.M.), and the other societies which supplanted the prewar peace establishment. At the same time, the Fellowship brought absolute pacifism, the total rejection of war, from its sectarian origins into the new peace movement. Henceforth, pacifists would constitute an important and well-organized wing of peace advocates.

The new antiwar coalition coalesced around the issue of preparedness and culminated in the American Union Against Militarism. From the beginning, the Woman's Peace Party had come out for: "Limitation of armaments and the nationalization of their manufacture," and "organized opposition to militarism in our own country."[12] Various groups and individuals within the Peace Party viewed with apprehension the mounting public clamor for a greater army and navy. They equated an arms build-up with militarism and war itself. Most active in this regard was the New York City branch of the Peace Party, led by Crystal Eastman. A graduate of Vassar College, she took a law degree at Columbia University, became a recognized authority on the legal aspects of industrial accidents, and managed the state women's suffrage campaign in Wisconsin. Her personal vitality stimulated each major organization of the progressive peace coalition in turn, and during the war she edited with her brother, Max, the irascible *Liberator*. At the outset of the defense controversy she urged the Woman's Peace Party to formulate a more definite program.

Antipreparedness became the chief theme of the annual conventions in January, 1916, and December, 1917. Discouraged in their efforts to mediate the European war, the women pacifists opposed the arming of America. They fought increased military appropriations and war profits.

They requested a joint committee of Congress to investigate the con-

---

* David Porter was on the National Council of the Y.M.C.A. from 1907–34, and then went into education; Fletcher Brockman was general secretary of the National Committee of Y.M.C.A. Associations of China, 1901–15, and the associate general secretary of the International Committee; Charles Hurrey became a secretary of the International Committee in 1900 and was a traveling secretary to South America in 1908; John R. Mott was student secretary for the International Committee from 1888–1915, general secretary from 1915–31, and was chairman of the executive committee of the Student Volunteer Movement from 1888–1920.

ditions of national defense. Some of them testified before congressional committees. Their Peace Party circularized pamphlets opposing arms increases and military training in public schools. Its New York branch protested a giant Preparedness Day parade of 100,000 soldiers and civilians in May, 1916, by placing opposite the reviewing stand a banner inscribed,

> There are only 100,000 of you.
> You are not the only patriots.
> 200,000 farmers, 500,000 mine workers and
> organized labor of America are opposed to
> what you and Wall St. are marching for.
> Are you sure you are right?[13]

By then antiwar patriots had another spokesman.

In the same November that pacifists founded the Fellowship of Reconciliation and Henry Ford financed a peace pilgrimage, the meetings at Henry Street House were formalized into an Anti-Preparedness Committee. The name was not precise, as its chairman, Lillian Wald, quickly pointed out. The committee included absolute nonresistants, some who advocated defensive war, and others between these extremes. Miss Wald herself was somewhat in the middle. She did not object to military defense as such; but she was against war and afraid of militarism, distressed to think that war would stifle social reform. The nation would be stampeded into conflict, she warned; absolute controls would supplant democracy; and as a belligerent, America would lose the initiative in peacemaking. Her fears were shared by the other members of the committee—distinguished social workers and thinkers such as Crystal Eastman, Paul Kellogg, Jane Addams, Frederic C. Howe, Alice Lewisohn, L. Hollingsworth Wood, Charles Hallinan, Louis Lochner, and James P. Warbasse.* As Oswald Garrison Villard wrote tersely,

> militarism withholds vast sums from the amelioration of the lot of the poor, the ill, the suffering, the wronged, the oppressed, and I am for bitter and harsh words about it now and always; I am for turning upon those who counsel that we shall plot to murder other nations and peo-

* Howe was a journalist, former Ohio state senator, municipal reformer, and Wilson's Commissioner of Immigration; Wood was a lawyer who was treasurer of both the F.O.R. and the A.U.A.M., and first chairman of the National Civil Liberties Bureau; Hallinan left woman suffrage work to do publicity work for the A.U.A.M.; Warbasse was a surgeon active in socialist and cooperative societies whose wife was a founder of the New School of Social Research and was active in the Woman's Peace Party; Alice Lewisohn helped launch the A.U.A.M. with a check for $1,000 in Nov., 1915. Other early and active officers included Hamilton Holt, editor of the *Independent*, and Amos Pinchot, a liberal lawyer and publicist.

22

ples either for offense or defense as true traitors to the spirit of the nation.[14]

Because many people agreed with Villard in 1915–16, the Anti-Preparedness Committee increased in a year from about 15 to 1,500 members, published and distributed about 600,000 pieces of literature, and spent $35,000. As it changed from a small committee into a broad organization, it was rechristened the American Union Against Militarism.[15]

The American Union changed its name and organization in response to the increased activity of preparedness forces. It circularized civic groups, unions, and Granges. It compiled a mailing list of everyone known to be remotely interested in peace. Its lobbyists in Washington worked closely with Congressman Claude Kitchen, Senator George Norris, and others; indeed, Senator William E. Borah later called it the "brains" of the peace movement.[16] Its greatest effort came in April, 1916, when it accepted a challenge made by Woodrow Wilson. Advocating greater preparedness at a rally in St. Louis earlier in 1916, the President had said that those people who differed with him should rent halls and take their case to the people. In reply, the American Union sponsored a mass meeting at Carnegie Hall on April 6. There, from a podium shared by representatives of social workers, labor, the National Grange, the Protestant and Jewish communities, and a Texas congressman, Lillian Wald satirized the current fears of German invasion as unreasoning and illusive, and attacked the preparedness forces. Militarism, the absolutism of military necessity, was invading the nation under the "seemingly reasonable term of 'preparedness,' " she declared. The only absolute pacifist speaking was John Haynes Holmes, and for the sake of argument he agreed with the others that "peace at any price is damnable." But, he queried, "what about the doctrine that is . . . security at any price?"[17]

From New York the American Union team traveled to Chicago, Kansas City, Pittsburgh, Cincinnati, St. Louis, Des Moines, Minneapolis, and Detroit, where it drew generally large audiences. In each city its rally was preceded by a papier-mâché replica of a stupendous armored dinosaur—"Preparedness." Walter G. Fuller, pacifist creator of the beast, explained that dinosaurs,

> all armor-plate and no brains, had no more intelligent way of living than that of "adequate preparedness." All their difficulties were to be met by piling on more and more armor, until at last they sank by their own clumsy weight into the marsh lands, such as one would expect to find at low tide at Oyster Bay.

He went on to say, "It is also considered likely that the dinosaur had no funny bone."[18]

Foreign policy was, after all, no laughing matter that election year. President Wilson was caught in the crosscurrents of European war strategies and embroiled in Mexican politics. In March he sent General John J. Pershing and a punitive expedition of 15,000 men in pursuit of a roving band of Mexicans under Francisco Villa which had killed Americans, apparently in retaliation for the recognition of Venustiano Carranza as president. Mexican and American troops clashed south of the border on June 21. Passions ran high. War seemed imminent. The tension broke suddenly when the American Union Against Militarism arranged for major city newspapers to print a first-hand account of the incident by Captain Lewis S. Morey which documented American responsibility for it. At the same time the peace group convened a joint commission of Mexican and American citizens to explore ways of reconciling national interests.* "The Carrizal episode does not constitute a just cause of war," the American Union insisted, and its advertisements triggered an outpouring of public opinion so great and so spontaneous that Wilson was moved to make overtures of conciliation.[19] President Carranza responded diplomatically. Negotiations took the place of threats, and war was averted. The American Union had some reason to believe that "the people acting directly . . . can stop all wars," and peace advocates had renewed confidence in their President.[20]

Throughout the year they supported Wilson with alternate reluctance or enthusiasm as he seemed to act against or speak for their principles. Sometimes it seemed even to Jane Addams, one of the President's most steadfast supporters, that he was "imprisoned in his own specious intellectuality, and had forgotten the overwhelming value of the deed."[21] His Mexican policy had provoked the peace advocates, but his decision to shelve the controversy won their applause. His naval program encountered their determined resistance, but by August, when preparedness was secured in Congress, his reelection campaign was generating peace and progressive sentiment. Peace leaders generally supported the

---

* The A.U.A.M. persuaded David Starr Jordan to chair the commission and authorized its expenses, including transportation, accommodations, and the salary of a stenographer. It met first in El Paso, Texas, but moved to Washington, D.C. American members besides Jordan included Moorfield Storey, a Boston jurist, and Paul Kellogg. Crystal Eastman, secretary of the A.U.A.M., served as secretary of the commission. Lincoln Steffens kept the White House in touch with the unofficial commission, which served as a transition to a Joint High Commission that met from Sept. 6, 1916, through Jan. 15, 1917.

24

President in the fall election. They believed that he shared their values from his different point of view. They trusted their influence with his administration. Disheartened by American occupation of the Dominican Republic in November, they were still elated by Wilson's message to Congress on January 22. Even after he broke diplomatic relations with Germany the next month, the American Union and the Woman's Peace Party cherished the hope that they might influence the President. They urged him to refuse passports to American travelers in the war zone and to call a conference of neutrals, but all to no avail. Walter Fuller's whimsical dinosaur was put in storage when the nation mobilized and went to war, and the last laugh belonged to no one.

In 1917 three events shook the progressive peace coalition and sifted it of all but wartime pacifists: the United States broke diplomatic relations with Germany on February 3; it declared war on April 6; and the first wave of oppressive conformism crested about September 1. In each case outstanding leaders resigned and the ranks of the movement were reformed. Some of those who accepted the war effort gave up peace work. Others gravitated to the older societies and the League to Enforce Peace, or founded the new Foreign Policy Association (1918). The constituency of the societies formed during the European phase of the war increasingly narrowed to the pacifists who created new, short-lived groups as they cast about for public support.

Attrition began when the President severed relations with Germany. Within a week it was reported that "there were no live elements" left in the Boston Anti-Imperialist League and some other peace groups.[22] Most of the executive committee members of the American Neutral Conference Committee resigned, leaving it in the hands of its two young founders, Rebecca Shelley and Lella Faye Secor.* More dramatic was the sudden resignation of one of the American Union's most ardent

---

* Rebecca Shelly (she later spelled it Shelley) was the daughter of a minister, took her B.A. in German language at the University of Michigan in 1910, and taught school in Michigan, Washington, and Illinois. An ardent suffragist, she was converted to peace work by Rosika Schwimmer and Louis Lochner in the winter of 1914–15 and went on the Ford Peace Expedition. Lella Faye Secor also was a native of Michigan who emigrated to Washington. There she made a career in newspaper work and through it became involved in the juvenile court, better babies, and woman's suffrage movements. She represented the *Post-Intelligencer* of Seattle on the peace pilgrimage. In the American Neutral Conference Committee they promoted the Neutral Conference for Continuous Mediation with the support of Oswald Villard, the active help of Emily Balch, and the sponsorship of distinguished progressives who wanted to keep the Woman's Peace Party Plan before the public.

25

spokesmen, Rabbi Stephen Wise, after a torturous council meeting. Emily Balch, Paul Kellogg, and others were stunned; but for three months they waged a determined holding action against intervention, censorship, and conscription.

Organizational lines were in flux that spring. The meager American Neutral Conference Committee was transformed into an Emergency Peace Federation which tapped a reservoir of antiwar sentiment when it placed a full page appeal for help in the New York *Times* and netted $35,000 in contributions.[23] Pacifists worked through several organizations, each with its own circle of supporters. Vivacious Crystal Eastman seemed to be everywhere, conferring with the ladies in the Woman's Peace Party, plying wealthy sponsors of the American Union for funds, inspiring the coterie of cultural radicals drawn to her brother's the *Masses*—antiwar artists John Sloan and Art Young and writers Floyd Dell and Randolph Bourne. Her resourceful husband, Walter Fuller, devised a postal card referendum which the American Union financed. One hundred thousand people in five congressional districts received circulars from their own congressmen, and they voted overwhelmingly against going to war and for submitting intervention to a plebiscite. Meanwhile, Louis Lochner joined Charles Hallinan in Washington, D.C., to lobby against conscription and censorship bills. Sensing that "the situation was increasingly critical," pacifists from several groups hastened to get appointments with the President. On February 28, Woodrow Wilson listened to them politely, even sympathetically, but his reply implied that America's destiny lay with intervention.[24]

There was nowhere to turn but to the people, and time was running out. The American Union expanded its staff, bringing Roger N. Baldwin from St. Louis where he had been secretary of the Civic League (Baldwin shortly would organize a wartime pacifist-socialist coalition and the National Civil Liberties Bureau from the ranks of the American Union). With the Emergency Peace Federation it sponsored an unofficial commission of experts in international affairs to explore alternatives to war, and it filled Madison Square Garden with war protesters. William Jennings Bryan added his voice to the cause, and Robert La Follette delivered what historian Merle Curti has called "one of the greatest speeches ever heard in a crisis in Washington."[25] David Starr Jordan was brought from the West Coast to chair the commission of experts; he rallied antiwar sentiment at one meeting after another, but he was conscious of a public mood running against him and carrying many peace advocates with it. On Palm Sunday he escaped from a large mob which broke through a police cordon and burst into the Academy of Music in Baltimore, where he was speaking. "It seems to me that exactly the same thing is going on here as in Germany in 1914," he wrote Bryan that day. "The fair weather pacifists make the same excuses for sliding into the abyss, and the faithful stand out without flinching as they did in Germany."[26] The next day he was addressing a large audience in Washington when he was handed news of Wilson's message to Congress requesting a declaration of war, which he read aloud. Knowing that the struggle to avoid war was lost, Jordan continued his efforts until Congress had actually resolved the issue four days later, on Good Friday.

Whereas Wilson feared world disaster from German victory, Jordan feared the demoralization of the United States, democracy's chief refuge. But when his nation had been committed he wrote, "There was now nothing to do but accept the situation and turn all our efforts to winning the war with the least possible sacrifice of the principles of democracy." Hoping that the President might glimpse prospects for peace denied to him, Jordan concluded a statement to the San Francisco *Bulletin* by asserting, *"Our Country is now at war and the only way out is forward."*[27] Peace workers like David Starr Jordan fell back on a second line of defense, the protection of individual freedom under the Constitution. As even that guarantee gave way to wartime hysteria, they retreated to a third line to employ the war as an instrument of freedom and justice.

Hoping to tap the idealism of these prowar advocates, pacifists created the People's Council of America for Peace and Democracy to advance civil liberties and democratic peace terms during the war. In April and May a few individuals (notably Roger Baldwin, Louis Lochner, and Emily Balch) developed the nucleus of an organization. They incorporated the remnant of the Emergency Peace Federation under Rebecca Shelley and Lella Secor, and they attracted antiwar Socialists such as Joseph Cannon and Morris Hillquit.* The council was formally launched at a huge Madison Square Garden rally on May 30–31. Even

---

* Joseph Cannon was a union organizer for the International Mine, Mill and Smelters' Union. Morris Hillquit had immigrated to the United States from Russia as a young man and rose to become international secretary of the Socialist Party and a popular candidate for mayor of New York in 1917. Although Socialists were prominent in the organizing committee, as of June 13 the staff was pacifist: Lochner was executive secretary, Miss Shelley was financial secretary, Miss Secor was organizing secretary, and Miss Elizabeth Freeman (a militant suffragist born in England and reared in America) was legislative secretary.

then it was something of a front organization: its organizers formed local councils and affiliated labor groups in an effort to build a popular farm-labor coalition that would supplant the pacifist-Socialist leadership. By August it claimed just under two million constituents, based on the membership of its affiliates.[28] Large meetings were held in New York, Chicago, Los Angeles, and elsewhere as the council prepared for a grand Constituent Assembly on September 1.

Clearly, the People's Council was associated with international socialism on war issues, but otherwise its program was familiar enough. Throughout the summer it campaigned for a quick peace on liberal terms, civil liberties, and repeal of conscription. It arranged a meeting in Washington with legislators who were interested in those programs. It participated in a New York conference to coordinate scattered legal efforts on behalf of conscientious objectors. Its economic demands were no more radical than maintaining fair-labor standards, curbing the high cost of living, and taxing war profits.[29] Its September 1 assembly was planned carefully to appeal to a broad spectrum of liberal thought. Nonetheless, it was billed as radical and subversive by fervent patriots and conservative labor leaders who disrupted meetings that summer and thwarted plans to hold the Constituent Assembly in Minneapolis.

Lochner, who was in the Middle West to make final arrangements, looked desperately for another meeting site as a special train bearing delegates rolled westward from New York. He tried to arrange for the use of a hall in Hudson, Wisconsin, among other cities, but was marched to the train station by a mob. The "Peace Special" pulled into Chicago on Friday night, the delegates still uncertain of their destination until Mayor William Thompson gave them his official protection. About two hundred delegates gathered in Chicago's West Side Auditorium the next morning, but they were interrupted by police taking directions from the governor. That night the pacifists met covertly in private residences, and even when the mayor reasserted his authority and encouraged them to meet again on Sunday, they concluded their business hastily in order to forestall intervention by national guard troops which the governor had sent from Springfield. "Not in any of the three speeches was one word said against the administration," a delegate reflected bitterly, "and yet we were being treated like criminals."[30] In view of such public and official opposition, the council did not seem useful even to some of those who had initiated the new peace coalition—Lillian Wald and Paul Kellogg, for example.

The American Union Against Militarism had been increasingly split

28

during the summer of 1917 by the efforts of Roger Baldwin, Norman Thomas, Crystal Eastman, and others to commit it to the cause of conscientious objectors. At no time was its membership entirely pacifist in the strict sense. Lillian Wald and Paul Kellogg feared that close association with peace-at-any-price war objectors, however desirable for the cause of civil liberties, would render the organization unacceptable to internationalists who felt compelled to support the war. They sensed, too, that the People's Council had a public image of "impulsive radicalism and [did] not represent the organized reflective thought of those opposed to war" characteristic of the American Union. Affiliation with the People's Council would preclude influencing nonpacifist liberals, as even Crystal Eastman had hoped to do.[31]

On August 20, in Miss Wald's absence, the executive board of the American Union voted to send delegates to the People's Council Assembly. She resigned, along with several others, despite a valiant attempt by Miss Eastman to hold the group together.[32] On October 1 the National Civil Liberties Bureau was formally separated from the society that had nourished it. It was agreed, moreover, that members of the executive board should not hold office in either the Civil Liberties Bureau or the People's Council (although some of them continued to be active in those groups). Indeed, the organization was renamed the American Union for a Democratic Peace. The way seemed open for "reflective" pacifists to cooperate with nonpacifist liberals, but the vision was illusory. In November, Crystal Eastman had a "long and thoughtful" talk with Walter Weyl, who was representative of the progressives on the staff of the *New Republic*. She concluded that pacifists simply could "not find a common ground on which to work with the pro-war liberals."[33] Thereafter the American Union was largely a paper organization. It had a nominal existence owing mainly to the efforts of Charles Hallinan and Oswald Garrison Villard. Hallinan still cherished the illusion that the society could become respectable, and he proposed that it sponsor an ambulance for France (he could imagine people saying, " 'Well, that's decent of them' ").[34] His proposal was spurned, whether from a sense of dignity or of futility it is not clear. Liberal pacifists during the war found more meaningful their affiliation with several other groups that were to last over half a century: the National Civil Liberties Bureau (subsequently the American Civil Liberties Union); the Woman's Peace Party (subsequently the American Branch of the Woman's International League for Peace and Freedom); the American Friends Service Committee ([A.F.S.C.] founded in 1917 to

29

provide humanitarian alternatives to fighting); and the Fellowship of Reconciliation. These groups absorbed the pacifist remnant of the progressive peace coalition.

> We are patriots who love our country and desire to serve her and those ideals for which she has stood . . . but we cannot believe that participation in war is the true way of service to America or to humanity. Nor can we persuade ourselves that it is right to do evil that good may come. To us war especially in its modern form is not so much a sacred call to give one's self as it is a stern necessity to do all in one's power to kill others . . . .
>
> —THE FELLOWSHIP OF RECONCILIATION[35]

The typical leader of the organizations formed between 1914 and 1917 had matured early in the progressive era; hardly one was under thirty when America entered the war. He was college educated and probably had a professional degree. He was a social worker, clergyman, educator, or publicist. He probably was a Protestant (although he might have been Jewish), and if he belonged to a peace church it was the most liberal, the Quaker one. He had been active in causes, particularly woman's suffrage (and, indeed, the pacifist might well have been a woman). He was action oriented and open minded. He was sympathetic to the kind of socialism typified by the Intercollegiate Socialist Society or the Christian socialist movement. He was joined by literary radicals who identified the war with the old cultural order and by anti-war socialists.[36]

As the war developed, the pacifist leader was joined, too, by a number of younger pacifists who, in the long run, were most important of all since they virtually staffed the pacifist movement after 1919: among others, A. J. Muste, active radical who became chairman of the Fellowship of Reconciliation and "Mr. Pacifist" to a cold war generation; John Nevin Sayre, never far from the center of the International Fellowship of Reconciliation and its American branch; Evan Thomas, outstanding conscientious objector of World War I and chairman of the War Resisters League (W.R.L.) during the Second World War; Kirby Page, the most influential pacifist speaker and writer of the interwar period; Ray Newton, organizer of farm and labor sentiment for the

30

Friends Service Committee; Frederick Libby, Florence Brewer Boeckel, and Dorothy Detzer, who wielded an influential peace lobby in Washington; Devere Allen, chief advocate of war resistance in the Socialist Party; and the leader of that party, Norman Thomas.

These pacifists had not been active in peace groups much before 1917, and they thought through the war question by themselves. They had not been active in domestic reforms, but were, indeed, just discovering social problems—some through college experiences, some through church work, and others in the fresh idealism of the Y.M.C.A., then promoting international concern through the Student Volunteer Movement. In short, the young pacifists encountered World War I when they were coming of age, just as progressives of a previous generation had awakened to social problems when they were choosing personal directions. It is hardly surprising that many of those whose pacifism commenced in the war years made peace work a vocation.

There were liberal pacifists of various hues, then, and their language and experiences differed significantly. The very corollary of conscience is, in the apt phrase of Rufus Jones, "a final farewell to uniformity," so that any analysis is hazardous.[37] Yet, to a striking extent, pacifists held certain similar values and premises. What they had in common that set them apart from war supporters was neither a covert conspiracy nor any discernible personality or social characteristics; they shared, rather, a distinctive view of the war and a disposition to elevate that view into a matter of principle.

They acknowledged that war calls upon men to sacrifice themselves for principles such as democracy, justice, nationality, and peace. Therein lay the idealism and virtue of the Great War, as liberal patriots insisted. Therein lay also its test. The criterion by which Norman Thomas, for example, judged the peace settlement was a moral principle: that "the central law of all wholesome life is reciprocity, mutuality," and that this law "follows from the social nature of man."[33] Man has the whole world as his social environment, Thomas continued, so a moral peace must remove barriers to world-wide human fellowship. The war aims stated by Wilson and Lloyd George in January, 1918, must be extended to apply that moral law. Open diplomacy should be followed by "an intelligent democracy"; neutralization of the seas should become coordination of waterways; removal of economic barriers should be followed by a free exchange of commodities and of thought, art, and knowledge; disarmament should be accompanied by the removal of nationalistic barriers to good will; national self-determination ought to involve the negation of imperialism; and the League of Nations should

31

become the parliament of the world. Thomas was hopeful for a brief time in 1918 because the war aims enunciated by Wilson seemed to be founded "upon the ultimate moral ground of things." To that extent he agreed with those who supported the war effort that men are responsible to society and to abstract principles.

Pacifists pushed the argument a step further, however, and inquired into the ultimate standards of social and philosophical values. Their ideals were couched in a bewildering variety of expressions and were applied as criteria of even national policy. Indeed, their notions about what is good were assumed so thoroughly that they became "axioms of . . . emotional nature," as Max Eastman put it.[39] Judgments about foreign affairs became intensely personal in the light of liberal values of the progressive era such as the pragmatic approach to choices, the democratic process, and the ultimate worth of the individual.

The leaders of the Fellowship of Reconciliation put their idea of human value in religious terms, agreeing with Norman Thomas that war is "absolutely opposed to Christ's way of love and His reverence for personality."[40] Although they did not often define personality they seemed to refer to a man's total being and latent possibility. They rejected the notion of prowar clergymen that fighting or even death could leave men undefiled, could even ennoble them. War immolates personalities, they said. It treats all men as objects. It kills some and regiments the rest; it thwarts their altruistic capacities even as it demands sacrifice; it teaches them to risk death in order to kill. In the oldest tradition of their faith, pacifists revolted "not only against the cruelty and barbarity of war, but even more against the reversal of human relationships which war implied."[41]

The doctrines of Love, Fatherhood, and Brotherhood and symbols like the Cross expressed the normative value of personality for pacifists. Even Jesus came to life in this respect: he "was a man and he gave us some very true and excellent ideals and principles of life," wrote Evan Thomas during an agonizing reappraisal of religion, ". . . more than that I don't care about."[42] Love, "as revealed and interpreted in the life, teachings and death of Jesus Christ," was the motif according to which Christian pacifists wanted to fashion their lives and society.[43] It was the theme of their theology. The justice, righteousness, and mercy of God, the crucifixion and resurrection of Jesus were aspects of absolute love. It was the standard of their ethics from which they derived their emphasis on the virtues of suffering for others, abjuring of violence, respecting personality, and seeking justice. Christians and humanists alike agreed

32

on the supremacy of love, although the official statements of the Fellowship of Reconciliation had a religious and New Testament bias.

Members of the Fellowship interpreted the kingdom of God as human society ordered by love. They understood the kingdom to be a realistic possibility for future society and, more important, a standard for present social living. They were convinced that Christianity is a way of life for the present rather than merely an ideal for the future. The kingdom symbolized to them a religious duty to live in "confidence in the power of Love progressively wrought out in human society . . . ."[44] Holding this doctrine, they concluded that it was not enough to avoid evil; they must seek to overcome it in the world. They avoided a dual standard of values, religious and social, such as nonresistants traditionally had held. They sought to propagate the City of God among men. Their sight was not upon the city, however, as much as upon their immediate duty to it. The Cross of Jesus was an important image throughout their literature precisely because it seemed to sanction sacrifice for the kingdom, suffering for others, universal love, and nonviolence.

If human personality was sacred to religious pacifists, it had nearly absolute value for some who stood on secular grounds as well—Roger Baldwin, for example, director of the National Civil Liberties Bureau. On trial for refusing to take the physical examination required in the draft, Baldwin said, "The compelling motive for refusing to comply with the Draft Act is my uncompromising opposition to the principle of conscription of life by the state for any purpose whatever, in time of war or peace."[45] At the same time, he felt an intense social concern. As Norman Thomas explained shortly after the war, the individual is a "product of the group, but the group is only valuable as it permits personalities, not automatons, to emerge."[46] Pacifists, unlike Spencerian individualists, supported social reform. But then, unlike those whose individualism derived from natural law, they believed that every man is of intrinsic value. Some of them reconciled individualism and socialism, for example, by assuming that man is essentially a social animal and that an individual's personality is most fully realized in altruistic impulses. In any case, they insisted that society should be judged in regard to whether it permits the full development of its members. The theme of the supreme worth of the individual permeated the publications of the Fellowship and writings of pacifists from Addams to Villard. For some it was in itself sufficient reason to refuse military service; for all it guaranteed the right of conscientious objection.

A closely related value was the democratic process of majority deci-

33

sion with its corollary of individual dissent. It was perhaps more obviously threatened than individual worth, and like abolitionists before them the pacifists won support on civil rights which they could not get on other issues. The American Union Against Militarism had come into being largely in the fear that war would undermine the political and social gains of a decade.[47] Its programs and techniques expressed the progressive faith in the power of public opinion and in government responsible to the people. Woodrow Wilson expressed the same political faith even as he pressed for policies that distressed the pacifists. Even in February, 1917, most members of the American Union's executive board preferred to leave foreign policy in his hands. Emily Balch disagreed; she mistrusted the executive in comparison with Congress, and thought it a bad precedent to give the President broad discretion.[48] Increasing numbers of pacifists shared her apprehensions as the administration geared up for war, although Crystal Eastman wrote in June of the President's wartime appointments,

> It [is] as though he said to his old friends, the liberals, "I know you are disappointed in me—you don't understand my conversion to the draft —my demand for censorship. I have reasons, plans, intentions, that I can't tell you. But as guarantee of good faith I give you Baker and Keppell and Lippmann and Creel, to carry out these laws. No matter how they look on paper, they cannot be Prussian in effect with such men to administer them."[49]

The guarantee was not sufficient. The National Civil Liberties Bureau and related organizations expanded their work rapidly, insisting that the civil rights of conscientious objectors to the war were linked to the democratic process itself; majority decision which rested on the suppression of minorities would be a thinly veiled tyranny. This exactly was the premise of those who wanted to keep the Civil Liberties Bureau within the American Union in the fall of 1917. It was within the scope of "any organization *against* militarism," wrote Edmund C. Evans, a Philadelphia architect on the executive committee. Norman Thomas added that no other national group was prepared to fight for "tolerance of minority ideas" which, he said, "is absolutely necessary for reasonable social progress."[50] Even those pacifists who wanted to separate the bureau from its parent organization valued its work, differing rather over the priorities of progressive goals in wartime and the tactics of maintaining a broadly liberal peace movement.

Pacifists in the People's Council of America who supported the Russian Revolution regarded it as a vindication of the democratic process, not the Bolshevik party or even, on the whole, Marxist economics. As

34

Max Eastman wrote, "what makes us rub our eyes at Russia . . . is the way *our own theories* are proving true."[51] Their vision of a progressive society foundered on the shoals of wartime conspiracy, however; and in the backwash of the September 1 assembly in Chicago, one delegate mused, "we knew how it must have felt to live in Russia during the old regime."[52] The metaphor was all the more poignant because liberal pacifists had admired also the Russian peace planks. They had demanded that a new diplomacy embody a "Democratic Foreign Policy" which should include freedom of press, petition, and speech, a progressive tax on war profits, and a "referendum on questions of war and peace."[53]

However impractical a referendum on war might appear (it proved no more plausible in 1917 than it would twenty years later as the Ludlow Amendment), most liberal pacifists were responsive to the pervasive currents of pragmatism. Norman Thomas heeded them at Union Theological Seminary, Randolph Bourne at Columbia University, Kirby Page at Drake University and at the University of Chicago—but, in fact, pragmatism was construed to support opposing positions on the war. John Dewey and the liberals aligned with the *New Republic* argued that since war prevailed, the intelligent thing to do was to participate so as to be present at that "plastic juncture" when history is being made—the peace settlement. Yet Randolph Bourne called this approach a rationalization of intellectual default; it was a sanction, not an application of pragmatism, he insisted. The tendency to judge things in terms of results typified all liberals; Bourne was atypical only because he was pessimistic about the consequences of national war.[54] Even liberal religious pacifists justified themselves on pragmatic as well as moral grounds: Kirby Page, working out his position while helping German prisoners of war in England, argued that war had to be judged as a social "method," and his friend Evan Thomas wrote that "on purely sociological grounds I would oppose the war."[55] Like Page and Thomas, a number of the professional pacifists of the interwar years had been impressed in college by the developing field of sociology and the prospect of "discovering concrete ways of getting [ideals] incarnated in actual institutions."[56] Their disposition to value pragmatic criteria in decision-making set liberal pacifists apart from sectarian and even Garrisonian nonresistants of the past, and lent special force to their distinctive analysis of the war.

Liberal pacifists concluded that World War I was a product of the European state system and that American national interests were best served by staying out. They identified its causes in European rivalries, in long-standing "misunderstanding, suspicion, fear, diplomatic and commercial struggle to which all nations contributed."[57] All the elements of later "revisionist" writing on the war question can be found in the antiwar literature of 1917–18. Pacifists and socialists alike stressed the role of commercial competition, imperialism, secret treaties, and war profits. Behind their rhetoric was a growing recognition of the power of nationalism with its psychological extensions of fear and pride which went beyond a strictly economic explanation and which enabled pacifists to distribute responsibility for the war among all the nations embroiled in it. Thus, young Devere Allen, a senior at Oberlin College, argued that there was no righteous side in the war. All nations shared the blame for its outbreak and the injustice and deceit which characterized the conflict. America could not rightfully fight for the freedom of the seas from German submarines when she had willfully allowed Britain to abrogate that freedom. In a struggle to uphold humanity and democracy the nation would have to give tacit consent to the Allies' illegal food blockade of Germany, their violation of Greek neutrality, and the desecration of Poland by Russia. In fighting German tyranny the United States would help preserve "the despotic internal politics of all the allied nations . . . ." Allen concluded: "In short, we fight against evil that is disagreeably successful, we strive to overthrow one sinner by the side of another sinner, of like kind, but of lesser degree . . . ."[58] Jane Addams, Kirby Page, and others found that their reports of Allied atrocities were resented by the public, which accepted a devil theory of warfare.

Pacifists shared a distinctive neutralism both because they distinguished between the mean motives of all warring governments and the high idealism of all the peoples that fought (as did Woodrow Wilson) and because they blamed all the belligerents for the war. They could not support an idealistic war on behalf of the Allies. Everything they knew of the war's origin pointed to a strictly European conflict with which the United States had no business. Private business, to be sure—war trade and finance—but neither national security nor American ideals were entrenched on one side or the other of no man's land.

In this regard pacifists were not intentionally isolationist. They consciously identified with Karl Liebknecht, Romain Rolland, and Bertrand Russell—with men and women in all belligerent nations who shared what John Haynes Holmes called an "international mind." Nicholas Murray Butler, president of Columbia University and of the Carnegie Endowment, had used that phrase in 1912, but he meant then

36

(and would mean thirty years later) no more than people's interest in foreign affairs.[59] Butler dreamed of an *international* world, but the wartime pacifists responded to a *trans*national allegiance. They recognized that there were in the world intense struggles for human dignity and decency, for peace itself, but they found these issues *within* each nation at war. Inside America, as well as in Austria, there was a struggle against economic privilege. Within Britain, as within Germany, imperialism was an issue. In Russia, as in Austria, autocracy was at bay. In France, as in Germany, public opinion was manipulated by the military elite. International war seemed to obscure the truly vital struggles of mankind. Holmes and Liebknecht, Rolland and Russell were neutral "not only in a political sense, but in an ethical and spiritual sense as well." They all refused to believe that, as Holmes wrote, "the present war involves any fundamental questions of liberty and civilization. Or, if such questions be involved to any appreciable degree, . . . [these men failed] to see that one side or the other in the conflict has any exclusive possession of the hopes and ideals of the human race."[60]

This transnational humanism characterized pacifists of every hue, from Walter Rauschenbusch to Eugene V. Debs, from Emily Balch to Morris Hillquit. It was the organizing principle of the Fellowship of Reconciliation and the Friends Service Committee. It was implied in the St. Louis resolution of the Socialist Party that American intervention was "a crime against the people of the United States and against the nations of the world."[61] The war seemed irrelevant because, in short, it seemed artificial. It did not concern the human needs with which pacifists identified, whether phrased religiously or socialistically. That is why Max Eastman found it "uninteresting for all its gore," and Bertrand Russell wrote, "It was trivial, for all its vastness."[62]

Their interpretation of the war gained the force of moral commitment from the values pacifists held. It set them apart from prowar internationalists (just as it would set them apart from isolationists after the war). In fact, the very ability to "honestly differ from the convictions and enthusiasms of one's best friends did in moments of crisis come to depend upon the categorical belief that a man's primary allegiance is to his vision of the truth and that he is under obligation to affirm it."[63]

But it was a desperate crisis. The war became an interior event for each pacifist. One after another described the anguish of being isolated in the midst of war idealism. Ministers felt the snapping of ties that had bound them to affectionate congregations. Social workers and reformers discovered how dependent on public approval they had become when they were denied it. The memory of suddenly being alienated from their fellow citizens remained painfully sharp for years, as Jane Addams found when she reflected,

> The pacifist, during the period of the war . . . was sick at heart from causes which to him were hidden and impossible to analyze. He was at times devoured by a veritable dissatisfaction with life. Was he thus bearing his share of blood-guiltiness, the morbid sense of contradiction and inexplicable suicide which modern war implies? We certainly had none of the internal contentment of the doctrinaire, the ineffable solace of the self-righteous which was imputed to us. No one knew better than we how feeble and futile we were against the impregnable weight of public opinion, the appalling imperviousness, the coagulation of motives, the universal confusion of a world at war.[64]

Perhaps worst of all was the haunting fear of actually becoming fanatical, of preferring theoretical consistency to recognition of real social situations, the apprehension of becoming what they were reputed to be.

Miss Addams could remember pacifists who traveled "from the mire of self-pity straight to the barren hills of self-righteousness" and hated themselves equally in both places. She recalled the temptation of that path herself. The position of the pacifist was "so devilish unhuman," as Evan Thomas put it when writing his brother from the army barracks at Fort Riley, Kansas, where he had been interred as a conscientious objector. He watched the soldiers, feeling the idealism that informed their ranks. "There is something about all this that gets me hard and I long with all my heart to be part of the crowd as I never have in civil life," he wrote.

> The comradeship one must give up, the being part of the fun and hardship of all this, yes of fighting and maybe dying along with the rest of your fellows on both sides in this huge tragedy makes my stand seem so terribly aloof, so terribly unhuman . . . . I will see it through only I no longer feel like criticizing even the Y.M.C.A. Their stand is human . . . and I'm not sure that we two have always understood the terrible pressure of this game.[65]

Pacifists mitigated this stress through their activity for war relief and civil rights and their common association in the Fellowship.

The Fellowship, alone in the progressive peace coalition, had not been formed to accomplish specific programs. It had been born of the increasing isolation felt by those who sought to apply Christianity totally, even to war, and its members were expected to "work out personally, and in their own way, the principles of the Fellowship."[66] Jane Addams joined a group of pacifists in Chicago. "We usually met in private houses on a social basis, as it were," she explained, "not so much because we felt that a meeting discussing the teachings of Jesus could be considered 'seditious,' but from the desire to protect from publicity and unfriendly discussion the last refuge that was left us."[67] Jessie Wallace Hughan, socialist and pacifist, wrote to Norman Thomas in 1917 that she wished the Fellowship of Reconciliation would sponsor some more conferences. "I feel the need of them these days," she said. "Don't you?"[68] Membership in the F.O.R. helped to sustain numerous pacifists during the war, to make their affirmation less lonely.

The society's emphasis on personal conscience implied that the initiative for peace action should come from individuals or local groups, rather than national officers. In many cases it did. Before and during the war local groups held discussion meetings and conferences, sent delegations to Washington to lobby on behalf of conscientious objectors unaffiliated with peace sects, and aided objectors. Members were in key posts in all pacifist groups. The F.O.R. would have formed a sort of interlocking directorate of pacifism, except that it did not formulate overall policy. War forced the central organization to become more active, although it did not change the basic principles of the Fellowship. "We are no mere anti-war society," the Fellowship's executive committee wrote,

> but a fellowship of those who by the method of love, seek the triumph of justice and the establishment of a social order based upon the will of God revealed in Christ Jesus . . . . Our great task is preparation for a worthy peace. This by no means implies that we shall keep silence on this war. Never more than now must we testify to our own conviction that the method of war is a grim and ghastly contradiction of those high ends for which our country has entered the conflict . . . . This war, then, is both the text and the occasion to preach the gospel of the way of love . . . .[69]

The society became more centralized as it used the war as "both the text and the occasion to preach" pacifism. It helped direct the efforts of local groups on behalf of conscientious objectors, contributed to the Friends' relief work, and early in 1919 joined the National Civil Liberties Bureau in urging members to protest the sedition law then being considered in the Senate. Annual conferences brought the active members of the F.O.R. together during the war. As many as 200 people gathered near New York City to consider the broad ideals of the organization and the future of religion in relation to education, economics, race relations, and the organization of peace work. They found a sense of comradeship and purpose in one another's company.

The single action most significant in uniting the Fellowship members probably was the founding in January, 1918, of the *World Tomorrow*, a high-quality magazine of the religious radical left. Although the society did not accept financial responsibility, all but one of the editorial board during the war were Fellowship members, and the first managing editor was Norman Thomas.[70] In September, 1918, the Post Office Department declared the magazine nonmailable under the Espionage Act because it contained a parable against hate by John Haynes Holmes, an article by Norman Thomas calling on President Wilson to stay American intervention in Russia, and a piece by Frederick Libby alleging that the Kaiser and Theodore Roosevelt worshipped the same God. The *World Tomorrow* was delivered only after the President had talked with John Nevin Sayre, an Episcopal minister who was already prominent in the F.O.R. and whose brother, Francis B. Sayre, was Wilson's son-in-law. The magazine was withheld briefly from the mail on two other occasions during the war.[71]

After World War I the journal urged pacifism in international, industrial, and interracial relations. It denounced the Treaty of Versailles but supported the League of Nations. It urged the United States not to intervene in Russia, Mexico, Nicaragua, and China. It supported disarmament but was skeptical of achieving peace by "mathematical ratios" of military power. Essentially, the *World Tomorrow* wrestled with the seeds of war in the social order. By the time it was discontinued for want of money in August, 1934, and its mailing lists were taken over by the *Christian Century*, it had become a weekly with a circulation of at least 16,000; and some topical numbers were distributed to 40,000 or more readers. Among its editors were Norman Thomas, John Nevin Sayre, Devere Allen, Anna Rochester, Reinhold Niebuhr, and Kirby Page.* The semiofficial spokesman of the Fellowship of Reconciliation, it became the "leading journal of liberal Christianity and Christian-motivated political radicalism."[72]

Thus, the Fellowship, like other new peace groups of the war years, acquired organization not only because it grounded isolated pacifists in a common faith but also because their notion of peace required exposition and realization. Through the *World Tomorrow*, a number of pamphlets, and letters from its guiding committee, the Fellowship of Reconciliation explored its motivating convictions during the war.

---

* Anna Rochester was a radical writer who eventually moved into the Communist orbit; Reinhold Niebuhr was a pastor in Detroit, Michigan, who became a prominent pacifist spokesman (until the mid-thirties) and a renowned theologian and professor of applied Christianity at Union Theological Seminary.

40

These ideas were not systematized, nor did they reflect the thinking of the total membership. But they formed a rationale which was expressed by many articulate pacifists who suddenly were faced with war. The interior event of each was the problem of all, and they explored together the religious ethic with which every pacifist wrestled alone. The vows they exchanged and the bonds they made would form the program and organization of postwar pacifism. A half-century later, John Nevin Sayre would sit before the firelight, almost alone of that "community of saints" whose measure he had first taken in common opposition to the First World War. His mind clear but far away, he would recall the long path traced by that "beloved fellowship" through which pacifists had endured.

II

War as an Interior Event

> The world's an orphans' home. Shall
> we never have peace without sorrow?
> without pleas of the dying for
>   help that won't come? O
> quiet form upon the dust, I cannot
> look and yet I must. If these great patient
>   dyings—all these agonies
>   and woundbearings and bloodshed—
>   can teach us how to live, these
>   dyings were not wasted.
>
> Hate-hardened heart, O heart of iron,
>   iron is iron till it is rust.
> There never was a war that was
>   not inward; I must
> fight till I have conquered in myself what
> causes war, but I would not believe it.
>   I inwardly did nothing.
>   O Iscariotlike crime!
>   Beauty is everlasting
>   and dust is for a time.
>
> —MARIANNE MOORE, "In Distrust of Merits"[1]

Many pacifists did more than endure isolation. The leaders whose pacifism matured between 1914 and 1919 were, "as a man . . . awakened out of sleep," suddenly alive to the "moral confusion and disorder that lie concealed in a civilization heavily weighted with materialistic aims."[2] The remnant of liberal pacifists emerged from the war impelled by the breadth of social concern and the activism characteristic of their progressive origins. But they harbored as well a more radical view of society and an ethic of conflict which proscribed the use of violence for social change. Thus, associating injustice with war, they hobbled the drive for social justice with a commitment to peace.

42

Some pacifists had been sharp critics of society before, of course, and these moved further to the left. Jane Addams's autobiographical writings can be read profitably as records of her recognition of injustice on successive levels of the social order, culminating in international war. Walter Rauschenbusch shared her experience, as did even the literary radicals around Max Eastman. Episcopal Bishop Paul Jones was hounded from his diocese of Utah for his socialism as much as for his pacifism, and John Haynes Holmes wrote in the fall of 1914 that the peace advocate must drop his "dilettante, academic, pink-tea" habits, join with labor, "and strike straight and sure . . . at the things which make war—first, militarism; second, political autocracy; and third, commercialism . . . armaments, dynasties, and exploitation."[3] Most significant for the future, however, were the younger pacifists who brought to domestic issues a heightened sense of social responsibility and a more radical view of society which they acquired from their wartime experiences. Norman Thomas was their classic instance, since he initially joined the Socialist Party because of its opposition to the war and its defense of the conscientious objector. Devere Allen and Kirby Page also became active Socialists, while others, including A. J. Muste and Evan Thomas, joined forces with labor. The war provided these young men with an impulse for reform.

The development of pacifist social ethics in a wartime context was strikingly evident in the lives of a group of college-age men who volunteered for the overseas war work of the Young Men's Christian Association while America was still at peace—notably Kirby Page and Harold Gray, Evan Thomas, Jack Sherman, Henry H. Crane, and Maxwell Chaplin. Bred amid devout surroundings, they had travailed over doubt, textual criticism, and subjectivity. In college they had caught "a certain idealistic interpretation of life which their Christian habits compelled them to take seriously at whatever the cost to their personal welfare."[4] The problem they faced in Europe was how to relate the war they experienced to the ideals in which they believed.

Neither Kirby Page nor Harold Gray, his younger roommate on the outward voyage in 1916, could have foreseen how difficult this problem might be or where its resolution would lead. Page had imbibed a strong Christian faith from his mother and especially from his wife, Alma, who had influenced him for several years before their marriage. Gray had been educated from boyhood in spiritual habits: "prayer, he was taught, is as normal and as necessary as eating."[5] As young men, Page and Gray had taught Sunday school classes in Disciples of Christ churches and had been active in Y.M.C.A. work. Page had been personal secretary to

43

the general secretary of the Houston, Texas, Y.M.C.A. and had rejuvenated the college "Y" association at Drake University. Gray's activity in the Y.M.C.A. had interfered with his high school studies, and even when he transferred to Phillips Exeter Academy in New Hampshire he was active in the student Christian group. The emphasis of student Christian work at that time was on personal religion and evangelism. Although social issues were not emphasized, the foundation for Page's and Gray's later radical and social Christianity was laid in the dedication and missionary zeal of their student days. Their motivating reverence for the Christian life was latent power which only needed to be given its social applications.

The European war did not at first intrude upon their ideas. Gray was among the first to join the student regiment at Harvard University, but he did not then anticipate a break in his education. Even when he went to work for the international Y.M.C.A. with German prisoners in England, in 1916, he volunteered out of evangelical devotion rather than concern about war. Page had not seriously considered pacifism either. He graduated from Drake University in June, 1915, and went on to the University of Chicago. The next year he was invited to become personal secretary to Sherwood Eddy, renowned evangelist of the International Y.M.C.A. Accepting the offer, Page found himself sailing with Eddy for evangelistic campaigns among the soldiers in the English war zone. Like Gray and millions of other Americans, he did not at first express any particular revulsion to war. As late as August, 1916, Page responded to the patriotic spirit around him. "Everyone is taking it in the most heroic manner," he wrote. "They seem to regard [war] as a piece of work that must be finished regardless . . . . It is a wonderful spirit, and I am learning many lessons."[6]

He and Harold Gray learned some of their lessons together as they visited army camps with Sherwood Eddy. They mixed with the soldiers while the evangel preached. They visited troop hospitals and felt that the war came closer there. In the streets of London they felt the grip of war psychology, listened to a crowd "roar with delight" as a German Zeppelin with its crew of thirty men fell in flames; they heard Englishmen demanding reprisal for the air raids, demanding German mothers and children in proportion to their own losses. Perhaps most impressive of all, they learned about war morality. Behind the lines, Page heard for the first time of Allied atrocities. In the camps and on the streets he and Gray cared for Tommies racked with loneliness. They saw the night lines and the soliciting. "Life was cheap," they learned; "morals were made for peace-times."[7]

44

This lesson struck these two sin-sensitive men. Page wrote the following spring of his shock and sadness on learning that 20 per cent of the American boys serving in the various ambulance corps had been dismissed because of venereal disease. "There is a common saying in Paris as follows," he reported, " 'The British are drunkards, the French are whoremongers, the Americans are both!' To put it mildly, the war is not improving morality."[8] Such reports shocked the naïve home front, too, and Page got into trouble for making them. Americans at home could go on believing in a glorious and honorable war, but for the secretaries in England the crusade began to lose its spangles.

The ethical problem of war was dramatized for them by personal contacts. The poetic lay near the surface of Page's mind and was stirred by his seeing from a train a soldier taking leave of his wife and child, and then seeing "in quick succession an orphanage and a cemetery."[9] Gray became intimately acquainted with German prisoners of war whom he found to be warm, responsive, and Christian. Sometimes it seemed to him as though the prison camps were havens of sanity in a war-frenzied island.

By late October, 1916, the two friends were thoroughly disillusioned with the war, and Gray was confessing to his parents his growing admiration for conscientious objectors. About this time they were joined by Evan Thomas, a tall, lanky lad who had left his seminary studies at Edinburgh to work with prisoners of war and who brought along pacifist convictions he had nurtured through his two years in Scotland. During the winter and spring the seven American Y.M.C.A. secretaries held monthly meetings at the home of their English supervisor, Dr. Robert Ewing. Each secretary agreed to read at least five hundred pages a month on the subject of the war, and to lead the discussion at one meeting. Evan Thomas led the January session on the individual's responsibility to the state, especially in the case of the conscientious objector. In light of Thomas's later experience, his was a prescient choice of topics.

Page characteristically put his ideas in the form of a manuscript, the first in a series of influential analyses of war which culminated in his *National Defense* (1931).[10] Early in 1917 he circulated among friends a revised draft of a manuscript called "War and Love." Perhaps indicative of the change in the American mood in the following year were the different responses to Page's pacifism by Dean Shailer Mathews of the Divinity School of the University of Chicago. In January, 1917, he thought the article "worthy of publication," expressing reservations only about the handling of alternatives to war. But in 1918 he criticized

Page's pacifism itself, which he said was "as if the Good Samaritan, if he had come down a little earlier, had waited until the robbers had finished with the traveler before he assisted him."[11]

What were the doctrines to which Dean Mathews could assent in January, 1917, but not a year later? Page personally did not suppose that the war was a simple struggle between good and bad nations. But neither did he emphasize the mixed motives of the combatants as did those men of the "international mind." For the sake of clearness he was willing to *suppose* "that Germany is altogether in the wrong and that America is altogether in the right in this present struggle."[12] In words that echoed the private thoughts Evan Thomas had been sending his brother, Norman, young Kirby Page tried to state what war is and what it involves:

> War is not an ideal, it has an ideal; war is not a spirit, it is waged in a certain spirit; war is not a result, it produces results. War is always and everywhere a *method*, and it is as a method that it must be discussed.[13]

The high ideals, spirit, and results for which Americans might be fighting were not the tests of the morality of World War I, he insisted; war must be justified by what it does.

It "inevitably involves" the law of military necessity that the end justifies the means, he continued; it requires atrocities and the wholesale destruction of life, the breakdown of values, the surrender of moral freedom. War as a method, he concluded, is the very antithesis of all that Jesus stood for. Harry Emerson Fosdick had argued that Christians living in an unideal world must compromise realistically in order to attain their very ideals. They dare not ignore the evil which is a part of them and their every choice, he had said. Page did not deny the reality of human weakness and sin, even in his own life, but he believed he ought never to compromise deliberately with evil. "All of us are human and sinful," he wrote, "and are constantly doing things that are unchristian, which does not remove us from the category of Christians." But neither does doing an unchristian thing make it less wrong.[14]

Page's manuscript had been thoroughly discussed when Harold Gray agreed to defend the conscientious objector and pacifist position at the April meeting of the secretaries. The issues he faced were somewhat more personal and less social than those raised by his friend. The question was not whether war was wrong. Everyone admitted that it was. The question was whether it was ethically necessary. Could a nation or an individual espouse an evil, especially the lesser of two evils, "as a means to an approved end?"[15] Gray's idealism was revealed in his con-

46

viction that a good alternative was available. His dilemma was to find it in either war or nonresistance. He seized a radical alternative, based upon his understanding of theology. His basic premise was that God never violates the right of choice which He has given man. This "eternal respect for man's right of choice" seemed to be testimony of the love of God "even as respect for personality must be the core of love." For this reason, "Jesus rejected the instruments of force as a means for founding the Kingdom and substituted the instrument of compelling love."[16] This position was more extreme than that taken initially by Kirby Page (although it was the essence of his last sermon, delivered almost half a century later). Furthermore, it avoided the dualism of traditional nonresistance. Because of human nature itself, violence cannot usher in love, peace, or righteousness, Gray believed; put this way, the issue was not refusing to do evil, but effectively doing good.

Gray's convictions demanded that he do something, but circumstances militated against action. He was physically and emotionally exhausted by the time his nation went to war; his family was deeply disturbed by his position and was insistent that he remain in England; Dr. Ewing urged him not to give up the "Y" work for which he was well qualified. Still, Gray believed that the Y.M.C.A. and the Red Cross were becoming mere "efficiency departments" of the army, and besides he wanted to apply some of his convictions to concrete problems. One evening in September, 1917, he decided with Maxwell Chaplin and Evan Thomas to resign and return to America. He came back to conscription and, eventually, imprisonment at Alcatraz for his uncompromising pacifism.

The pacifist "Y" secretaries had evaluated World War I at close range and according to a Christian ethic, and they naturally extended their analysis to social and economic questions. Their views became more radical as they became more firmly pacifist. As young men they had shared the ideas of middle-class America: religion was mostly personal, society was oriented toward progress and gradual reform, and capitalism was the flexible instrument of a mobile society. In wartime England they began to suspect that the existing social order was based on the same ethic of force which had produced international conflict. The abstractions they debated at length were all mixed up with the personal quandries that awaited them in America.

By the time he left England, Harold Gray thought he might go to South America and associate with some industrial mission in order to "work out some great social principles on a small scale in a new social order."[17] He was conscripted instead. In army camps and prisons he

47

continued to dream of a new order, but he was painfully aware of his need for training and realism. When and if he were released, he wrote in July, 1918, he would be found "in the best school of social science of which the country can brag."[18] By November he was dreaming of working out his ideas in some agricultural project and, indeed, he did experiment with a communal farm in Michigan after his release and further education. Evan Thomas went to prison as a pacifist, too, and subsequently worked with labor in an effort to prevent violence in a strike at Paterson, New Jersey. Maxwell Chaplin was similarly influenced, although he expressed his social concern as a missionary to China rather than as a reformer at home.

Meanwhile, Kirby Page was finding his social and economic views changed by his wartime pacifism. He had been interested in social questions in college, but his solutions to immigration and slum problems, for example, were remedial rather than revolutionary. He did not blame capitalism as a system for them. His principles of social reform then, as later, were "Jesus' principles of the fatherhood of God, the brotherhood of man, the love of man for man," but as a young man he interpreted them to mean "the obligations of the strong to help the weak" voluntarily.[19] His views remained conventional as late as 1916 when he observed the social contrasts in New York City. Children played merrily on the waterfront, he noticed, oblivious to their dismal surroundings. Maimed and wasted bodies in a free clinic showed him "the awful effects of sin, ignorance and carelessness."[20] Four years and a war later he would have meant the sin and negligence of the economic stewards; in 1916 he almost certainly referred to the poor.

Between 1916 and 1920 the war forced Page to relate his Christian idealism to a specific social problem. Like Gray, he found other applications of that ethic. Furthermore, just as he had looked at violence as a method he began to think in terms of the social system and of "the fundamental evils therein, one of which is war."[21] He soon discovered, however, how very little he knew about any of the social problems of his day. He determined to take graduate work in sociology, economics, and philosophy in order to understand the structure of his society. His subsequent study was mostly informal, though, and was initiated with the help of Sherwood Eddy.

The evangelist had rejected the absolute pacifism of his personal secretary during the war, but he was troubled by "grave doubts and misgivings of conscience." After long thought he recanted his prowar attitude, vowed never to take part in any future conflict, and promoted this pacifism until in the thirties he abandoned it under the shadow of

48

Nazi Germany. Even before he became an absolute pacifist, Eddy had been disturbed by certain implications of war. He later wrote:

> Behind the grim Medusa's head of the carnage at the front in World War I, I began gradually to see the symptoms of a world which at heart is hostile. As an abscess may become the focal point of a diseased and poisoned body, so the war became to me the symbol and evidence of a sick and envenomed social order. Beneath the conflict I saw a world of perpetual strife between classes, races, and nations . . . . I saw that wars were the logical and almost inevitable result of the whole competitive economic system, which is fundamentally a war system and, therefore, ever in unstable equilibrium.[22]

Thus led from international to social discord, he determined to fight for "social and industrial justice." He envisioned the formation of an intellectual elite which could furnish "the brains, the leadership, the facts, and the writing to capture the press and arrest the attention of the people . . . ."[23] He wrote to Page, urging him to resign the church he had taken and put his life for the present in the "social fight." He would guarantee Page's support for 1921 so that his secretary would be free to do research, "furnishing munitions for those of us who are speaking, and, where possible, joining in the campaign yourself." In a burst of vaguely directed enthusiasm, Eddy concluded, "I am coming back to fight!"[24]

The opportunity appealed to Page, and he joined Eddy as soon as he was able to leave his church. It was a chance for him to study and write. To his wife he wrote, "such a crusade . . . appeals to all the deepest instincts within me." He had long applied the principles of Jesus to personal living; he now sought to apply "the methods of Jesus to social and economic life."[25] He was led eventually to socialism and to a career as a free-lance writer and speaker, a social evangelist.

Other young pacifists underwent a similar reorientation in their social views. William Fincke, a Presbyterian minister, left Greenwich Church in New York because of trouble there arising from his opposition to the war. He went to France with the first Presbyterian hospital unit, and his ship was torpedoed and sunk on the crossing. Warfare confirmed his pacifism and expanded his social concern. When he returned home he became director of the Presbyterian Labor Temple in New York, was active in the Duquesne, Pennsylvania, steel strike of 1919, helped to found Brookwood Labor College at Katonah, New York, and was active in the Farmer-Labor and Socialist parties. Edmund B. Chaffee's experience was similar to Fincke's in that he lost his associate ministry at the Greenwich Presbyterian Church because of

49

his pacifism, and in 1921 became director of the Labor Temple. From his wartime experience as a pacifist, young A. J. Muste became concerned to make his "fundamental convictions operative in the field of social and specifically of industrial relationships . . . ."[26] His opportunity came in 1919 with the textile strike in Lawrence, Massachusetts. There, as chairman of the strike committee and in conjunction with two other pacifist ministers, Cedric Long and Harold L. Rotzel, Muste was active in preventing violence by the workers. He was subsequently made executive secretary of the Amalgamated Textile Workers Union, chairman of the faculty at Brookwood Labor College from 1921 to 1933, and in 1937 he replaced Chaffee at the Labor Temple.

In the war years numerous Christian pacifists became intensely aware of the gulf between contemporary social conditions and the ideal which they conceived. They found in the very failure of the world to accept their principles a challenge and an obligation to apply them. "Only by such faithfulness," they were convinced, could "the spirit of love be woven into the very fabric of personal and social life."[27] Members of the Fellowship of Reconciliation believed in the practicability of the kingdom of God, and in the possibility of practicing love and brotherhood even in a warring world. Pacifism, for them, was an ethically necessary and practical extension of the gospel of love to social problems, especially to war. It heralded both an ideal and a method of social reform. Groups, as well as individuals, responded to the challenge to practice pacifism actively, and they also shifted leftward as they organized war relief and the defense of civil liberties.

The work of the American Friends Service Committee on behalf of conscientious objectors illustrated a relationship between civil rights and relief. The committee itself was organized in response to the needs of Europe and to the ethical demand for an alternative to fighting. Friends' service in World War I was originally conceived of as volunteer, and not as a legally required substitute for fighting; it was no way out. When they organized in April, 1917, the committee members expected that the draft law would give Friends complete exemption. They felt that they "could not accept exemption from military service and at the same time do nothing to express their positive faith and devotion in the great human crisis."[28]

Although English Friends first felt the strains of war, leading American Quakers realized its implications from the beginning. The English Friends formed committees to administer comfort and counsel to conscientious objectors, aid to aliens and their families, a volunteer ambu-

50

lance unit to soldiers, and relief to refugees and war victims. Friends in America almost immediately began contributing significantly to English work, and even underwrote four young men who volunteered for the English Friends' Ambulance Unit, in which they served with distinction. A continuation committee representative of different Quaker branches was appointed at a Friends National Peace Conference in July, 1915, and shortly before the American declaration of war it printed in leading magazines and newspapers a message urging the use of new techniques of conciliation and altruistic service. "The alternative to war is not inactivity and cowardice," it declared. *"It is the irresistible and constructive power of goodwill."*[29]

The American Friends Service Committee was organized in an effort to implement that declaration in wartime. Representatives of the Philadelphia Yearly Meeting, the Friends General Conference, and Five Years' Meeting met at the Young Friends Building in Philadelphia, an occasion historic in establishing cooperation among these branches of Friends. The immediate purposes of the A.F.S.C. were to assist English Friends in relief work in devastated areas of France and to plan opportunities for service in lieu of the expected exemption from the army. At Haverford College an Emergency Unit of relief workers had already been organized by Dr. James Babbitt, the physician, and Rufus Jones, a professor of philosophy. Jones, then in his fifties, had been recapturing Quaker history and renewing the pacifist faith for over a decade; Henry Hodgkin had stayed in his home while planning the Garden City Conference, and Jones himself was a charter member of the F.O.R. With the help of his close friend Grayson Mallet-Provost Murphy, chief of the American Red Cross in France, arrangements finally were made for the Quaker unit to work in cooperation with the civilian service of the Red Cross.

The members of Reconstruction Unit No. 1 who assembled at Haverford during the summer of 1917 represented the larger branches of American Quakers and a small number of others who shared Quaker views on war. Some members of the unit who would become active in the postwar peace movement included William I. Hull, Lucy Biddle Lewis, Frederick J. Libby, and one whose scholarship would be enlisted for pacifism, Roland H. Bainton.* The first group of fifty-one

* William Hull was a Friend who had taken his Ph.D. at Johns Hopkins (1891), had studied in Europe, and had returned to teach history and political science at Swarthmore College. He had attended the first two Hague conferences (1899 and 1904), was an official of the Church Peace Union and the F.O.R., and

men and three women sailed for France early in the fall.

There the unit was under the jurisdiction of the American Red Cross, but it merged with the English Relief Unit already on the field. More Americans arrived until they numbered 340 in comparison with 210 British. Administration came largely into American hands.[30] The Service Committee spent over one million dollars in France. In Aisne, Somme, and Oise the workers plowed, seeded, and harvested crops. They repaired farm equipment, restocked farms, and rebuilt whole villages. They furnished medical and dental services, and they left to France as a memorial the Châlons maternity hospital at Châlons-sur-Marne after having stocked it with Red Cross supplies and endowed it with a staff. In many other ways the men and women of the red and black double star, the emblem of Quaker service, entered into the life of the French.

The work begun in France was extended throughout devastated Europe, ending in Austria in 1927. The Service Committee worked with the English Quakers, the American Relief Administration, the American Red Cross, the Jewish Joint Distribution Committee, other smaller relief agencies, and European governments. It was instrumental in the postwar feeding of over one million German children, and in combating severe famine in Russia from 1920 to 1925 (especially in Samara Province). It fought tuberculosis in Austria, typhus in the Vilnyus district of Poland, and malaria and cholera in Buzuluk Ooyezd, Russia. It established an agricultural college in Poland, and objected to the food blockade of Germany by the European Allies. It was regarded as an expert corps of the American Red Cross in France, and was asked by Herbert Hoover to administer relief in Germany. About $25,200,000 worth of aid was donated to the committee's work in the form of cash or gifts in kind.[31]

Mennonites and Brethren also undertook programs of positive action. As meek as they sought to be, Mennonites were often fearfully punished for not supporting the war effort. As civilians some were flogged, tarred, and feathered; in some instances their houses were

---

was chairman of the Pennsylvania Committee for Total Disarmament. By 1926 he was a member of almost every major peace society in the country. His wife, Hannah Clothier Hull, was active in the Women's International League for Peace and Freedom, and the Committee on Militarism in Education (C.M.E.).

Lucy Biddle Lewis, of Philadelphia, was active in the W.I.L.P.F. and the A.F.S.C. Frederick Libby became the founder and executive secretary of the National Council for Prevention of War (N.C.P.W.), and was on the national council of the C.M.E., and of World Peaceways. Roland Bainton became a distingushed historian and professor of church history at Yale Divinity School.

painted yellow or even burned. Upon occasion they arranged with their communities to support the civilian Red Cross in lieu of buying liberty bonds, but many Mennonites (and Brethren) objected to the Red Cross and the Y.M.C.A. Both were allied with the war, they thought; to give them money seemed to be only another way of subsidizing the conflict. Besides, these organizations distributed to soldiers tobacco and other things objectionable to many pious sectarians.

Nonetheless, Mennonites and Brethren responded to the idealism of the Great War. Many did not doubt the righteousness of the cause, but felt prohibited by their gospel from participating in it. Others deplored the war and its attendant suffering. Charity was not merely a response to war sentiment; it was a principle imbedded in Brethren and Mennonite history and associated with nonresistance. Even so, it seems to have been greatly stimulated by the war. Many nonresistants felt a gnawing desire to take part in the positive idealism of the moment. When their desire could not be expressed through public organizations which seemed to compromise their piety, they founded agencies of their own or worked through the Friends Service Committee.*

Other agencies spent more money and fed more people, but the Friends contributed two great intangibles. In America they stimulated unity and social concern among the peace churches, and thus set an example of constructive pacifism. In Europe they left immeasurable hope and good will. When German children received the cards with which they might secure food, they read on the reverse side:

> To the Children of Germany:
>   A greeting of Friendship from America, distributed by the Religious Society of Friends (Quakers), who have for 250 years, and during the several years of war just ended, maintained that only service and love, not war and hatred, can bring peace and happiness to mankind.[32]

A professor at the University of Frankfort remarked to Quaker worker Caroline Norment that evaluation of the work would have to wait twenty years. The real test would come, he suggested, when children would ask, " 'Who were those people who came and fed us and why did they do it?' If they are answered truly in terms of the message on the food cards, the result should be the development of strong anti-

* A Mennonite Relief Committee for War Sufferers was formed in December, 1917, in order to systematize relief work. Mennonites supported also the American Committee for Armenian and Syrian Relief working with the Red Cross in the Near East, and organized six relief committees to work in southern Russia. After July, 1920, these groups were coordinated by a Mennonite Central Committee in Elkhart, Indiana.

war sentiments."[33] That in succeeding years the German children were given answers contrary to the Quakers' only throws the pacifists' efforts into sharper contrast to the need they sought to meet.

In the United States the results of relief work were more lasting. A precedent had been set for constructive pacifism during peace time and in World War II. Many pacifists became convinced that their refusal to bear arms obligated them to explore what William James had called moral equivalents for war. In stimulating unity among the peace churches and a broad postwar social awareness, the Service Committee's relief work was, as Professor Elbert Russell concluded, "epoch-making in the history of American Quakerism."[34]

At the urging of some Friends who had "discovered the seeds of war in our social order," the Philadelphia Yearly Meeting created a Social Order Committee. If love is applicable in personal and international life, the committee held, it should be operative in the intermediate social and industrial life. Whereas nineteenth-century Friends had emphasized mercy in a static world, modern Quakers should help direct a changing society. Accordingly, the Social Order Committee created study groups on labor conditions and the causes of poverty, the democratization of industry, distribution of wealth, and traditional Quaker concepts of simplicity. A number of Philadelphia's leading businessmen in the study groups sought to practice the enlightened capitalism they discussed. This social concern was formalized in the reorganization of the Friends Service Committee in 1924 into four sections: foreign service, home service, interracial work, and peace work. Quaker leaders were among those who emerged from the war with increased social concern arising from their war experiences.

The traditional position of nonresistance, submission to the state and withdrawal from conflict, increasingly seemed to be inadequate to the total crisis of 1917–18. Patriots were expected to rise to the idealism of a militant cause, the defense of civilization itself. Men were drafted into the army, to be sure, but their term of enlistment was referred to as military *service*. Pacifists might refuse to support the war, but they nevertheless felt impelled to serve that cause for which others were fighting; peace was the organizing principle of relief programs. Still, many who were engaged in humanitarian efforts (like Jane Addams, who enlisted support for the relief work of Herbert Hoover's Department of Food Administration) found in the service of "Bread" only a tentative alternative to nonresistance and fighting. Having discovered the seeds of war in the social order, they found in pacifism an

54

impulse to social reform; and justice was the organizing principle of civil-rights work.

The historic peace churches thus tried to look after their own conscientious objectors. Quakers and Mennonites appointed committees and secretaries to visit members, to correspond with them, and to bring their problems to the attention of the War Department. The Brethren took an official position against noncombatant military service after January, 1918, but this position was compromised because leaders who visited Brethren objectors in army camps did not always advise taking the traditional nonresistance position.[35] The three sects increasingly coordinated their efforts to secure good treatment of their members, and to clarify or change the conscription law to meet the objections of absolute nonresistants.

They sought also some form of civilian alternate service for those pacifists who had reservations even to noncombatant work under the army. The rules and regulations prescribed by the President for local and district boards on June 30, 1917, provided that each inducted man would be in the military service of the United States from the time he reported at a cantonment. Accordingly, leaders of the Friends Service Committee outlined a plan for a reconstruction unit under Red Cross civilian administration, and urged that it be recognized for noncombat duty. When it became apparent that the War Department would not validate their relief work soon, the Service Committee sought exemption for its workers. All men but one in Indiana were granted transfers of jurisdiction by their home boards to draft boards in and about Philadelphia. The men were then rejected from service on physical or religious grounds, and were permitted by district boards to leave the country for work "of national importance."[36] Because of the unsatisfactory nature of this arrangement and the threat of having its men recalled to face the second draft, however, the Service Committee continued to cooperate with Brethren and Mennorites in pressing for civilian alternative service.

Other organizations sprang up even before war was declared in order to defend the rights of conscientious objectors who did not come under the protective aegis of the peace churches and civilians who were threatened by an overwhelming pressure for patriotic conformity.*

---

* These organizations included the League for Democratic Control, Boston (A. J. Muste, chairman; and Harold L. Rotzel, a Friend, organizing secretary); the Young Democracy of New York City (Devere Allen, secretary); the Young People's Socialist League of Chicago; the American Liberty Defense League of

These groups were staffed largely, though not entirely, by pacifists. One wing of the Union Against Militarism had organized as the National Civil Liberties Bureau with headquarters in New York City and an office in Washington. On October 1, 1917, the bureau assumed an independent existence and it expanded into the single most significant organization in the field of civil liberties.

L. Hollingsworth Wood, a New York lawyer and prominent Quaker, was its able chairman and Walter Nelles was its attorney, but its wartime accomplishments were largely the work of its intrepid director, Roger N. Baldwin. Although he was sentenced to a penitentiary for refusing to do military service, Baldwin was allowed to return to New York and straighten out the bureau's files, which Department of Justice agents had scrambled in a raid. His integrity won him friends everywhere: once he was locked out of a Newark, New Jersey, prison where the warden had given him the job of watering the plants near the entrance, and he had to ring the bell and ask to be taken back. It was, indeed, difficult to keep him out of anything he felt he should be in.[37]

Friends of the Civil Liberties Bureau were concerned lest democracy be lost in the struggle to secure it. When Socialist leader Eugene V. Debs was convicted of having violated the Espionage Act and given a ten-year sentence, Norman Thomas warned in the *World Tomorrow,* "Unless a people retains its liberty to discuss freely according to conscience, it loses its soul."[38] The editor was not merely speaking in defense of a minority position. Indeed, he applied the doctrine of civil rights to the aims of the minority itself. He was aware of the danger

> that the radical, like the reactionary, will forget liberty. He has a remedy for the world's ills which will save it despite itself. Moreover he has usually been the victim of oppression, no school in which to learn tolerance.[39]

Thomas admonished liberals to remember that it is possible "to enact wise economic legislation which will make for general prosperity and still leave men a race of helots."[40] Civil liberty seemed to him paramount over economic or even military success. In this respect, Thomas represented the others actively working for the Civil Liberties Bureau.

Their first concern was for the conscientious objectors to military service. They cooperated with other groups to popularize the legal rights and procedures of objection. Norman Thomas unofficially spoke

---

Chicago; the Bureau of Legal Advice, New York City (Frances Witherspoon, secretary); the National Civil Liberties Bureau; the Friends of Conscientious Objectors in New York City; the F.O.R.; and sectarian groups such as the Friends, Brethren, and Mennonite.

for them through the Fellowship of Reconciliation *News Sheet* when he urged all young men to register for the draft and express their conscientious scruples within the process. Baldwin had refused to cooperate with the draft at any point, and half a century later pacifist advice to objectors would be divided; but in 1917, Thomas argued that to resist prior to induction would be to obstruct a constitutionally enacted measure. Such obstruction would be denying the democratic principle. Political protest should proceed through the regular channels of society, he thought.

> It is a great and solemn responsibility at any time to decline assent to the requirements of the state; and democracy cannot be saved from anarchy except on the principle that we render obedience to the common will . . . up to the limit at which the strain of assent reaches the absolute breaking point. Of that point each person must at last be judge.[41]

More technical advice was given directly to objectors.

The Civil Liberties Bureau collaborated with the Fellowship of Reconciliation to aid conscientious objectors in detention camps in forming study groups and to provide them with chaplains and encouragement. In June, 1917, it asked the Federal Council of Churches to urge upon the War Department care and fairness in treating objectors and to help provide understanding among the churches. The council failed to act decisively.

Probably the most important work of the bureau was to publicize mistreatment of objectors. In general, it held, the War Department was "liberal and shrewd" in dealing with its obdurate charges; the department tried honestly to prevent brutality, although it did not always succeed. During the war at least one hundred cases of physical cruelty were reported to the bureau. These cases included beatings, bayonetings, torture, and unreasonable confinement. The worst conditions reported were at Camp Meade, Camp Funston, and Fort Riley, all under Major General Leonard Wood. Protests directly to the department resulted in investigation and amelioration in some cases.

The Civil Liberties Bureau objected most strenuously to the abuse of solitary confinement for those who refused even prison work. Representatives of the bureau visiting Forts Leavenworth and Jay found conditions generally good, except for the use of solitary confinement. It was often administered as punishment, sometimes with a bread-and-water diet, although sentences were usually short. At Fort Jay three men were handcuffed to their cell windows, standing on tip-toe during working hours because they refused to do prison work which they re-

57

garded as a recognition of their military status. After the bureau's visit these men were transferred to Fort Leavenworth. There, even after the Armistice was signed, men were being manacled in a standing position for nine hours a day and were kept in solitary confinement. Secretary of War Newton Baker refused to believe pacifist reports of these conditions, and they were not changed until Nevin Sayre spoke to President Wilson in December. As a result of this conference such treatment was abolished for all those in military prisons. Harassment by Civil Liberties Bureau members Norman Thomas, L. Hollingsworth Wood, John Haynes Holmes, and John Lovejoy Elliott greatly irritated the War Department, which protested that good conditions prevailed. Before the objectors were released, however, the army had admitted the truth of many of the bureau's contentions and had made some improvements.[42]

Civil rights and relief work were twin facets of the heightened social conscience that characterized the antiwar movement in many lands. Premysl Pitter's revulsion from war during his service on the Italian front made him the moving spirit of the postwar Czech peace movement and the founder of a children's home in Prague. Pierre Ceresole conceived of his international peace army for social service while in a Swiss jail for refusing to serve in the army. Friederich Siegmund-Schultze, former pastor to the Kaiser, worked with Allied prisoners of war during the war and afterwards both stimulated religious pacifism in Germany and founded his *Soziale Arbeitsgemeinshaft* in East Berlin. Henri Roser reached the front in the French army; but reflection and theological studies afterward led him to resign from the reserves, propagate pacifism, and serve a slum parish near Paris. British pacifists expressed social concern in innumerable ways—a Muriel Lester in settlement work, a George Lansbury in the Labour party. The Dutch Kees Boecke found his career as a violinist interrupted by the war, but founded a Brotherhood House at Bilthoven, near Utrecht, Holland. There in October, 1919, men and women from London and Berlin, Paris and New York, who were motivated by a similar devotion to pacifism and social work founded the International Fellowship of Reconciliation.

Meanwhile, a similar conception of the war's origin and of peace terms linked American pacifists with British left-wing labor, antiwar German Socialists, and the Russian Petrograd Council. The radical peace and justice movement of the post-1914 era was, indeed, international from its inception. In the United States the chief agencies of

58

this first united front were various civil liberties bureaus and the People's Council of America.

The council had been a project of the remnant of the progressive antiwar coalition and moderate Socialists, of course. Its initial burst of enthusiasm had been quashed in the debacle of the September assembly; and by October, 1917, it was apparent that liberal and radical forces were to be divided for the duration. Pacifists still hoped to win the prowar liberals to a new American Union Against Militarism. The People's Council lost the support of large contributors, cropped its grand design, and concentrated on building local support. Throughout the fall it increasingly represented Socialists and radical labor. From its ranks, to a large extent, came a national conference of labor, Socialist, and radical movements in February, and a second one in May. These conferences responded specifically to the example of the British labor movement, and James Maurer was delegated to attend an inter-allied Socialist and labor conference in London. Maurer personified the combination of peace and labor's justice. A Socialist since 1898 and president of the Pennsylvania Federation of Labor from 1912 to 1928, he had been on the executive committee of the American Union, was temporarily chairman of the People's Council in September, 1917, and would remain active in the F.O.R. throughout his life. His reputation went before him, and he was denied a passport to England.

The People's Council maintained contacts with antiwar Socialists and labor leaders in Europe, however, and it was the chief defender of Soviet Russia in 1918–19; but it never quite lost the marks of liberal progressivism. Its program remained virtually unchanged after the summer of 1917. Scott Nearing became chairman that fall on the understanding that the council would work for "industrial democracy," but when he was asked if that meant socialism he replied, ' No."[43] Its platform at the end of the war included the restoration of civil liberties, amnesty for political and industrial prisoners, self-determination for and nonintervention in Russia, and disarmament; and it quoted remarks of President Wilson in support of each liberal plank. By that time, however, the council had become a paper organization, inactive because the threat of reprisal attended its every project. Sensing new possibilities in November, 1918, Lochner and Nearing offered to resign in favor of a new administration "unfettered by the opprobrium which surrounds our names and our activities."[44] Their caution was well taken in view of the Red Scare in the offing; hardly two months later investigator Archibald E. Stevenson detailed the organized pacifist movement for the Overman Subcommittee of the Senate Committee of the Judiciary because "of its direct connection with the subsequent radical movement, which is the thing which is of most importance before the country today."[45] The pacifist who associated with Socialists in the People's Council or elsewhere was tarnished indiscriminately with a radical image.

The pacifist believes that the means and the end are so intimately related that it is impossible to get a coordinated and cooperative world by destructive methods that violate personality and increase antagonism and distrust.

—PAUL JONES, "The Meaning of Pacifism"[46]

The true nature of that so-called radicalism is important; it derived from the pacifist's reflection upon wartime society in terms of his own experience. Isolation was painful enough, but in fact he was the target of persecution because of his opposition to conscription and his association with political radicals. He promised not to obstruct the war effort, but his skeptical neutralism was itself a crime. The conviction of Eugene Debs sealed that. Scott Nearing reported after a cross-country trip in the winter of 1917 that public meetings to urge an immediate peace were impossible in the face of opposition led by the American Defense Society with the connivance of local police. Under the circumstances, he concluded, propaganda work must be conducted in print. Even that procedure was challenged, as Socialists and the pacifist editors of the *Masses,* the *Nation,* and the *World Tomorrow* discovered. Nearing himself was indicted under the Espionage Act for writing *The Great Madness,* a book which restated the socialistic view of the war.

The pacifist's meetings were broken up; his friends were harassed, run out of town, flayed, and imprisoned; his literature was withheld from the mails, his headquarters raided, conscientious objectors humiliated or worse; and the President he trusted seemed to keep his own peace. Early in the war, and before nationalism was virulent, the People's Council printed in facsimile a Russian peace appeal, together with an English translation and this note: "the original copy of the Bulletin from which this reproduction is made was smuggled over to this country—though not, as in the old days—smuggled *out of Russia*, but, as in these strange, new days—smuggled *into America!*"[47] Pacifists now looked upon their earlier warnings as prophetic. The American Union had said in 1916 that "militarism is the real danger" of war, and Randolph Bourne was not alone two years later in describing the "inexorable union of militarism and the State," or in fearing that "War is the health of the State" apparatus.[48]

By the time of his death in 1918, Bourne's ideas were as familiar to liberal pacifists as was the sight of his hunched back and tortured features. He distrusted religious moralism only less than complacent liberalism, but he came to conclusions similar to those of Christian pacifists. Like some of them he broke with many of the assumptions and friendships of his past, and he groped toward a more radical view of reform. He tried to thrust back of Dewey's instrumentalism, now a lever for preserving the old order, he thought, to the spirit of William James with its "gay passion for ideas, and its freedom of speculation."[49] The trouble was that the ideas did not seem to lead him anywhere. In the summer of 1917 he wrote autobiographically of a "friend" whom the nation could not mobilize. The friend loved his country but he was not nationalistic. He would register (as Bourne did), but he did not know what he might do if he were drafted. He was apathetic to both military service and absolute objection. He found no honor in alternative service, and his "horror of useless service may make even the bludgeoning of himself seem futile." So the friend might go off to war without enthusiasm, idealism, or hope. In one translucent sentence, Bourne revealed his bewildering sense of uselessness. The work "so blithely undertaken for the defense of democracy will have crushed out the only genuinely precious thing in a nation," he wrote, "the hope and ardent idealism of its youth."[50]

Out of his emotional despair, Bourne gave the antiwar movement its most trenchant analysis. He assumed that the ruling classes use the instruments of the state and its military authority to exploit those whose allegiance it commands. There was nothing new in his description of economic injustice or even its connection with war, but he went on to identify violence as the essence of war and authoritarianism as the essence of the state. Where a state identifies itself with democratic forms, the authority of conformism takes the place of violent, physical force. Wartime patriotism is, therefore, the obverse, the domestic counterpoint, of military force. Violence and authoritarianism are essentially and equally objectionable.

This thesis was given its classic statement by Bourne, but it was

61

echoed in the literature of liberal pacifism. It introduced a political and ethical note into the antiwar socialism of Eugene Debs, Max Eastman, Scott Nearing, and especially Norman Thomas. Only three weeks before he applied for membership in the Socialist Party, Thomas had written that he feared its tendency to bind the individual. "The ultimate values in the world are those of personality, and no theory of the state, whether socialistic or capitalistic, is valid, which makes it master, not servant of man," he wrote.[51] He did join just because he feared "the undue exaltation of the State" and believed that those were "days when radicals ought to stand up and be counted."[52] He was a radical pacifist before he was a Socialist, and his distrust of violence and authoritarianism would leave its mark upon the party in the future. Max Eastman was no absolutist—like most Socialists he was against World War I specifically—but his fervor against that war modified his radicalism. Later he recalled, "A similar thing happened . . . to a good many American socialists. The reality of armed conflict in Europe dampened the proletarian-revolutionary part of their credo, and stepped up to a high pitch the antimilitary part."[53] They emerged a "more skeptical, and more alienated group."[54]

Bourne's understanding was reflected, too, in Kirby Page's influential analysis of war as the method of violence, and in the declarations of pacifists in the Fellowship of Reconciliation. Their enemy was war itself, and they concluded that war was the result of the whole competitive economic system. War could be linked to the whole "causal circle," wrote Vida Scudder, and the pacifist who made the connection would be forced into a "constructive social radicalism."[55] Under the circumstances it was radical enough to express skepticism of the war or the social system of which it was a part. When conformity is an instrument of war, as in 1917–19 it was, then skepticism *is* a crime. The liberal pacifists stood accused as a group. In their alienation they discovered that what made their pacifism radical was their objection to violence and authoritarianism equally.

This discovery pointed to an ethic of conflict which looked for the implications of war as a method and related the instrument to its objectives. As Kirby Page wrote, it must be judged by what it does because that is inseparable from what it is for. Jane Addams rued the "pathetic belief in the regenerative results of war."[56] Violence could not deal with the causes of fighting, she said. Scott Nearing agreed, and declared that in the name of liberty and humanity he was against violence in any cause. The agnostic Max Eastman found himself mindful of the "mangled bodies and manic hatreds implied by the lyric word violence so dear to humdrum petty-bourgeois dreamers like George Sorel . . . ."[57] The religious Evan Thomas was persuaded of the hypocrisy of war-blessing churches largely because he had assumed that "Protestant Christians do not believe that the end justifies the means" and had learned in Britain of "the terrible downward shove war gives to everything . . . ."[58]

Thomas came to the "out and out nonresistance basis" at the same time that he drew apart from the theology and religious vocation he had assumed as a youth. He was reading a good deal of H. G. Wells now, and he wrote, "Even though I admit that I still am governing my conduct from a scale of relative [rather] than absolute values, nevertheless I still maintain that I can't imagine any scheme of relative values demanding that an individual give up the freedom of his conscience to the extent that the military system demands . . . ."[59] Even wars for relatively good ends made absolute demands upon people, he argued; the military is the apotheosis of authoritarianism. Evan Thomas retained a purposefulness that he would need in his months of prison, a faith in God "or in an absolute truth" denied to Randolph Bourne. But he recognized, too, that any action had only relative value, so that his pacifism acquired a pragmatic cast. He found himself reevaluating his position at each new step of the way. Like other liberal pacifists, he felt personally obligated to judge the merits of claims made on his citizenship and "the value of war for ideal ends."[60]

John Haynes Holmes labored at length to meet this requirement, arguing that the logic of force is that it can defend and liberate men, but the fallacy of force is that it actually brings new forms of conflict and is the *sine qua non* of tyranny. On the very eve of national commitment, Holmes had stood in his pulpit to deny that war is ever justifiable. Even fighting to end war itself was illusory, he preached. Good will and compassion are volatile sentiments which war dissipates. Suspicion and hate are malleable instincts which war forges. Internationalism dissolves in the crucible of nationalism. He did not ask the members of his congregation to disavow their nation's part in arms, but only to preserve in their church a sanctuary from the conflict. They did, and Holmes continued his active ministry, writing prolifically and making two especially important contributions to pacifist thought: On the one hand, he opposed the idea that Allied victory alone would make real peace possible. On the other, he advanced the thesis that nonresistance was a practical alternative to war as well as a religious obligation.

Holmes shared the singular neutrality of the "international mind" and the conviction that World War I missed the sources of twentieth-century discontent. But what if the crusade were actually waged in a righteous cause against an evil foe? What if Germany did represent militarism and the Allies democracy? What then could the war accomplish? Holmes argued that because of war's ironic and tragic natures, as wave swelled on khaki wave, peace and liberty would be drawn steadily into the undertow of violence. The irony of war as a social phenomenon was that "through its very effectiveness, it propagates itself." The more noble it seems the more it fastens itself on honorable men. "In other words, the better this war is in character as a war, the more it will tend to convince people that there are such things as holy wars, and thus to adjust their minds to the permanent acceptance of war as a factor in social progress . . . ."[61] In his writing this irony was overshadowed by his tragic understanding of history that the most idealistic reliance on force invariably creates opposing force and ends in violent contest. Men must learn that the means determines the end, he concluded. They must find alternatives to fighting.

It is important to note that Holmes's concept of nonresistance prohibited coercion of any kind except the force of reason, love, and example (passive resistance). Nonviolent coercion, as it later came to be known, was far from his thinking in 1918. Yet he held one of the tenets of what later was called nonviolent action, that "nonresistance" should be constructive. But would it work? In *New Wars for Old* (1916), Holmes gave historical examples of nonresistance.[62] He held that Lao-tzu, Buddha, Isaiah, and Jesus had prophesied it for their respective religious traditions. He showed that it had been held by religious minorities throughout most of western civilization. He speculated that if the estimated billion followers of Taoism, Buddhism, Judaism, and Christianity had been faithful to the prophetic vision of their religions, war would have been impossible in 1914. Holmes did not show that force had been overcome by the prophets' lives. He did not argue that nonresistance had protected the minorities which adhered to it. He begged his own question of practicability. Granted that peace was ideal, and that nonresistance was in the world's prophetic tradition, what would it avail under fire? Granted that wars would cease if men would not fight, what would it gain in wartime? At this point he substituted assertion of the effectiveness of nonresistance for demonstration.

The further examples with which Holmes supported his argument were generally either isolated or irrelevant. His defense of nonresistance was the weakest part of his writing precisely because it was defensive. He seemed to be debating, while prowar liberals were exhorting. He argued, for example, that all he needed to show in order to prove his point was that nonresistance *might* achieve security better than force. Since he had demonstrated that force invariably breeds insecurity, his logic was tight. But his statement was unconvincing.

The whole argument is like a debate between Holmes and Scott Nearing in 1922 for the benefit of the socialist work of the Rand School in New York. The subject of the debate was, "Can the Church Be Radical?" Holmes took the affirmative. He hedged with forensic technicalities, made a cautious defense, and sought to put the burden of proof on the negative side. Nearing accepted the burden willingly, spoke boldly on the negative, and concluded with a ringing appeal to his audience not to waste their time in the churches when they could be radical only as individuals. Holmes's case may have been sound, but it did not seem to fire his audience with enthusiasm.[63]

Nonetheless, his futile attempt in 1916 to establish the social utility of nonviolence suggests how far he had stretched what he called nonresistance. He shared something of Harry Emerson Fosdick's distrust of ethical dualism and inclination to make the pragmatic a test of the ethical. This tendency was only latent in Holmes's thought; although he challenged the war effort and sought alternatives to it on practical grounds, the context of his writing was religious. He rescued the doctrine of nonresistance from the negativism and passivism implicit in its title, perhaps, but he did not dramatize it as a practical alternative to winning the war.

Holmes's major contribution to pacifism in wartime was his argument that violence would result in violence; that the means would determine the end; and that, therefore, fighting could not fulfill the high ideals of patriots. This position struck at the core of liberal prowar sentiment, based as it was on faith in social progress. It struck a responsive chord with liberal pacifists, convinced as they were of the importance of social justice. Indeed, their heightened sense of responsibility changed the focus of pacifism. It grounded their refusal to fight in an assumption that underlay their idealism, the basic premise that would separate nonresistance from nonviolent direct action—that pacifism is socially relevant. As yet that premise was hardly more than a gratuitous assumption, only as secure as their faith, no more demonstrable than John Haynes Holmes's assertion. As yet it represented mainly an inward struggle for direction. After the war that assumption would lead a generation of pacifists into diverse activities which would affect their own understanding and raise questions about the efficacy

65

of love and good will to supplant hate and exploitation. They would reassess the progressive faith and the social gospel as well as the tradition of nonresistance.

If some of their statements have an unduly evangelical ring today, that is because the rhetoric of pacifists changed. But in putting their ethic in such boldly Christian terms, the members of the Fellowship of Reconciliation gave their pacifism a religious cast which would be challenged in the succeeding decade. The very impulse to social action predicated by their ideals would lead them to expand their organization, to associate with secular peace advocates, and to coordinate the antiwar movement; this active position inevitably would tempt some of them to ask how religious the pacifist ethic need be. If their initial statement of social obligation has an unreal optimism for modern minds, that is partly because it had been applied only to war, and partly because it was rooted in a progressive faith that has since been challenged. But in even assuming that pacifism is relevant to the struggle for justice, they projected themselves into the great social movements of their time, working for international order, industrial democracy, and better race relations; this involvement invariably would lead some of them to ask whether coercion might sometimes be necessary for reform, and whether the state itself might inevitably impede progress.

Pacifism was thus recast by World War I in several senses. It had a new personnel, including not only outstanding Quakers but also other liberal Protestant ministers and social workers; it had a new organizational structure; and it had broadened assumptions. Twentieth-century pacifism was historically oriented to liberal values. The progressive background of the liberal pacifist reinforced these values even as it socialized them and added a disposition toward political action. In 1917–18 the pacifist began to view war as an integral part of an unjust social order. The instruments of political control involved at least the latent threat of violence, he discovered, and these were in the hands of classes opposed to change. Behind even the system of democratic majority decision he found the tacit sanctions of violent force. To his political right and left were activists for whom violence appeared to be the ultimate authority.

But if the pacifist remembered anything from World War I it was that violence and authoritarianism were precisely what threatened his every liberal value. Against them he began to define an ethic of conflict, dealing with force as an instrument for social control and rejecting violent means. For a generation and more pacifists would evaluate choices in terms of the relationships of "ends and means," and in fact, the phrase would acquire a sanctity independent of tough-minded analysis. The new pacifist ethic was not fully articulated in its inception because the war was brief; the fetters of conformity were shortly removed; and the professional peace advocate felt free again to fight militarism without, it seemed, challenging the state.

Only a few pacifists perceived the dilemma that their impulse to far-reaching reform might come in conflict with their refusal to sanction violence in any cause: John Haynes Holmes, searching for ways to rationalize the passivity out of pacifism, perhaps searching for a Gandhi; Kirby Page looking for nonviolent methods of social change; moderate socialists warding off a Bolshevik-Communist line; Harold Gray and Evan Thomas on a hunger strike at Fort Leavenworth. Even those men forgot the dilemma once the war was over and they returned to normality or took up again the traditional instruments of social change. Liberal pacifists would face it again, however, in the agony of defining the road to power that split the Socialist Party in 1934, and in the fight against war and fascism; they would meet it in the sixties in working for civil rights and in opposing war in Vietnam. The terms of the dilemma were exposed in World War I. A willingness to grapple with them would characterize liberal pacifism in the twentieth century.

Peace as a Lonely Affirmation

... nothing in this Act contained shall be construed to require or compel any person to serve in any of the forces herein provided for who is found to be a member of any well-recognized religious sect or organization at present organized and existing and whose existing creed or principles forbid its members to participate in war in any form and whose religious convictions are against war or participation therein in accordance with the creed or principles of said religious organizations, but no person so exempted shall be exempted from service in any capacity that the President shall declare to be non-combatant . . . .[1]

Harold Gray and Evan Thomas were 2 of perhaps 3,989 objectors to war who were drafted.[2] These nearly 4,000 men claimed exemption in army camps, although 20,873 inducted men had been granted non-combatant classification by their local boards, and an indeterminable number had claimed exemption which their boards had refused. There are no figures for the men who refused to register and were sentenced by civil courts, although some of them were later inducted into the army.[3]

The figure of four thousand conscientious objectors can be compared with that of nearly three million inducted men to show the relative numerical insignificance of resistance to the military. Nevertheless, the President and the War Department, under Secretary Newton D. Baker, feared that the number of objectors might swell and obstruct the war effort. Therefore, the department avoided antagonizing objectors more than was necessary to maintain over-all discipline, while it placed tests on their sincerity and restrictions on their freedom in order to discourage the horde of slackers which, it imagined, would take advantage of any exceptional leniency. Beyond that point it seemed to leave the problem for matters of greater moment.

The four thousand objectors can be compared also with the estimated 171,000 draft evaders to show that, numerically, the pacifists were much less a threat to the war effort than real evaders It is apparent that the objectors were forthright and law-abiding in comparison with many others. They could not reconcile war with their highest ideals, but they accepted the penalties of the laws to which they objected. "Yet it was these men," Norman Thomas justly complained, "who did not so much as try to avoid the draft who were most vehemently denounced as cowards and slackers."[4] More important, these men had to relate themselves to the wartime state.

At the time of the Armistice the objectors had been assigned as follows:

        1,300 were accepted for noncombatant service
        1,200 were furloughed to service in industry and agriculture
          99 were furloughed to Friends' reconstruction work
         450 were court-martialed and imprisoned
         225 remained in camps, objecting to combat service
         715 remained in camps, objecting to combat or
                noncombatant military service
        _____
        3,989

Besides the 450 objectors sentenced by court-martial, 1 had been acquitted in trial, and 53 had been released from sentences by reviewing authorities and the Judge Advocate General.[5]

Ninety per cent of the conscientious objectors were native-born Americans. They were generally recognized by army psychologists as being mentally superior to average soldiers, despite the fact that less than one-fourth had graduated from high school, and only 3 per cent were college graduates. Furthermore, objectors possessed the normal attributes of personality, as well as of mind.[6]

Statistics are but the framework of the story of American conscientious objectors in World War I. In relation to the experiences and convictions of these men, ciphers were as meaningless as was the epithet stamped on Harold Gray's discharge papers, "character bad.' " Like the phrase, the figures were a bureaucracy's disinterested judgment. The importance of conscientious objection for subsequent American pacifism cannot be contained in numerical tables; it entails, on the one hand, a brief description of the government's policy to which pacifists objected, and, on the other hand, analysis of the assumptions governing conscientious objectors.

The term "conscientious objector" apparently was borrowed from England by the War Department. At first it designated only those who

69

shared creedal convictions of a church having nonresistant doctrines, but the term was soon applied to anyone who refused military service on the grounds of conscience. In this regard the Selective Service Act of May 18, 1917, virtually applied Civil War provisions and failed to deal with important aspects of modern conscientious objection. Its terms applied only to members "of some well-recognized religious sect or organization whose existing creed or principles forbid" participation in war "in any form." It applied only to members who shared those religious tenets, and it exempted them only from combat duties.[7] Its inclusive provision of military service for all and its exclusive application to members of recognized peace sects were modified through other acts of Congress and executive orders, but changes were made reluctantly and with little evidence of a larger understanding of the pacifist point of view.

The Selective Service Act was unacceptable to many sincere religious objectors because the noncombatant work to which it referred was regarded in practice as military service. Nearly a year passed after President Wilson signed the act before he specified noncombatant activities, and then (March 20, 1918) they included units that were patently supportive of the fighting: the medical corps, quartermaster corps, and engineer service.[8] Friends' relief work was not at first included. Another act of Congress was required before the War Department felt authorized to furlough objectors to civilian service.

Moreover, the act pointedly excluded all but members of the historic peace churches, making the test of sincerity the personal and corporate history of nonresistance. The administration's apprehension of a wave of evaders masquerading as converts was transparent; social ethics was to be frozen at its *status quo* ante bellum. As a matter of fact, the exemption provision had been broader in the National Defense Act of June 3, 1916, when it defined the objector as one who conscientiously held religious beliefs prohibiting participation in war, and whose sincerity would be established as the President might prescribe.[9] The War Department's difficulty lay in determining sincerity, and so during hearings on the 1917 Selective Service Act, Secretary Baker recommended the restrictive definition that was finally adopted. Pacifists discussed their objections with him and lobbied in Congress, but to no avail. Late in April, John Nevin Sayre wrote to the President asking that exemption be extended to individuals rather than organizations. Wilson replied that this was "impossible . . . because it would open the door to so much that was unconscientious on the part of persons who wished to escape service."[10] Consequently, the army found itself burdened with men who refused to fight because of personal convictions, but were not members of any religious body. Some such men proved as uncompromising as the most rigorous religious nonresistants; they certainly underwent as grueling tests of conviction as any others.

After all, a few thousand pacifists were but one of a multitude of problems facing a nation at war. The government had to train and transport three million fighting men; it had to gear the labor and ideals of about ninety million people to war. Conscientious objectors were handled in connection with the mobilization of the army and in rough proportion to the trouble they caused. They got a generally humane and flexible policy from civil administrators and superior military officers; they were subject to treatment ranging from forbearance to outrageous brutality at the hands of petty officers whose main concern was to see that orders were obeyed and who often were unsuited to tasks involving diplomacy and understanding. Pacifists were governed by policies which changed as the government learned more about them.

Three and one-half months after initial registration the Secretary of War directed that all conscientious objectors should be segregated from soldiers within camps and treated with "respect and consideration." The order was framed partly in the hope that judicious treatment would draw objectors into the army (the results of the policy depended upon the officers who implemented it; Major General J. Franklin Bell at Camp Upton, New York, for example, succeeded in enlisting a number of men, especially socialists).[11] The segregation order was aimed also at eliminating the confusion and distraction which objectors introduced into the ranks of soldiers, and at meeting the concerns of some pacifist churches.

Furthermore, in December, 1917, the Adjutant General of the Army found it necessary to order that "personal scruples against war" should be considered as constituting conscientious objection. "Conscientious scruples" against war were accepted as grounds for noncombatant service under an executive order of the President of March 20, 1918.[12] Thus, nonreligious objectors were recognized and treated in the same way as sectarian nonresisters. Except for those sentenced to prison, objectors remained segregated in army camps until June, 1918. At that time provisions were made to furlough some of them into agricultural and relief work.

Under the farm-furlough system the Secretary of War was empowered to grant furloughs without pay and allowances to enlisted men, and this was extended to conscientious objectors. Subsequently, 88 of them were recommended for Friends' reconstruction work abroad, 15

71

for reconstruction hospitals where soldiers were being rehabilitated for civilian life, 341 for noncombat or combat service, and 1,500 for farm or industrial furloughs.[13] The War Department suggested that the program be administered by an adjutant of the department, but after much correspondence and discussion established the fact that military operation would be unsatisfactory to most objectors, civilian administration was established under the very able commissioner, R. C. McCrea, of Columbia University.

Objectors accepting farm furlough agreed to work at the prevailing rate of wages in the community where they were employed (usually about forty or fifty dollars a month). They would turn over any amount above a private's pay, plus subsistance (about thirty dollars), to the American Red Cross. In many cases objectors returned their earnings to the government, or applied it to relief work. Either the farmer or the objector had to pay railroad fare from camp to the site of work. Conscientious objectors were not usually furloughed to their home communities, but the department did try to see that they were placed where they would be free to worship in their own ways. In Iowa and Ohio especially there were resentment and hostility to furloughed pacifists, but the army made it clear at the outset that they were employed in national service and were under military supervision. For the pacifists' ears, farm furlough was a civilian administration; for the public's information, it was a military institution. This kind of juggling made the problem difficult for the army, which, authorities agree, was more patient and understanding of objectors than were some religious leaders.

With a plan of alternate civilian service acceptable to all but the most "absolute" objectors, the War Department found itself faced with other serious problems. How should it fairly select objectors for its program? How could it weed out the insincere? Examples of unwise if not malicious treatment were being reported, and confusion surrounded the objectors. It seemed obvious that ordinary officers could not give a considered or uniform judgment on their nonresisting charges.

On June 1, 1918, Secretary Baker constituted a board of inquiry to examine all conscientious objectors for their sincerity and to recommend them for various types of service, including farm work and also Friends' reconstruction work in France. The board was composed, as Rufus Jones wrote, of "serious, high-minded, kindly disposed men, who honestly endeavored to do the impossible, i.e. to decide after a brief interview with the men, who among them was sincere and who was insincere."[14] The first chairman of the board was Major Richard C. Stoddard. He was ordered to Europe in the middle of August, 1918,

72

and was replaced by Major Walter G. Kellogg, judge advocate, United States Army. The other members of the board were Julian W. Mack, a judge of the United States Circuit Court of Appeals, and Harlan F. Stone, the dean of Columbia University Law School. The board visited each camp holding conscientious objectors and talked briefly with those who were not under court-martial charges and who had either refused or been denied noncombatant service. When they had the consent of the camp commander they examined also men under charges but not yet on trial. They interviewed all types of pacifists. Men who had been certified by local boards as belonging to nonresistant sects, "religious objectors," were generally tested for the consistency of their professions, habits, and church history. Political or "individual objectors" were tested for the consistency of their convictions against "warfare in any form."

 Crush out the fly with your thumb and wipe your hand,
You cannot crush the leaden, creaking machine,
The first endorsement, the paper on the desk
Referred by Adjutant Feeble to Captain Dull
For further information and his report.

Some men wish evil and accomplish it
But most men, when they work in that machine,
Just let it happen somewhere in the wheels.
The fault is no decisive, villainous knife
But the dull saw that is the routine mind.

—STEPHEN VINCENT BENÉT, *John Brown's Body*[15]

The professions and convictions of objectors were the most important things about them. Laws, provisions, and government boards are relevant because they were formed in response to the idea of nonresistance and because they forced the holders of that idea to explore its ramifications, often for the first time. Again and again pacifists had to draw the lines beyond which they would not obey the military. Each order forced them to define anew for themselves the implications of nonresistance; each decision required them to redefine their relationship to the state. In action their logic was often reduced to absurdity or, from another point of view, heroism.

Conscientious objectors of all sorts agreed that on the basis of their

73

notions of right and wrong for themselves and society they would refuse to participate in war, at least in combat service. They therefore
agreed to deny the rights of even the state at war to dispose of them
without regard to their convictions. The obligation not to participate in
war and the consequent duty of civil disobedience—these common
minimal assertions mark the various ramifications of conscientious
objection.

It would be a serious mistake to discuss objectors solely in terms of
logic and theology, or to stereotype them rigidly. Jane Addams wrote
with considerable insight that the term "conscientious objector" did
not apply to many objectors.[16] She probably distrusted the nuances of
the phrase rather than its literal meaning. She wrote that it was too
rigid and individualistic. In a sense it suggested doctrinaire obstruc-
tionism; it seemed to neglect the social concern of many objectors and
their instinctive rather than reasoned action. The phrase is settled upon,
however. It is precise and descriptive. It may be used with the understanding that many things motivated any one conscience, that there
were many sorts of objections, and that there was, therefore, a bewildering variety of pacifist responses. Some objectors started mod-
erately and then tried to stiffen up. Some began obdurately and then
softened their resistance. Noncombatants objected only to actual killing; absolutists refused even farm furlough. Here an objector would
not bear arms or wear the uniform but would police his own area and
cook for other pacifists; there a man would refuse to work at all.

This variety of motives and reasons characterized objectors as a
group and as individuals. The sensitive Harold Gray underwent acute
mental distress precisely because of his difficulty in choosing among a
variety of motives and reasonable alternatives. For this reason, and
like many objectors, he cannot easily be classified. For example, in
Walter Kellogg's categories of objectors—religious, idealistic, and political—Gray might fit as an idealist who undertook to solve the world's
ills with kindness and believed in human goodness. But on the other
hand, he believed also in human sinfulness. Though not a member of a
nonresistant sect, as a Disciple of Christ he belonged to a church with
a strong pacifist minority tradition; he himself was motivated by religious convictions. Though not a card-carrying Socialist, he became
increasingly aligned with those Socialists who abjured violence. More
important, he stressed the duty of opposing conscription from the secular point of view of the absolute right to political freedom. Perhaps
Gray's thought was more encompassing than that of most others, but
it illustrates the difficulty of classifying pacifists.

Another illustration of this difficulty is the distinction made between "religious" and "individualistic" objectors, between those who were members of well-recognized pacifist sects and those who were not. This distinction proved meaningless in individual cases. Because of the wide latitude of beliefs within some sects, a member of a nonresistant church might hold doctrines identical to those accepted by a member of another church, or of no church at all. Either might or might not take the Bible literally, emphasize Christ's example, believe that God's way is love, or hold that the God-inspired conscience should not be conscripted. In practice, official distinctions broke down. As Norman Thomas noted, "It was not even possible to distinguish between 'sincere' and 'insincere' objectors save by the pragmatic test of the amount of suffering they should endure for their beliefs."[17]

To the army, however, the distinction seemed useful in dealing with groups of objectors. General Enoch H. Crowder, provost marshal, reported to the Secretary of War at the end of 1917 that religious and "other" objectors were entirely distinct classes, legally, morally, and practically. The general wrote:

> They are legally distinct because the act of Congress expressly recognizes and gives a legal status to the one, but wholly ignores the other. They are morally distinct, because the one obeys what he regards as a divine mandate . . . while the other is merely choosing to accept the loose and untried speculation of modern theorists . . . . They are practically distinct, because the one includes an ascertainable group of individuals, registered in their sect, definitely fixed on May 18 . . . and not capable of enlargement at will; while the other may include any one whomsoever has chosen, after May 18 last, to make profession insincerely, of an opinion opposed to war . . . .[18]

Even admitting the General's bias, he was correct in asserting that religious objectors in the army's sense were ascertainable. For this reason statistical data are available for them. A survey of over 1,000 conscientious objectors in army camps revealed that about half were Mennonites (554), about one-fourth were members of various pacifist sects (if one includes Quakers), and the rest were either members of denominations not necessarily pacifist (206) or were not affiliated with any denomination (55). It appeared, moreover, that an overwhelming majority of religious objectors understood the Bible literally and objected to war because it was forbidden in the Scriptures, by church and creed, or by Christ and "the Commandment."[19] Figures such as these led observers to associate Biblical literalism with religious objectors. This association was perhaps reasonable, although it undoubtedly had exceptions.

75

The difficulty was that many Quakers and many men who were not of nonresistant churches were not literalistic, although they were motivated by religious convictions.

Moreover, it was concluded generally that those men who were "religious" objectors in the restricted sense of the word were nonresistants; that is, they opposed war rather than the government, and they tried to accommodate themselves to the military world without compromising with it. The difficulties with this generalization are two-fold. In the first place, a number of members of churches officially supporting the war were themselves nonresistants, as was, for example, Harold Gray. Secondly, nonresistants sometimes found themselves resisting the government as obdurately as even the political objectors. This fact is cardinally important because it means that the relationship of individuals to the wartime government was evaluated from various pacifist positions, and that *the limits beyond which individuals would go did not necessarily correspond to the bases for their pacifism.* Opposition to conscription and a high valuation on individual freedom were characteristic of pacifism of all doctrinal kinds.

The problem of identifying "political objectors" further illustrates the difficulties of classification. The War Department estimated that they constituted about 10 per cent of all objectors, but the figure was meaningless by definition because the category was so vague.[20] It often included "all men who on economic or rational rather than religious grounds opposed enforced participation in war," and thus denoted the basis for objection; but it sometimes referred to men against a specific conflict, and then denoted the *instance* of objection.[21] In either case, most of those involved were Socialists who believed that "modern wars are at the bottom sanguinary struggles for the commercial advantages of the possessing classes, and that they are disastrous to the cause of the workers, their struggle and aspirations, their rights and liberties."[22] Many of them never appeared on Selective Service rolls because they were imprisoned under the Espionage Act or for failure to register for the draft. Ammon Hennacy spent nearly eight months in solitary confinement in Atlanta for distributing antiwar leaflets and then was prosecuted for refusing to register. He was one of hundreds of war resisters who were labeled lawbreakers for the reason that

> there could be no such thing as a political offense in a democracy; each man was arrested for breaking a law and tried as a criminal. Any other course might have laid the government open to the charge of suppressing a minority, which was to be avoided. The reformer in politics

knew only too well how to deal with the reformer out of politics. The latter was hoist by his own petard.[23]

The Socialist was often well educated and intelligent, and this assured him of harsh treatment. Considering all his advantages and his incessant talk of democracy, Walter Kellogg recalled, "you were bound to feel differently about him than you may have felt about the Mennonite . . . . He who should help, hinders and obstructs; he who should lead, by his example incites others to revolt."[24] Kellogg disagreed with the Socialist's explanation for the war, of course, but he could not understand why the radical would not accept the majority interpretation. In part it was because Kellogg did not distinguish clearly between the instance of socialistic objection—the specific war—and the grounds of it.

There were at least three major doctrinal bases for conscientious objection to military service which can be distinguished by *the authority adduced* for disobedience of the state rather than by the point at which disobedience was asserted. At one extreme were those who rested their cases upon philosophical or political principles. At the other extreme were those who objected to fighting because of a literal response to scriptural or creedal injunctions. In the center were those liberal Christians who objected to military service from a mixture of religious, humanitarian, and philosophical grounds.

A major basis of conscientious objection was the doctrine that the unrestrained (but responsible) individual is of supreme worth, and that the state is a corrupting appendage to the community. Those who held this view opposed conscription per se as well as killing. Their position was most precisely put by Roger Baldwin who refused to obey any statutory direction of his "choice of service and ideals" on the grounds that the principle of conscription was "a flat contradiction of all our cherished ideals of individual freedom, democratic liberty, and Christian teaching."[25] He refused "any service whatever designed to help prosecute the war." Although he recognized that everyone renders "involuntary assistance to the war in the process of . . . daily living," he rejected all services consciously accepted, whether fighting among the trenches, buying war bonds, or raising crops "under the lash of the Draft Act." Holding such absolute convictions, he confronted the draft by choice. He refused to take a physical examination, and thus waived the possibility of being rejected or being called too late to serve in the war. A civil court sentenced him to one year in prison.

Norman Thomas wrote to Clarence M. Case in 1921 that "conscientious objection by radicals was based rather on objection to conscription than to killing,"[26] but, in fact, motives were usually mixed. Indeed, only a few objectors opposed conscription per se. Of their type, Walter Kellogg, chairman of the board of inquiry, deridingly reported:

> The State, the Army, the Church, any Institution is . . . merely a name. Persons are what is real—and persons alone. The vague verbal thing called the State with its empty verbal product, the Army, are not real enough to impose any commands upon him, the Real, the Fundamental, the person. He cannot, therefore, submit to conscription . . . .[27]

It is not necessary to discuss *reality* in a philosophical sense in order to understand what these objectors were asserting. Most of them did not carry their position to the anarchism in which it logically ended (as Garrisonian no-government men had done). In part this was because they thought in concrete and personal terms when they were faced with specific decisions to make. In part, too, it was because they held an ethic which stressed social value but, nevertheless, placed the ultimate responsibility for ethical decisions upon the person.

One value to which men are responsible, according to this group of objectors, is the social welfare. In this respect *individualistic* was an inaccurate description of the radical objector, for he felt an intense social concern. Like Baldwin, he wanted a fellowship of free men. With Norman Thomas he believed that "social institutions are failures unless they can secure the maximum of co-operation with the minimum of coercion." In a true sense, Thomas concluded, the individual is a "product of the group, but the group is only valuable as it permits personalities, not automatons, to emerge."[28] To this value both the individuals and the state itself are responsible, and by it individuals must judge the state. Evan Thomas wrote his brother from camp, "I am a C.O. not because I believe fighting is wrong [although he did] but because no free man can be conscripted."[29]

Only three months earlier, Evan Thomas had been working with German prisoners of war. He respected them, but he was disturbed by the extent to which they seemed to have lost the sense of worth of the individual in their national idealism. Moral intolerance frightened him as much in Americans as in Germans, and the only alternative he could see was "individualism and love, which make individualism and collectivism ultimately one and the same thing."[30] His thoughts were crystalizing now. He acknowledged his responsibility to help change the social milieu in which, for example, both wealthy and poor sought property at the expense of greater values such as social concern, love, and freedom. His analysis of the economic order paralleled his view of war. He felt duty-bound to challenge both in the only way he knew, by denying the absolute authority of the state over the individual; but he did not come to grips with the question of how a national policy of nonresistance to force could advance the cause of peace and justice. In his thought the ethical obligation of conscientious objection expressed a personal impulse toward social action, rather than a well-defined social program.

Thomas and Baldwin were compassionate men in whose thought philosophical and religious motives were mixed. They challenged the absolute authority of the state because they believed that it often fettered people. Many who began as religious objectors to war emerged as radicals because their camp and prison experiences illustrated the authoritarianism of the wartime state. Some who had not been Socialists before the war embraced Marxism. A few philosophical anarchists who regarded government as an instrument of class oppression turned to communism. Roger Baldwin was probably correct in thinking that the war experience of most objectors had not led them to theorize about the state, class struggle, or "coercion." The result, he wrote, had been "more pragmatists and fewer theorists" among reformers.[31] Some of the most articulate leaders did announce their utter loss of confidence in political methods and in the state as an institution; they turned to the labor movement or to international socialism in order to advance social values which the government seemed to have spurned. Meanwhile, numerous men were quietly challenging the state without theorizing about it. The philosophical objectors said at least that the state is not the ultimate authority for the individual. Not only is government subject to the will of the people in aggregate, but the people themselves have no right through it to conscript an individual because men are ethically committed to other values than popular decision.

The largest number of conscientious objectors based their actions on scriptural and creedal injunctions rather than on rational grounds and social value. For example, Maurice Hess, a Dunker, told a judge:

> I do not believe that I am seeking martyrdom. As a young man, life and its hopes and freedom and opportunities for service are sweet to me. I want to go out into the world and make use of what little talent I may have acquired by long and laborious study.

> But I know that I dare not purchase these things at the price of eternal condemnation. I know the teaching of Christ, my Savior. He taught us to resist not evil, to love our enemies, to bless them that curse us, and do good to them that hate us. Not only did he teach this,

79

but he also practiced it in Gethsemane, before Pilate, and on Calvary. We would indeed be hypocrites and base traitors to our profession if we would be unwilling to bear the taunts and jeers of a sinful world . . . rather than to participate in war and military service. We know that obedience to Christ will gain for us . . . eternal life. We cannot yield, we cannot compromise, we must suffer.[32]

Hess was more concerned with "eternal condemnation" than were some objectors, and he had different church traditions, but otherwise his reasons were typical of the sectarians. In his mind the issue was neatly drawn between obeying Christ and obeying the state, and the former claimed his full devotion. Other sectarian pacifists drew the issue differently, but maintained the same allegiance.

Many International Bible Students, for example, opposed conscription because according to scriptural revelation the imminent return of Christ had made carnal warfare unnecessary for them, the elect. Followers of "Pastor" Charles T. Russell, an evangelist who died just before the war, the International Bible Students constituted about 6 per cent of the objectors examined by the board of inquiry.[33]

The Molokans, a group of Doukhobors from Arizona and California, on the other hand, believed in the direct and sometimes physical revelation of the Holy Spirit. They had immigrated to America from Russia on the understanding that they would be free from military service. They believed that they had been warned by the Holy Spirit not to register for the American draft or to have anything to do with the war. The eligible men among them frankly presented their claims to their local board and to President Wilson. Because they refused to register, thirty-four were sentenced to civil prison, some were subsequently inducted, and six were sent to Fort Leavenworth, Kansas. There they became the sectarians best loved by their fellow objectors. The Molokans did not argue about religion. They read their Bibles, sang, and walked about. They joined readily in games; they were keenly interested in education. They were prepared to die for their quiet convictions, but they did not in any way threaten the national war effort. They were punished for obeying creedal beliefs rooted in generations of suffering; they were imprisoned for holding to that which alone gave meaning and value to their way of life.

The irony of that kind of punishment in a war to save democracy was tragically illustrated in the case of an inducted nonresistant who refused to don military uniform or do any kind of service for the army because he believed that these things were forbidden in the Bible. He was imprisoned at Alcatraz with other members of his sect, where he

80

was kept in the prison dungeon for about five days under gruelling conditions. He was later transferred to Fort Leavenworth where he contracted pneumonia and died. Jane Addams wrote of him:

> He had originally and continuously taken his stand against putting on the uniform, and when his wife arrived at Leavenworth to take away the body, to her horror she found that body, at last unable to resist, dressed in a soldier's uniform. Her representative who came to see me, with his broken English could convey but feebly the sense of outrage, of unfairness, of brutal disregard of the things of the spirit, or the ruthless overriding of personality which this incident had aroused among thousands of Doukhobortii.[34]

What qualities made religious pacifism so obdurate? Whatever it was, obedience to creedal and scriptural injunctions led many plain men to suffer great physical cruelty and social disapprobation in order to assert their allegiance to supranational values.

Harold Gray was quartered with such men upon his arrival at Camp Custer, Michigan. They were mostly Russellites and Mennonites, he wrote, who took their Bibles "with painful literalness," and seemed to be entirely lacking "in anything like a modern interpretation of the Cross."[35] Indeed, he observed, the Cross did not seem to play much part in their thinking; their devotion was directed by the words of Scripture.

Gray found the sectarians sincere but dull, as did a nonreligious objector, Ernest L. Meyer. The Mennonites with whom Meyer was placed were kindly, but their religion seemed to him rather grim. They crowded around the tent stove on frosty nights to read their Bibles and discuss the Word, to pray ponderously and to sing—always to sing. They sang their hymns loudly and seriously. This particularly irritated Meyer, who liked laughter and literature, until on his first night in a cell at Fort Leavenworth the Mennonites eased his apprehension by singing the old hymn, "For This Is Like Heaven to Me." Meyer joined lustily in the singing, forgetting for the moment his hatred of those voices that had driven him mad "in the noisy holiness of the Crusaders' colony."[36]

Meyer spent much time with the Mennonites; he said he lived "with sanctity in the doldrums." But then he reflected that the radical objectors in their tents were spinning "webs of different materials and perhaps just as gray and tedious. The difference would be merely a difference in jargon . . . ."[37]

There was an important element of truth in Meyer's reflection. Despite the great differences between them, both radicals and sectarians sought security in a hostile world, and both were devoted to ideals other than those of their compatriots in arms. Neither group was understood or accommodated by the government. Major Walter Kellogg regarded the sectarians as generally ignorant and isolated people, "dull and almost bovine."[38] Although he recognized the superior intelligence of radical objectors, he had only more contempt for their refusal to serve. Kellogg could not accept any absolutistic objectors because his judgments were based on a different set of values than theirs. He valued common sense and realism; they valued absolute truths. He thought of social idealism as being synonymous with the Allied cause; they judged the Allies by their ideals, whether a free society, for the radicals, or God, for the sectarians. Kellogg, a government official responsible to the majority of the people, thought of the national community and the state as identical. The objectors, on the other hand, represented minority groups opposed to the war, and they were conscious that the state was an agency distinct from their communities. For the major, the nation was sovereign; for the objectors, the nation was responsible. Radicals and sectarians, absolutists and noncombatant soldiers, all asserted their right to hold values different from the prevailing norm.

A few objectors held a middle ground with respect to their reasons for refusing military service. They were religiously motivated, but they were not members of nonresistant sects (except for some Quakers). They had a spokesman in young Erling H. Lunde who said in his court-martial defense that he was "out of the rut of orthodox thought," but that in refusing to become a soldier he was prompted by "deep religious and moral convictions against war, which includes militarism and conscription."[39] In 1920 the Conference of All Friends, representative of international Quakerism, defined in retrospect the position taken by the middle group of conscientious objectors:

> The fundamental ground of our opposition to war is religious and ethical. It attaches to the nature of God as revealed in Christ and to the nature of man as related to Him . . . . The only absolutist ground for an unalterable and inevitable opposition to war is one which attaches to the inherent nature of right and wrong, one which springs out of the consciousness of obligation to what the enlightened soul knows ought to be.[40]

In place of a rational analysis or church doctrine the conference substituted a religious ethic.

This ethic was shared by objectors other than Friends, and not by all Quakers. It had at least five facets. It involved respect for personality which, it assumed, war debases; it held that suffering for another was a higher virtue than conquering him by force, although both might in-

volve self-sacrifice; it held that violence would be overcome by its opposite, love, rather than by its likeness, force; and it asserted that ethical
living means not only avoiding but also overcoming evil. In these four
ways the ethic was aligned against war. Its fifth characteristic was its
demand that each individual discover his ethical responsibility for himself in every situation. This meant to some objectors that they should
not participate in warfare, and should seek to overcome war.

Those who held this religious ethic found themselves taking the same
actions as radical and sectarian objectors, but for different reasons.
The radical, for example, sought to protest against conscription (which
he believed was an integral part of the war system)—Roger Baldwin
took his first opportunity to object to the draft. Religious objectors also
opposed conscription, but they came to distinguish their actions from
mere protests. Thus, in the summer of 1918, Kirby Page wrote to
Harold Gray at Fort Riley, Kansas:

> Of course you will agree that Christ was not concerned primarily with
> making a protest against the evils of his day. What he was concerned
> about was overcoming those evils, and of course, that is your purpose
> in the stand you have taken against war. If I put the emphasis in
> making the maximum protest, I should preach a sermon next Sunday
> morning that would cause me to be locked up before night. I believe
> that I can do more to help overcome war and the war spirit by another
> approach. Of course, if it came to a question of compromise, I should
> not hesitate one moment, for with you I am an "absolutist" to that
> degree. If I had not been entitled to exemption on legal grounds, I
> should certainly be where you are today . . . .[41]

Gray and Evan Thomas exemplified the religious idealist in this respect.
They resolved the problem in the same way as did Page, distinguishing
noncompromise from protest. But their resolution came only after considerable mental and physical suffering.

At Fort Riley, Gray and Thomas were joined by Erling H. Lunde
and Howard W. Moore in a hunger strike. Their action was not taken
suddenly. Late in July about fifty objectors who refused to perform
regular camp duties or to build their own separate facilities were left
in a vacant field with tents, inadequate water, and no toilet facilities.
Three times a day they were escorted a quarter of a mile to draw raw
rations which each man was expected to cook for himself with only his
mess kit for equipment. Most of them refused rations on these terms,
and so after about three days of fasting they were permitted to cook
collectively. Some twenty men still refused to work, but they accepted
the hospitality of the others. The little tent colony existed about three

83

more weeks in that fashion. Naturally there were disputes with the army officers, who insisted on addressing their charges as "privates," but more distressing was the rancor between the objectors who held varied and intense convictions about where "to draw the line." After a protracted dispute, the majority decided that food should be provided only to those who helped with the work.[42]

Thomas, Gray, Lunde, and Moore were left with unenviable alternatives. They could join with the others, but that seemed to mean "working with the military." They could accept raw rations, but even then they would be accepting the "technical status of soldiers" and getting an impossible diet in return (the rations provided were intended for use in large kitchens, not in the field). They chose not to eat. They argued that since they were refusing conscription, the government should either free them into civilian jurisdiction or imprison and care for them. In any case, it should cease to treat them as truculent soldiers. For a time their objective shifted from prepared food to outright liberty. They were through with the pretense of being civilians in army camps; they wanted to break conscription itself; they would not eat until they were released; and they sent a statement of their intention to Secretary Baker.[43] On August 19, Thomas and his three friends refused to eat until released from military status. Ironically, the next day one of his brothers, Ralph, was wounded in action in France.*

The army was solicitous of the strikers' health, now, and the doctor even resorted to force-feeding them milk and eggs through a tube. On September 1 a colonel ordered Thomas in the name of the United States Army to eat. He refused. Gray began to reconsider. It seemed to him that his friend's position was extremely tenuous, that it might be construed as an assertion of the right of suicide, and that at all events the original meaning of their strike had been lost. A major arrived from Washington and talked with each man at length, promising, among other things, improved conditions for the objectors at camp. Gray abandoned his strike with the mental reservation that he would await an order he might conscientiously refuse to obey. The object of protesting conscription had given way to a desire to clarify his position.

Norman Thomas immediately wired his appreciation to Gray, even as he had assured them all of his support, and Evan felt the mounting

---

* Ralph Thomas enlisted with great enthusiasm in the army, and was eager to see action. He was wounded above Vesle, France, by an exploding German shell, and three weeks later still regretted missing "the most exciting of all war events—an advance." His letters home revealed his increasing disillusionment with the war, however, and a warm admiration for Evan Thomas.

84

pressure to give in. He paced the hospital room nervously, his green eyes lost in thought. Another tube-feeding, more promises from the major, and he relented. Lunde and finally Moore came around. After a short time in the hospital they were returned to camp.

By this time, Gray had come to the conclusion that there was nothing wrong in doing his own cooking and cleaning, and that he would be wrong in refusing to care for himself. He was not a philosophical anarchist; he believed that the state had the right "to enforce sanitary and health regulations, to imprison criminals for the purpose of reforming them, and to conscript capital . . . for the common good."[44] He did not agree that the state had a right to conscript men for service to which they were conscientiously opposed. The trouble with the hunger strike had been that it confused the right of compelling service to the wartime government, which Gray denied, with government regulations that he accepted. Thomas came to similar conclusions.

Shortly after the hunger strike, Gray was commanded to do some work around Fort Riley which clearly contributed nothing to the maintenance of his own person. He refused, and was sentenced to twenty-five years' imprisonment at hard labor and committed to the disciplinary barracks at Fort Leavenworth. Evan Thomas was court-martialed for refusing the order of an officer to eat, found guilty, and given the same sentence (the original terms of life imprisonment in both cases were reduced by Major General Leonard Wood, as Norman Thomas wrote, "in his mercy").[45]

Finally, Gray and Thomas found their situations clarified. At Leavenworth they worked gladly. Gray contrasted his work as a hospital attendant which he was doing, as he said, "under compulsion," with the labor that he had been required to do at Fort Riley "under conscription."[46] At Fort Riley he had been ordered to work as a soldier; in prison, he thought, rejection of military service was recognized. Prison ended Thomas's confusion, but not his trials. On November 8 he again refused to work, but this time he was clearly supporting a group of religious objectors who themselves had refused prison work and had been manacled in solitary confinement. From then until some time after Christmas he was in solitary every other two weeks on a bread and water diet, and was forbidden to read or write (except for an occasional letter to his mother which usually was not delivered). As a direct result of his protest, the publicity given to it, and a resulting conference between Nevin Sayre and the President, manacling in all military prisons was abolished, and conscientious objectors were brought out of solitary. As soon as he had registered his objection, in June, Thomas had known

85

that "it became absolutely necessary . . . to work out the relation of the individual to society." Only after months of experimenting which somehow he bore with good humor, was he able to work out in action and to his own satisfaction his conviction that "freedom and love and truth were always dependent on each other . . . [so that] no free man can be conscripted or submit to the army machine."[47]

Whether or not Thomas and Gray rationalized their actions, it is important to appreciate how their religious ethic affected their conscientious objection, inasmuch as they were representative of the religious idealist. Because they believed that ethical living meant more than avoiding evil, they sought an ethical way to strike at evil, in this case at war through conscription. Because they held that suffering was more virtuous than fighting, they chose to starve in protest. Because their ethic involved searching within their own minds, weighing the advice of others, and evaluating the implications of the Bible, Thomas, Gray, and their friends went through considerable mental anguish in order to relate themselves ethically to their nation. This evolvement of their position is significant because it reveals the impulse to social action which came to characterize pacifism and to distinguish it from traditional nonresistance.

A half-century later numerous conscientious objectors would call themselves war resisters and would apply the principle of political effectiveness in their search for relevance and consistency. They would push the point of objection back to registration, challenging the Selective Service System with mutilated draft cards and mass demonstrations. They would work through organizations designed to encourage resistance, not merely to protect their civil rights. There would be other differences, too, in the role of the United States in world affairs, in the role and perceptions of young people, in the new media making the tensions between ideals and realities nationwide, immediate, and often intolerable, and in increased social permissiveness. Not the least important would be the development of pacifism itself as a technique of social change. A war objector tracing that notion back through history would stumble upon Evan and Norman Thomas, Harold Gray, Ernest Meyer, Roger Baldwin, and their friends tortured by familiar questions: Do I have a right to deny the claims of my state on my own authority? "Is the singular, moral witness the best way personally to affect history? Should effectiveness be considered at all? . . . To what extent are my decisions political and moral decisions?"[48] How should I relate to those who accept the call to arms? At what point and on what basis should I draw the line of noncooperation?

To some of these queries he would answer differently than they (his movement would be no more unified than theirs), but to others he would respond the same; for in the final analysis, he was like the religious idealist, the radical, and the sectarian of World War I in asserting an ethic which demanded a measure of freedom from his state. Beyond all hope of striking at the evil of war, every objector came at last to conclude with Ernest Meyer:

> We live in society, but we live first of all with ourselves, and we could not live honestly or at peace with ourselves if we had taken human lives in war when all reason [and all religion, others would have added] cried out against it. So much we have attained.[49]

Right or wrong in refusing to fight, objectors asserted that pacifism was a duty for which they were willing to suffer. At the very least they were "pleading for the social value of Heresy."[50] If the will of the nation is truly the ultimate ethical authority, then pacifists were but a "slightly bedraggled fringe on the robe of Mars."[51] But if men owe their first allegiance to anything other than public opinion, then conscientious objection was an important affirmation of that duty.

For many it was a lonely affirmation. Every sincere objector sought for himself some basis upon which to choose between alternative and conflicting loyalties, whether according to a political philosophy like that of Roger Baldwin, or scriptural injunctions like those of the Molokans, or a religious principle like that of Harold Gray. If the anguish of decision was more poignant for objectors than for other pacifists, that was perhaps because they had almost no constructive alternatives to military service. This situation bred in some of them a sense of futility which was heightened by their isolation. It was perhaps more difficult for them to accept the test of social relevance that marked pacifists for their role in the postwar peace movement.

PART TWO

Pacifists between the Wars

"If the Nations Used Donkey Sense!"

A widely distributed cartoon later published in the Emergency Peace Campaign's *No-Foreign-War Crusade*, 1937.

IV

The Dynamics of Peace Advocacy*

> Peace is within reach for the first time in history. Instantaneous communication between the responsible heads of governments and simultaneous distribution of information to the people of all nations are now possible. International relations can be watched and guided from day to day. Machinery exists for the peaceful settlement of disputes. There is ready at hand an organized peace movement, capable of concerted action.
>
> —FLORENCE BREWER BOECKEL[1]

Charles Clayton Morrison, editor of the *Christian Century*, was not very encouraging when, early in 1920, he wrote Kirby Page about publishing *The Sword or The Cross*. "I sometimes think there is less interest in constructive peace than before the war," the editor reflected; "We have been much more seriously brutalized by the war than we know." Much later in the year he added, "Your book will be read by the esoteric few. The mood of the time is anything but congenial with pacifist doctrine."[2] Nevertheless, Morrison joined the crusade against war and sought to implement the ideals which World War I had not realized: peace, justice, and internationalism. Throughout the twenties and into the thirties, the organized peace movement gained strength, building on the nation's disillusionment and frustration with the peace settlement. Pacifists were active in attempts to secure peace (as reflected by Morrison's statement that he had been taught to see more deeply into the nature of war by two "mere boys," Harold Gray and Kirby Page). Their effectiveness in mobilizing public opinion in order to affect foreign policy was largely a function of the dynamics of the peace movement itself, however, and in particular of the relationship between

* This chapter is designed to provide a conceptual frame of reference for the narrative history of the interwar period.

91

the constituencies of each peace society and the specific publics it cultivated.

Woodrow Wilson sailed the Atlantic with copies of the Treaty of Versailles while Page wrote to Gray, "Most of our friends are quite pessimistic over the peace treaty. Many people are beginning to doubt that this was 'the war to end war?' "[3] Most pacifists had reached that conclusion before the Armistice. They had consistently advocated the peace implied in Wilson's Fourteen Points even though they insisted that fighting would tie the settlement to "the old self-convicted diplomacy." Some of them had joined prowar liberals in the Foreign Policy Association, one of the few American groups to send advice to the peace conference throughout its deliberations.* Others promoted a league and liberal peace through the Woman's Peace Party, which in most respects avoided criticism of the government. Its leaders participated in an international conference in Zurich, Switzerland, beginning in May, 1919, which kept in touch with the Paris negotiations and also perfected the organization of the Women's International League for Peace and Freedom.† The American women were disappointed with the treaties. They, like most pacifists, had been isolated only from the prevailing nationalism which, they feared, characterized both conflict and settlement. Their varied ideals—secular and religious, socialistic and sectarian—produced a similar position for them all, a stance apart. For one reason or another they viewed the international order from a different perspective than that of traditional diplomacy. In this they were perhaps like Wilson. Ironically, the pacifists and the President were equally dominated by their international visions, they who from the first would not fight and he who at the last would not compromise. His bitter experience reinforced their conviction that the war would both aggravate the need for international and social change and place in control of all nations those most wedded to the *status quo.*

---

* The Foreign Policy Association originated in a meeting in Apr., 1918, and reflected Paul Kellogg's dismay with the lack of a coherent liberal force for a democratic peace. For some time it was known as the Committee on Nothing at All and had the nucleus of the old American Union Against Militarism. As the Armistice neared, peace aims could again be freely discussed, so the committee became the League of Free Nations Association and, subsequently, the Foreign Policy Association.

† The Zurich meeting was the outgrowth of a provision made by the International Congress of Women which met at The Hague in 1915 that delegates from each national section should meet in conjunction with the peace conference. It had been expected that the settlement would be held in a neutral country; and when Paris was chosen, the women met at Zurich in order to mitigate the distinction between the vanquished and the victors.

They were not surprised, therefore, to find that at the very moment of victory "any attempt at bold and penetrating discussion was quickly and ruthlessly suppressed as if men had no right to consider together the social conditions surrounding them."[4] In Chicago members of the International Workers of the World were tried for sedition, and in New York the Socialist Rand School was harried by an investigating committee of the state legislature. Race riots and strikes engendered hatred and misunderstanding. The Red Scare, a hysterical apprehension of radicalism, excited patriots across the country and resulted in the deportation of hundreds of innocent aliens. Jane Addams incurred incrimination because German women appealed to her and the President's wife to help replace 3,000 of their milk cows which had been sent to Belgium. In some respects, she wrote, it seemed more difficult to be known as a pacifist in 1919 than it had been during the war.[5]

Most disappointing to peace workers was the mood of the country, "anything but congenial with pacifist doctrine," as Morrison wrote. They were not disturbed merely that the Senate rejected the League of Nations, for many of them had serious misgivings about that world organization; they feared, however, that the United States had rejected international cooperation as well. John Haynes Holmes noted that less than one year after the peace conference all the great powers were arming for the next war. He asked whether "man, face to face with the challenge of peace, has found himself unwilling to pay the price which peace exacts; or, if willing, has been ignorant of what this price has really involved."[6]

A number of writers concluded that Americans in the decade after the war were unwilling to pay the international price of peace or the social price of justice. Norman Thomas observed the "almost total failure of a stalwart minority of liberals to function" in either wartime or postwar crisis.[7] Walter Weyl, who had contributed *The New Democracy* to the political understanding of the progressives, returned from Paris to describe his generation of reformers as "tired radicals." Vida Scudder wrote later from Wellesley College of distressed friends, of "broken and scattered ranks of reformers." Some of them, like Anna Rochester and Grace Hutchins, who helped to edit the *World Tomorrow* in the early twenties, eventually turned to the Communist party as a substitute for liberal reform. Vida Scudder concluded:

> There is a worse type of Depression than the economic; such was shared by most people who in the pre-war period had joyously hailed what seemed the rising forces of social redemption. The Great War had not made the world safe for democracy; intelligent reformers

93

had never expected it to do so, yet it was not easy to watch the surging flood of disillusion which threatened to submerge the idealism and drown the hopes of the world, not to see the reforms on which hope and effort had centered, hardly with exception halted or destroyed. Those ten exhausted years were the most discouraged I have known, and I say this in 1936.[8]

One of the changes that most bothered her was the shattering of the prewar assumption of "inevitable progress." The very reformers who before the war had been deluded by the idea that peace was inevitable were those who after the war were most tempted to conclude that peace was impossible. They were the "tired radicals" who had tried reform and tasted defeat. As author John Chamberlain concluded, they were of little use to the younger radical, "the fledgling who has the courage of inexperience."[9]

A younger generation of peace workers arose, however, and while many of them assumed religious certainty or a vague faith in the ultimate triumph of good, the most prominent were not bound to a conception of "inevitable progress." They tended to agree, instead, with Florence Brewer Boeckel, educational director for the National Council for the Prevention of War, who wrote in 1930 that there were two errors equally dangerous: to assume that peace will come in any case, and to assume that peace cannot possibly be achieved. She urged, rather, that although the threat of war persisted, "peace is within reach for the first time in history."[10] Miss Boeckel was not an absolute pacifist, but her search for realistic grounds for peace characterized the more significant pacifists. These men and women looked at the "scrapped ideals" and "withered hopes" of the peace settlement and concluded with Kirby Page that "we who believe there is a better and more practicable way out than by violence and bloodshed . . . see in the present upheaval of the world a vindication of our position."[11] Page was a radical pacifist, but his determination to find an alternative to war characterized all those who organized the peace movement of the twenties and thirties.

American peace workers took part in a world-wide effort. Supporters of the League of Nations in the United States, for example, united with others in Estonia, Hungary, India, and elsewhere through the International Federation of League of Nations Societies. English-speaking women cooperated with Egyptians, Dutch, Italians, and Japanese, to name a few of the groups in the Women's International League for Peace and Freedom. They learned of each other's work and aspirations through their journal, *Pax International*, which Madeline Doty, the wife of Roger Baldwin, developed and edited until 1931. Emily Greene

94

Balch held all the most influential offices of both the national and international W.I.L.P.F. at one time and another, and she succeeded Jane Addams as international president. The United States Section of the organization in 1930 took upon itself the pledge of $500 a month that Miss Addams had kept for nearly a decade: "although the WILPF had been born of the Travail of Europe, it was nurtured by America."[12] Nonetheless, the executive committee remained overwhelmingly European, and its headquarters were in Geneva.

Similarly, the Fellowship of Reconciliation maintained close touch with the International Fellowship of Reconciliation, largely through John Nevin Sayre. Chairman of the American section in 1935–39, and co-executive secretary in 1924–35 and from 1940–46, he was also for several years prior to 1941 chairman of the Council of the I.F.O.R. He was active in other ways, too, contributing financially and many times sailing to Europe. In 1921 he toured Germany with four other members of the International Fellowship to carry a message of postwar reconciliation to Berlin and other German cities. In 1936 he helped organize the "Embassies of Reconciliation," visits to prime ministers of major European countries by Fellowship representatives who appealed for a new peace conference. Americans cooperated in the International Fellowship, but they did not dominate it. It undertook many conferences and much work in which they helped only financially. Its headquarters and its executive officers were European.

By 1938 the *Peace Year Book* listed 109 international organizations, including professional societies but not including groups promoting relief and friendship between only two nations. Most of them had their headquarters in Switzerland, although many were staffed in England and France, and a few each in Holland, Belgium, Austria, and the United States. All of these groups promoted internationalism and peace, although for perhaps two-thirds of them peace was incidental to professional and technical cooperation. In seven countries there were organizations to coordinate peace work. The peace movement was international and diversified.[13]

The American organizations devoted to peace in the interwar period were many and varied. A Commission on the Coordination of Efforts for Peace listed 12 international, 28 national, and 37 local peace societies in the United States. In addition, it found 2 international, 56 national, and 51 local groups which were not primarily peace societies, but promoted internationalism through special committees (these included many churches). Another 120 bodies were organized for purposes somehow related to peace advocacy.[14] Peace was promoted from

95

Madison Avenue to Main Street. In New York the Brooks-Bright Foundation and in Boston the American School Citizenship League sponsored oratorical and essay contests. In Cincinnati, Ohio, the Peace Heroes Memorial Society tried to supplant the school-boy image of dashing, courageous military figures with equally heroic civilians. Stores were urged not to stock military toys. Edward Bok, a leading Philadelphia publisher, sponsored a $50,000 prize for the best plan for world peace; the contest received nationwide publicity, and the better suggestions were published. World Peaceways, founded in 1931 and directed by Mrs. Estelle Sternberger, tried commercial advertising techniques such as posters, free space in magazines, a newspaper column, and a weekly radio program of news analysis.*

For each established organization there were numerous individuals with their own projects—unsophisticated people like Ashton Jones who proposed in 1935 to paint his wife's car white, name it "World Peace Car," and equip it with radio, victrola, loudspeaker, and religious records. To the car he would hitch a "nice, comfortable, trailer house" which he would build. Then he would deliver peace messages "in song, on records and in person several times a day to the idle around our industrial centers, in parks and on crowded street corners in our cities and villages."[15] Jones was sincerely altruistic, but he was also most naïve in his choice of a vehicle for peace work.

As World War I became a memory, and then a revised memory, peace organizations became increasingly active. Their speakers toured the college circuit; their literature was circulated among the churches; their conferences drew representatives of all social classes; their young people campaigned for peace from town to town each summer; their spokesmen claimed partial credit for victories in the Washington Conference and the Pact of Paris, and looked hopefully toward American participation in the World Court and the League of Nations. In the Protestant denominations peace became an important concern. By 1934, indeed, the secretary of the Commission on International Justice and Goodwill of the Federal Council of Churches, Walter W. Van Kirk, claimed that organized religion had renounced war.[16] Significant magazines, such as the *World Tomorrow*, the *Nation*, and the *Christian Century*, were evangels of peace-making. It was symbolic of the confidence

---

* Mrs. Sternberger was also executive secretary of the National Council of Jewish Women. It is of interest to note that Franklin Roosevelt developed a plan for the Bok contest, one which Mrs. Roosevelt credited with "being the basis on which he built other plans for world peace in later years." *This I Remember* (New York: Harper & Bros., 1949), pp. 23–24, 253–66.

96

felt by peace advocates that, in 1928, Florence Boeckel published a book which she called *Between War and Peace,* and that two years later she phrased another title, *The Turn Toward Peace.*

Leaders in peace societies judged their success by the response they evoked among the public. They had no way of measuring the millions of Americans who were unaware of or unconcerned with international issues, or who opposed the official solutions of the organized movement. These millions would become significant in the formulation of national policy only when the clouds of war rolled in to obscure the international vision. Then the weaknesses of the crusade against war would become apparent. But in the decade and a half after the Treaty of Versailles, peace workers sensed instead the growing strength of their world-wide movement.

It has been estimated that the core of the peace movement consisted of less than one hundred professionals who directed their organizations from Washington or New York headquarters.[17] The peace groups have been classified in various ways. Allan A. Kuusisto grouped them according to their activities into national service, denominational, and women's organizations with committees on international relations; endowed national organizations with educational and study programs; and the "inner core of the peace movement," eight groups which had educational and legislative programs.* Elton Atwater divided peace advocates according to their programs into those emphasizing military preparedness for peace, those advocating cooperation with other nations, disarmament, and support for the League of Nations, absolute pacifists who opposed all war, and socialists who believed that war had its basic roots in capitalism.[18] Like the differences among religious bodies, those among peace groups were largely matters of emphases. In this regard organizations which sought to educate the public in international understanding generally have been distinguished from those which sought to influence the government to adhere to international agreements and organizations or to curb military preparations.

Some organizations did make significant contributions to the study of foreign affairs. Acting on the policy that "the actual facts concerning international relations . . . constitute the best possible argument for lasting peace and improved international understanding," the World

---

* The eight were: the Fellowship of Reconciliation, Women's International League for Peace and Freedom, National Council for Prevention of War, Committee on Militarism in Education, League of Nations Association, National Committee on the Cause and Cure of War, Public Action Committee, and World Peaceways. The American Friends Service Committee surely should be added.

97

Peace Foundation made available monographs on arbitration, the League of Nations, and the Kellogg-Briand Pact.[19] Another body, the Institute of Pacific Relations, established central offices in Honolulu and committees in each nation concerned with Pacific affairs. It promoted mutual understanding through informal discussions of delicate issues, including the Oriental exclusion clause in America and rising nationalism in China. The Foreign Policy Association specialized in research in international affairs. Its staff conducted a radio program and a speakers bureau and prepared *Foreign Policy Reports* which were used in many universities and colleges as required material for international-relations courses. Its resources were also applied to specific problems, as in 1934 when President Carlos Menieta of Cuba invited the association to organize a commission of scholars to study the social and economic problems facing his island.

The best financed organization which emphasized understanding through study and publication was the Carnegie Endowment for International Peace. The guiding assumption of the Endowment was stated by the director of its Division of Intercourse and Education, Nicholas Murray Butler, who wrote in 1924, "The Division has never had any illusion as to the length of time it will take to raise the opinions and the ambitions of men to a place where international war will become so unlikely as to be almost impossible." The Endowment did not expect to discover any "patent device for the elimination of war," he added.[20] Its goal was to change men's minds with regard to war; its path was education.

Both the assumptions and the methods of the Endowment differed from those of peace societies which sought to influence government directly. These groups promoted international organizations and agreements, and tried to curb war preparations, believing, as Florence Boeckel wrote, that "the peace movement has apparently escaped from the red-herring theory that human nature is what needs to be changed and has definitely turned its attention upon governments as the agency [*sic*] responsible for war."[21]

In this hope the members of the Women's Peace Society sponsored a constitutional amendment which would deprive the United States of its war-making powers, and the members of the Women's Peace Union (W.P.U.) promoted an amendment to require a national referendum on a declaration of war. Leaders of the Committee Against Militarism in Education fought military training in congressional halls and on campuses and joined other groups lobbying for disarmament. Other peace-minded citizens sought to commit their government to arbitration treaties, the League of Nations, the World Court, and the Kellogg-Briand Pact. Internationalists operated not only through established peace societies such as the Women's International League for Peace and Freedom, the League of Nations Association, and the American Foundation (for a World Court), but also through special groups. Thus, seventeen organizations formed in 1921 a National Council for the Limitation of Armaments which established headquarters near the meeting place of the Washington Conference on disarmament, and lobbied for arms reduction. A number of women's organizations formed the Women's World Court Committee in order to put pressure on the American government to join the World Court. These allied groups were not themselves peace societies. They included, among others, the American Association of University Women, the General Federation of Women's Clubs, the National Board of Young Women's Christian Associations, the National Federation of Women's Clubs, the National Federation of Colored Women, the Women's Christian Temperance Union, and the Girls' Friendly Society in America.

The tendency of other groups to identify themselves with various aspects of the peace movements indicated a widespread interest in peace and internationalism in the interwar period. Farm and labor groups, denominations and fraternal orders, Sunday school and mission associations, the National Student Federation and the American Federation of Teachers, the Socialist Party and the United States Chamber of Commerce—all were enlisted at one time or another in the cause of peace. They drew ideas, literature, and speakers from the established peace societies.

This same tendency was basic to the dynamics of the peace movement. Precisely because each peace organization presumed to work in the national interest it cultivated various segments of public opinion in support of its approach. Moreover, each peace society represented a constituency which combined a distinctive point of view (such as pacifism) with either a social characteristic (such as being feminine, religious, or socialistic), or a functional program (such as fighting the Reserve Officers' Training Corps [R.O.T.C.], publicizing peace, and lobbying). All the groups were related to one another because their leadership, membership, and goals overlapped, so that in relation to any given policy the peace societies themselves constituted a series of publics, or segments of potential support; and success or failure was largely a function of their relationship. The organizational basis of peace advocacy became especially important in the thirties because Franklin Roosevelt then did not give foreign policy the personal leadership that he would after war broke out in Europe, or that Woodrow Wilson had exercised in World War I. Strong pressure groups were proportionately more effective in directing an otherwise divided public opinion and in representing it to a Congress which still had a formative voice in foreign affairs. The political strength of the peace movement was related to its ability to maintain unity among groups with divergent interests and points of view.

Where in this movement were pacifists?

To visualize one answer to this question, draw a line representing the peace movement between the First and Second World wars. Divide it into segments representing various peace organizations. One might then label the element at the far right as the American Peace Society, or perhaps the Carnegie Endowment. Merle Curti did this, in effect, by describing these organizations as most conservative, interested in securing peace without changing the *status quo*. One might then label that segment of the diagram at the far left as the Fellowship of Reconciliation. As Curti described its members,

> the radicals insisted that peace could be obtained only by altering in fundamental ways the existing political and economic status quo . . . that the war system could be finally abolished only by personal resistance and absolute refusal to fight under any circumstances.[22]

This view of pacifists was and is widespread. It knows them as most ready to change society, most obdurate, most extreme of all peace advocates, men who not only want peace but will not fight. But this does not sufficiently describe the relation of pacifists to other peace workers.

For another view, form a triangle representing the peace movement. Divide the triangle into segments representing various groups by drawing lines from its apex to its base. At the base of the diagram the pacifists will be isolated on the far left: at the apex, however, they will join with all others. This was more nearly the case. Pacifists preserved their distinctive position while they worked in other units of the peace crusade. They even attempted to coordinate and unify the whole effort. They supported most peace programs, many of which they helped to direct. They sought especially to promote internationalist attitudes, and to influence government directly to curb militarism and participate in world organizations.

Involved in virtually every effort to stave off war and basically internationalistic, liberal pacifists supported and often led coordinating agencies for the peace movement. They became increasingly dependent on these formal coalitions for access to the general public, and their

100

political influence was impaired when the coordinating bodies became divided over public policy. Loosely related in the twenties, peace societies with varying programs increasingly aligned in two blocs in the next decade. One side was led largely by Clark Eichelberger and the League of Nations Association and was financed by the Carnegie Endowment for International Peace; it increasingly supported collective security even at the risk of American involvement. The other consisted of a coalition of pacifist leaders in the Fellowship of Reconciliation, the Women's International League, the American Friends Service Committee and the National Council for Prevention of War who agitated for strict neutrality with nondiscriminatory embargoes against all belligerents in order to keep America out of war. The changing role of pacifists in the interwar peace movement can be expressed in terms of the public-constituency relationships within and between their organizations.

LET THE PEACE FORCES OF THE WORLD UNITE[23]

Pacifist groups cooperated informally because their membership, leadership, and goals overlapped. The classic example of this cooperation was the central pacifist organization, the Fellowship of Reconciliation. Active members of the Fellowship were officers in most other pacifist societies of national significance (see Table 1). John Nevin Sayre, for example, was not only successively executive secretary and chairman of the F.O.R. and chairman of the International Fellowship of Reconciliation, but he was also a member of the political committee of the National Council for Prevention of War, vice-chairman and a financial sponsor of the Committee on Militarism in Education, a major supporter of the American Civil Liberties Union and chairman of the Peace Section of its Continuation Committee, president of the National Peace Conference (1935–38), president and financial backer of the *World Tomorrow*, and a founder of Brookwood Labor College. His wife, Kathleen Sayre, was on the governing board of the War Resisters League and active in the W.I.L.P.F. Nevin Sayre was exceptional only in the range of his interlocking interests.

Not only did pacifists cooperate individually; the Fellowship itself worked officially with other organizations, including the Church Peace

Union, the National Council for Limitation of Armaments, the Women's International League, American Friends Service Committee, and National Council for Prevention of War. It exchanged mailing lists with other groups, such as the Committee on Militarism in Education. The historic peace churches—Mennonites, Brethren, and Friends —were represented in the Fellowship through an intermediary organization, the Pacifist Action Committee (December, 1929), but the A.F.S.C. associated with the Fellowship also through an official representative. Just because it conceived of peace as the absolute and total abolition of war, the Fellowship was led to support almost any anti-war program, including disarmament and world organization. This disposition gave pacifists the leverage of initiative and comprehensiveness that made them leaders in the general peace movement.

The concerns of that movement in the 1920's were largely legalistic and organizational. The precedents for peace-keeping were the prewar international conferences on arbitration (The Hague Conferences of 1899 and 1907) on the one hand, and the related League of Nations on the other. The two approaches to peace were logically compatible, but were divided in the United States by the tradition of unilateral foreign policy, jealously guarded by the irreconcilables in the Senate. Accordingly, the peace movement itself divided sharply over the question of strategy. One wing pushed the World Court, as a form of organization with which the United States could associate without being committed to the League of Nations. Another wing pressed for the outlawry of war by international agreement on the grounds that a World Court was meaningless without guiding law, and that law by treaty was a form of unilateral action. The denouement of the divided peace effort is well known: the World Court plan was defeated, largely because of its alleged relationship to the League; and the Kellogg-Briand Pact outlawed offensive war, but did not effectively enter the tradition of applied international law. Leading pacifists were among those who had tried in vain to join the wings of peace advocates into a coherent political force.

During the spring of 1925 several prominent pacifists consulted with advocates of the alternative peace plans. Two of them, Leyton Richards and Frederick Libby, flanked outlawry stalwart and fellow pacifist Charles C. Morrison at a dinner during an F.O.R. conference in Columbus, Ohio. There Libby explained the Quaker way of getting agreement without compromise by probing a question until understanding is reached. He thought he sensed some understanding in Morrison's voice, although scarcely three weeks later at another meeting

Fellowship of Reconciliation	Fellowship of Youth for Peace	War Resisters League	World Tomorrow	Emergency Peace Campaign	National Peace Conference	National Council for Prevention of War	Women's International League for Peace and Freedom	American Friends Service Committee	Committee on Militarism in Education	Pacifist Action Committee	Women's Peace Society	Women's Peace Union	
●		●	●	●	●			●					John Nevin Sayre
●	●	●	●	●					●	●			Jessie W. Hughan
●		●		●			●						A. J. Muste
●		●	●	●			●						Devere Allen
●		●	●	●			●						Kirby Page
●	●	●											Paul Jones
●		●		●		●							Dorothy Detzer
●		●		●			●		●				Ray Newton
●	●	●	●										John Haynes Holmes
●	●						●						E. Raymond Wilson
●		●			●		●						Norman Thomas
●	●	●								●			Kathleen Sayre
?					●					●			Carrie C. Catt
●					●		●						Clement Biddle
?					●	●				●			Lucia Ames Mead
●			●										Gilbert A. Beaver
●		●					●		●				Clarence Picket
●								●					Tucker P. Smith
?		●						●		●			Edith Bryce Cram
?					●						●		Jeanette Rankin
●			●				●						Edward W. Evans
?		●						●					Frank Olmstead
●				●	●		●						Frederick J. Libby

Table 1. SELECTED MEMBERS OF THE FELLOWSHIP OF
RECONCILIATION WHO WERE ACTIVE IN OTHER PEACE SOCIETIES

the editor of the *Christian Century* lashed out with a brilliant and un-compromising speech for pure outlawry of war.[24] About that time, James T. Shotwell, director of the Carnegie Endowment's Division of Economics and History, was bringing pacifists into conversation with supporters of the World Court and the League. On the basis of such conversations, Kirby Page and Sherwood Eddy, with the help of Ray-mond Robbins and F. Ernest Johnson, called a meeting of leading peace advocates for June 3. Twenty-seven of them discussed every aspect of the controversy in three all-day sessions and then appointed a small committee to evaluate a compromise proposal from the out-lawry group.* Another exhausting day of discussion on the nineteenth produced a "Harmony Plan," which was approved by the original group one week later and released to the press in mid-July.[25]

Page's hopes were high. The "Harmony Plan" would end the battle of priorities by linking the basic ideas of outlawry with the entrance of the United States into the existing World Court, he thought. It urged the United States to enter the Permanent Court of International Justice immediately on the basis of the reservations proposed by Presidents Harding and Coolidge, but with the understanding that the nations of Europe should call an international conference to negotiate a general treaty outlawing war as a crime under the law of nations. Were no con-ference called in two years the United States might withdraw its adher-ence to the World Court; should no conference be called in five years the American government would be obligated to withdraw. The inter-national conference should outlaw war and also create a code of international law based upon equality and justice between all nations. The plan did not challenge the right of national self-defense, and its signatories represented their personal, not organizational, views.

The plan was ingenious, but its authors could not evoke compromise merely by incorporating all positions. Page had hoped that Senator Borah and President Coolidge would agree on the compromise. He also expected peace societies to back the plan with enthusiasm. He

---

* The committee included pacifists Kirby Page and Norman Thomas, outlawry advocates Salmon Levinson and Charles C. Morrison, and World Court support-ers James Shotwell and James G. McDonald (chairman of the Foreign Policy As-sociation; he was sceptical of the compromise); it was chaired by John H. Clarke, president of the League of Nations Non-Partisan Association. Pacifists at the June 3 meeting included (besides Page, Eddy, and Norman Thomas) John H. Holmes, Nevin Sayre, Wilbur Thomas (A.F.S.C.), and Halford Luccock (contrib-uting editor of the *Christian Advocate*). Raymond Robbins was a lawyer active in the old Progressive party, and Ernest Johnson was executive secretary of the Federal Council of Churches.

was disappointed in both respects. Borah campaigned against participation in the World Court without promoting any alternative, despite the fact that he and Salmon Levinson (the Chicago lawyer who had helped formulate the outlawry of war idea) had given pacifists the impression that they would support it.[26] Borah was sensitive to the pressure for adherence to the World Court which was coming from the peace societies; it appears likely that he sought to weaken that pressure by seeming to favor a compromise.

The "Harmony Plan" produced acrimony among peace advocates themselves. For some it became a new symbol of division; for others it was a third alternative, and so it threatened to weaken both the camps it was designed to support. The Federation of Business and Professional Women's Clubs withdrew from the Women's World Court Committee to support the new scheme, for example, and Laura Puffer Morgan, associate secretary of the National Council for Prevention of War, wrote from the Mountain States that the "Harmony Plan" was drawing popular support from the Court itself.[27] Frederick Libby wrote Page that he approved the plan as an educational device, but cautioned against introducing any new bill when the President and two-thirds of the Senate seemed to favor a pending one. On the other hand, outlawry proponents complained bitterly that the World Court group was lobbying "with practically no reference to our Harmony Peace Program."[28] The plan had been contrived in the first place only because each contending wing thought that a compromise might favor passage of its own program, as Charles DeBenedetti has perceptively shown:

> The division between the Outlawrists and the bulk of the American peace movement was irreconcilable. If it did nothing else, the Harmony Plan did demonstrate this. The assumptions and expectations which each side held toward America's position in the postwar world were simply too antagonistic to be amalgamated in a common agreement.[29]

The experience was an understandably bitter one. John Haynes Holmes was "shaken to the marrow" by it, and Salmon Levinson wrote: "To me it is sickening. If christian [*sic*] civilization has not enough brains and morality to cope with war, God help it."[30]

The dispute faded from public view after the Senate sidetracked American participation on the basis of reservations. It rankled through personal correspondence, though, occasioned a futile exchange of articles and letters between Morrison and Page in 1927–28, and left

105

Levinson deeply embittered. After promoting their program independently for three years, the outlawry of war group won the Kellogg-Briand Pact. Borah lent his support since it did not involve any tangible commitments abroad. Kirby Page sought to broaden the vision of this group, even as he had tried to widen the base of World Court advocates. "The *idea* of delegalizing war is the freshest and most vital one" of the recent peace movement, he wrote, but the outlawry of war *movement* was wholly inadequate.[31] It relied too much on judicial measures. It seemed hostile to the League of Nations. It left America isolated from international currents.

Page had helped to organize the "Harmony Plan" precisely because of his radical position against war. Believing that war had its origins in a multitude of causes, the pacifist author-evangelist supported all approaches to peace and argued that each would be sterile in isolation. The very division of the peace movement represented a fatal acquiescence in nationalism, he insisted. Token allegiance to an international order of law and organization was wishful thinking.

Pacifist groups cooperated with others on specific projects besides the World Court and the outlawry of war. Their active Committee on Militarism in Education was formed with nonpacifist support for the purpose of fighting R.O.T.C. The substantial National Council for Prevention of War was formed from a 1921 council supporting disarmament. With an able staff directed by pacifist Frederick Libby, it became the most effective pressure group of the peace movement, to which it brought the combined influence of national civic organizations not themselves peace societies (such as the American Farm Bureau Association and the American Association of University Women). The National Council was intended to bridge the division among peace societies. Gradually it became an organization with the role of congressional lobbying and with policies of its own, but that only dramatized the difficulty of obtaining broad consensus in the late thirties. Meanwhile, there was besides spasmodic cooperation on specific programs a continuous endeavor to coordinate peace efforts formally.

The War Resisters League originated about 1924, for example, partly as an attempt to found a coordinating pacifist committee. It failed in this role because of differences in the constituencies and programs of its affiliates, and developed instead its own program of taking pledges to refuse military service.* A succession of coordinating com-

* The W.R.L. grew out of a committee of the F.O.R. which developed in 1922–23, adopted the name of the recently formed War Resisters International (then

106

mittees followed: a Federation Committee of Anti-War Groups, organized by Clarence V. Howell in 1923; the Pacifist Action Committee, organized by the A.F.S.C. in 1929; an Emergency Peace Committee in 1931; the Inter-Organization Council of Disarmament and its successor, the National Peace Conference in 1932 (reorganized in 1935). Pacifists warily boycotted the communist-dominated American League Against War and Fascism, founded in 1935, but they launched a crusade of their own, enlisting a wide range of peace organizations in an Emergency Peace Campaign (1936–37) to support neutrality legislation and international economic cooperation. That campaign was well organized and relatively free from bickering. It was the most important coalition in the history of the American peace movement before the Vietnamese war, and despite its leaders' internationalism it was "a leading cause of the wave of isolationist sentiment which swept the country in 1936 and 1937 and produced the demand for strict neutrality legislation."[32]

It was only part of the antiwar sentiment, though. Support dwindled by the fall of 1937, as peace groups returned to familiar grooves of action and polarized on the issue of neutrality. All elements continued to be represented through the National Peace Conference, but within one year its chairman, Walter Van Kirk, was wondering whether it was really worth the effort.[33] Despite overlapping goals and officers and the need to reach the general public in order to advance their constituents' view of the public interest, pacifist leaders were unable to sustain a program of coordinated leadership in the peace movement.

> Unquestionably, the rather general disunity in the ranks of the peace forces has tended to induce weakness and at times an almost fatal ineffectiveness . . . .
>
> —DEVERE ALLEN

> These pressure groups . . . put down their roots only where there was an already existing climate of opinion favorable to their point of view.

---

called P.A.C.O.), and urged the creation of a separate organization. The American group was affiliated with the international one, as were the F.O.R., the Women's Peace Union, and the Women's Peace Society, each of which retained emphases besides war resistance.

Public opinion rose from the depths of isolationism to acceptance of war . . . . as the inevitable reaction of the public to events abroad . . . .

—JOHN W. MASLAND[34]

Since the pacifist-oriented wing of the movement itself was composed of a series of constituent groups, any peace program vied for support with all others. Despite the overlapping membership and underlying assumptions of various societies, their coordination was based on a tenuous consensus about priorities. An effort new to any group—even a project to cooperate with others—would drain limited resources and funds for which it competed with other peace advocates. Every joint project had to meet two criteria: (1) was it consistent with the tenets of the groups it enlisted, and (2) would it strengthen their position with the publics they cultivated? Potential cooperation was, therefore, largely a function of the public-constituency relationships of member organizations.

The constituency of the National Peace Conference, for example, represented the spectrum of the peace movement: at one time seventeen peace organizations were affiliated with it. The conference was briefly important when in 1936 and 1937 it was funded by combined grants of $15,000 a year from the Carnegie Endowment and the Carnegie Corporation. The Endowment was interested in the N.P.C., presumably because it might coordinate the peace movement during the European crisis. It was interested, too, because the National Peace Conference had another seventeen affiliates, national civic organizations which represented direct links to segments of the middle-class public.* By 1940 the N.P.C. claimed forty groups with a total membership of 45 million people (some of which overlapped).

Its program represented an amalgam of its constituents' goals, those tenets upon which all would agree. It favored international disarmament, control of the munitions industry, revision of immigration policy, civilian formulation of policy, and the abandonment of traditional neutral rights to trade on the seas. It took over the last phase of the Emer-

* N.P.C. affiliates included, besides peace groups: the American Association of University Women, the Central Conference of American Rabbis, the Council for Social Action of the Congregational and Christian Churches, the Commission on International Justice and Goodwill of the Federal Council of Churches, the National Board of the Y.M.C.A., the Federation of Business and Professional Women's Clubs, the National Student Federation, the Women's Christian Temperance Union, and others.

gency Peace Campaign, which was to popularize international economic cooperation. As a pressure group its function was to popularize internationalism and to help define the terms of policy debates through its access to civic affiliates.

One member of the N.P.C., the National Council for Prevention of War, was itself a cooperative agency. It developed distinctive aims and became virtually the congressional lobby of the pacifist wing, with a budget which at its height amounted to over $100,000 per year. Most contributions to its work were small, and about half of its funds came from Quakers. Its journal, *Peace Action*, had a circulation of over 20,000; it published several books, over 1 million pieces of literature, and conducted a regular radio program; its motion picture department actually affected some movie releases between 1935 and 1939. An able staff developed a capacity to mobilize broad support from farm and labor organizations in a matter of days; it used congressmen on its radio program, sometimes writing their scripts; and it was close to commentators like John Flynn. It achieved a resounding success early in 1927 when it provided the initiative and organization for the mobilization of public opinion—especially the legal profession—that forced President Coolidge to arbitrate differences with Mexico and so to avoid a threatening war. A few years later it cooperated with Dorothy Detzer, the incisive lobbyist for the Women's International League for Peace and Freedom, in order to provide the initiative and supportive staff for the Senate Munitions Inquiry. Moreover, it sought to mobilize its affiliates behind strict, nondiscriminatory neutrality legislation and even experimented with backing peace candidates for election to Congress.

In all these respects the N.C.P.W. was useful to pacifists when they tried to shape the public interest in foreign affairs. But it also illustrated their role as peace activists. They were trying to persuade and mobilize public opinion according to their definition of the public interest. Ostensibly a clearinghouse for thirty-two national organizations, the National Council had an essentially pacifist constituency which valued its channels to specific publics such as farm, labor, and civic organizations, and the Congress. These groups, in turn, valued the N.C.P.W. to the degree that they believed that it was able to define and advance a broad liberal consensus on the national interest in foreign affairs.

The supportive relationship between the constituents and publics of the two major coordinating agencies was thus circular. The peace groups cooperated to the extent that the central organizations offered access to the general public. But specific publics—civic and interest groups—affiliated with the National Peace Conference and the National Council to the extent that they were broadly representative of the peace movement. Loss of support from these affiliates, lack of cooperation among peace societies, or a restricted definition of the public interest served could break the circle.

The coordinating agencies were not exceptional in having a constituency different from the public whose interest they served, for this situation was also true of each constituent group. Small coteries such as the feminists in the Women's Peace Society and Women's Peace Union, or the relatively few secular conscientious objectors in the War Resisters League addressed themselves to Congress. A handful of persons in World Peaceways addressed themselves to the public, securing $800,000 worth of free advertising space to inculcate mass hatred of war. The strong Peace Section of the American Friends Service Committee had a dedicated constituency of concerned Friends, but its public included not only Quakers but also leadership elites in the public at large. These people were cultivated through institutes of international relations for teachers, students, ministers, civic leaders, and, after 1933, labor leaders. Young people gave summers to the A.F.S.C. peace caravan program, touring towns across the country in search of a popular base for the peace movement. Meanwhile, the relatively influential Women's International League for Peace and Freedom represented about 12,000 American women (1936), and it lobbied in the United States and at the League in Geneva for programs which it presumed were in the national interest.

The constituency of the Fellowship of Reconciliation was essentially religious and liberal in the sense of being ecumenical, theologically modern, and socially concerned. Well over half of the members were ministers. Others included students, teachers, Y.M.C.A. and social workers, missionaries, and professional people. Its officers were significant precisely because they brought to nonviolence a concern for social action and to neutrality the sanction of internationalism. They sought to bring Christian bodies to social action and to infuse reform groups with the ethic of Christian pacifism.

The constituency was defined by membership, since members accepted the religiously couched F.O.R. statement of principles. But the leadership conceived of the members largely as channels through which to focus the attention of the religious community upon areas of conflict (thus, in 1935 the F.O.R. kept 3,034 "contacts" on its roles in addition to its 4,271 "active" members). There was a concerted effort to enlist denominations, the Federal Council of Churches, and individual ministers. The *Christian Century* and the *World Tomorrow* were agents of this attempt, and the pacifist fellowships formed in various churches were its offsprings. Harry Emerson Fosdick and other nationally known ministers signed pronouncements intended to enlist the support of clergymen who were polled, solicited, and surfeited with information on specific issues. To a large extent the Fellowship was successful in getting liberal Protestant churches to renounce war.

Because its leaders were socially concerned, however, the Fellowship was conscious of quite another public—reform and labor groups. Leading pacifists were active in movements for social reform (see Table 2). Some of them could be found on picket lines, if not in union offices. Others helped found labor colleges to cultivate the Christian ethic along with leadership skills among unionists, were associated with the League for Industrial Democracy, or worked in the Socialist Party. Toward the end of the thirties civil rights began to supplant labor as field work for pacifists.

If social involvement was a prerequisite of enlisting labor and liberals in the cause of peace, it sometimes paid off by providing an entre to those publics and reinforcing the long-standing pacifist tradition of the Socialist Party. Thus, in the terribly bitter and divisive national convention of 1934, pacifists Norman Thomas and Clarence Senior of the Socialist center beat off attacks by the cautious right and the radical left wings, driving through a Declaration of Principles against war and fascism written by pacifist Devere Allen. Thomas was forced to support the embattled revolutionists in the Spanish Civil War, but one year before conservatives organized the America First Committee, he had put together a Keep America Out of War Congress with the support of pacifists and all left-wing groups except the Communists.

Participation in an antiwar Left permanently affected American religious pacifism. It made necessary the definition of nonviolence as a technique of social change which would underlie the civil rights movement of the sixties. Immediately in the thirties, however, it broadened the public to which pacifists appealed for support without substantially adding to their constituency (relatively few F.O.R. members were laborers or radicals, and the War Resisters League was not yet significant). This development made the pacifist coalition within the F.O.R. as tenuous as that between pacifist organizations. The broader the alliance— the more publics and the larger resources it could command—the more tenuous it became. It was ever more difficult to satisfy the tenets of all groups; the larger public threatened the narrower constituencies; and

111

the pacifist coalition became more and more dependent upon public approval for its political success.

This coalition was strongest in 1935–37 when the various pacifist groups cooperated to secure neutrality laws and when they had the support of nonpacifists, such as those represented in the National Peace Conference and the National Council for Prevention of War. Even in those years the coalition was weakening, however, as the world situation darkened. The ineffectiveness of the League of Nations during the Japanese occupation of Manchuria and more poignantly in the Italian invasion of Ethiopia and the Spanish Civil War lent credence to pacifist fears that it represented a new alliance for the *status quo* and not a genuinely international organization. Frederick Libby, among others, shifted his support to strict neutrality. As American ships came under fire in China he became ever more suspicious of the administration which refused to apply neutrality laws there. Cooperation in the National Peace Conference on programs for international economic cooperation hardly masked the division over America's political role in the world.

The coalition broke in 1937–38, initially over the Ludlow Amendment controversy. This provision to require a public referendum on any declaration of war had been proposed in Congress for fifteen years. Not until 1937 did it appeal strongly to the antiwar coalition, though, and then mainly as a way of throttling executive initiative. In October the N.C.P.W. launched an all-out campaign for its adoption.

This action decisively drew the line between pacifists and those peace societies which, having given up neutral rights on the seas, were gravitating toward collective security. The National Peace Conference struggled on, but its goal of neutrality legislation "to reduce the risk of entanglement in foreign wars, and not to obstruct the world community in its efforts to maintain peace" was compromised.[35] If pacifists were able "to reduce the risk" of war by hobbling the President, they would "obstruct the world community in its efforts" to restrain aggressors with sanctions. Clark Eichelberger, director of the League of Nations Association and member of the N.P.C. steering committee, continued to handle its Campaign for World Economic Cooperation (1937–38); but at the same time, being acutely sensitive to aggression in Austria and Czechoslovakia, he organized committees to build support for sanctions against aggressor states only. His colleague on the steering committee, Frederick Libby, joined forces with Norman Thomas in renewed attempts to keep America out of war through strict neutrality. They won unsolicited support from isolationists, with whom in all other

Fellowship of Reconciliation	War Resisters League	League for Industrial Democracy	Socialist Party	American Civil Liberties Union	Labor Union Official or Worker in Strikes	Brookwood or Other Labor College	League for Independent Political Action	Labor Temple, New York City	Committee on Militarism in Education	N.A.A.C.P., Urban League, CORE, etc.	Social Action Agency of a Church	
●			●		●				●			John Nevin Sayre
●	●	●	●									Jessie W. Hughan
●		●		●	●	●		●		●		A. J. Muste
●		●	●	●	●	●		●				James Mauer
●	●	●	●									Devere Allen
●		●	●	●							●	John Haynes Holmes
●	●	●	●			●		●				Norman Thomas
●	●	●	●			●		●				Tucker P. Smith
	●	●	●	●								Clarence Senior
●		●	●	●		●	●					Harry Laidler
●	●			●								Roger N. Baldwin
●				●						●		L. Hollingsworth Wood
●		●	●			●						Kirby Page
●				●						●		Claud Nelson
●	●			●							●	Charles Webber
●		●		●								Howard Kester
●						●			●	●		George Collins
●			●		●	●	●					William Fincke
●					●		●					Laurence Hosie
●		●	●	●							●	William Spofford
●										●		James Farmer
●										●		George Houser
●										●		Bayard Rustin

Table 2. SELECTED PACIFISTS WHO WERE
ACTIVE IN MOVEMENTS FOR SOCIAL REFORM

respects Libby was at odds. His N.C.P.W. itself was split on this issue, and it became ever more clearly the tool of a pacifist coalition. But precisely to the extent that it no longer attracted nonpacifists, it lost a measure of importance to pacifists. The A.F.S.C. and the F.O.R. continued to support antiwar efforts, but they did not initiate or lead. They turned increasingly to the task of preparing their organizations and conscientious objectors for war. That is to say, they attended more to the interests of their constituents and less to those of the general public.

In the case of the F.O.R. this tendency was reinforced by its declining rapport with Socialist reformers. On the one hand the Fellowship had been straining its resources in the cause of neutrality and serving labor less. Besides, labor had won important concessions by 1937, and the threat of class struggle had died. Then, too, the Socialist Party had been riddled with factionalism and had supported militancy in the Spanish Civil War. Norman Thomas campaigned vigorously against intervention in 1940, but he no longer considered himself to be an absolute pacifist (and, in fact, he reluctantly accepted the war effort after December 7, 1941). As the F.O.R. lost something of its radical public, it concentrated on its essentially liberal-religious constituency, building it up numerically and preparing it for wartime.

The change in public-constituency relationships within the pacifist coalition between 1937 and 1941 can be illustrated graphically by two charts. The first was prepared by pacifists Ray Newton and Kirby Page for discussion at the Emergency Peace Campaign Council on March 2, 1937 (see Table 3). The plan envisioned a comprehensive policy-forming center for the peace movement which would represent organizations and geographical areas. The movement would tap special publics and a grass-roots peace public as well. Its directors would both represent and mobilize a broad range of publics in the interest of peace. That was the key assumption: that the organized peace movement represented a definable but general public interest.

Events in the following two years shattered that assumption. When the peace societies polarized over collective security, no coherent political program could encompass their various tenets. Consequently, the coordinating agencies failed to affiliate other publics to the movement and therefore threatened to drain support from pacifist societies without the compensation of public power (real or illusory). This declining spiral was not a mechanical process, since personal, organizational, and ideological loyalties had become habitual; but it seems to have been effective. By 1941 pacifists had turned inward, as the second chart suggests (Table 4). It was prepared for the War Resisters League. The

114

Table 3. PLAN FOR A GREATER AMERICAN PEACE MOVEMENT*

A Basis of Discussion with the Expectation
That Something Better Can Be Worked Out

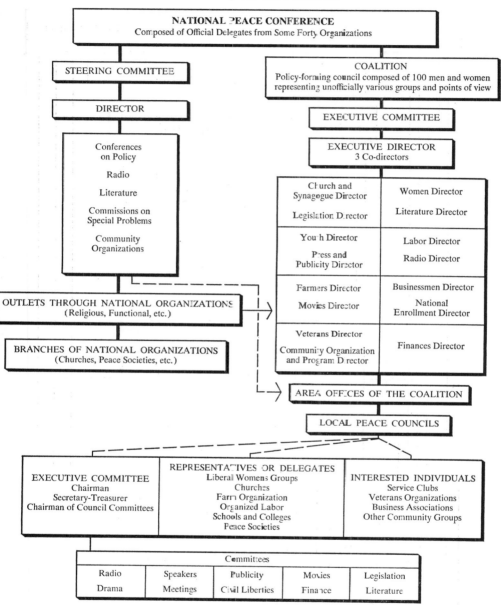

NATIONAL PEACE CONFERENCE
Composed of Official Delegates from Some Forty Organizations

STEERING COMMITTEE

DIRECTOR

Conferences
on Policy

Radio

Literature

Commissions on
Special Problems

Community
Organizations

OUTLETS THROUGH NATIONAL ORGANIZATIONS
(Religious, Functional, etc.)

BRANCHES OF NATIONAL ORGANIZATIONS
(Churches, Peace Societies, etc.)

COALITION
Policy-forming council composed of 100 men and women
representing unofficially various groups and points of view

EXECUTIVE COMMITTEE

EXECUTIVE DIRECTOR
3 Co-directors

Church and Synagogue Director	Women Director
Legislation Director	Literature Director
Youth Director	Labor Director
Press and Publicity Director	Radio Director
Farmers Director	Businessmen Director
Movies Director	National Enrollment Director
Veterans Director	Finances Director
Community Organization and Program Director	

AREA OFFICES OF THE COALITION

LOCAL PEACE COUNCILS

| EXECUTIVE COMMITTEE
Chairman
Secretary-Treasurer
Chairman of Council Committees | REPRESENTATIVES OR DELEGATES
Liberal Womens Groups
Churches
Farm Organization
Organized Labor
Schools and Colleges
Peace Societies | INTERESTED INDIVIDUALS
Service Clubs
Veterans Organizations
Business Associations
Other Community Groups |

Committees				
Radio	Speakers	Publicity	Movies	Legislation
Drama	Meetings	Civil Liberties	Finance	Literature

* Drawn from "Blueprint—Plan for a Greater American Peace Movement," probably by Kirby Page for the Emergency Peace Campaign, in Feb. or Mar., 1937. Emergency Peace Campaign papers, box 3, SCPC.

Table 4. THE INTERRELATIONSHIP OF PEACE SOCIETIES SEEN IN THE ORGANIZATIONAL TIES OF THE WAR RESISTERS LEAGUE*

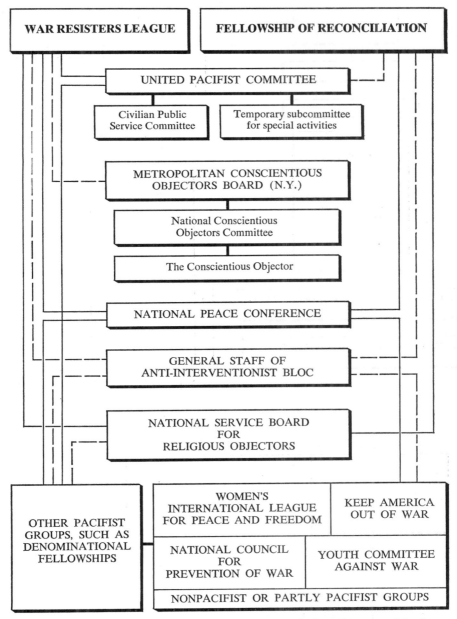

| WAR RESISTERS LEAGUE | FELLOWSHIP OF RECONCILIATION |

UNITED PACIFIST COMMITTEE

| Civilian Public Service Committee | Temporary subcommittee for special activities |

METROPOLITAN CONSCIENTIOUS OBJECTORS BOARD (N.Y.)

National Conscientious Objectors Committee

The Conscientious Objector

NATIONAL PEACE CONFERENCE

GENERAL STAFF OF ANTI-INTERVENTIONIST BLOC

NATIONAL SERVICE BOARD FOR RELIGIOUS OBJECTORS

OTHER PACIFIST GROUPS, SUCH AS DENOMINATIONAL FELLOWSHIPS	WOMEN'S INTERNATIONAL LEAGUE FOR PEACE AND FREEDOM	KEEP AMERICA OUT OF WAR
	NATIONAL COUNCIL FOR PREVENTION OF WAR	YOUTH COMMITTEE AGAINST WAR
	NONPACIFIST OR PARTLY PACIFIST GROUPS	

* Drawn from "WRL Relationships with Other Groups," organizational chart prepared by the War Resisters League in 1941. W.R.L. papers, SCPC.

pacifist coalition is as clearly represented as ever, but it is depicted in terms of constituent interests—the conscientious objectors, for example—rather than in the public interest.

The pacifists' assumption that their conception of foreign relations was in the national interest remained strong, but for the duration it was not organizationally coherent (and that is to say it was not politically operative). Consequently, pacifist groups lost interorganizational cohesion and influence in foreign affairs just when Franklin Roosevelt cautiously began to identify his charismatic personality with support for the victims of aggression, the very policy that had already robbed pacifists of political effectiveness. After two decades in which they had won enduring respect and achieved a pervasive influence in American social and international thinking, the mood of the country was once more "anything but congenial with pacifist doctrine."

PART THREE

Beyond "The Last, Blind War"

"The Road Back?"

Vaughn Shoemaker, chief cartoonist for the Chicago
Daily News, won his first Pulitzer prize in 1938 for this
cartoon, which predicted World War II.

V

The Search for an Antiwar Public

All night they marched, the infantrymen under pack,
But the hands gripping the rifles were naked bone
And the hollow pits of the eyes stared, vacant and black,
When the moonlight shone.

. . . .

"It is eighteen years," I cried. "You must come no more."
"We know your names. We know that you are the dead.
Must you march forever from France and the last,
    blind war?"
"Fool! From the next!" they said.

—Stephen Vincent Benét, "1936"[1]

The memory of World War I became formative in the thinking of State Department personnel and advocates of collective security in the thirties, but it was operative particularly for the pacifist. For two decades he tended to universalize the war and apply it to other events. He used it to popularize his view that wars are both futile and irrelevant to the fundamental social issues of his time, and that the United States could stand aside from a European state system based on force of arms. The revised version of the First World War provided a vehicle for inculcating that view. It could not convey that strong internationalist impulse which was a corollary of the liberal pacifist's humanism, however; and so, to the extent that his memory of the war was accepted by the public, it encouraged isolationism.

Revision took on every literary form. During and just after the war the romantic treatment of battle was redrawn in bitter and sceptical lines by Europeans Erich Remarque in *All Quiet on the Western Front* and Henri Barbusse in *Under Fire*; and by Americans E. E. Cummings in *The Enormous Room* and John Dos Passos in *Three Soldiers, Journey's End*, and *Pathos of Glory*. Other novelists, short-story artists, and

121

poets joined in the farewell to arms. Meanwhile, the story of propaganda was written and the true-sources-of-atrocity stories were disclosed by Philip Gibbs in *Now It Can Be Told*, Arthur Ponsonby in *Falsehood in Wartime*, and Harold Lasswell in *Propaganda Technique During the World War*. The public hardly needed pacifists to conclude from such books that it had been duped.

In the thirties, investigations into the operations of munitions makers stimulated new revelations, including H. C. Englebrecht's *Merchants of Death, One Hell of a Business*, and *Revolt Against War*, George Seldes's *Iron, Blood and Profits*, and Richard Lewishohn's *The Profits of War*. A new generation of muckrakers probed collusion on an international scale. At that time, also, peace advocates put forth books of pictures—Kerr Eby's *War*, and *The Horror of It*, arranged by Frederick A. Barber. Eby did not subscribe to pacifist doctrine, but he shared the sentiment that "lawful, not to say sanctified, wholesale slaughter is simply slobbering imbecility." He had served with the army engineers. What he drew he had seen, and his drawings and etchings claimed the pathos of it, the emptiness of men and boys who "underneath had some vague idea of purging the world of an evil" but who "died for less than nothing." His bandaged columns trudging back from the Argonne front, "pencil sellers, class of '17," might have been Stephen Vincent Benét's infantrymen under pack. For Eby in 1936, as for Benét, those shadows of men flinched not only from the "last, blind war," but also from the next.[2]

Many of these books and others were recommended by pacifist groups like the Fellowship of Reconciliation in the conviction that "the primary necessity at the present time is the education of the general public in regard to the attitudes and action required for the elimination of war and the organization of peace."[3] Books of all kinds, on international issues, economics, history, and religion, were useful. Pacifists were hopeful of mobilizing an antiwar public, and their goal was twofold: to convince people of the futility of war and of the importance of international cooperation. The starting point of the educational peace campaign, however, and the subject most interesting to the public, was the Great War.

Most important were the new historical interpretations of its origin and of American intervention. In major studies, Harry Elmer Barnes, Sidney B. Fay, and Bernadotte E. Schmitt repudiated the sole-guilt theory of Versailles and suggested that war had originated in the social attitudes of all countries and in a general failure of diplomacy in 1914. C. Harley Grattan in *Why We Fought* and Walter Millis in *The Road to War* debunked wartime explanations of American involvement and heroes such as Colonel Edward M. House, Walter Hines Page, and even Woodrow Wilson. Pacifists naturally used the new history to support their old ideals. Like Barnes, they approached history with "a hatred of war in general and an ardent desire to execute an adequate exposure of the authors of the late World War."[4]

For this reason they welcomed the judgment of Barnes and Fay that the Allies shared responsibility for the war with the Germans. For the same reason they were displeased that historian and peace advocate James T. Shotwell did not come fully into the revisionist camp. Director of the Division of Economics and History of the Carnegie Endowment, and a leader in the drive to secure a more effective League of Nations, Shotwell distrusted the pacifist position, feeling that "negation is a weak platform for times of crisis, when the call is for action."[5] Bernadotte Schmitt also was apprehensive that pacifists were drawing from his work conclusions different from those which he had intended, and were using his account of the war's origin to promote their own ideas about war's cure. His concern was justified; pacifists emphasized the underlying causes of war such as nationalism, alliances, and fumbling diplomacy, which he had explicitly acknowledged, but they minimized the diplomatic history which had led him to place primary responsibility for the war on the Central Powers.[6]

Pacifists had in Kirby Page their own historian of the war. He wrote reportorially from a wide range of secondary sources and memoirs. His major literary weakness was a penchant for long quotations. When in 1931 he dealt with the war's origins he briefly recounted the events of 1914; quoted at length from Schmitt, Fay, and British historian G. P. Gooch; and added the results of his poll of one hundred historians on the question of war guilt.[7] He was a popularizer of historical revisionism who neither doubted the significant responsibility of German leaders nor blamed them alone for the war. He attributed it, rather, to a variety of causes, just as he promoted a broad and thorough-going peace movement. His books, *War: Its Causes, Consequences and Cure* (1923), *The Abolition of War* (written with Sherwood Eddy in 1924), and *National Defense* (1930), were widely circulated.[8] The first one, *War*, was endorsed by Sidney Gulick on behalf of the Commission on International Justice and Goodwill of the Federal Council of Churches, and was recommended to Y.M.C.A. personnel by John R. Mott. Some 85,000 copies were given away to ministers, Y.M.C.A. secretaries, college faculties, and members of the F.O.R. and the Fellowship for a Christian Social Order. Samuel McCrea Cavert, subsequently general

123

secretary of the Federal Council of Churches, wrote that over 100,000 copies were circulated the first three months (compared to a sale of slightly more than 60,000 of Walter Millis's *The Road to War* in its first year). He added that it had "probably done more than any other single publication to bring the ministers and other Christian leaders sharply face to face with the question as to what they are going to do about war."[9]

That was, after all, Page's intention. He began by discussing the fundamental causes of the conflict—economic imperialism, militarism, alliances, secret diplomacy, and fear—thus anticipating Fay's opening chapter by half a decade. He then emphasized the war's futility in moral and material losses; described the international measures, processes, and spiritual requisites for peace; and challenged churches and Christian people to renounce all war. The next year he published a Christian catechism of liberal pacifism.

 . . . I must say that the more I consider war, its sources, methods, and results, its debasing welter of lies and brutality, its unspeakable horror while it is here and its utter futility in the end to achieve any good thing that mankind could wish, the more difficult I find it to imagine any situation in which I shall feel justified in sanctioning or participating in another war.

—HARRY EMERSON FOSDICK[10]

Pacifists cultivated church groups more assiduously than any other segments of public opinion between the world wars. They found an increasingly receptive audience, since the problem of war and peace was as important in Protestant opinion as any other issues, including prohibition and the fundamentalist-modernist controversy. Furthermore, this concern was so thoroughly internationalist that when the desire for peace seemed to lead along the narrow path of national isolation in the late thirties, the witness of the churches became divided and confused.[11] Until that time, however, pacifists in the Fellowship of Reconciliation were acknowledged leaders in this area of church thought because their organization had been both internationalistic and religiously oriented from its inception.

In 1922, Kirby Page and Nevin Sayre called together twenty-four ministers and prominent laymen to discuss the responsibility of churches in war. After three hours of discussion, a committee consisting of Page, Harry Emerson Fosdick, and William P. Merrill penned "The Churches' Plea Against War and the War System," which was signed by over 150 prominent clergymen.* Page wrote later that it was probably "the first proclamation of conviction by an influential group of American Christians—Protestants and Catholics—that . . . the spirit of war and the spirit of the Gospel are anticlerical, and the first appeal by prominent churchmen that the crisis of decision between war and Christ be recognized and stated."[12] Many such declarations were to follow.

Page originally had suggested that those who signed the "Churches' Plea" might acknowledge a change in the thinking of those who had supported war in 1917. Fosdick objected, warning that Henry A. Atkinson, general secretary of the Church Peace Union, had even asked to include a statement sustaining the earlier war position. Page agreed to let the matter rest. His first objective had always been to marshal the churches against war, not to align them against supporters of World War I:

> The Church will never withdraw its sanction and support of war until it comes to feel intensely that war—all war is necessarily and inevitably violently unchristian and absolutely opposed to the spirit and method of Jesus Christ. Such a feeling is now almost entirely lacking in the Church . . . . The reason for this is that when Christian people think or talk about war, they think and talk about the courage and sacrifice *called forth by the war* and not about *war itself*. Only when the Church fixes its thought on war itself—a means to an end—and realizes the brutalities and atrocities that are always and everywhere a part of war, and as a consequence begins to regard war with an utter loathing . . . will it withdraw its sanction and support of war and set itself resolutely to the task of finding a better, a Christian way out.[13]

Sometimes led by pacifists, as in this case, church leaders increasingly thought in terms of war itself, loathed war, withdrew their sanction of it, and sought ways to maintain peace.

The shift in church opinion was first noticeable about 1923–24. It crystalized in the next decade, and the *World Tomorrow* exaggerated only slightly when it announced in 1934 that "unqualified repudiation of war is now becoming commonplace in religious conferences."[14] That

---

* Fosdick was the pastor of Riverside Baptist Church in New York City and a prominent clergyman who recanted his support of war formally in 1923; Merrill was president of the board of trustees of the Church Peace Union.

very autumn two thousand people at the Des Moines Convention of the Disciples of Christ passed by a two-to-one majority a resolution framed and defended on the floor by Harold E. Fey:

> We believe that war is pagan, futile and destructive of the spiritual values for which the Church of Christ stands. We also believe that it is a violation of the solemnly pledged word given by the United States and other nations in the Pact of Paris . . . . As Disciples of Christ we therefore disassociate ourselves from war and the war system, and hereby serve notice to whom it may concern that we never again expect to bless or sanction another war.[15]

A number of leading Disciples had struggled toward that declaration, but none could have been more pleased than Kirby Page to have the victory come at his alma mater.* The next year pacifists, led by Ernest Fremont Tittle and Henry Hitt Crane, seemed to capture the General Conference of the Methodist Episcopal Church which declared that it would not endorse, support, or participate in war.† This position was reaffirmed when the northern and southern wings of the church were joined in the uniting conference of 1939. Among Methodists, too, pacifism was introduced by a core of leaders who had pressed forward in district conferences, in the Commission on World Peace of their church, and in the young people's Epworth League formed in 1935.[16]

Walter Van Kirk was one Methodist clergyman who, although not himself an absolute pacifist, had reason to suspect that Christians individually and collectively were committing themselves "to the pacifism of the early church."[17] After nearly ten years as secretary of the Department of International Justice and Goodwill of the Federal Council of Churches, he compiled the pronouncements of war which had been made during his tenure by church assemblies, conferences, synods, and conventions. He compared them with the statements of preachers who had "presented arms" in the Great War, and he concluded that religion was "parting company with Caesar." They were written, he found, by

---

* These leaders included, among others: Peter Ainslie, founder of the Christian Unity League; H. O. Pritchard, secretary of the Board of Education; James A. Crain, secretary of the Department of Social Education and Social Action; Harold Stone Hull, the Pacific Coast secretary of the F.O.R.; Charles C. Morrison, editor of the *Christian Century*; A. E. Cory, director of the (Disciples) Pension Fund; Stephen J. Cory and Kenneth I. Brown, presidents of the College of the Bible and Denison University, respectively; and Harold E. Fey.

† Ernest F. Tittle was the distinguished minister of the First Methodist Church, Evanston, Illinois (since 1919); Henry H. Crane, close friend of Kirby Page since their Y.M.C.A. service during World War I, was the prominent minister of Elm Park Church, Scranton, Pennsylvania (from 1938 to 1952 he was in Detroit, Michigan).

126

committed internationalists who were convinced of the sin and futility of war.

Polls taken in the mid-thirties seemed to confirm the antiwar bias which Van Kirk ascribed to the churches.[18] The largest and most carefully organized one was conducted in 1935 by a subcommittee of the newly formed Council for Social Action of the Congregational-Christian Church. This "Peace Plebiscite" was intended to stimulate as well as to measure opinion. It was preceded by a period of debate and discussion among about 2,800 cooperating churches, and ballots were sent only to churches requesting them. The plebiscite was taken November 3–10 and 177,050 returns had been tabulated by Christmas, a total which represented about 20 per cent of persons on the participating churches' membership rolls, and about 72 per cent of the churches' average attendance. In the plebiscite only 10 per cent of those replying expected to support any war the United States might declare, or any war against an internationally recognized aggressor. The most popular alternative was to accept war only after the "utmost use of every agency for peace" (the 42 per cent who favored this position were mainly also for a bigger army and navy and against cooperation with the League). About 48 per cent expected not to fight, or to fight only if the United States were attacked. The editors of *Social Action* concluded that "since prospects for invasion in the near future are very slight, it would seem that the government can expect little war support from approximately one-half of those voting in this Plebiscite."[19] That assumption proved to be the Achilles heel of pacifism as a political force after December, 1941.

Two of the most useful polls were conducted among ministers and seminary students by the *World Tomorrow* in 1931 and 1934 and were used by Walter Van Kirk to buttress his conclusions. Both were largely the work of Kirby Page, but were sponsored by a number of distinguished clergymen representing various denominations. Both made use of elaborate forms which were sent to 53,000 and 100,490 ministers, respectively. In both cases replies were tabulated by machine and attested by certified public accountants. Of the 19,372 people responding to the 1931 poll, 62 per cent held that the churches should go on record as refusing to sanction or support any future war; 52 per cent said that they intended not to sanction any future war or to participate as an armed combatant (43 per cent would sanction or participate in a war "clearly for defense"); and only 45 percent could "conscientiously serve as an official army chaplain on active duty in wartime." A clear majority favored entering the World Court, taking the initiative in arms

127

reduction, and abandoning armed intervention to protect American lives and property.[20] The 1931 questionnaire was limited to the problem of war. It was sent to members of major denominations except Jews, Roman Catholics, Lutherans, Southern Baptists, or Southern Methodists. Northern Methodists and Disciples of Christ were the most strongly pacifist.

The 1934 sampling of opinion on war included some denominations not previously polled. It was coupled with a questionnaire on economic and political attitudes. Of the 20,870 replies in 1934 about 67 per cent wanted the churches to refuse to sanction any war, 62 per cent would not themselves sanction or participate in any future war (36 per cent could support a war clearly for defense), and only 41 per cent would conscientiously serve as a chaplain in wartime.[21]

Kirby Page was careful to point out some weaknesses of the polls. The 1931 survey had excluded important religious bodies. Probably ministers who opposed war most keenly replied in larger proportion than others, so that the ministry as a whole was "probably less hostile to the war system than these tables would seem to indicate."[22] The questionnaire method is inherently weak, anyway, he continued, because it seeks to resolve complex questions into either-or choices. Besides, people make errors, and interpretations of questions vary.

There were two qualifying aspects of the polls which Page did not mention. It is significant that although the number of questionnaires sent nearly doubled, the number of replies increased by only 1,498, and the total pacifist response increased only slightly. Page was right in thinking that the more pacifist-minded ministers would respond more readily to the poll. In the second place, Page did not emphasize the widely acknowledged point that the ministry was much more pacifist than the laity. Whereas 63 per cent of the Congregational-Christian clergy responding to the plebiscite indicated that they would not sanction any future war, only 15 per cent of the laity took the same position. A wide gulf separated the two elements of the churches on this point, despite the fact that the public was more international and peace-minded than ever before.[23]

Nevertheless, when all caution is exercised, the fact remains that pacifism made a significant impression upon the Protestant clergy by 1931, and that its appeal increased up to at least 1934. Young people in the churches probably were influenced by pacifism less than their ministers and more than their parents. Pacifists were well placed in student Christian organizations, including the Y.M.C.A. They enlisted not only prominent ministers but also distinguished teachers and scholars in leading schools of theology.* They occupied strategic places in social action and social education committees from which they helped to write church pronouncements and to distribute literature on war and international affairs. They were not lost in their denominations largely because they were united through the Fellowship of Reconciliation, which itself had ties to the Federal Council of Churches and other interdenominational bodies. Like a spider's web, the lines of pacifist influence were gossamer threads that spanned indifferent space and derived whatever tensile strength they had from the fact that they were joined to one another.

It is clear that pacifists were a small minority in every church, even in those, like the Disciples and the Methodists, which took strong antiwar stands. But church members often accepted the vigorous leadership of the minority on the war question. This acquiescence was of great consequence during the five years before Pearl Harbor when the policy of American neutrality was debated. It was important, too, in shaping government policies on military build-up and the treatment of conscientious objectors. Most important, perhaps, it helped to shape the attitudes of Protestant churches toward war. By 1941 pacifism had become a respectable, although definitely minority, position in Christian ethics.

American churches never again supported a war in the crusading spirit of World War I. Even at the end of a year of conflict in November, 1942, the executive secretary of the Department of Research and Education of the Federal Council of Churches, F. Ernest Johnson, wrote that "to a large and influential portion of the Protestant leadership war had become anathema before the blow fell at Pearl Harbor, and no clear 'testimony' in support of the war has taken form in Protestant circles." This restrained critic of pacifism further explained that the origin of this attitude toward war was to be found in "the pacifist crusade which swept the country in the twenties and thirties . . . ." He wrote,

* These educators would include, among others, Professors Roland Bainton, Jerome Davis, and Kenneth Scott Latourette at Yale Divinity School; Bruce Curry, Arthur L. Swift, and (for a time) Reinhold Niebuhr at Union Theological Seminary; Arthur E. Holt, Dean Charles Gilkey, and President Ozora S. Davis at the University of Chicago Theological Seminary; Henry Cadbury, Nels Ferre, and Dean Willard L. Sperry at Andover Theological Seminary; Adelaide Case at Columbia; Earl Cranston at Colgate University and the University of Redlands; Georgia Harkness at Garrett-Biblical Institute (previously at Elmira and Mt. Holyoke colleges); and Walter Marshall Horton at Oberlin College.

Its strength lay very largely in the fact that those who became purveyors of its philosophy were among the most intellectual, liberal, and socially minded, and therefore the most broadly influential, of the ministerial leaders. The movement had the support of some of the most ably edited religious journals, and it produced a pamphlet literature of a vigorous and convincing sort. The influence of the spoken and written word, unsupported by vested interest of any kind, has perhaps never been so strikingly demonstrated. True, the pacifist movement blended at the fringe with political isolationism. Among the college populations served by the Christian student movements the line between religious pacifism and a broad ethical internationalism was not clearly drawn. But Christian pacifism became an indubitably authentic movement, the influence of which is strongly felt in the religious life of America now that we are in the war.[24]

What special appeals did pacifists make to Christians besides the general pleas of the peace movement? What claims upon religion did they advance? The spectrum of pacifist theology ran from Catholic to Unitarian, from Jewish to peace sectarian; and even within liberal Protestant circles it included a broad range of beliefs. On one point pacifists agreed—war is an unethical use of force. "War is inherently and essentially a supreme violation of Jesus' way of life," Kirby Page insisted. "In short, war is sin—hateful to God and abhorrent to every Christian conscience."[25]

The pacifists' indictment of warfare was as total as modern war itself. It was documented by their accounts of the causes and effects of World War I. It was a powerful assertion that war, at least, is a form of force wholly in conflict with the ideal of the kingdom of God within men or in society, and that it is a method which violates the essential nature of God and man as revealed in the life of Jesus. Like the evangelists of abolition in pre-Civil War years, therefore, pacifists challenged religious men with an either-or proposition. They had no doubt which alternative to choose. They said, with Alfred T. DeGroot, "Christianity is Pacifism!"[26]

That statement was the original premise of Christian nonresistance, as defended by the historic peace churches; but World War I had changed its application in ways that began to challenge other premises of nonresistance, such as the relation of church and state. As early as 1919 the Mennonite Church formed a Peace Problems Committee. As this committee succeeded the Military Problems Committee of 1907–19, so, too, an antiwar program supplemented the nonresistance concern of the church. The new committee expressed its interest in international affairs as well as in conscientious objectors. It sent letters to government officials regarding compulsory military training, naval reduction, and foreign policy on Nicaragua, Mexico, and China. The committee participated with Friends and Brethren in a series of informal meetings beginning in 1922, and in 1935 it helped form a Continuation Committee of the historic peace churches.[27] The Church of the Brethren also was stimulated by World War I to reevaluate its peace position, and it developed activities that went beyond its traditional nonresistance, even acting as a political pressure group on foreign policy questions. The general conference of the Church of the Brethren took increasingly adamant stands, finally condemning all war as sin. Brethren were thus tempted to abandon their old position that the church and state operate on separate ethical bases. For many of them this abandonment meant accepting the wars of the state; for others, however, it required using the influence of the church to affect policies of the government. By the time of the Second World War statements of the Brethren in annual conference had shifted "from nonresistant pacifism toward the modern pacifism of political reform and the abolition of war."[28]

Even as Mennonites became more concerned with social and political reconstruction following the war, they tried to draw a distinction between themselves and pacifists. The leading Mennonite thinker on this subject, Guy Franklin Hershberger, complained that pacifists too frequently saw peace as an end in itself. They were often too optimistic about achieving it, he averred, and they frequently failed to appreciate that the state is essentially an organization which maintains order by coercion in a sinful society. The pacifist would compromise, therefore, with the methods of the state: "Nonresistance, love, and the cross give way to nonviolent coercion or nonviolence, which in its essence is a form of warfare."[29] Mennonites' social action was severely limited by their belief that ultimately the Christian should express his faith by nonconformity to the world in life and conduct, and should refuse any forms of coercion to achieve justice. However much the Mennonite churches were influenced or challenged by pacifist social concern between the wars, officially they never wavered from their sectarian conception of absolute nonresistance.

Most Christian pacifists were thoroughly within the currents of twentieth-century American religious life. They drew from and contributed to the evaluation of liberal religion between 1920 and 1940. Their theological positions were formed in the context of the stagnation into which the social gospel seemed to have fallen in the twenties.

Leading pacifists were vitally concerned about the problems of an industrial and urban society, and they committed themselves to increas-

131

ingly radical solutions. They also held doctrines common to mid-nineteenth-century evangelical religion: the Fatherhood of God and human solidarity, the immanence of God, the sanctification of man, the doctrines of love, and the kingdom of God. Pacifists were sons of a science-minded generation, though, and their world view altered some of the earlier doctrines: the authority of the Bible rested on its illumination of experience rather than on its prescriptive truth; human solidarity was a sociological fact and a democratic ideal as well as a religious proposition; the sanctification of man and the kingdom of God were relative possibilities; and the applications of love might be judged pragmatically.[30] As pacifists reinterpreted the social gospel they stressed the practical evaluation of each conflict situation. This position made it possible for them to hold a prudential, or pragmatic, social ethic within the framework of their religious doctrine. They evaluated direct social action on practical grounds, but they ruled out violence—war in particular—on the grounds that it violated the moral order as revealed by Jesus.

Pacifists further modified the optimistic and rationalistic view which, they assumed, religious liberals had initially found in science. Their own categories of thought were basically historical. The authority of the Bible for them derived from its effect on history as well as its insight into contemporary experience. They rejected the doctrine of inevitable progress. They understood Jesus as a historical revelation of the nature of God and man. They meant by Fatherhood of God the self-denying Creator and Redeemer, active in history. Man, they felt, is potentially good or evil; his development is influenced by his social and physical environment and his ideals. Because he is essentially a child of God, however, he has latent goodness, will, and responsibility. Pacifists concluded that it was the responsibility of Christians to choose the kingdom of God, an *ideal* which was antithetical to the existing economic and international order and to traditional methods of changing social conditions by violence. They criticized the Christian church for having sanctioned injustice by maintaining the *status quo* and for having traditionally aligned itself with the state in war. They explored the early church's pacifist witness and dated its "fall" from its alliance with Constantine the Great. They traced the history of dissenting sects which had continued to witness in their own communities to the uncompromising Christian ethic despite persecution by orthodox churches.[31] Pacifists believed that the "rediscovery" of the historical Jesus and the early church in the face of the indiscriminate violence of modern warfare forced modern churches "either openly to repudiate much that

132

Jesus believed and taught or boldly to endorse his fundamental positions."[32]

War is not sacrifice; it is killing, they said. War is now the most malignant social evil of all because it includes all forms of social injustice and corporate inhumanity. The warring government resorts to lies, fear, and hate, they continued. It conscripts whole populations, and it necessarily enlists the churches. It cannot serve the ends of freedom because it is tyrannical. War is a vicious circle in which the response to evil by destruction issues in more war; evil plus evil equals evil, was their formula. War is unlike the police function, pacifists contended, because nations fight under no judicial process or superior sanction, and their object is not to restrain but to destroy. Modern war is total, in which there can be no distinction between the home and the battlefield, or between the innocent and guilty. As John Haynes Holmes summarized it, war is the organized use of physical force to kill wholesale and indiscriminately for national self-interest.[33]

Essentially, liberal pacifists rejuvenated the ancient idea of the just war. They did not invent this concept, of course. Indeed, the doctrine is both historically and logically a compromise between pacifist absolute rejection of war and religious sanction of it. Pacifists contributed to the modern concern with the just-war theory by focusing the attention of churchmen on the issues of international conflict and by totally rejecting the war method on the grounds that modern war is futile. It should be renounced not only because it is sin, Kirby Page concluded, but also because it is "ineffective . . . and is self-defeating in its very nature." For the liberal pacifist in the 1920's this was not an abstract proposition. It appeared to be a pragmatic judgment based on historical evidence: "Consider the World War," Page advised.[34] That was reality; a just war, on the contrary, had become only a theoretical possibility.

That conclusion was implicit, too, in a 1940 report of the Ethics Committee of the Catholic Association for International Peace (C.A.I.P.), founded in 1927, which considered that it was "conceivable but . . . very unlikely" that the war activities of Hitler and Stalin might so threaten civilization "as to create a moral obligation of active participation by the United States."[35] By then a few Catholics had begun to argue that a just war, in the sense long sanctioned by church usage, was virtually unthinkable under modern conditions.* They doubted

---

* The "just war" is defined as one which "must be waged by a sovereign power for the security of a perfect right of its own (or of another justly invoking its protection) against foreign violation in a case where there is no other means available to secure or repair the right; and must be conducted with a moderation

133

that one side would be wholly right and another wrong. They did not expect means for peaceful settlement to be exhausted before fighting began. They said that the very concept of civilized weapons was as obsolete as the musket, and that war no longer excluded unarmed and innocent populations. According to the conditions laid down by the church, these Catholics argued, a modern war cannot be justifiable.[36]

Catholic pacifists occasionally advanced this point of view through the church's organ of social protest, the *Catholic Worker*. The little group around Dorothy Day took a consistently neutralist and antiwar stand, even after the United States declared war against Japan. Its thinking was largely nonresistant, if not Tolstoyan, but it sponsored the formation of the somewhat broader Pax, a fellowship of objectors to modern war which in 1940 became the Association of Catholic Conscientious Objectors. The previous November the Jesuit weekly, *America*, published the results of a poll of over 50,000 students in 182 Catholic colleges and universities. More than one-third of the students expected the United States to be drawn into the European war. What would be their duty in such a case? Some 12,000 claimed that they would volunteer for military service; 21,000 would serve only if conscripted; and 18,164 pledged that they would refuse to fight. Students voted fifty to one against American participation in war. They were ten to one of the opinion that intervention would not contribute to enduring peace.[37]

These students and other Catholic pacifists were a small minority in their church. Far more representative of informed Catholic opinion was Charles G. Fenwick, president of the Catholic Association for International Peace and professor of political science at Bryn Mawr. He wrote in 1937 that not only was a just war possible, but that a fundamental weakness of American foreign policy was the refusal to distinguish between "which party is right and which is wrong in time of war."[38] He noted that several modern Catholic theologians had argued that a war can be just in the absence of peaceful alternatives for reaching a just settlement. To the extent that neutrality legislation denied the national obligation to protect a victim of international injustice, he con-

---

which, in the continuance and settlement of the struggle, commits no act intrinsically immoral, nor exceeds in damage done, or in payment and in penalty exacted, the measure of necessity and of proportion to the value of the right involved, the cost of the war, and the guarantee of future security." Charles Macksey, "War," *The Catholic Encyclopedia*, XV (New York: The Encyclopedia Press, Inc., 1913), 550. Pope Pius XII defined international justice in terms which Germany explicitly violated. Giuseppi Valentini, "Pius XII," *ibid.*, *Supplement II* (New York: The Gilmary Society, 1950).

cluded, American foreign policy was not ethically sound. Fenwick did not differ significantly with Catholic pacifists in his interpretation of a just-war theory. He disagreed sharply with their interpretation of international events.

They, like Protestant pacifists, were reading into 1939 the lessons they had gleaned from the First World War: that divided responsibility had produced it, that its apparent altruism had been hypocritical, and that its victory had been Pyrrhic. One Catholic professor wrote that the presumption of injustice "in an offensive war" is so great in the modern world that the Christian needs sure evidence to the contrary—the assurance of the Pope—before he can participate in war without sinning.[39] The theological appeals made to the churches represented, therefore, the notion that pacifism is rooted in the real world as well as in religious ideals. Numerous Protestant ministers wrote with self-assurance that virtually all modern wars are offensive, and that they are sinful in their tragic futility.

> The old-time missionary engaged in preaching the Gospel of Christ to the Chinese was not more impervious to the teachings of Buddha than are the majority of Americans, occupied today in proclaiming abroad their religion of peace, to the meanings of European political principles.
>
> —FRANK SIMONDS, *Can America Stay at Home?*[40]

One assumption held by pacifists, as also by other peace advocates, was that a willingness of peoples to fight had been a prerequisite of World War I. Expressed as nationalism, chauvinism, militarism, or fear, this disposition had to be changed if peace were to obtain. Accordingly, pacifists cultivated internationalism and a frame of mind which John Haynes Holmes called "the will to peace."[41] Page wrote in 1923, for example, that fear had been an underlying cause of the conflict. Economic imperialism, alliances, secret diplomacy, militarism—all had aggravated the insecurity felt by Germans, French, and Russians alike. The whole of Europe was a huge armed camp, he wrote, and fear "more than any other factor caused the war."[42]

In his enlarged treatment, *National Defense*, Page wrote that nationalism had accentuated fear and had been the chief cause of the World War. He agreed with Norman Thomas, who had written that

135

the patriot's fear of alien nations was aggravated by his devotion to his native land.[43] Nationalism both created social loyalties and divided peoples, Page wrote; citizens were bound both to uphold national honor and to avenge it; men organized for public good and for war. The extreme form of nationalism, chauvinism, was spread by professional militarists, patriotic societies, and the sensationalist press in every land. Thomas and Page both emphasized their belief that economic and political considerations had induced the Great War. In this respect, governments were the responsible agents, and the peace movement should seek to influence government policies. They insisted, however, that ultimately distorted ideas of national sovereignty and security made war possible.

Liberal pacifists thought that social attitudes could be changed. They denied that fighting is instinctive in men. There is always an assumed reason or an emotional appeal for conflict, they argued; people have to be aroused to fight. Pacifists conceded that the modern state marshals patriotism against foreign and domestic foes, but they noted that the nation itself is a recent historical development. National loyalties had been learned; they might be superseded. Leading pacifists believed also that modern capitalistic civilization encourages aggressive responses among men and nations. They asserted, however, that the duty of the "Christian patriot" was to resist insane public opinion. The true patriot must influence his people. Since war was thought to be largely a state of mind, the peace crusade became a "battle of opposing ideals."[44] Consequently, the largest efforts of the peace movement went into the dissemination of information about foreign affairs and the creation of international-mindedness.

In an effort to create intelligent public concern for world affairs the Peace Section of the American Friends Service Committee contributed two especially striking educational programs, peace caravans and institutes of international relations. It began its work along traditional lines when it was established as one of the four departments of the reorganized A.F.S.C. in 1923–24. It supported the campaign for United States entrance into the World Court, formed an affiliated Interracial Peace Committee, and scheduled speaking arrangements for Thomas Que Harrison, a former soldier who was traveling and lecturing for the Fellowship of Youth for Peace, an F.O.R. affiliate. A distinctive program emerged in the summer of 1926, though, when a few students were sent out to speak on the subject of peace.

The peace caravan burgeoned in the next fifteen years as 1,200 young people gave their summers to voluntary work for peace. The program was directed by Ray Newton. During the war he had lost his job at Phillips Exeter Academy because of his pacifism, had served with the Quaker relief project in Europe, and had been executive secretary of The Young Democracy, a postwar youth organization. Newton came to the Peace Section in June, 1927. He held a three-day training conference at Haverford College in Pennsylvania for the twenty-one college students previously selected, and sent them off in pairs in second-hand model-T Fords. In California and Colorado, the Midwest and New England they drove from town to town, distributed peace literature, and talked to clubs and churches wherever they found an audience.[45]

Under Newton's direction the caravan program was extended to a Student Peace Service which operated a year-round program, sending field secretaries to colleges during the winter to form study groups and recruit summer volunteers. National depression cut finances but often caravanners raised much of their funds themselves, as in 1938 when each volunteer brought $100 along. In the shadow of war, in 1940, the A.F.S.C. sponsored 119 students from 55 colleges, representing 26 states, 20 denominations, and 8 nationalities. Twenty-three teams of itinerant peacemakers educated communities on international issues; most of the teams also worked on some community service project.[46]

The caravan program reached thousands of people, mainly in the rural Midwest. In 1930 alone caravanners estimated that each of twelve teams reached about 6,000 people.[47] Many of these people undoubtedly were more impressed by the spirit of the young peace workers than influenced by their campaign. Probably the most lasting effect of the program was the interest aroused in the volunteers themselves; certainly this enthusiasm was very important to the Peace Section. The caravan program was, however, only one of several ways to promote international peace through education.

A second approach, the institutes of international relations, grew out of the peace caravan program. Ray Newton extended the summer conference in 1930, mainly for caravanners and other peace workers. For two weeks sixty people studied the political, economic, social, and religious aspects of peace. They were led by a faculty which included Henry T. Hodgkin of the British F.O.R., Frederick Libby of the National Council for Prevention of War, Clarence E. Pickett of the A.F.S.C., and Devere Allen and Reinhold Niebuhr, authors and editors of the *World Tomorrow*.[48] The conference turned into an institute.

Subsequent conferences brought increasing attendance and other distinguished leaders. In 1940 the total registered at eleven institutes

137

was 2,282; in 1941 a total of 1,542 people attended institutes for five days or more. Several thousands more people each year came to evening lectures. Registrants were mostly teachers, students, ministers, and leaders of civic organizations, in that order.[49] The faculties included many nonpacifists, since the primary aim was to cultivate intelligent concern for world affairs, but pacifist leadership was well represented. E. Raymond Wilson, who had come to the Peace Section in 1931 as traveling secretary, was made dean of institutes four years later. Grants from national foundations supplemented the A.F.S.C. budget. In 1933 a Haverford institute was organized in cooperation with the Pennsylvania Federation of Labor and the Central Labor Union of Philadelphia. Mainly for labor leaders, it was followed by another the next year. In 1934 a deliberately interracial institute was established in Atlanta, Georgia, with Claud Nelson of the F.O.R. as field secretary. The institutes seemed so strong by 1941 that six of them were put on a year-round basis. Each had its own field secretary to develop activities "focused toward building an informed, articulate public opinion for world peace."[50]

The Peace Section was less directly involved in a third kind of imaginative public education, an independent news service. From 1929 to at least 1933 it cooperated with the Baltimore Yearly Meeting (Friends) to support the work of Lucy Meacham Thruston. This peace journalist sent news articles to 450 newspapers (1933) every two weeks. Her material went mainly to rural papers in Maryland, Delaware, Virginia, West Virginia, and North Carolina, whose subscriptions varied from 2,000 to 50,000. She supplied, in addition, a biweekly news release, *The Trend of World Affairs*, to as many as 2,000 teachers, club leaders, and Sunday school teachers.[51] In 1933 the A.F.S.C. aided the more ambitious No-Frontier News Service, undertaken by one of the outstanding pacifists of the period, Devere Allen.

Allen was a writer by inclination and a reformer by conviction. His social concern was expressed especially in socialism and pacifism. "With reiteration," he wrote in 1930, "I have borne down upon the needs of a more drastic opposition to war, the war system, and its perpetuators."[52] His "drastic opposition to war" began in 1917. Even before America declared war he founded and edited the *Rational Patriot*, a journal of some Oberlin College students who denied that soldiering was the highest form of patriotism, even in wartime. Although he was heckled by most students, Allen continued to put out his pacifist journal until in 1918 he moved to New York City with his wife, Marie Hollister Allen, to become secretary of a new organization, The Young

Democracy. There he began a long and fruitful association with Ray Newton and edited the journal, the *Young Democracy*.

In 1921 he joined the staff of the *World Tomorrow*, of which he was the managing editor until the fall of 1924, an editor until 1931, and again in 1933. Associated with John Nevin Sayre, Anna Rochester, Grace Hutchins, Kirby Page, and Reinhold Niebuhr, Allen was instrumental in making the *World Tomorrow* one of America's most vigorous little magazines of the 1920's. He wrote serious articles, humor, and poetry. His poems were sometimes tender, often sardonic. His various columns represented the crest of his literary powers. They were charged with both wit and social concern.

Also in the twenties, Allen began to analyze pacifism. He turned to its historical roots and, in 1930, published a major history of the American peace movement, *The Fight for Peace*. His work was not only a history, however; it was also an analysis of the peace crusade which purported to show that radical pacifism is ultimately the only answer to war, and that international harmony and domestic social reform are two facets of the same movement. He also edited a collection of articles, *Pacifism in the Modern World* (1929), which was intended to demonstrate the relevance of the pacifist approach to all social problems.[53] He insisted that pacifists be realists, that they recognize the fact of power struggle even though this made day-to-day judgments not less but rather more difficult.

While he was with the *World Tomorrow*, Allen had vainly urged the other editors to include a four-page section carrying news of the worldwide peace movement. At the same time he had become aware of the need to coordinate American peace organizations, to make them more aware of international developments, and to reach beyond the paid circulation of the magazine. On a European trip in 1931 he developed a bold plan to increase American awareness of the international problem of peace and war. He talked with leaders like Madeline Doty, of the Women's International League for Peace and Freedom at Geneva; Bjarne Braatoy, who was active in both the peace and the labor movements, and was formerly an editor of the *Labor International*; Reginald Reynolds, secretary of several Indian associations in England and a confidant of Mohandas K. Gandhi; and Marcel Van Diest, a Belgian who printed a monthly news report on reform groups throughout Europe. Allen was impressed with the amount of material on international affairs that was available through liberal channels. In America he found through his contacts with the *World Tomorrow*, John Haynes Holmes's *Unity* magazine, the labor and the religious press, and the peace groups that there was a market for news of international affairs from a liberal point of view. The editor needed only an agency through which to funnel news to those who wanted it, an agency which could then both coordinate the American peace movement and integrate it with the world-wide effort.[54]

Again he approached the *World Tomorrow* staff. In particular, he mentioned an agreement he had made with the War Resisters International for the *World Tomorrow* to use regularly material that flowed in fourteen languages into the International's office, provided only that there should be no discrimination between groups of various religious or atheist views. Incredibly, it seemed to him, the American magazine would not accept this basis. It insisted upon giving international news a Christian emphasis. The paper was moving toward a weekly basis, too, and may not have wanted to venture in two new directions at once.

The following year, Allen edited the *Nation* for Oswald Garrison Villard. There, too, he presented his plans for an international relations section of the magazine. It should devote eight pages to world affairs, he urged; it should include articles, one page of advertising, and reports of world progress and problems and of peace organization. The staff was cautious, and when in 1932 Allen alienated Villard by running for senator from Connecticut on the Socialist ticket, the news project was frustrated a second time.[55]

In November of the following year, Devere and his wife launched a bold experiment in journalism and in peace work which lasted until 1955. They started the independent No-Frontier News Service (subsequently Worldover Press). By 1955 the service was supplying international news and analysis to nearly 700 newspapers and magazines in 62 countries. The Allens estimated that the total circulation of client papers using their material reached well over 12 million people. They used hundreds of periodicals to add to their perspective of world events, but they relied upon 40 regular overseas correspondents and 60 special correspondents (sometimes reporters, but often professors or writers) for their own news and analysis. They sent regular weekly bulletins and special reports to religious, labor, peace, and private newspapers. A fortnightly newsletter, the *World Interpreter* (subsequently *World Events*), was sent to ministers, teachers, other individuals, and libraries. In the world crisis of 1939 the Allens themselves operated a European Bureau in Belgium; during the Second World War they initiated a Latin American Bureau in Mexico (1942–44).[56]

Worldover Press was not operated as an organ of pacifism. It collected and distributed news of the peace movement, of social and cultural progress, and also of conflict around the globe. Although it published items before the regular news agencies upon occasion, it was not relied upon for everyday news. Although it indirectly reached millions, its influence on public opinion cannot be measured. Worldover Press was important to many people for its insight into news treated only casually, if at all, in standard journals. It was vital to the peace movement, which it put in contact with international events. Historically, the news agency was most important because it represented the clearest understanding in the peace crusade of the significance of international reform. Its editor believed that peace would be advanced through professional reporting and analysis of world events. In this respect Worldover Press represented, also, the assumption that pacifism is rooted in the real world as well as in religious ideals.

The educational and political work of leading pacifists mirrored that assumption. Kirby Page sometimes wrote of war as though it were the abstract question, "Is it sin?" But his answer was framed in terms of historical consequences—the memory of World War I. He investigated and publicized also the conditions leading to war. Trying to be realistic as well as religious, Page and his fellow liberal pacifists sought to educate the public in international affairs. Believing that uninformed and narrowly nationalistic peoples had been easily led into World War I, they hoped to create an aware and broad-minded electorate. Ironically, perhaps, they helped to lay grounds for public acceptance of collective security in the face of a totalitarian threat to the international order to the degree that they successfully communicated their internationalism, just as they inadvertently contributed to isolationism to the extent that they established World War I as proof of war's essential futility. On the eve of the Second World War that they had labored to prevent, pacifists would find themselves misunderstood by both collective security advocates and isolationists, each of whom drew strength from different strains of pacifist evangelism. In the 1920's, however, the world still looked open-ended, and pacifists tried to persuade people of the futility of war *and* the reality of one world.

Their efforts were not confined to organizations such as the F.O.R., the A.F.S.C., or Worldover Press. They spoke often across the country, touring the college and civic-club circuits. They arranged with the George H. Doran Company to publish a series of small books on Christianity and world problems. Local branches of organizations such as the Women's International League became nuclei for community discussions of foreign affairs. Pacifists hoped to influence opinion through their own magazine, the *World Tomorrow*. Whole issues of it were

141

devoted to specific areas of conflict. Editorials and articles often dealt with international problems. The magazine reached a limited audience, however—mainly people already interested in these questions. Its editors assumed that they were mobilizing liberal sentiment to influence foreign policy decisions, and the *World Tomorrow* became an instrument of pacifist efforts to deal with governments as the responsible agents of war and peace. In order to influence national policy, pacifists had to mobilize specific interest and opinion groups, so that the search for an antiwar public turned upon issues such as neutrality legislation, world economic cooperation, regulation of munitions makers, military training programs, and disarmament. The path away from the "last, blind war" led pacifists into the issues of the next one.

VI

Disarmament and the Devil Theories

The only way to abolish War is to abolish preparations for War.[1]

Assuming that governments are the agents of war and peace, pacifists in the United States sought to influence domestic as well as foreign policy. A few of them tried to obstruct the war-making power by constitutional amendment, but they got little public encouragement. Others fought to limit armaments, prevent compulsory training in public schools, and curb the activities of munitions makers. They worked closely with the rest of the peace movement on these issues, and they found an antiwar public which could be organized in response to them. In the political battles of the thirties pacifists were sometimes portrayed as the dupes of subversive interests. They, in turn, were tempted to identify their opponents as "vested interests."

Some antiwar activities were decidedly utopian. The Women's Peace Union wanted to make war unconstitutional, for example.* On its behalf Lynn J. Frazier, senator from North Dakota, introduced a constitutional amendment in every Congress from 1926 to 1937. It read:

> SECTION 1. War for any purpose shall be illegal, and neither the United States nor any State, Territory, association, or person subject to its jurisdiction shall prepare for, declare, engage in, or carry on war or other armed conflict, expedition, invasion, or undertaking within or without the United States, nor shall any funds be raised, appropriated, or expended for such purpose.

* The Women's Peace Union was organized for this purpose as a result of a debate over tactics within the Women's Peace Society, which Fanny Garrison Villard had founded in Oct., 1919, as a place for absolutely pacifist women disgruntled by the moderate stand of the W.I.L.P.F. on disarmament and free trade. The W.P.S. was discontinued about 1934, and the W.P.U. was inactive after at least 1941.

143

SEC. 2. All provisions of the Constitution and of the articles in addition thereto and amendment thereof which are in conflict with or inconsistent with this article are hereby rendered null and void and of no effect.

SEC. 3. The Congress shall have power to enact appropriate legislation to give effect to this article.[2]

In 1929, Frazier argued that the amendment would bring the United States into line with the spirit of the Kellogg-Briand Pact; but, in fact, that agreement had never questioned the right of defensive wars and had been based on the assumption that unilateral disarmament was unthinkable. War had not only the sanctity of being constitutional, but also the appearance of being necessary.

The amendment which the Women's Peace Union had drafted in 1923 and peddled to Congress each year was endorsed by pacifist organizations including the Women's International League, the War Resisters League, and the Fellowship of Reconciliation. None of these groups campaigned for the measure, however, while conservative peace societies followed the lead of Frederick J. Libby of the National Council for Prevention of War who repudiated disarmament by example. The Frazier Amendment was introduced on the commonly held assumption that the United States could quarantine itself from international ills; it lent substance to charges of isolationism which were hurled at pacifists.

A proposal which became known as the Ludlow Amendment proved more popular, although little more defensible, than the Frazier Amendment. Congressman Louis Ludlow, of Indiana, introduced in the House of Representatives in 1935, 1937, and 1938 a constitutional amendment providing that a declaration of extraterritorial war and the taking of property for public use in time of war would have to be validated by a national referendum.[3] The measure had not originated with Congressman Ludlow, however. As early as 1922, Edward Voight, of Sheboygan, Wisconsin, had introduced an amendment to the Constitution to submit declarations of war to the people. The following year, Mrs. Winnifred Mason Huck, of Chicago, introduced House Joint Resolution 423, "authorizing and directing the President to inform other nations that the United States will delegate to its peoples the sole power to declare war against any nation that shall delegate the same power to its people."[4] Resolutions favoring constitutional amendment for war referendum were introduced in every subsequent Congress through the Seventy-fifth (1938), when Robert M. La Follette, Jr., brought it up for himself and the isolationist core.[5]

144

As war became an increasingly real possibility in the thirties, the Ludlow Amendment was advocated to impede presidential initiative in foreign affairs and to obstruct collective security. Like proposals to limit armaments and to regulate munitions makers, it came to be viewed less in the context of disarmament and more in relation to neutrality. Like the Frazier Amendment, it assumed that America could remain isolated from world wars, and it further implied that Americans would prefer to do so. Walter Lippman, among others, argued that the idea was unrealistic. It would prevent the President from using the diplomatic threat of force, he said, and compel the United States to wait for actual invasion; but it would not really clip the war-making power of a headstrong President. Such a man could violate peace without declaring war.[6] Pacifists felt obligated to give official support to the measure despite its utopian character. Indeed, they felt bound to give token allegiance to virtually any antiwar plan.

Even Kirby Page flirted with the utopian. He drafted a plan for a peace department of the government whose administrator would hold cabinet rank, like the Secretary of War. The Department of Peace would maintain an international university to train specialists in foreign affairs—a West Point or Annapolis for peace. It would operate an "International Friendship Training Corps," comparable to the U.S. Army's Reserve Officers' Training Corps, and it would provide 1,000 professors of international relations to American colleges and 5,000 instructors in foreign affairs for high schools. As the military operated Citizens' Training Camps, so the peace department would conduct 100 summer institutes in international relations (no doubt on the A.F.S.C. model). As the navy sent its fleet to foreign seas, so the peace department would conduct tours of friendship to and from the United States. It would also establish about 40 information centers abroad; produce and distribute magazines, posters, films, and books; and support an exchange program of students and teachers. Its budget might be $1 million.*

Page probably did not take his plan too seriously. It was a whimsical project that had the merit of being logical, if unobtainable. It was in-

---

* Page, *The Renunciation of War* (New York: Doubleday, Doran & Co., Inc., 1928), pp. 24–25; and *National Defense*, pp. 308–14. In the sixties, programs similar to some features of Page's plan would be administered by the United States Information Agency (having information centers abroad, distributing books, films, and radio programs), the Peace Corps, the Agency for International Development (financial and technical assistance), and the Department of State's Bureau of Educational and Cultural Affairs (student and teacher exchanges, cultural tours abroad, aid to schools and colleges). Congress appropriated $59 million for the Peace Corps alone in the fiscal year ending June 30, 1963.

tended to show the irony of peace workers vainly competing with the government-subsidized military to influence public opinion. Page sent a rough draft of the plan to Devere Allen who commended it as a comment on military budgets, but discouraged offering it as a serious alternative. It would be useless even if it could be obtained, he said, and in our society it could not be adopted: the masses, not the leaders, are the only sure grounds for peace.[7]

The scheme was given fleeting prominence in 1934 when George E. Bevans, minister of the First Presbyterian Church in Fairmont, West Virginia, became enthusiastic about it. A bill similar to Page's plan was introduced in the Senate by Matthew M. Neely, one of Bevan's parishioners.[8] Leaders in the peace movement gave little support to the bill, arguing that the Department of State was the appropriate agency of any President really concerned about peace. The problem, they averred, was to curb the military. That Page's plan would not do this was illustrated with unintentional irony by a high school newspaper in California which claimed enthusiastically:

> An American, Mr [sic] Kirby Page, has worked out a peace plan which can be set into operation without disarmament. He does not ask us to destroy anything or to give up at once any part of our program for military preparedness. His program for peace can be put into operation right along side of our program for national defense.[9]

It is little wonder that, with such publicity, Page did not campaign for the peace department. He was already involved in the antipreparedness cause.

The first postwar political activity of the peace movement was to limit the military establishment on the assumption that an arms race had been an underlying cause of World War I. Three months after the Armistice the American Union Against Militarism was roused from its somnolence ("incredible as it may seem," its officers admitted) by a campaign to resist peacetime conscription.[10] Its executive committee voted to concentrate all its efforts on that single issue, and set up a lobby in Washington. It found a focal point in the bill endorsed by Secretary of War Newton Baker on August 3, 1919, which would have given all eighteen- or nineteen-year-old boys three months of compulsory military training. "There is no flubdub about democracy in the Baker-General Staff bill . . . ," wrote the executive secretary. "It is a straightforward unpretentious Prussian bill . . . ."[11] That argument and a demand for economy cut across many sections of public opinion, so that in the Army Act of June 4, 1920, Congress cut back Baker's requests in every respect, omitting entirely universal military training.

146

Secretary of the Navy Josephus Daniels also flaunted the mood of a Congress already anxious to return to normality by proposing in 1918 and 1920 a three-year expansion program designed to give the United States a fleet second to none. For the navy that proposal represented the logic of defense (which was already yielding a new naval race). For the Wilson administration it offered a thinly veiled alternative to a League of Nations. On December 14, 1920, William Borah offered the Senate another alternative when he introduced a joint resolution urging the President to call an international conference for the limitation of armaments. The new adminstration resisted congressional encroachment on its executive discretion in foreign affairs, but Borah's resolution and parallel hearings in the House gave impetus to mounting public support for a conference.

That support became clear in February when delegates to the convention of the National Women's Party tried to decide how to use their newly won suffrage. A minority of women, failing to carry the organization for disarmament, withdrew and formed their own Women's Committee on World Disarmament. Working swiftly, they staged mass meetings on Easter Sunday and a disarmament week in May. In cooperation with existing women's organizations, such as the Women's Christian Temperance Union and the League of Women Voters, and with new disarmament groups, they distributed literature, sponsored speaking tours, sent delegations to the President, and elicited resolutions for Congress and the White House. They were spurred by revelations about military gas in Will Irwin's *The Next War* and about germ warfare in a widely distributed sermon by Harry Emerson Fosdick. They warned of increased taxes and economic crises. Borah was delighted with their work. The Washington Conference which Warren Harding finally summoned on August 4 resulted from demands for economy within the government and from Secretary of State Charles Evans Hughes's perception of the diplomatic interests of the United States, Japan, and Great Britain; but both Hughes and the disarmament bloc in Congress had valuable leverage in organized public opinion. The astute Secretary of State continued to manipulate this lever during preparations for the international conference which met in November and afterward in seeking congressional ratification of its agreements. His dramatic opening speech and the program he unfolded were calculated, in part, to secure maximum popular support.

As so often thereafter, the very existence of a politically oriented peace movement broadened the bases of decision-making and turned foreign policy decisions into political issues. Public support became im-

147

portant to all factions interested in the government, and one index of the movement's effectiveness was the activity of organizations marshalled against it—the Army and Navy Club, for instance, and the Navy League. The former was created in 1920 explicitly to counteract "the tide of anti-preparedness and pacifism."[12] The Navy League acquired a new lease on life because of the threat to naval strength which it perceived in the Washington Conference. The *Army and Navy Journal* was disturbed by "the undercurrents of powerful propaganda . . . to discredit and emasculate the national services."[13] The response of these groups was to organize their own propaganda. Once it understood the importance of public opinion to naval programs, the Navy League set out to popularize the navy, consciously emulating the techniques of the prewar German navy league.

Meanwhile, the Washington Conference stimulated the development of the Navy League's particular bête noire, the National Council for the Limitation of Armaments. Disarmament became an institutionalized aspect of the peace movement when that group became the National Council for Prevention of War on October 31, 1922. Only the name changed. The program, presuppositions, and personnel remained the same. Frederick J. Libby was at the core of both of them.

The son of a country doctor and a schoolteacher, Libby acquired a native Maine stamina, wit, and practical bent that prepared him for three decades of organizational work. In his youth he acquired, too, experiences in education and internationalism which he tied together as perhaps the leading peace worker in the twenties. Between his graduation from Bowdoin College in 1894 at the age of nineteen and the First World War he had been a high school principal, a seminarian and ordained Congregational pastor, studied for a total of three years in Europe, toured the Pacific world, and taught on the faculty of Phillips Exeter Academy. In 1917 he applied for Y.M.C.A. work with prisoners of war but was rejected because of his membership in the pacifist F.O.R. He was accepted by the Friends' reconstruction unit, though, and sailed for France on the Fourth of July, 1918. His experience there confirmed his inclination to work full time for peace, and in 1921 the A.F.S.C. employed him to educate the public on European needs. Libby soon set his own course for disarmament. He was a small man, built close to the bone as a Maine fence hugs the land, but his personality and energy were expansive. He was generous with his friendship even to those with whom he differed, although he never willingly gave up a vote in a political fight, whether to the Navy League or within his own organization.

148

Libby had voiced the need for a broadly representative disarmament council as early as April, when only small committees with limited constituencies were in the field. By June several influential Friends shared his concern. They formed the Friends Disarmament Council as a nucleus for the larger clearinghouse for which they hoped. One of them, Harold Evans, won the support of Christina Merriman, executive secretary of the Foreign Policy Association, who invited numerous civic organizations to be represented at a meeting in Washington on September 8. By then invitations had been issued to the international Conference on Limitation and Reduction of Armaments, and Libby recognized that it was "a natural rallying point" for his group.[14] The new council even took its name from the conference, and prepared to channel public support through each member organization. Even though he knew he would have to raise money for the council's work, Libby quickly employed able staff members who worked together well into the thirties.* By the time the Washington Conference opened at the Pan American building on November 12, 1921, they were settled in an office two blocks away and just across Seventeenth Street from the State, War, and Navy departments.

From this vantage point the National Council issued a biweekly *Bulletin* which had a circulation of 5,000 in December, posters, letters, press releases, articles, and 30,000 copies of a pamphlet by Will Irwin, *War On War*. It sponsored essay contests; operated a speaker's bureau; and organized Christmas, 1921, as Peace Day. Perhaps most effective were the forty-one public forums conducted by Laura Puffer Morgan four afternoons a week. Most sessions of the Washington Conference

* Most important were Florence Brewer Boeckel, who developed publicity and educational programs; Glady Gould (Mackenzie), who ran the busy office; and Laura Puffer Morgan, who became the council's expert in foreign affairs. She was the wife of a newspaperman who died in 1921, and she had been active in the American Association of University Women as president of the District of Columbia branch, a vice-president at large, and legislative representative. Mrs. Boeckel had done newspaper work, edited the *Suffragist,* and had been a founder and publicity director of the National Women's Press Club.

Harold Evans was a member of the A.F.S.C. and the F.O.R. and Miss Merriman was active also in the League of Women Voters and the New York Clearinghouse for Disarmament.

Besides the civic, farm, religious, educational, and women's groups represented at the Sept. 8 meeting, there were two labor unions. Samuel Gompers, president of the American Federation of Labor, stayed out and formed a General Committee which would offer an alternative to what he considered the radical pacifist leadership of the National Council. The full list of participating organizations is included in Frederick Libby's autobiography, *Fighting for Peace* (New York: Fellowship Press, 1969).

149

were closed, and so the forums, which featured foreign as well as American speakers, became a popular and important source of information. As Libby recalled years later, the forums and news releases "kept the Washington Conference before the public, and at the same time introduced our infant Council to Washington and the world."[15]

However naïvely the public might have received the completed naval armaments agreement and related treaties, both big and small navy men knew they had only opened the question of naval power. The nations achieved a staggering cut-back in capital ships; but cruiser strength, auxiliary craft, and personnel remained undetermined, and these naval elements were linked to foreign policy. The National Council accordingly addressed broad international problems in its *Bulletin* while it fought for reductions in naval personnel in the spring of 1922. This contest revealed the presuppositions of the contenders, even as it roused them to a long dispute.

The U.S. Navy and the Navy League regarded the treaty ratio of 5:5:3 for capital ships of the United States, Great Britain, and Japan as defining the minimum American needs, and concluded that the nation should build up to the treaty provisions in order to achieve parity with the British Empire. Moreover, the league's officers regarded congressional parsimony on naval requests as evidence of public ignorance, of misplaced values which would sacrifice adequate defense to economy. They launched a major propaganda campaign to reorient the people. The National Council, on the other hand, regarded the treaty as defining maximum naval strength, and concluded that the nation should cooperate with others to scale fleets down from the treaty. Moreover, peace advocates were apprehensive of the navy's contemplated expansion. Economy had been an effective keynote in the recent disarmament campaign, but they knew it would be temporary and that the people would have to be educated to more basic issues of war and peace.

Libby's staff members now took over the work of the American Union Against Militarism, which finally suspended its activities.[16] They expanded their educational programs, prepared the first comparative analysis of navies produced by any peace movement, and organized the American version of "International No-More-War Day" on the anniversary of the beginning of World War I. Public meetings were planned and 200,000 posters were distributed through member organizations. The Navy League retaliated with its Navy Day on Theodore Roosevelt's birthday. The occasion was supported by the administration and the navy. It was replete with massive newspaper coverage, newsreels, official statements, and public fanfare. Rivalry between the two pressure groups was cemented, even as Libby's experiment in national coordination changed its name to the National Council for Prevention of War and developed into an independent organization.

Competition for the public continued. The Navy League had its "Day" annually, occupied a building near the N.C.P.W. office, and lobbied hard for naval increases. Nonetheless, its membership fell for five years, and it was easy to conclude that the mood of the people "was pacifist," ready to support the National Council and similar peace societies.[17] Libby was the only pacifist on the N.C.P.W. staff then, in any strict sense of the word. Few of its member organizations were pacifist, and the council did not even press for unilateral disarmament, but the word stereotyped everyone who favored limitation of arms at all and carried over the wartime implication of disloyalty.

It was just as easy for peace advocates to castigate all supporters of naval increases as militarists, and equally misleading. By the end of 1927 the nation had spurned the League of Nations and the World Court, and President Coolidge's Geneva Conference had failed to yield disarmament agreements. Pacifists once had paraded the slogan, "Scrap the Battleships and the Pacific Problems will settle themselves," but those problems looked worse than ever.[18] Many people were ready to conclude with the President himself that stronger defense was a necessary alternative to international accord. Peace organizations and the Navy League group campaigned intensely throughout 1928, with the National Council forming a legislative reference service for congressmen and mobilizing public opinion. Early the next year, Congress passed a bill that substantially reduced Navy requests but still authorized the largest naval construction since 1916.

> Is the reader aware that there is in existence in this country a well-organized movement to militarize the tone and temper of our national life? Is he aware that militarism has already become a vested interest, economic as well as political and social? . . . Is he aware that the vested interest resorts to methods of aspersion and overt attack in order to intimidate those . . . who oppose its efforts to get a strangle hold on our schools . . . .
>
> —JOHN DEWEY

151

> Anyone willing to pursue the . . . lists of Communist organ-
> izations and leaders named side by side with "Peace"
> organizations and leaders, as cooperating and official sup-
> porters of such Communist-organized and controlled affairs
> as the various Congresses against War . . . cannot doubt
> that the Pacifist and Revolutionary movements are linked
> together by hoops of steel.
>
> —ELIZABETH DILLING[19]

Pacifists meanwhile were investing their greatest single effort in "disarming the minds of American youth."[20] From its beginning the Fellowship of Reconciliation had viewed education as the basic instrument
for the cultivation of internationalism. At an early date the National
Council surveyed textbooks used in public schools, demanded that they
be "disarmed" of jingoistic nationalism, and sponsored a conference on
promoting international peace through the schools.* Moreover, pacifists
had always opposed universal conscription as the antithesis of democracy, as the opening wedge of militarism. Distrusting conscription and
cherishing the educational influence, they were committed to resist the
military training in public schools which was encouraged under the
National Defense Acts of 1916 and 1920.

The War Department was authorized to fund and staff Reserve Officers' Training Corps in colleges and universities. Students taking at
least two years of military training and supplementary service were
given a commission in the army reserve. Although originally billed as a
training program, the R.O.T.C. soon served principally as a recruitment
and public relations device. In return for participating in it the host
schools might receive military equipment useful in gymnasiums and
instruction, cavalry units, armories, and scholarship aid in the form of
cadet subventions. By 1927, R.O.T.C. was mandatory in eighty-six colleges and universities, elective in forty-four more, and had been extended also to high schools in fifty-three cities.[21] A long list of public
and private schools without R.O.T.C. units received equipment and aid
from the federal government because of military training they offered.

Pacifists had resisted the program from its inception, but by 1925 it
had become a visible target of attack which alarmed also some educators and politicians. That spring the F.O.R. distributed 159,000 copies
of a pamphlet written by Winthrop D. Lane at the urging of Nevin

---

* The week-long conference took place in San Francisco following June 28,
1923, with over fifty countries represented. A World Federation of Education Associations was formed, and it was agreed that May 18 should be celebrated by
schools throughout the world as International Goodwill Day.

Sayre. Referring to official sources, Lane documented and attacked the use of R.O.T.C. to popularize military training and indoctrinate students with the War Department's point of view.[22] The Lane pamphlet set a pattern for subsequent literature. It also defined the task of the Fellowship's new Committee on Militarism in Education which led and coordinated the drive against compulsory military education from 1925 to 1940.*

It had an independent organization and membership, although it was tied to the F.O.R. by birth and leadership. Nevin Sayre was an active chairman and Oswald G. Villard, treasurer; and both of them were major financial sponsors of the committee. Successive secretaries were men close to the Fellowship: E. Raymond Wilson, Roswell Barnes, Tucker P. Smith, and Edwin C. Johnson.† The C.M.E. even shared an office with the F.O.R. in the twenties, and it used mailing lists compiled by the Fellowship and Kirby Page for its first contacts.[23] It enlisted prominent churchmen and educators who were outraged by the extension of compulsory military training into the schools. It antagonized other educators because it established subgroups on many campuses, kept meticulous track of R.O.T.C. programs across the country, and publicized both campus controversy and the suppression of dissent.

The committee helped to focus latent resistance of teachers and students to military training programs. Faculties at the University of Minnesota, Cornell University, and the University of Washington, among others, voted against compulsory drill.[24] The University of Texas faculty voted overwhelmingly against the establishment of an R.O.T.C. unit, but the decision went over their heads to the state legislature. Faculty members at Ohio State University, after full debate and investigation, expressed a slight preference to make drill optional; but less than one week later and following charges of disloyalty from the R.O.T.C. colonel and the clear will of the administration, they reversed themselves decisively. The Board of Trustees promptly served notice that students and teachers who chose to remain at its institution were expected to accept its definition of policy. The administration went further and dis-

---

* Congress passed a peacetime conscription bill in Oct., 1940, and the C.M.E. disbanded as of Nov. 1, 1940. Even so, Nevin Sayre and others continued its work, mainly through the F.O.R.

† Wilson was head of the A.F.S.C. Peace Section and its official liaison with the F.O.R.; Barnes was associate secretary of the Commission on International Justice and Goodwill of the Federal Council of Churches and an F.O.R. member; Smith was a former Y.M.C.A. general secretary, a socialist and director of Brookwood Labor College, a member of the executive committee of the W.R L., and in 1934 assistant treasurer of the F.O.R.; and Johnson was on the executive committee of the W.R.L. and the Brookwood extension department.

153

missed a sociology professor who had opposed compulsory drill, despite formal protests from thousands of students and the faculty which had just voted its wish.[25] College students elsewhere opposed the compulsory features of the R.O.T.C., and a strong minority challenged the program itself, but they were as frustrated as their teachers.[26] Even criticism of programs frequently was quashed upon complaints from unit officers. College administrators had a variety of reasons to defend the compulsory program, including alumni or legislative support, financial advantages to the school, and their own understanding of patriotic service, but their support had little to do with student-faculty preference or with education.

Pacifists objected to the R.O.T.C. because it appeared to be a device for introducing militarism—authoritarianism and indoctrination—into the educational process under the guise of social and civic societies. Consequently, they attacked it both for its so-called military value and for its popular, nonmilitary appearance. War's tragic mask was obscured by comic romance, they said, and playing war contributed to neither good soldiers nor realistic peace.

College catalogs often described military courses in terms of drill, military courtesy, marksmanship, and some technical classes. Early R.O.T.C. manuals themselves were full of evidence that the object of military training was to inculcate a martial spirit. Pacifists quoted them (and challenged the public to distinguish them from similar statements of the Prussian general, Friedrich von Bernhardi):

> We live in a world governed by Divine laws which we can neither alter nor evade. And in this world of ours force is the ultimate power.
>
> During the course of a great war every government, whatever its previous form, should become a despotism.
>
> An armistice should never be granted at the instance of a defeated foe. It is a confession of weakness, of inability to clinch the victory.
>
> This inherent desire to fight and kill must be carefully watched for and encouraged by the instructor.[27]

When students at the College of the City of New York printed excerpts from a chapter on "The Spirit of the Bayonet" in a *Manual of Military Training*, it was called in and the offending section removed. "But why?" pacifists asked. "Of what use to emasculate Mars on the drill field when it cannot be done on the battlefield?"[28] They argued that the program was not designed to fit men for battle, but rather to prepare them for "the war system"; it cultivated the belief that war is inevitable and that internationalism threatens preparedness; it trained men to submit to authority and even extended suppression of dissent to the host academic community.[29] If that was the real import of military training in school, its opponents said, then it was insidious.

R.O.T.C. had another, more inviting face for which pacifists reserved their best satire. Congressman Ross Collins of Mississippi relied on c.m.e. materials in the annual appropriations debate as he scored the program for lavish waste. Pretty co-eds were selected to be honorary colonels or cadet sponsors, he noted; they were given uniforms and sabers; they formed rifle teams, reviewed the boys, and presided over social affairs. A unit in Maine opened a dancing school and one in Alabama formed a horseback-riding class for young women. Cadets wore snappy dress uniforms, put on public parades and reviews, dispensed trophies, staged mock battles, and appealed to school pride. They had their own honorary fraternity, Scabbard and Blade. They turned military horses into polo ponies and were credited by the *Princeton Alumni Weekly* with bringing a postwar "renaissance" to the game.[30] Congressman Collins pointed out that relatively few reserve officers were recruited from all this effort, and he pronounced it "foolishness."[31] The c.m.e. detailed the techniques used to popularize military training. "So This Is War!" it exclaimed. Combat is not child's play, pacifists insisted, and defense policy should not be a matter for the emotions.

In the early thirties the c.m.e., together with the Methodist Episcopal Church, tested the cases of several students who were suspended because they refused to take the compulsory R.O.T.C. course on the grounds of their conscientious objection to war. In one case the Supreme Court refused to overturn an adverse judgment of the Maryland State Court of Appeals.[32] In a case involving two students at the University of California, the Court held that exemption from wartime service was a constitutional immunity which did not affect the right of a university to require military training.[33] These decisions were in accord with the Court's validation of conscription in *Arver* v. *United States* in 1918 and its denial of citizenship to aliens who would not swear to bear arms in defense of the country. In both *United States* v. *Schwimmer* (1929) and *United States* v. *Macintosh* (1931) it held that exemption from military service is a privilege granted by Congress, not a right under the Constitution.[34]

The c.m.e. campaigned in vain after 1926 for legislation to prohibit compulsory military training courses by withholding federal funds either from schools or from R.O.T.C. units where the program was mandatory. In 1934 it drafted a bill to require that military training should be elective under the National Defense Acts of 1916 and 1920. Bills

155

introduced by Senator Gerald P. Nye of North Dakota and Congressman Paul J. Kvale of Minnesota won strong endorsement from churchmen, educators, civic groups, and important newspapers, but not from Congress.[35] By the mid-thirties war had been loosed on the world again. Pacifists shifted their lines from antipreparedness to neutrality, and the c.m.e. joined their general campaign against conscription in 1939–40.

The committee had been encouraged by scattered victories, and it could claim some credit for thwarting Junior r.o.t.c units in high schools, but it never seriously threatened military training in the colleges. In 1928 it was cheered by a report that the Girl Scouts had abandoned their old uniforms as too militaristic, scant comfort in its over-all campaign. By 1931 it knew of sixty-five high schools and colleges that had dropped military training completely, but the War Department had replaced them with others. About one dozen more had made it elective, following the lead of the University of Wisconsin in 1923.[36] North Dakota prohibited compulsory drill in state-supported institutions in 1937. Elsewhere the committee counted as many defeats as victories. Peace advocates faced a military establishment with large resources of finances, influence, and congressional good will. Even foreign affairs favored the military, for to the extent that Americans accepted defense spending, they were persuaded by international developments more than by anyone's propaganda.

For their troubles, Libby, Page, Sayre, and their friends in the movement were assailed by patriotic extremists as subversives. The charge was ridiculously false, but it had a way of obscuring the issues they were trying to dramatize. For reasons not altogether clear, the Communist party conspiracy had a credibility far in excess of its power between the wars. One did not have to be an extremist to be deterred by that devil theory; caution alone sufficed to suppress dissent, bar speakers, and close minds.

Grounds had been laid during the war and the subsequent Red Scare. Files compiled then by the Lusk committee of the New York state legislature, the National Security League, the American Legion, and others were used later to produce blacklists circulated among the Daughters of the American Revolution or the notorious "spider web chart" prepared in the War Department. There, in the Chemical Warfare Service, Brigadier General Amos A. Fries chaffed under the threat to his branch which disarmament posed. He lashed out at Frederick Libby in 1922, calling him a Communist sympathizer. The next year his office released a chart which traced connections between various peace, social welfare, and religious groups and their leaders, and purported to show that "The

Socialist-Pacifist Movement in America Is an Absolutely Fundamental
and Integral Part of International Socialism."[37] The chart, with its web-
like lines of influence, was reproduced in the Dearborn (Massachusetts)
Independent. It caused a furor among the women's groups it designated, including the League of Women Voters. Secretary of War John
W. Weeks finally recalled it with an apology for the "errors" it contained, but for many years it was used surreptitiously to give "official"
sanction to extremist charges.

Each President of this period had his difficulty with zealous patriots.
Calvin Coolidge was caught briefly in sparring between the War Department and the National Council for Prevention of War over the cele-
bration of a national Defense Day; he escaped by appointing the Fourth
of July as the day requested by the military, thereby diluting mobilization with a holiday mood. Herbert Hoover was charged by the Navy
League with ignorance of defense needs, if not apathy to them. Franklin D. Roosevelt received complaints that the naval intelligence section
was disseminating irresponsible charges of Communist affiliation, and
he finally ordered an investigation. His naval aide reported that the
Navy was "not the source" of the offending information.[38] Often private individuals implied the existence of official information they did
not have or sent to the government accusations which then became
parts of official files; but executive departments were, for the most part,
scrupulous in refusing even to acknowledge the existence of confidential information about citizens. Roosevelt advised the military also to
remain silent in the face of criticism from peace advocates:

> Nobody wants to put a censorship on the admirals but I really think
> that it is far better not to answer the professional pacifists than it is to
> "hit" and assail them. Replies only create a controversy. Perhaps with-
> out letting it appear that this is a suggestion of the Commander-in-
> Chief, you can spread the word abroad.[39]

General Fries was, therefore, exceptionally outspoken on politics, certainly on the Communist conspiracy theory. Nonetheless, numerous
persons connected with semipublic groups took advantage of their freedom from official responsibility to exploit their public image.

Nevin Sayre was prohibited from speaking on the campus of the
University of Oklahoma in 1926 after he had been described by a lieutenant colonel of the U.S. Infantry as "more dangerous than an open
communist," but the army held that its officer was speaking as a private
citizen.[40] The R.O.T.C. unit at Ohio State University attacked a student
pastor and reserve chaplain for his criticism of compulsory training,
and it prepared a formal investigation until the War Department or-

dered it stopped. Similar incidents were reported around the country, particularly after the R.O.T.C. fraternity, Scabbard and Blade, circulated special alarmist bulletins warning of Communists in disguise and organizations formed "by direct order" of Moscow.[41] The aim of these subversives, it was repeated, was to confuse and collectivize American youth and to weaken national defense. The president of the Reserve Officers' Association, Pennsylvania Department, alerted other chapters to a "close-working alliance" between Ross Collins, chairman of the House Subcommittee on Army Appropriations, and "the Soviet-loving Pacifist, Frederick J. Libby of Notorious Communist leanings. This points toward the justice of the conclusion that certain present Congressional leaders have shamefully entrusted the sacred charge of our National Defense to the soiled hands of our enemies within."[42]

Professional patriots sold pamphlets, data sheets, and lists of people they regarded as dangerous. They formed groups such as the Key Men of America (Dealing with Radical and Subversive Movements) and the Industrial Defense Association. The Military Order of World War I and especially the American Legion were vehicles of smear campaigns aimed at pacifists and based on the ubiquitous lists of radicals. In their lexicon pacifists were slackers and advocates of reductions in the defense budget, and were disloyal. The persistent exclusion of peace advocates from some podiums finally occasioned a revolt among the Daughters of the American Revolution in 1927–28. Peace advocates often found their right to speak challenged by local Legionnaires, and they frequently challenged their critics to debate. Page was particularly adept at extemporaneous give and take, and, besides, he was an effective and much desired Christian evangelist. Extremists predictably called him and his friends false prophets. In her vicious book-length index to so-called radicals and their organizations, Elizabeth Dilling wrote that the sincerely misled Christian pacifist was "ignoring the fact that those most dominant in influencing, financing, boring from within, if not actually controlling the great majority of pacifist societies are Socialists and Communists who appear in the clothing of sheep crying 'Peace! Peace!' when there is no peace while they themselves, like ravening wolves, are agitating 'class struggle,' 'class war,' civil wars and bloody revolution."[43]

Charges like these were all the more ludicrous in the light of the acrimony between pacifists and Communists. Plans for a Conference on Filipino Independence in 1926 were disrupted, for example, when Nevin Sayre noticed Communist connections on the organizing committee, and the F.O.R. withdrew. A few years later when Anna Rochester, Grace Hutchins, and Scott Nearing became for a time Communist party members, they resigned from the Fellowship, feeling that the two groups were "thoroughly inconsistent."[44] Pacifists were tempted to cooperate with Communists in a united front against war and fascism in the thirties, but even then they competed separately for the antiwar left wing. Fights to control youth organizations became especially bitter. Kirby Page, whom the American Legion regarded as one of the most dangerous subversives, became "the most persistent and articulate critic of cooperation between Communists and Christians."[45] Nevertheless, in their campaigns against military expansion pacifists were exorcised along with other devils of the Communist conspiracy theory. All too often these exercises in futility detracted from a realistic appraisal of public policy.

In one respect, at least, the disarmament campaigns were useful: they were fulcrums from which pacifists organized segments of the public and developed political leverage. Military training, for example, was a particularly useful issue among young people or groups concerned with education, such as church conferences and social action committees. Pacifists traveled and spoke under the auspices of both the C.M.E. and the F.O.R. They gave a visible alternative to compulsory soldiering to thousands of youths who saw them debate R.O.T.C. officers and Legionnaires, who joined groups affiliated with the C.M.E., or who depended upon it for information. Pacifists won support, too, from people who agreed only on their right to be heard over the objections of patriotic extremists. The C.M.E. never sponsored war resistance, but ten years of its work could not have failed to influence the antiwar pledges which students took in the mid-thirties.

Similarly, pacifist influence on Capitol Hill in the thirties was grounded on experience in the disarmament campaigns of the previous decade. In 1923, Libby's N.C.P.W. staff was supplemented when Dorothy Detzer came to Washington as national secretary of the Women's International League. She was one of those whose lives World War I changed. She had worked beside Jane Addams then without becoming a pacifist, had suffered personal loss, and had joined the Friends' reconstruction unit in France. A few weeks at home in the all-too-pleasant routines of postwar America prompted her to return to relief work where the daily questions were life and death in famine-stricken Russia. When she came back again to the United States she was radically convinced that peace and freedom were corollaries. She entered full-time peace work. Miss Detzer became America's foremost "lady lobbyist," aggressive but diplomatic, possessing stern principles and *savoir-faire,* backed by a vociferous segment of public opinion and wise in the ways of committees and pressure groups.

Women in Germany and Scandinavia, the United States, and especially Great Britain pressed for total universal disarmament in conjunction with the work of various League of Nations commissions in the twenties. The w.i.l.p.f. was particularly concerned to prohibit chemical warfare. Prospects looked bright when Labour leader Ramsey MacDonald became Prime Minister and gentle Herbert Hoover became President. The two heads of state quickly agreed on preliminary terms that allowed MacDonald to call a five-power London Naval Conference intended to complete the work of the Washington Conference. For months the delegates labored to define acceptable ratios of naval strength, the United States retaining parity with Great Britain.* All the while, Miss Detzer kept up a stream of letters to the President and encouraged a flood of mail to the State Department demanding that it abandon parity for "real naval disarmament." Department officials frankly complained about the volume of letters. President Hoover finally called Miss Detzer in and asked her to examine a sheaf of dispatches on the conference which documented the government's good faith and the complexities it faced. She did not challenge his intentions, but rather questioned his objectives, insisting that he would have to abandon the principle of parity in order to make significant progress. "I can't," he fairly whispered. "I can't."[46] Indeed he could not, for two days earlier, on April 22, the United States had signed the treaty. Hoover called a special session of Congress and secured ratification.

Pacifists were not entirely pleased with the conference. One group of them concluded:

> Many of the peace groups should be openly repentant over their earlier and naïve acceptance of the principle of parity which is now written into the laws of nations and which gives the navalists an undue advantage in our national councils for years to come.
>
> If any lesson at all can be learned from history, it is the lesson that disarmament by agreement is an elusive will-o-the-wisp . . . it is high time that the peace agencies drop their efforts to follow official leading, and strike out boldly and realistically for disarmament by example. Disarmament, to our minds, is not a *summum bonum* of the peace crusade; but it is of great importance psychologically and the fight must go on.[47]

* The American delegation was headed by Secretary of State Henry L. Stimson, and included Secretary of the Navy Charles Francis Adams; Charles G. Davies, Dwight Morrow, and Hugh S. Gibson, ambassadors to Great Britain, Mexico, and Belgium, respectively; and Senators David Reed and Joseph T. Robinson.

160

Realistically, there was not much to do but follow Hoover's lead until in January, 1931, the League of Nations Council decided to convene the World Disarmament Conference for which it had prepared so long on February 3, 1932. Peace groups were encouraged to "strike out boldly" for public opinion.

The Women's International League budgeted about $50,000 for its campaign from March, 1931, to July, 1932.[48] Like its European counterparts, it used the device of a popular petition as a reason to send delegates to the President, interview local officials and sponsor demonstrations. Every meeting was designed to produce telegrams and petitions. The women secured national publicity with their Peace Caravan, a motorcade which left Hollywood late in June bound for the nation's capital. It made front-page news in each of the 125 cities along the way where the women stopped to speak. When it reached Washington almost four months later it had grown to about 150 cars. It was met by about 60 more and proceeded to the White House under police escort and led by the *Navy* band. There the women presented Hoover with a petition bearing 150,000 signatures.[49] Other organizations circulated petitions, too, and the w.i.l.p.f. held many meetings during the opening months of the conference. No amount of international good will could bring the negotiations out of the morass of conflicting national interests, however. Even Hoover's startling proposal to abolish offensive weapons and reduce all armaments by one-third did no more than to revive interest in the conference. It adjourned in July.

The women repeated their petition campaign during the second spring of the World Disarmament Conference, from February to June, 1933; but this time they directed it to the new administration. As before, they stressed the need for economic relief as well as for international order. They sent "Peace Messengers" on speaking tours throughout the country, searching their files for contacts, and making new ones as they went. State and local chairmen proved to be the "backbone of the campaign," but the national organizers formed new local branches and community councils on international affairs in whatever out-of-the-way places they could.[50] They frequently crossed the paths of representatives of the N.C.P.W. or the F.O.R. The National Council had more than fifty workers on its payroll by this time, and had lists of some 125,000 contacts and 2,500 newspaper editors to whom it sent frequent bulletins on disarmament. Even in 1930 it had been mailing about 1,000 packages of peace literature a month, and the tempo of the movement had increased since then.[51]

All of this effort had little effect on the new administration (although the President acknowledged receiving an "immense" number of petitions), and none on the negotiations in Geneva, which were finally broken off in the spring of 1934.[52] The race to prepare for the next war was no longer restrained, even in the popular imagination. Peace advocates found more than a temporary value in their work, however, as the secretary of the w.I.L.P.F. campaign noted: "From every point reports show the strengthening of interest in peace and the formation of permanent groups for study and work, either as a branch [sic] of the Women's International League or as independent committees."[53] The extension of pacifist organization became increasingly significant as the peace movement shifted from a united effort on behalf of disarmament to a divided approach to neutrality legislation.

Early in 1930 pacifists had formed a Pacifist Action Committee in order to build solidarity among their groups, principally by anticipating the requirements of another war. It was a purely advisory body designed to strengthen war resistance among pacifists.* One year later it was supplemented by an Emergency Peace Committee to "coordinate, develop and concentrate 'left-wing' peace opinion" on political issues.† The peace committee advocated, besides universal disarmament, repudiating the sole-guilt clause of the Treaty of Versailles, canceling war debts and reparations, recognizing the Soviet Union, and entering the World Court.[54] It was a board of strategy for pacifist organizations, and it became virtually a left-wing caucus when pacifists joined other peace advocates in an Interorganization Council on Disarmament in April, 1931. More than twenty-eight groups were represented, including the most active ones.[55]

At last leaders of various persuasions found common cause. As long as they kept to disarmament they were able to act with near unanimity —framing resolutions of support; sending delegations to the White House, State Department, and congressional hearings; sponsoring demonstrations; and supporting observers in Geneva. In the fall, though,

* The Pacifist Action Committee grew out of a conference of pacifists called by the Peace Section of the A.F.S.C. in Dec., 1929. It began meeting, probably, in Mar., 1930. Devere Allen was chairman, and its members included representatives of the A.F.S.C., F.O.R., Brethren, W.I.L.P.F., and W.R.L. Minutes of the Pacifist Action Committee, Mar. 21, 1930, to May 20, 1932, A.F.S.C. Archives, Peace Section files, Haverford College.

† The Emergency Peace Committee was formed Apr. 13, 1931, after a preliminary meeting on Mar. 30. It represented the A.F.S.C., F.O.R., W.I.L.P.F., Methodist Peace Commission, Socialist Party, League for Industrial Democracy, and *World Tomorrow* (other groups joined later). John Nevin Sayre was secretary; Clarence Pickett, chairman; and Norman Thomas and Dorothy Detzer were vice-chairmen. Minutes of Apr. 13, 1931, in John Nevin Sayre papers, and correspondence in the A.F.S.C. Archives, Peace Section files.

162

their attention was preempted by Japanese aggression in Manchuria. Some dissonance appeared in their deliberations, particularly over the question of withdrawing the ambassador from Japan and the relationship of American and League of Nations diplomacy. Even then, however, a majority of the Interorganization Council agreed on a number of propositions, including an embargo on arms to Japan and China, support for the Stimson doctrine of non-recognition of territorial changes made by force of arms, and close cooperation with the League of Nations.

The council divided more sharply over what programs it might urge upon the political parties the following spring. The pacifist left-wing wanted to go beyond generalized endorsement of the Kellogg-Briand Pact, World Court, League of Nations, disarmament, and conferences on economic problems. It favored also "drastic reduction" of the American defense budget, tariffs, and inter-Allied war debts; protection of persons and property abroad "by pacific means only"; and "immediate recognition" of the Soviet Union. Neither side would accept the program of the other, and so the council recommended no platform at all, despite the fact that it had agreed to sponsor a peace conference in Chicago during the political convention period.[56] By autumn it had returned to its original design as an organization for education and conferring. Six months later it dissolved, thus ending another major attempt to coordinate the whole peace movement.

The Interorganization Council on Disarmament foundered because the campaign for disarmament itself had failed. More precisely, it became irrelevant because disarmament had changing terms of reference. It seemed less and less to be a useful device for limiting international conflict. "Disarmament by example" would have been possible only where nations felt free to emulate; but by the time Japan invaded Manchuria and Hitler rearmed Germany, most European statesmen had concluded that modest defense needs were unique to the Western Hemisphere. Disarmament by parity and ratio had always been an expression of concurring and relative national interests (as leading pacifists had known); and that fact should have been clear when France demanded an Anglo-American alliance as the price of disarmament after World War I. It was implicit in President Roosevelt's offer not to obstruct a collective security system operating under the League of Nations in return for a disarmament program substantially as proposed by Hoover. Accordingly, Roosevelt supported domestic legislation, also originally suggested under Hoover, which would have given the President authority to embargo arms to selected nations.

163

In this sense the disarmament conference occasioned the reintroduction of the alternative of collective security into the consideration of American foreign policy, and from that time forward the peace movement gradually divided. Pacifist agitation for disarmament continued, but increasingly it was subordinated to support for neutrality. Disarmament, like defense, always had been an instrument of national policy; and in the mid-thirties peace advocates realigned over basic, prior policy questions.

The disarmament campaign itself had obscured these policy issues, in part by identifying war with vested interests within the nation—the munitions makers. In 1921 a League of Nations Commission investigated the European armaments industry and charged it with influencing public opinion with false reports, deliberately fostering an armaments race, bribing government officials, and instigating war scares. Only the commission's conclusions were published, and not the evidence upon which they were based.[57] Little was written to document its charges until the thirties when a spate of information spilled from British and American presses. In England the Union of Democratic Control, founded just before World War I by journalist Norman Angell and Labour party leader Ramsay MacDonald, published *The Secret International* in 1932 and *Patriotism Ltd* the following year. These extensive pamphlets and other books stressed the international cartels in armaments with emphasis on European firms.[58]

 We certainly are in one hell of a business where a fellow has to wish for trouble so as to make a living, the only consolation being, however, if we don't get the business, someone else will. It would be a terrible state of affairs if my conscience started to bother me now.

—FRANK SHERIDAN JONAS, munitions agent for Remington Arms and Federal Laboratories, Inc.[59]

In the United States a joint congressional-cabinet War Policies Commission was created in 1931 to hear and discuss plans to equalize the burdens of war and prevent war profiteering, although pacifists suspected that it was more interested in planning for national mobilization. It reported to the Senate in March, 1932, recommending that, among other things, in time of war individuals and corporations should be taxed at the rate of 95 per cent of all income over the previous three-year average, after allowing necessary capital expenses for expansion for war purposes. If the nation conscripts lives, the commission asked, why shouldn't it confiscate property also? The question went unanswered, for the commission's recommendations were buried in committee, but an account of its hearings was published in *Death and Profits* by Seymour Waldman, formerly on the New York *World* staff, and then an editor for the National Council for Prevention of War.[60]

Then, in December, 1933, the national board of the Women's International League decided to concentrate on regulation of the munitions industry the following year. When Congress convened, Dorothy Detzer enlisted the help of George Norris. He went down the whole list of senators to find just the right one to handle the issue, and he finally suggested Gerald P. Nye of North Dakota. Miss Detzer, with Frederick Libby and Jeanette Rankin, Estelle Sternberger and Nevin Sayre, gave the Nye committee close support, developing material for it, helping to line up support in Congress, and publicizing its disclosures.* Dorothy Detzer recommended her trusted friend, Stephen Raushenbush, as the chief investigator. The young instructor in economics at Dartmouth College was subsequently attacked as a Socialist and New Dealer, but he was warmly defended by committee members who pointed out that his politics did not affect his intelligent and diligent service, and that anyway he was a registered Republican (although apparently not like some other Republicans, Gerald Nye remarked).[61]

The Nye committee capitalized on its staff's work and on public interest. It initiated legislation on the taxing of war profits, regulation of war industries, and neutrality provisions for commerce and private travel abroad during time of war. It charged that private armament interests circumvented national policies as defined in arms embargoes and treaties, sold weapons to both sides in time of war, bribed government officials, lobbied for military appropriations and against embargoes, stimulated arms races between friendly nations, and thrived on excess profits and favoritism from the government. The committee con-

---

* Miss Rankin was the first woman elected to Congress (from Montana) and voted against declaration of war in both world wars; Miss Sternberger headed the peace publicity organization, World Peaceways.

Members of the Nye committee all were to be found later in the isolationist bloc. They included: Walter F. George of Georgia, Bennett Champ Clark of Missouri, Homer T. Bone of Washington, James P. Pope of Idaho, Warren Barbour of New Jersey, and Arthur H. Vandenberg of Michigan (a co-sponsor of the resolution authorizing the investigation).

cluded, too, that American arms companies had arrangements with British firms to exchange patents and to divide profits and sales territories. It held that the international armaments industry influenced defense and foreign policies of the government, but that the United States was powerless to prevent or regulate shipments of weapons to warring nations in violation of embargoes. It seemed to provide a sordid context for the case of William B. Shearer, who had revealed in 1930–31 that shipbuilders had subsidized him to wreck the Geneva Disarmament Conference of 1927.

In exposing numerous abuses the committee revealed a paradox which William T. Stone, Washington representative of the Foreign Policy Association, ascribed to "the dual character of the munitions industry." He explained:

> Munitions firms are private corporations responsible to shareholders, whose chief concern is the prompt payment of dividends. Dividends can be paid only out of profits, and profits depend on the sale of war materials in the world market regardless of political or social consequences. At the same time munitions firms receive government aid in time of peace in recognition of the part they are expected to play in the mobilization of industry for war. Yet governments, when they encourage the development of the domestic munitions industry, are not only involved in the abuses of the industry but are forced to effect compromises with their own policies.[62]

Peace seemed to be threatened by the association of profit-making and semipublic functions in the same industry. In this limited respect, at least, many people were convinced that capitalism was a cause of war.

Pacifists encouraged that conclusion. The National Council joined other groups in publicizing the investigation, even producing a play based on testimony before the committee, *Repeat Hearing.* Journalist George Seldes wrote *Iron, Blood, and Profits,* a detailed exposé of the "world-wide munitions racket," which was frankly publicized as "the most sensational story since the War." He had help from the National Council, Women's International League, and Foreign Policy Association as he traced the activities of armament manufacturers during and since the First World War and concluded, "No reason for war remains except sudden profits for the fifty men who run the munitions racket."[63] The same year, 1934, H. C. Englebrecht and F. C. Hanighen published *Merchants of Death,* which was chosen as a Book-of-the-Month Club selection and enjoyed a large sale. Their book was a documented story of the arms industry. The authors rejected the picture of a ruthless conspiracy to promote war, but they documented every charge made by the League Commission in 1921. They blamed managers of war industries

166

for blindness to the social consequences of their work rather than for ruthlessness. *Merchants of Death* impressed Senator Nye, who used its material in his speeches.[64]

The disclosures of the Nye committee aroused great public interest. At its outset, President Roosevelt had written that "the private and uncontrolled manufacture of arms and munitions and the traffic therein has become a serious source of international discord and strife."[65] Secretary Hull cooperated in the investigation, although he tried to guard the integrity of confidential sources of information, and the administration appealed for ratification of the Geneva Convention on International Trade in Arms and Ammunition and in Implements of War. When the Senate did ratify the convention in May, 1934, it implicitly accepted the premise that abuses of the private munitions industry threatened the public peace. Other plans, such as a government monopoly of munitions, total disarmament, and wartime taxation, made the same assumption.

Various polls taken in 1934–35 suggested that many private citizens mistrusted the role of munitions makers. In the Congregational-Christian Peace Plebiscite 90 per cent of the church members replying favored government controls of some kind.[66] This vote probably reflects the wide publicity given to the Nye committee. It suggests also that large numbers of people accepted a devil theory of war, at least to the extent that they attributed it to the machinations of private vested interests.

In the radical rhetoric this interest was frequently said to be the essential cause of modern war. Even Frederick Libby attributed Navy League policy to "powerful personalities and corporations," although he recognized broader causes of war.[67] Not all pacifists were as sophisticated as he was. " 'NATIONAL HONOR,' another way of saying PROPERTY, must be respected," mocked a flyer of the Women's Peace Society; "Every American Boy Who Enlists or Is Drafted to carry this country's banner into the Far East would march to the clink of coins—with the insignia of 'big business'—the dollar sign upon his sleeve."[68] Socialist Gus Tyler added that the worker would not commit suicide for "his boss and his bosses' nation." If "the capitalists fling the workers into war," he wrote, "the laborer with backbone, common sense and class feeling will answer with the determined opposition of his organized power."[69] Pacifists of this conviction were about as unprepared to face the complex policy questions of the thirties as right-wing extremists who portrayed the whole peace movement as a subversive Red network.

The Political Economy of Conflict

Among the many forces which create those suspicions which perpetuate and increase armaments are the economic and commercial rivalries of today. . . . This competition cannot be stopped. It will be intensified. It will grow more bitter. The question is, will it remain in the commercial sphere, or will it become political?

—JAMES G. McDONALD[1]

One did not have to postulate a clique of bankers and munitions makers responsible for war in order to stress its economic origins, as Charles Beard demonstrated in his *The Devil Theory of War*.[2] Even the most public-spirited banker would have seen that American prosperity depended on Allied success in the First World War, he wrote. National economic interest, rather than private vested interests, led the country into war. Variations of this theme were found in the writings of other revisionist historians. As Beard's good friend, James T. Shotwell, wrote: "The tendency to find in economics the chief, if not the sole, cause of war has grown in the United States in recent years and has almost become an axiom in the thinking of the younger generation."[3]

One did not have to be a pacifist in order to oppose imperialism and trade barriers, or to advocate currency stabilization and a redistribution of markets and resources by agreement. Even the most conservative peace societies saw that peace for America depended on international economic stability. The Carnegie Endowment for International Peace, for example, authorized as much money for a specific survey of Austrian resources as the Committee on Militarism in Education ever had in its annual budget. A study guide on the causes of war copyrighted by the Church Peace Union devoted half of its twelve chapters to economics. "Can you think of any political situation that is not involved in some economic cause or consequence?" it asked. Apparently, no one could.[4] The National League of Women Voters published its own extensive analysis of the *Economic Causes of War*.[5] There *was* a common identification of the importance of economic competition underlying national conflict, as Shotwell observed. There was also a latent difference of opinion among peace advocates about the possibility of disarming economic rivalry.

James Shotwell had been a member of Woodrow Wilson's Inquiry, the secretive group picked to research possible World War I settlements. At Versailles he had helped to frame the labor sections of the peace treaty, including the International Labor Organization (I.L.O.). He learned from the British the value of establishing a political instrument instead of a specific but limited agreement: the I.L.O. was designed to provide for continuous negotiations between labor, employers, and governments outside of traditional diplomatic channels. Shotwell later promoted this idea in the League of Nations with regard to disarmament and economic changes, but he found that his political conception of the league was countered by a juridical notion written into its charter. In 1919 he became general editor and enterpreneur of the Carnegie Endowment's massive international series on the *Economic and Social History of the World War*, and shortly afterward was appointed director of its Division of Economics and History. Shotwell operated comfortably and informally in the circles of departments of state as well as of scholars. He associated with Norman Davis, Stanley Hornbeck, and Cordell Hull; with James McDonald of the Foreign Policy Association; Raymond T. Rich of the World Peace Foundation; and with Newton D. Baker, Clark Eichelberger, and others in the League of Nations Association.

The *History* which Shotwell organized dealt mainly with the cost and effects of the conflict. It showed him that war under modern conditions produced aftershocks so massive and so unpredictable that it was no longer a logical extension of politics. As the research progressed, the economic aspects of war increasingly appeared to be complex and related to every other aspect of national security. Shotwell became convinced of the imperative need for instruments to encourage the peaceful interdependence predicated by modern economics as an alternative to old national rivalries. He advocated carefully prepared international conferences on economic questions under the League's auspices. When such a meeting proved fruitless in 1927, he said it was because its delegates came without authority to bind their governments. He, no less than Cordell Hull, hoped that enlighted self-interest could reinforce the international order, although he was less committed than Hull was

169

to the specific solution of tariff revision. Together they hoped that the London Economic Conference of 1933 might be an opportunity to deal officially with economic problems which were aggravating the world-wide depression. President Roosevelt interpreted American recovery as an alternative to international economic stabilization, however, and so the conference was futile. Shotwell mused years later that "if F.D.R. had seen the demonstrations which I watched in Berlin, he might have paused before disrupting the forces of liberalism in Europe."[6]

Liberal pacifists by this time sensed the crisis of liberalism in the failure of internationalist capitalism. Their organizations had lobbied throughout the twenties against what they called American imperialism in Latin America and the Philippines. They had urged downward tariff revision, cancellation of war debts and reparation, stabilization of international currency, and equal access to underdeveloped areas. In the thirties they urged that world markets and resources be opened to the highly industrialized totalitarian states through lowering of trade barriers and reorganization of the mandate system. Pacifists did not guarantee that this would prevent war, but they warned that failure to relieve economic pressure in these countries would certainly result in a second world holocaust. They added, *"The utmost emphasis should be placed upon the fact that Germany, Italy and Japan cannot themselves by peaceable means bring about the required change. Only the favored nations have power through pacific processes to provide release from economic strangulation."*[7]

The notion of a world conference for economic change thus appealed to all wings of the peace movement. It was pivotal in their unification under the aegis of the National Peace Conference after the failure of disarmament in 1934. It was the basis upon which societies aligned with the Carnegie Endowment were brought into the greatest single pacifist effort between the wars, the Emergency Peace Campaign of 1936–37:

> A new policy of neutrality by itself is not enough. The basic cause of war is economic. Before enduring peace can be achieved, drastic adjustments in economic relationships among nations must be brought about. Industrialism has made various countries highly dependent upon one another.
>
> While industrialism is unifying, nationalism is divisive . . . . If the handicapped powers are shut out from favorable access to the resources of favored countries, they are subjected to extreme economic privation. And the greater their distress the more belligerent they become.[8]

170

During the campaign pacifists interpreted the world economic conference as an instance of neutral initiative in foreign affairs. Shotwell and his friends tied it to the League machinery and collective security. The almost universal appeal of liberalizing the international economy, like that of disarmament, could not overcome the divisiveness of the neutrality controversy.

As that debate clarified into opposing sides it became clear that not only the world position of the United States but also the efficacy of the liberal institutions planned in the Wilson years was at issue. Isolationists had never recognized any alteration of the traditional struggle for power in Europe and had concluded shortly after the war that liberal institutions could be maintained only inside a fortress America. They never gave Wilsonian liberalism a chance. Pacifists had worked for the League of Nations and the World Court, but they became suspicious that this international machinery was but a new instrument for traditional diplomacy. They valued internationalism, but the political economy of Europe looked more nationalist each year.

In 1932, before the neutrality controversy was really underway, the Foreign Policy Association invited Sir Norman Angell and Bruce Bliven to address its annual dinner on the subject, "What Causes War?" Bliven —pacifist, socialist, and president of the *New Republic*—argued that war sprang from the rivalries of capitalist nations. Angell pursued the theme with which he had stirred a generation before the First World War: the cause of war was the illusion that sovereign nations can live together without any rules but their own. He denied that capitalism itself promotes war, arguing on the one hand that victory cannot ensure profits in the light of modern economics, and on the other that capitalism is a rational organization of resources whereas nationalistic war is the product of unreasoning passion. Bliven replied that "capitalism lies behind the nationalism, that the interests of the capitalist are what produce the insistent, insidious, persuasive, automatic, almost unconscious propaganda, all the time, that our country is better than others and that we have to enforce our superiority in some way on them with military strength."[9] A number of pacifists had predicted for years that international capitalism was a contradiction in terms, and that the only escape from war would be "the reorganization of our whole social system on the basis of production for use and not for profit, with the needs of the world and not of particular nations in view."[10]

Norman Thomas had anticipated the revelations of the Nye committee on the munitions industry when he wrote that "the particular form of modern trade which tends directly to promote war is the trade in

171

armaments by private interests."[11] He had supported every attempt to lower trade barriers, but he doubted that it could be done. He had decried Allied imperialism when it was dramatized during the war by Russia's publication of secret treaties with Britain and France. Nothing would be more tragic, he had written, than to conclude the war with a "financier's peace."[12] It seemed to him by 1924 that his worst fears had come true. The very forces of nationalistic economic rivalry which had caused the war were embodied in the postwar policies of the Allies, he wrote. How could one expect anything else?

Thomas, together with Kirby Page, argued that the social structure of unrestrained economic competition makes social-mindedness and internationalism virtually impossible, and that the very persons who have most at stake in existing trade barriers are those who have the largest measure of influence on foreign policy. Moreover, the sovereignty exercised by capitalistic states arises partly from the need to establish order and to maintain the economic system. To this extent there is a vested economic interest in preserving sovereignty itself against the encroachments which any international system (political or economic) must make in order to be effective. Page did not discuss the nature of nationalism in noncapitalistic Russia; he might have found, as Reinhold Niebuhr did, that power structures are not confined to capitalistic states. In any case, Page's observation of the vested interest in nationalism held by an economic class did lead him to doubt the efficacy of efforts to liberalize economic policies.[13] Thomas added that even if international capitalism could triumph over western nationalism, it would open new sources of conflict with the exploited areas of Asia and Africa. Socialists equated exploitation with capitalism, of course, and contrasted them both to the ideals of peace and justice.

A Socialist analysis of war contributed to the pacifist's analysis of international affairs at a time when he was rethinking the policy of neutrality. Perhaps equally important, dilemmas he shared with Socialists influenced his choice of a model of social conflict and its resolution. Throughout the twenties pacifists were increasingly involved in social reforms and were associated with the labor movement and the Socialist Party. This new public severely strained the constituent basis of the Fellowship of Reconciliation in 1929–31. Moreover, its leaders found that their pacifism was challenged as they encountered the issues of class conflict and revolutionary change. The theory of nonviolence which emerged from left-wing polemics in the mid-thirties was based on a model of domestic, class conflict; but, combined with a distinctive

172

analysis of the international scene, it produced a pacifist rationale for neutralism which sustained liberal pacifists where even Socialists opted for war.

> The writer . . . must begin, therefore, by stating two positions which represent the two poles of his thought. One is that the use of physical violence in international life has impressed itself upon his mind as an unmitigated and unjustified evil. The other is that some form of social compulsion seems necessary and justified on occasion in all but the most ideal human societies.
>
> Between these two positions a line must be drawn somewhere . . . .
>
> —REINHOLD NIEBUHR[14]

It is impossible to gauge the percentage of Socialists in pacifist organizations. Kirby Page's judgment that "a considerable majority" of the Fellowship's members supported the Socialist Party probably was based on a poll of the F.O.R. in 1932 which revealed that of 1,709 members replying, 75.1 per cent preferred Norman Thomas for president, 20.4 per cent favored Hoover, 2.9 per cent chose Roosevelt, and 1.6 per cent went with the Communist candidate, William Z. Foster. Page estimated that radicalism gained strength among pacifists in the following two years.[15] Whatever may have been the proportion of Socialists in the Fellowship, it probably was greater in the War Resisters League, a small, nonreligious pacifist society. The rest of the peace movement accepted Socialist support, but did not court it. Numerous pacifist leaders were active Socialists, though, and this affiliation was important both because of the effect of socialism on their thought and for their influence in the Socialist Party. They might have agreed with the party's line on war, but most of them came to its support because of their experience in social reform.

Leading pacifists who gathered around Norman Thomas included Kirby Page, who resigned as secretary of the executive committee of the League for Independent Political Action in order to devote more time to the Socialist Party and the F.O.R.; Devere Allen, Socialist candidate for senator from Connecticut in 1936 and Labor party candidate for governor in 1938; Jessie Wallace Hughan, Socialist candidate for secretary of state in New York in 1918 and for lieutenant governor in 1920; Harry Laidler, director of the League for Industrial Democracy; Clarence Senior, national secretary of the Socialist Party after 1929; Powers Hapgood of Indiana, and Darlington Hoopes of Pennsylvania, both on the national executive committee of the party; and Paul Jones, Sherwood Eddy, Vida Scudder, James Mauer, John Haynes Holmes, and Reinhold Niebuhr, to mention only a few.

Socialist-minded pacifists did not confine their attack on laissez faire capitalism to its alleged propensity for war. They said that capitalism also had plunged the West into depressions, had carved the rest of the world into private dominions, and had deprived the working man of human dignity and liberty. The very individualism which had freed the middle class from feudal restraints had created class cleavages and subjected labor to new contraints. They added that the laissez faire economics which had created the huge American industrial complex had strewn unnecessary misery in its wake. They concluded that the profit system born in the handicraft era was inadequate for the age of the machine. Technology had made society as much more interdependent as it was productive, wrote the director of the Labor Temple in Brooklyn, and individualistic competition had become out of date.[16]

To their economic criticisms of capitalism these pacifists added social and moral ones: the system produced mass poverty, they said; it subjected laborers to intolerable working and living conditions; together with urbanization it depersonalized life and labor; it fostered greed, exploitation, and hypocrisy among all classes; it engendered class hatred and violence.[17] These criticisms were more often assumed than documented. They were shared by many liberal churchmen who took for granted the judgments of the preceding generation of the social-gospel movement and whose attack on capitalism was tied to their dissatisfaction with industrialism and urbanism. Often the critics did not distinguish between these things. They tended to assume uncritically that the failings of industrialization and urbanization were the fault of the capitalistic system and could be cured by a different social and economic organization.

The work of Norman Thomas and Reinhold Niebuhr is especially important, therefore, because by the turn of the decade they were dealing explicitly with the relationship of capitalism and industrialism in terms of the distribution of power.* The essence of Thomas's criticism

---

* Niebuhr supported World War I at first, became disillusioned by the excesses of religious patriotism, and turned against it in the twenties. As a pastor in Detroit his criticisms of capitalism and organized religion made him popular among

174

of capitalism was that it had subverted democracy by denying real, that is economic, power to the mass of workers. For all intents and purposes the owners ruled the system. This meant that the power in a capitalistic state was largely in the hands of those who were not affected by the failings of industrialism and urbanism. They were not likely to give up that power voluntarily, if history were any guide. Those who sought remedies through government to industrial and urban problems lacked the authority to act. Thus, according to Thomas, the concentration of power in a capitalistic class minimized social change and denied political liberty to workers.[18]

The importance that Thomas attached to his analysis of capitalism in terms of power relationships is indicated in his emphasis on "industrial democracy." He and the League for Industrial Democracy staff departed from theoretical and doctrinaire socialism. Their pragmatism was more in line with the tradition of Eugene V. Debs than that of Daniel de León. This emphasis marks Thomas's insistence that power must be democratically dispersed in a socialistic state, a point at which he differed sharply from Communists and even radical Socialists. It is also the basis on which he opposed company unions. To the degree that labor does not organize itself, he argued, it lacks real power and therefore lacks real liberty. To the extent that workers accept company paternalism they postpone the achievement of industrial democracy.

The decreasing power of unions even in the early depression years combined with the restlessness and aggressiveness apparent in workers made Thomas and his friends hopeful that the Socialist Party might lead a powerful movement of labor and the middle class to alter capitalism significantly.† This fact is very important for an understanding

---

young people and familiar to religious liberals. In 1926, Kirby Page persuaded Sherwood Eddy and Nevin Sayre to contribute with him toward Niebuhr's salary if he would come to New York, do free-lance work, and help to edit *World Tomorrow*. Page also negotiated with Harry Ward at Union Seminary to secure Niebuhr there on a part-time basis. When Niebuhr did join the faculty of Union in 1928 he signed on also with the pacifist magazine as an editor, a position he held until the periodical was discontinued in 1934. His early thinking is best traced in articles and book reviews for that magazine and *Christian Century*, in his *Does Civilization Need Religion?* (New York: Macmillan Co., 1927), *Moral Man and Immoral Society: A Study in Ethics and Politics* (New York: Charles Scribner's Sons, 1932), and *Reflections on the End of An Era* (New York: Charles Scribner's Sons, 1934).

† Eventually the appeal of the party was weakened not only by factionalism but also by the social programs of the New Deal (and the increased power of industrial unions, of course). By 1950 many specific reforms that Socialists had long urged were in effect. Labor had a measure of economic power that modified capitalists' control, and government had become something of an arbitrator be-

of the position of Thomas and those pacifists who supported him. In order to appeal to labor and the middle class on whom the party relied for voting strength, he had to present a program that was realistic in the sense of being reasonable, or workable, which is probably the reason why the 1932 party platform emphasized specific reforms rather than ultimate goals. At the same time he had to secure the organizational and financial strength of Socialists for whom any realistic program had to take into account the doctrine of class struggle.

The Socialists assumed that, ultimately, the goals of labor and capital could not be reconciled. Thomas's own analysis led to this view, since it posited a significant change in the distribution of power. To the nation he said that limited competition would be compatible with a "cooperative commonwealth," but to the party he conceded that even such moderate socialism could be achieved only by the aggregate power of the proletariat. The party itself symbolized the ideal of labor solidarity in a political contest. It had a mythic value which Thomas recognized. It supported unions and strikes partly to sharpen the workers' own sense of economic conflict. Underlying its factional disputes in the early thirties was a feeling that liberal institutions were inadequate and that class struggle was imminent, a sense of urgency which seemed to be confirmed by events in Europe.

Since the doctrine of class struggle was assumed by orthodox Socialists, the problem for pacifists among them was formulated as class struggle or class war. That is to say, what is the road to socialistic power? Bitter factional battles were fought throughout the Western world over the approach to, rather than the goals of, socialism. In this context those Socialists who were also pacifists advocated political organization; unionization; cooperatives; and nonviolent, direct action, such as strikes. These techniques were not obviously effective early in the depression, and the question of the proletariat's road to power increasingly disturbed those who took socialism seriously. Reinhold Niebuhr asked whether they should choose "peace or justice" if they could not have both. "What shall we do about civil war?" queried Kirby Page. Norman Thomas denounced revolution but also confessed that

---

tween large economic blocs. Thomas still advocated socialism, but he stopped running for President and even said that government control could be consonant with some private enterprise and competition. Kirby Page joined the Democratic party, and wrote that he no longer considered government ownership of industry necessary for its socialization. The problems and moods of the fifties were far from those of the mid-depression years when numerous liberals accepted the Socialist's idea of the economic causes of war and his critique of capitalism itself.

176

"for the workers merely to renounce violence with no substitute in sight would be to play into the hands of the oppressor."[19] The issue was of more than academic interest to pacifists. Committed to peace and justice during World War I, they had become increasingly and officially involved in the labor struggle. Whether Socialists or not, liberal pacifists eventually had to face the prospect of employing violent force in the interest of social justice.

Pacifists' initial reform efforts after the war were hesitant. They tried to spread Christian charity and social intelligence, hoping that a Christianized social order would emerge. They asked themselves, "Can the capitalistic system be stripped of its abuses by a process of democratization and made to serve a beneficent purpose in the social order consistent with the spirit of Christianity?"[20] They thought it could. Only the Socialists among them doubted the efficacy of intelligent good will; and even they, like Roger Baldwin, Norman Thomas, and Harry Laidler, the executive director of the League for Industrial Democracy, confined their initial work to discussion, education, and a few political gestures.[21]

An early Fellowship of Reconciliation pamphlet cited the example of "a woman in one group [who] is taking needy girls into her home as servants, giving them education and training."[22] The F.O.R. self-consciously used the union label on its literature and considered preparing a special statement of its principles for use among the working class. Members were troubled by the seeming paternalism of such efforts, however, and by the suspicion which labor harbored toward idealists. Some of them were bothered, also, by the fact that they were caught up in the very system they criticized. Time and again they debated about what to do with unearned income that came to their members and even to the Fellowship. Why was their testimony in the industrial struggle less clear than in the case of war, they wondered. One member wryly suggested, "Perhaps it is because we smell of dividends."[23]

The American Friends Service Committee experimented with groups to study property and investment, organized relief programs in the blighted Allegheny coal fields, and eventually developed rehabilitation programs there.* Economic issues were featured in early F.O.R. con-

---

* Beginning in 1929 mining people were taught nearly forgotten arts of furniture-making, weaving, and other handicraft skills. College-age young people were brought to mountain work camps where they built recreation centers, cleared areas for playgrounds, and studied industrial relations. The Department of Interior called upon the national secretary of the Service Committee, Clarence

ferences and literature, and radicals often spoke from its platforms. Leading pacifists were prominent in the labor movement and other social causes. Instead of bringing the "needy" to their homes, as did the woman cited in the F.O.R. pamphlet, they joined the "servants" in the field. Like her, though, a number of interested pacifists tried to give workers learning and training. They were active in labor education, and founded the first resident workers' college in the country, Brookwood Labor College, at Katonah, New York.

William and Helen Fincke founded Brookwood in 1919 as an experiment in the application of Christian principles to the use of property, community living, and education. John Nevin Sayre resigned his church to help, and six other F.O.R. members joined the faculty. Two years later the Finckes converted their large tract of wooded land in Westchester County into a labor college in an effort to provide American labor with trained, responsible leaders who would come from the ranks of the workers. The control of the institution was soon put into the hands of a board of directors composed of labor leaders. At least one Fellowship member, author and poet Sarah Cleghorn, remained on the faculty, in addition to A. J. Muste, who directed the college from 1921 to 1933. The question of the use of violence in the labor struggle split Brookwood in 1933 when a number of students and faculty members became more radical than the board of directors. Muste was succeeded by Tucker P. Smith, assistant treasurer of the F.O.R., who directed the college until it disbanded in 1937.[24]

Workers' education became a widespread movement in America in the two decades following the founding of Brookwood. Other resident colleges were formed, and enrollment increased at city commuters' schools. Pacifists took part in some of them. George Collins, a field secretary for the F.O.R., was vice-president of the Denver Labor College. Clarence Senior, on the national committee of the War Resisters League and after 1929 the national secretary of the Socialist Party, was the director of the Cleveland Labor College. Charles C. Webber, F.O.R. secretary for industrial affairs, organized a small labor college in Allentown, Pennsylvania, in 1931; and Albert McLeod, an editor of *World Tomorrow*, went to Nova Scotia in 1933 to establish a workers' school there. When Myles Horton returned from studying the folk high schools of Denmark and organized the Highlander Folk School at Monteagle, Tennessee, he secured among its officers Rein-

---

Pickett, to help plan Subsistence Homesteads under the Tennessee Valley Authority, and the committee operated a Homestead of its own (Penn-Craft, in Fayette County, Pennsylvania).

"Pencil Sellers, Class of '17," by Kerr Eby.
Courtesy Yale University Press.

Upper left: A. J. Muste. *Upper right*: John Nevin Sayre.
Lower left: Norman Thomas. *Lower right*: Devere Allen.

Peace and disarmament parades held in New York City, 1916.
Lower photograph courtesy National Archives.

Upper: C.O.'s cooking their meal in an open field, Fort Riley, Kansas, 1918 (*left to right*: Harold Gray, Howard Moore, Evan Thomas, and Erling Lunde). *Middle*: C.O. tent camp, apart from army barracks, Fort Riley, Kansas, 1919. *Lower*: Disarmament petition float of the W.I.L.P.F., 1932.

These "peace" stamps are representative of the 144 National Library of Students' Peace Posters, done by high school students throughout the United States in 1940.

Courtesy National Council for Prevention of War papers, Swarthmore College Peace Collection.

Upper left: Kirby Page. *Upper right*: Ray Newton.
Lower left: Frederick J. Libby. *Lower right*: Dorothy Detzer.

Upper: Roger Baldwin leading 3,500 students from Barnard, Union Theological Seminary, New College, and Teacher's College in the Oxford Pledge, April 12, 1935. *Lower*: Antipreparedness demonstration with "Jingo" the dinosaur, 1933.

Jane Addams (*right*) and unidentified friend in 1932, probably at the Women's International League for Peace and Freedom petition campaign for international disarmament.
Courtesy Swarthmore College Peace Collection.

hold Niebuhr, Norman Thomas, Sherwood Eddy, and Kirby Page.[25]

Christian pacifists shared with liberal churchmen the initial hope that they could make the social gospel fulfill the promise of prewar years by organizing it, and their greatest achievement in the twenties was the Fellowship for a Christian Social Order (F.C.S.O.). Its name and statement of principles suggested the continuing influence of Walter Rauschenbusch:

> We believe that according to the life and teaching of Jesus, the supreme task of mankind is the creation of a social order, the Kingdom of God on earth, wherein the maximum opportunity shall be afforded for the development and enrichment of every human personality; in which the supreme motive shall be love; wherein men shall co-operate in service for the common good and brotherhood shall be a reality in all of the daily relationships of life.[26]

This statement, and the name of the organization as well, illustrated also the fact that it was modeled after the Fellowship of Reconciliation. Kirby Page and Sherwood Eddy founded it in 1921 in order to join pacifists and reform-minded Christians who were not pacifists in a common exploration of the meaning of Christianity for industrial society.[27]

The national committee of the F.C.S.O. was not an advisory body but, rather, a group of sponsors—virtually a roster of the social-gospel movement. Page hoped that its founding would "become the most significant event in awakening the Churches to their social obligations ever held in this country."[28] The organization neither passed resolutions nor attacked specific social evils. It had no formal membership campaigns, and yet about 1,200 persons joined by June, 1923, and 2,410 were at least nominal members in 1928. Graham Taylor, editor of the foremost journal of social work, the *Survey,* probably expressed the satisfaction of many older progressives when he wrote to Page that "the lone voices crying in the wilderness to which I responded in my early manhood, have become a chorus as is conducted by the Fellowship [for a Christian Social Order], . . . and by the Fellowship of Reconciliation."[29]

Page operated freely within the organization. Besides writing pamphlets such as *Industrial Facts and Collective Bargaining,* he prepared a study course on *Christianity and Economic Problems* for the Federal Council of Churches.[30] In 1922 he wrote an analysis of the United States Steel Corporation's labor and financial policies for the *Atlantic Monthly.*[31] He moved about the country organizing local groups and conferences from which to originate demands for specific reforms.

179

Leaders of the social gospel in prewar years met in fellowship with their younger colleagues, including active members Reinhold Niebuhr and Paul Douglas. They discussed and approved workers' ownership programs. They persuaded Arthur Nash to install the Amalgamated Clothing Worker's Union in his textile business in Cincinnati, and they were "thrilled" that their success had come through educational and spiritual processes.[32] Donald Meyer rightly observed that the dominant mood of the F.C.S.O. was its "ethical glow." Like socially minded Protestants generally, it hoped to convert businessmen to apply Christian ethics to industry. "It did not discuss important tactical and systematic issues," Meyer added, "but social-ethical needs in the society."[33] The members of the F.C.S.O. had in this case upheld unionization, however, and although they seemed naïvely optimistic, they had committed themselves to an important tactical point regarding the reorganization of society.

Individual pacifists were found on the picket lines. A. J. Muste, Cedric Long, and Harold Rotzel gave striking leadership to the textile workers in Lawrence, Massachusetts, in 1919. Muste was elected chairman of the strike committee. The three F.O.R. ministers helped to keep the workers nonviolent in the protracted conflict despite the agitation of labor spies. Muste went on to become general secretary for the Amalgamated Textile Workers Union (1919–21), and Long became secretary of the Cooperative League of the United States. William Spofford of the Episcopal Church League for Industrial Democracy successfully mediated the 1925 strike of silk workers in Paterson, New Jersey, with the cooperation of local pastors. Norman Thomas, A. J. Muste, George Collins, William Spofford, William Simpson, and John Haynes Holmes provided a virtual F.O.R. staff in support of the 1926 textile strike in Passaic, New Jersey. They helped create an Emergency Committee for Strikers Relief in that strike, and rushed help to Gastonia and Marion, North Carolina, where in 1929 incipient unionization led to violence and murder. There James Myers spoke on behalf of the Federal Council of Churches in support of the workers whom Muste tried to organize, and for whom Spofford solicited relief. Pacifists worked with other liberals in support of labor, of course, but they seemed to be leaders in these cases, at least. Through their journals, the *Christian Century* and especially the *World Tomorrow*, they agitated incessantly for greater economic justice and civil rights for labor.[34]

As late as 1924 the Fellowship was unprepared to implement a

180

recommendation of its committee on pacifist strategy that it should cooperate with organized labor and Socialists in order to build a broad alliance against war. Two years afterward it reappointed George Collins as field secretary on the understanding that he would "devote the major emphasis of his work to . . . situations of conflict, particularly those of industry and race." Collins intended to steer a course between labor and management, but the sympathies of the F.O.R. leaders were very much on the side of labor.

Strikes demonstrated the needs of workers and, too frequently, the obdurateness of employers. More and more pacifists became convinced of the need for labor organization; they were committed to that demand which, more than any other, employers resisted in the twenties. Violations of civil rights and partial military law led even politically moderate pacifists to support workers in Colorado mining areas in 1928. The F.O.R. rented the municipal auditorium in Denver to publicize labor's point of view. It also let the Emergency Committee for Strikers Relief of Colorado circularize its membership roll for a financial appeal, and was gratified to learn that the Fellowship's list had brought the highest cash returns of any used. The following year it sent a representative to a discussion of the organization of 300,000 textile workers in the South.[35] The Fellowship was clearly convinced that unionization and economic justice were requisites of industrial peace. It was, moreover, addressing itself to a public much broader than its religious constituency.

> I have rounded out my ten years on the World Tomorrow because I have been devoted to it, and profoundly believe that human relations can never be put on a higher level until we learn to fight radically for social progress by non-violent methods . . . . I have always been able to subordinate the difficulties and not let them bother me, with one exception. That is the ministerial-preachy-exclusively-Jesus emphasis of my comrades. I hold to a religious view of life, but I have little bent toward official Christianity . . . . and it seems to me that this continuous Jesus emphasis is justly offensive to equally fine people of other faiths, and, moreover, leads to a perilously close reliance on Jesus in an authoritarian sense.
>
> —DEVERE ALLEN[36]

181

Devere Allen had been frustrated repeatedly by what he called the "Christocentric impulse" of the *World Tomorrow*. When he joined the staff in 1921 its subtitle read, "A Journal Looking Towards a Christian World." That irritated him, but he got a change two years later to "A Journal Looking Toward a Social Order Based on the Principles of Jesus." When Kirby Page was brought to the magazine in 1926 the subtitle was changed again to read, "A Journal Looking Toward a Social Order Based on the Religion of Jesus." Allen continued to urge Page, Sayre, and Niebuhr to drop the exclusively Christian emphasis. His efforts were rewarded, finally, when the magazine went on a weekly basis, beginning September 14, 1932, and dropped the subtitle altogether. Subtitles were only the symptoms of the issue which continued to divide pacifists long after the *World Tomorrow* had been discontinued.

Even in the Fellowship of Reconciliation, with its high proportion of Christians, there was considerable debate over the religious basis of pacifism.* The organization encountered several problems in formulating a statement of its principles—how specific a pacifist pledge to include and how to explain it, what to say about social problems besides war. But the issue of religious emphasis proved to be most troublesome throughout the twenties. In 1922, after polling the members, the council revised the original statement slightly. It repeated the accepted religious doctrines of the Fellowship: love as revealed in "the life, teachings and death of Jesus," the kingdom of God as love extended to the social order, and the religious duty of men and women to practice love in their lives. The council then inserted a paragraph condemning war and the existing social order because they violated these principles and "hinder the development of character into the likeness of Christ." It called for changes in the spirit of men and in the structure of the social order in loyalty to Jesus and humanity.[37] At the outset, the Fellowship was clearly religiously oriented.

Even then there was dissatisfaction. A. J. Muste reported for a committee of members that, although there was no question of the Christian basis of the Fellowship, some way had to be found to make its message appeal to more people, specifically organized labor and non-Christian reformers. These groups failed to understand the theologically couched Fellowship statement, he said, or if they understood it they feared that

---

* In 1929 about 88 per cent of F.O.R. members belonged to some church, and 75 per cent of them attended church regularly. They were mainly Methodists, Friends, Congregationalists, Presbyterians, and Episcopalians. Don M. Chase, "What Sort of People Are Pacifists?" *World Tomorrow*, XII (Feb., 1929), 84.

it implied agreement with "certain dogmatic formulations of Christianity," and perhaps also a close association with the churches.[38]

About the same time the F.O.R. was developing a substantial following among young people, which it organized into the Fellowship of Youth for Peace. The youth became increasingly restive. Their own statement of purpose was explicitly a humanitarian desire to abolish war. It did not enumerate religious principles, insisting, "It will be our aim to let no interest of self, family, creed, class, nation or race separate us from our fellow men." In May, 1925, the Fellowship of Youth for Peace separated from the F.O.R., mainly on the basis of the religious issue, although also, no doubt, because the young people wanted to organize their own movement. In their attempt to be inclusive they even abandoned the explicit pacifism of their parent organization. They said, simply, that trust and good will were "infinitely superior" to suspicion and violence.[39] They could not maintain a separate organization, however, and a year later were reunited with the Fellowship of Reconciliation, admitting that "getting away from a religious basis and an absolutist position on war had been a mistake."[40] Absorption of the youth fellowship seemed to be a victory for an exclusively Christian emphasis; actually it brought the debate back within the changing Fellowship.

In 1928 the F.O.R. adopted an associate membership for those who would not take an absolute war-resistance pledge but did share the general philosophy of pacifism, and on that basis it absorbed the Fellowship for a Christian Social Order. Not everyone was pleased with the result. F. Ernest Johnson, the executive secretary of the Federal Council of Churches, and one who originally had suggested the merger, was irked because absolute pacifism was retained in the statement of principles. He resented the provision for associate membership which, he said, virtually invited the nonpacifist "to join the Fellowship church on probation until he shall have no difficulty with its creed."[41] In any case, the merger emphasized the broadening interests and constituency of the Fellowship of Reconciliation, and it accentuated the difficulty of maintaining an exclusively religious basis.

On March 23, 1929, the governing body of the Fellowship, the national council, gathered in New York City. Changes were in the wind. The question of religious tenets had been revived. Mr. and Mrs. Charles Thomson had begun to promote the F.O.R. and its ideals in Latin America. There was general agreement on the need for administrative reorganization. Proposals had been made for developing numerous local Fellowship groups, and for expanding the industrial and race-relations work begun in the South. But few members of the council anticipated how decisive its meeting would be.

Shortly after opening the meeting, Paul Jones, executive secretary for ten years, read his letter of resignation and immediately left the room "to catch a train." As council members recovered from their consternation the other secretaries present, Nevin Sayre, Amy Blanche Greene, and Howard Kester (secretary for the South), offered their resignations in order to permit a thorough study and reorganization of the Fellowship. In the months that followed pacifists redefined their goals and methods.[42]

Conditions in 1929 were different from those prevailing when the F.O.R. was formed in 1914–18, Jones had told the council. The Fellowship would have to apply its principles to current problems if it were not to become "simply the antithesis of the American Legion." Members of the council concurred in wanting to apply pacifism to industrial and racial conflicts, and to support the Latin American work. They agreed that the staff needed to be reorganized. They voted to retain Nevin Sayre and Amy Blanche Greene as secretaries, to employ part-time secretaries for southern race-relations work, and to hire a full-time secretary for industrial relations and youth work.[43]

Policy questions were more troubling than administrative ones. They were broached by the executive committee when on May 25 it recommended to the council:

> That the application of the fellowship principle of non-violence to the method of war as expressed in the fourth clause of the Statement of Purpose is arbitrary and negative.

> That the limitation implied by the use of the word Jesus in the Statement of Purpose tends to make the Fellowship exclusive and sectarian.[44]

On Sunday, September 14, the annual conference of the F.O.R. at Haverford, Pennsylvania, adopted a resolution which had originated in the executive committee "that the Council of the Fellowship is requested to add to its numbers during the year from among Catholics, Jews, and others not now represented and also consider the problem of broadening the basis on which the Fellowship rests."[45] The religious issue had assumed major proportions.

Critics of the traditional statement of principles agreed with F. Ernest Johnson that its religious provisions represented "pacifist fundamentalism." They denied that the Christianity of the Fellowship was its unique characteristic. What was distinctive about the F.O.R.,

184

they said, was its program of applying the spirit of love to situations of conflict and its development of ethical social techniques. The Fellowship was essentially religious, but its members might find sanctions for pacifism in other religious leaders or even in other ways than "by reference to any historic figure." J. B. Matthews, formerly a professor of Biblical literature at Howard University and subsequently employed as an executive secretary of the F.O.R., caustically called the preoccupation with Jesus an "archeological interest." More generous critics noted that Christianity as an organized religion was itself a barrier to the reconciliation of many human beings. Charles Thomson reported that the religious aspect of the statement often impeded his work with Latin American Catholics. Devere Allen argued that a majority of the national council favored a change, and predicted a major crisis and perhaps a split in the organization if the question were not resolved. He added, ruefully, "I sometimes wonder if we aren't repeating the old creedal schisms on another plane."[46]

John Nevin Sayre, more than any other man, modified the inevitable change of emphasis. His dedication to the International Fellowship of Reconciliation had won for him a respectful hearing. He was not inclined to be doctrinaire himself, and he recognized a potential source of pacifist strength in non-Christian idealists. He pointed out that the Fellowship had originated from a specific desire to apply the principles of Jesus to the problem of war, although its members had soon reached the conclusion that war was bound up with all social questions. The understanding of the Fellowship was definite, he said, because it was derived specifically from the prophetic life of Jesus. This was the common denominator which its members interpreted and applied for themselves. To eliminate that reference altogether would be to dissolve the bonds of the Fellowship. Sayre acknowledged the desirability of bringing non-Christians and even nonpacifists into a working partnership with the Fellowship. But this association with others should not take the place of the distinctive message of the F.O.R. which was, he felt, that ethical social techniques proceed from religious insight. The Fellowship must be essentially but not exclusively Christian, Sayre concluded.[47]

This difference of opinion involved the question of whether pacifism as an ethical code of action was necessarily religious, and the larger problem of whether to revitalize the social gospel through a more pious or a more pragmatic ethic.

Critics of the religious statement avoided this way of putting the question by arguing that the F.O.R. should not bar those who held other

185

religious allegiances or even derived their ways of life from impulses which were not commonly called spiritual. In other words, religion was defined so broadly that it encompassed almost any sanction for pacifism. In fact, their very criticism of exclusiveness betrayed their assumption that ethical behavior need not be sanctioned by any authority outside of experience. They wanted to make room for pacifists who were motivated by pragmatic considerations as well as, or instead of, spiritual impulses. In this respect they reflected the weakening of authoritarianism in American Protestantism.

Those on both sides of the question were anxious to compromise. When the national council failed to resolve the problem it sought the advice of the membership. Another poll was taken. By September 5, 1930, almost 1,500 members, about one-fourth of the total membership, had voted. A statement omitting any religious reference was clearly unacceptable to most. There was a slight preference to add a reference to other spiritual leaders, but the difference between that and keeping the statement as it was seemed "hardly decisive." A subcommittee drafted a compromise statement which was adopted without major change at the annual conference in December.[48]

This statement was far less theologically worded than the previous one. God was mentioned only in the last sentence, and then as the source of strength and light. Christianity was referred to only in the context of the founding of the Fellowship. Jesus was mentioned as exemplifying the spirit of love in action. Members had been inspired by other religious leaders as well, the statement said, and in "other ways." The first paragraph of the 1930 statement of principle combined doctrines which previously had been enumerated separately and it phrased them much less theologically than before. The whole statement was calculated not to offend anyone; yet it was a strong, positive statement of religious faith.

It did not satisfy everyone. Nevin Sayre and Kirby Page feared that the change in wording might presage a weakened religious impulse, whereas Roger Baldwin and others wanted all religious references removed. The religious question was discussed again in 1933, but differences of opinion were lost in a new alignment of Fellowship members over the problem of applying pacifism in the class struggle.

The religious and economic issues were intimately related, however. The change of religious emphasis between 1920 and 1930 reflected a maturation of pacifist theology and the development of a pragmatic philosophy of social ethics. Outstanding pacifists reinterpreted the social gospel from a historical point of view and stressed the practical

186

evaluation of each situation of conflict in the light of Christian ideals. This new interpretation made it possible for them to hold a prudential, or pragmatic, social ethic within the framework of their religious doctrine. Although they challenged other Christians to "follow unswervingly the way of life exemplified by Jesus," they emphasized social action in concert with non-Christians. Liberalizing the statement was requisite for fuller involvement in the social-justice movement. It was an important step for pacifists who wanted to broaden their social concerns and accommodate left-wing publics.

It was a step taken while American complacency was eclipsed by the depression. Numerous people lost their savings, farm income sank to a new low, unemployment figures soared, and hardship became widespread. Under the new pressure of insecurity labor was roused from somnolence, and after 1933 it was increasingly organized. Industrial conflict was intensified. Socialists sensed a revival of class consciousness among workers. The social conflict seemed more imminent than international war to most pacifists.

John Nevin Sayre, executive secretary of the F.O.R., weighed many of these things in his mind in the summer of 1931 as he read a telegram from Arnold Johnson, a Union Seminary student who had gone to Harlan, Kentucky, representing the American Civil Liberties Union and the Fellowship of Reconciliation. Johnson had cabled in part,

> ANOTHER CAR DYNAMITED SUNDAY NIGHT STOP OPERATORS IMPORTED TWENTY EIGHT MORE THUGS SATURDAY STOP FRIENDS AMBUSHED LEAVING HUFFS HOME THIS MORNING ONE SHOT NOT SERIOUSLY STOP AUTHORITIES REPORT THUGS WILL GET ME AND DYNAMITE HOME STOP AM CHANGING RESIDENCE BUT STAYING HARLAN STOP SITUATION DANGEROUS.[49]

Sayre and the Civil Liberties Union both telegraphed Governor Flem D. Sampson of Kentucky, requesting protection for Johnson and those supporting the coal strike in Harlan. They also gave the story to the Scripps-Howard Newspapers. Sampson promised that Johnson would be protected, but he evaded the larger issue of curtailing the terrorism used against strikers.

The miners were starving, but determined to win, Johnson reported. They had not been supported by the United Mine Workers Union and could turn only to the International Workers of the World. Twenty of their leaders were being held without evidence on triple murder charges. "They are political prisoners," Johnson wrote.[50]

One month after his telegram to Sayre, Johnson was given a measure of protection; he was jailed. Kirby Page had been in Harlan about the

187

first of August and had written a story about it for the *Fellowship News Letter*. His account was published in the *New Republic*, the *Christian Century*, the *World Tomorrow*, and the *Nation*, and he was interviewed by Scripps-Howard reporters. Indignant national opinion bore upon Harlan where Arnold Johnson, a young and impressionable pacifist, was writing from the county jail:

> The cockroaches are plentiful. It's beans and cabbage and cabbage and beans. We freeze or sweat. One cold follows another. But this is jail. So what can one expect?
>
> I often observe that these men approach their trials with an optimism and a degree of uncertainty which characterizes liberals. But the reality of lifes [*sic*] problems is here. The realism and idealism of common men is astounding. My faith in the working class increases. As a class, these men look not to liberalism.[51]

Being on the union firing line infected Johnson with radical social passion.

Acting with labor in specific cases influenced the members of the executive committee of the Fellowship, too, to take a more positive role in labor disputes. They wanted to see economic justice, and they were equally concerned to mitigate industrial conflict. With these two considerations in mind they had sent Johnson as their representative to Harlan. The same interests led them to employ Charles Webber as field secretary for industrial affairs and Howard Kester as field secretary for the South. Webber, former assistant director of field work at Union Theological Seminary in 1924 and Methodist preacher of the Church of all Nations in New York City, attempted in 1931–32 to implement Fellowship ideals in the strike-torn town of Nazareth, Pennsylvania. He intervened in the strike, and he also tried to interest the community in industrial conciliation.[52] Kester, the southern secretary, did valiant relief and organizing work in the vicious strike of coal miners in Wilder, Tennessee, in the summer of 1932.

He reflected the feeling of a number of F.O.R. members when he declared that "the terrific power of the antisocial forces in the South has steadily driven the Fellowship into the position of a revolutionary movement."[53] Thus, by the thirties the Fellowship of Reconciliation had passed from individual to official applications of its principles; in addition to matters of ethical behavior it was concerned with the strategies of achieving social justice and resolving conflict.

The depression deepened during the years that Arnold Johnson, Charles Webber, and Howard Kester were experimenting with techniques of social change. Insecurity mounted for all economic groups, but especially for labor, as union membership continued to decline until 1933. Even in the first year of the New Deal there was a question of whether the promises of the labor sections of the National Recovery Act would not be offset by the fact that it was administered largely according to corporate advice. The conditions of workers would improve only with their own efforts, it seemed, and they faced a still hostile public. Pacifists wondered whether they had a right to counsel nonviolence under these circumstances. They were convinced that social conflict could be resolved only by achieving a measure of justice. What if justice could not be accomplished peacefully?

Late in November, 1934, a member of the council of the Fellowship of Reconciliation was trying vainly to organize a program of labor education among the mill workers in Passaic, New Jersey. She wrote to Kirby Page out of a frustration that went beyond her failure to establish a specific program. She revealed the anxiety that haunted many pacifists who were in contact with labor. "I live in this situation here filled with the hates, deceits, treachery, political corruption etc. of some of the workers and at the same time in the midst of the oppression of the owners," Frances Perry wrote. "I want to be clear and to have a working principle of truth in this area in which we are all concerned and when I get over into that F.O.R. group, it all seems so unreal in terms of my situation and of what can be done."[54]

She sealed her letter. The door opened and a friend, a labor organizer named Anna Kula, came in with two striking workers. While Frances Perry got ready to go to supper with them, they talked bitterly in her sitting room about a worker who had supported his boss against the union. They planned to give the man a beating. Their pacifist friend said nothing. Later she reflected,

> Someday perhaps we, Anna and these workers and I, shall have experienced life enough together and I shall have learned enough of truth and goodness in my own spirit so that in such a situation I can put to work the principles in which we believe as pacifists. It will take a long time for me to have the quality of life, which is of sufficient strength and beauty to bring goodness out of evil and it will take a long time for me to be so a part of life that I earn the right to speak of these ultimates. Until then I cannot go about speaking to other groups about pacifism . . . .[55]

Out of her own experience, Frances Perry had raised a question which became crucial for all liberal pacifists. Friendly critics in the churches, like F. Ernest Johnson and William Adams Brown, had insisted that wartime pacifism was an individual decision and not a

189

matter for group action. Perhaps this characterization was true of pacifism in the struggle for economic justice. If violence were necessary to end oppression, could socially concerned pacifists conscientiously counsel peace? This question split the F.O.R. council in 1933–34 and divided the Socialist Party in 1934. As a question of ethical strategy it involved not only social concern, but also political and economic assumptions that would be applied to wars as well as to class and racial strife.

190

Requirements of Peace and Justice

> . . . the F.O.R. must choose, and now, whether it is to disappear into the limbo of useful but no-longer-significant enterprises, or must speedily adapt itself to new world conditions and enter upon the struggles that are, in this century, to determine the course of world development. This will involve the widening of our economic interests and devotions, the building up of effective cooperation with the forces of labor, the education of our people in the various countries in the basic issues troubling the world, and the reinterpretation of our spiritual position so that it focuses directly on the problem of social change toward the left, but without violence.
>
> —Devere Allen[1]

Twenty-three members of the national council of the Fellowship gathered at Union Theological Seminary early in March, 1933, in order to consider the resignation tendered by one of their executive secretaries, Joseph B. Matthews. There were more people present than usual. They disposed of routine business quickly and focused their attention upon a memorandum by Nevin Sayre, the other executive secretary. As he outlined his view of the issues facing them, Sayre must have recalled the March council meeting four years before when Paul Jones had resigned. He concluded his opening remarks and offered his resignation, too, in order to give the council freedom of action. For the next ten months the two secretaries were symbols of the dilemma glimpsed during World War I: pacifists' impulse to far-reaching reform had come in conflict with their refusal to sanction violence in any cause.

J. B. Matthews, as he was known, was one of the most colorful characters ever to join the pacifist movement, although he traveled only a short way with it.* In college he had accepted the challenge of the

---

* Matthews subsequently was a Communist but reacted negatively and be-

191

Student Volunteer Movement to evangelize the world "in this generation," as Kirby Page, Harold Gray, and Evan Thomas had done. They had gone to Europe where they were confronted with the problem of war. He sailed westward to teach native ministers in Java, where he encountered cultural and religious pluralism and Dutch imperialism. He returned to America after the war with his religious and social outlook broadened but with his missionary zeal unabated; he was receptive to the social gospel.

For several years Matthews studied languages and taught the Old Testament, but the intricacies of Arabic, Hebrew, Aramaic, and Sanskrit did not divert his attention from social issues. Postwar disillusionment with Wilsonian liberalism led him to pacifism. He was a delegate to the First World Youth Peace Congress in Holland in the late twenties, and was elected its chairman, much to his surprise. He was quick to accept the position of executive secretary of the F.O.R. in 1929. Soon his pacifism was grounded in politics rather than in religion, though, and his associations became increasingly radical. He was at home in no group, and he gave allegiance to no one cause. He maintained connections with such mutually antagonistic organizations as the F.O.R., the Communist Party Opposition, the Revolutionary Policy Committee, and the Militants of the Socialist Party.

When the depression seriously reduced F.O.R. financial resources, the council divided administrative responsibilities between Sayre and Matthews. The former was in charge of the "development of education and activities relying on moral persuasion," both by strengthening the spiritual basis of the Fellowship and by applying pacifism in conflict situations.[2] Matthews was responsible for "propaganda and activities leading to political pressure" such as organizing public opinion, assisting unionization, working with the League of Industrial Democracy, and participating in strikes. The Fellowship was trying to tie together precedents such as those set by Sayre in the Committee on Militarism in Education, by A. J. Muste in Brookwood Labor College, by Arnold Johnson at Harlan, Kentucky, and by Howard Kester elsewhere in the South; and it was attempting to coordinate its social action. In this respect the F.O.R. implicitly recognized the validity of pressure, including some forms of coercion, but it was not clear about the limits of force

---

came, in 1938, the director of research for the special Committee on Un-American Activities (in which he continued until 1945). He estimated at that time that he had been connected with 58 organizations (an officer of 28) and 9 publications. Matthews, *The Odyssey of a Fellow Traveler* (New York: Mount Vernon Publ., Inc., 1938), pp. 72–76.

which it could accept. Its ambiguity was exposed by J. B. Matthews.

He continued to speak widely and to join groups. His speeches became more radical. He frankly identified himself with Communist front organizations at a time when Kirby Page, Norman Thomas, and Reinhold Niebuhr warned against having any associations with Communists. Matthews increasingly spoke of the inevitability of a violent contest between capitalism and the proletariat, and he interpreted the division of Fellowship work so as to sanction his virtual exclusion of any religious emphasis. Some members complained that he did not reflect their impression of the F.O.R. In March, 1933, he offered his resignation, Sayre added his, and the council tried to determine its position on the role of the Fellowship.

At the outset an old issue was raised again because Matthews expressly denied having any religious basis for what he did. He argued that the Fellowship should be broad enough to accommodate even nonreligious leadership. He charged Sayre with proposing a new basis of membership which would exclude non-Christians, of wanting to make the F.O.R. a " 'duplicate' of the church."[3] That charge was unjustified. Sayre took the same position that he had outlined in 1929, defending the religious orientation of the F.O.R. as being in line with its origin, its statement of principles, and its membership. He had no desire to exclude non-Christians, although he believed that the distinctive feature of the F.O.R. was that it tested its goals and methods by the demands of Christian ethics. A number of influential council members concurred in Sayre's analysis and agreed, also, that Matthews was not qualified for leadership on that basis. Of those who favored retaining the secretary, only Roger Baldwin and Walter Ludwig opposed the religious basis of the F.O.R. The others argued that whatever Matthews *said* about religion, his sacrificial devotion to the cause of social justice was itself spiritual. The discussion turned on whether Matthews was really a religious person and on the limits of exclusiveness, rather than on the essential nature of pacifism.[4]

Another fundamental cleavage in the council also was clouded by irrelevancies. Matthews correctly ascertained that whereas he accepted nonviolence as a tactical consideration, Sayre believed it as a matter of principle. He made Sayre's view seem more dogmatic than it was, however, by contrasting it with his own "realistic" personal philosophy. His faction persuaded a number of council members who were religiously oriented and opposed to any violence that criticism of him was tantamount to an attack on the social-action emphasis developed by the F.O.R.[5] Nonetheless, a close reading of the full debate in the council

193

reveals that revolutionary means, and not a reform orientation, was at issue.

No council members recorded any qualms about the first three articles of Matthew's creed. They apparently accepted the class character of society, an organized rather than individualistic approach to antiwar action and social change, and an anticapitalist emphasis. Some of them were uneasy when the secretary opted for "a coercive rather than persuasive technique in social change," for "minimizing and mitigating, for the sake of effectiveness, the inevitable violence which accompanies social change," and for "a revolutionary (in the sense of fundamental change) overturn of existing social controls, believing that constitutional or legal processes can be relied upon only slightly . . . ." Most members of the council disagreed with Matthews's conclusion:

> The technique of non-violent resistance is secondary to the aims. The most effective piece of non-violent resistance in the world today is the educational system when used by capitalism to prevent the spread of radical ideas. In the United States today it is 98% effective as a non-violent resistance movement to prevent revolutionary change. As between capitalism using non-violent resistance for injustice and communism using violent resistance against injustice, I am with the latter.[6]

This assertion was delusively appealing in 1933. The decay and failure of capitalism seemed obvious to many people then. The proletariat had not overturned the system anywhere except in Russia, however, and European socialism was suffering significant reverses. It had bid for power in Italy and Germany only to be repulsed by fascism, which numerous American liberals understood to be a dictatorial form of capitalism. In the United States the electorate had rallied to a party which Socialists still regarded as conservative. These things called for some explanation. The "educational system when used by capitalism," the "non-violent" coercion of labor by courts and legislatures, and the economic power of the propertied class seemed to radicals like Matthews to preclude the peaceful achievement of justice.

Given the power structure in America, they said, nonviolence would most likely operate to confirm economic injustice. Violence was undesirable, of course, and should be minimized, but it would inevitably occur when there was basic social change. Justice was more fundamental than peace because it was a prior condition of peace. The duty of pacifists was, in this view, to support revolutionary change even if it was somewhat violent.

It is not clear to what extent radicals such as Matthews actually expected the demise of capitalism in a social revolution in the United

194

States, and to what extent this became a shibboleth employed in the maneuvering for position characteristic of left-wing politics. In these years, certainly, some liberals, some of their critics, and even some of President Roosevelt's advisers viewed a revolutionary movement as a distinct possibility.[7] The fact that it was advanced by radicals forced more moderate Socialists to take the question of the road to power seriously. Whatever were their private convictions, Norman Thomas and Devere Allen in the Socialist Party and Kirby Page and Nevin Sayre in the F.O.R. were forced by left-wing politics to deal with the revolution as a real issue; they therefore maneuvered for position on the basis of real political convictions about an illusory view of the future. If this was so, then it follows that the student of their assumptions must treat their intense and prolonged controversy as real and significant, even if artificial.

Most of Matthews's opponents in the council agreed that capitalism had failed and that fundamental social changes in the direction of socialism were desirable. They expected changes to come. Some denied that social change must be accompanied by violence; they all felt that the distinctive function of the Fellowship was to oppose violence in the class struggle, even as it had opposed international war. But what social action should the F.O.R. take? On this they could not agree. Some, like Vincent Nicholson, formerly the executive secretary of the American Friends Service Committee, opposed coercion in the spirit of war, or "ruthless antagonism." The Fellowship should stress conciliation, not class-consciousness, they said. Others, like Kirby Page, justified "nonviolent economic coercion" and insisted that the radical economic point of view should be retained. Sayre took a middle position. The F.O.R. should concentrate on noncoercive "practical methods" of persuasion, he thought. It should experiment with techniques of "moral suasion" in conflict situations by groups which would be willing to suffer for their courage and adventure. Individual members should freely engage in political and economic pressure. "At any rate," he concluded, "the Fellowship should take the absolute stand of resistance to and non-cooperation with every method of war and military action, now and forever; but . . . it should leave the door open for more discussion and experience before reaching decisions on its attitude to non-military and non-death-dealing forms of pressure."[8]

The March discussion came to an inconclusive end. Matthews's resignation was tabled because the council was evenly divided on it. The June council meeting was no more decisive, and so the question was referred to the annual conference of the Fellowship at Swarthmore,

Pennsylvania, in October. The fall meeting was merely an enlarged version of the confused national council. Heated dispute among the sixty-eight members present resulted in little agreement even upon what issues were dividing them. What was distinctive of the pacifist position they were trying to apply? Was it nonresistance or nonviolence? Were pacifists opposed to coercion, to killing, or, as Reinhold Niebuhr was saying, merely to hating? The answers to these questions would affect their influence in neutrality controversy and in domestic reform movements after World War II, but Edmund Chaffee conceded that "arguments moved in circles. The issues were difficult to state."[9]

When it became obvious that the conference did not know the mind of the Fellowship, it was agreed that another referendum of the membership should be taken on the points of dispute. Late in November a questionnaire was mailed to over 6,000 members. On December 16, with 996 replies tabulated, the council met to hear the results. It was one of the largest meetings in the four years since the 1929 referendum, and it lasted some six hours.[10]

Eighty-one per cent of the members replying to the poll reaffirmed the primarily religious character of the Fellowship. Balloting on possible forms of social action revealed that virtually all members would accept the methods of "love, moral suasion, and education" to bring about a more just social order. Seventy-nine per cent of them would, in addition, side with the workers and underprivileged. Forty-three per cent would work through noncoercive methods, but 47 per cent would use nonviolent political and economic coercion, while an additional 10 per cent would sanction violence if necessary. Less than 2 per cent would participate in class conflict.[11] These findings were confirmed by answers to another question which showed that 90 per cent of the members believed that the F.O.R. should "hold to non-violence in the class war as well as in international war." The final question asked what position a secretary of the organization should be allowed to take: 34 per cent would call for his resignation if he advocated violence, and 50 per cent would have him step down if he participated in violence.

In view of the overwhelming mandate of the members replying in favor of nonviolent action, it was perhaps surprising that less than half of them would remove the secretary for advocating violence. This division was reflected in the council, too, where voting was very close until the Matthews faction was clearly defeated and had withdrawn.* The

* The council finally accepted Matthews's resignation by a vote of 18:13, but it retained Sayre by 16:11 (1 formally abstaining and apparently 2 not voting).

196

crisis was followed by resignations. By January, 1934, ten members had resigned from the council, and sixteen had left the Fellowship. Howard Kester resigned as secretary for the South, although Charles Webber stayed on as industrial secretary. By July the F.O.R. reported 53 resignations. It claimed, however, that it had added 924 new members, had paid a "long-standing debt of several thousand dollars," and had sponsored a nationwide series of forty conferences on pacifism and war.[12]

Administrative reorganization was completed by the fall of 1934. Sayre was elected chairman and freed of administrative duties so that he could give his full attention to speaking and soliciting. Harold Fey became executive secretary and editor of a new monthly journal, *Fellowship*, which succeeded the *World Tomorrow*. A new secretary for the South was appointed, and about twenty active members agreed to act as "field representatives" without pay. They would present the Fellowship message in their communities, counsel local groups, and solicit new members. By the spring of 1935 the F.O.R. had offices in New York City, Atlanta, and Los Angeles, and claimed to have about 7,000 members.[13] It emerged from the 1933–34 crisis with a more congenial staff ready to take on a larger program. Had the outcome been otherwise, it is not likely that pacifists would have played a significant role in foreign policy in that decade. Certainly, there would have been no Emergency Peace Campaign. As it was, leaders of the F.O.R. became increasingly involved in the politics of neutralism and nonviolent action.

Meanwhile, they met J. B. Matthews on another front, in the Socialist Party. During the twenties that organization had become a faint shadow of the militant party of Eugene V. Debs. It was sustained mainly by New York Socialists who dominated the needle trade unions and controlled the *Jewish Daily Forward*. Beginning with Norman Thomas's presidential candidacy in 1928, and especially after the election of Clarence Senior as national secretary the following year, the party organization was strengthened, finances were put in order, and membership was increased. In the early years of national depression, Socialists sensed the restlessness of labor and bid for its support. By 1935 organized workers had flexed their muscles in important strikes; young laborers began to turn to the Socialist Party for political leadership on such a scale that American Trotskyists found their own efforts to win unions of no avail. Following the example of their French comrades, they dissolved their Workers Party of the United States and in 1936 joined the Socialist Party, whose left wing seemed to hold the key to the organized proletariat.

Four factions emerged in the Socialist Party between 1928 and 1936.

197

The New York Socialists and their supporters elsewhere constituted the old guard. They were dogmatically Marxist, but they viewed Russia as a traitor to the Socialist ideal. They were very much concerned that the party take correct theoretical lines, but were little inclined to expand its influence beyond their own bailiwicks. They feared that orthodox socialism might be diluted by the liberals with whom Norman Thomas associated, but they were equally anxious lest the party fall into the hands of Communists. In short, they thought of it in terms of their own struggles against the nascent Communist party in 1919–20, and of what had been their bold program under Debs and Morris Hillquit during World War I.

Socialists grouped about Norman Thomas often were referred to as the progressive wing of the party. Some of them, like Harry Laidler and Jessie Hughan, had been members before the war. Most had joined during or after the war, as did Thomas himself. They were mainly American born, well educated, and middle class. They were not Marxist in a doctrinaire sense; although they assumed the reality of economic determinism and class struggle, they wanted to make the Socialist Party a vital movement relevant to American democratic ideals. They distrusted Russian communism. Their political approach was pragmatic and therefore changeable.

The third major group was known as the militants, probably from the 1934 proclamation, *Towards a Militant Program for the Socialist Party of America*. Its members constituted the left wing of the party in the thirties, and they therefore forced the progressives into a centrist position. The militants were young people who, according to Murray Seidler, "were embittered and disillusioned by the depression. Their ilk was coming to all of the radical parties during this period . . . . They viewed themselves as radical Marxists who opposed gradualism and reformism."[14] They were impressed by the Russian experiment. The militants were thus dissatisfied with the moderate and pragmatic progressives of the party, and they also despised the old guard which seemed to them little short of reactionary. So long as the right-wing New York Socialists remained within the party, therefore, the militants and progressives united against them.

A fourth faction, much smaller than the others and on the periphery of the party, was the Revolutionary Policy Committee. This group was formed just prior to the Detroit convention of the party in 1934. It was more radical than the militants, whom it regarded as being suspended between reformism and true revolution. It defended the Soviet Union and differed with Communists only on tactical matters which it considered, nevertheless, to be very important. The executive committee of the Revolutionary Policy Committee included nominal pacifists William Chamberlain, instructor of philosophy at Buffalo University; Francis Henson, secretary of the student division of the Y.M.C.A.; Irving Brown, a graduate student at Columbia University; and two former secretaries of the F.O.R., Howard Kester and J. B. Matthews.

Factionalism was rife as members of the Socialist Party gathered in Detroit on Friday, May 31, 1934, for their eighteenth national convention. Morris Hillquit had died the year before and the old guard was weakened but no less determined to control the party, whereas its opposition on the far left, the Revolutionary Policy Committee, demanded a radical change. Membership had increased by 7,000 since the previous convention, and more representatives of labor were present; but the picture was not wholly encouraging, for social democracy had been liquidated in Germany and Austria. Clarence Senior insisted, "It is no longer a question of existing by drifting along. It is either win in the near future or perish!"[15] In this atmosphere of urgency pacifist Devere Allen wrote the *Declaration of Principles,* which divided the factions of the party.

He began with a ringing call to action:

> The Socialist Party is the party of the workers, regardless of race, color, or creed. In mill and mine, shop and farm, office and school, the workers can assert their united power, and through the Socialist Party establish a cooperative commonwealth forever free from human exploitation and class rule.
>
> If the workers delay and drift, they will prolong the period of their enslavement to a decadent capitalism.[16]

He followed this statement with an incisive, although traditional, critique of capitalism and defense of socialism. When he dealt with the road to socialist power, Allen raised two issues that caused vehement debate: the questions of international conflict and class war.

His position on war virtually reaffirmed the St. Louis Proclamation of 1917, in which the party had opposed World War I. He defended it, now, by citing similar statements by European unions and labor parties. He interpreted the wartime resistance advocated in the *Declaration* to mean a disciplined general strike. He explained that "massed war resistance" was "known to thousands of trade unions abroad and to pacifists everywhere as the standard means of differentiating between individual, isolated conscientious objection after war comes and the organized preparation, by demonstration and strike and united non-co-operation, of war prevention."[17] The old guard denounced this aspect of the 1934 *Declaration* as being too pacifistic. That charge was ironic because former leaders of the New York wing, Morris Hillquit and Charles Ruthenberg, had written the 1917 proclamation. Thomas complained that the latter-day attack was "a rationalization of the bitter disappointment of the Right-wing Old Guard at losing to a large degree its control over Party machinery."[18]

With regard to the second issue, class struggle, Allen wrote in the *Declaration*:

> In its struggle for a new society, the Socialist Party seeks to attain its objectives by peaceful and orderly means. Recognizing the increasing resort by a crumbling capitalist order to Fascism to preserve its integrity and dominance, the Socialist Party intends not to be deceived by Fascist propaganda nor overwhelmed by Fascist force. It will do all in its power to fight Fascism of every kind all the time and everywhere in the world, until Fascism is dead. It will rely, nevertheless, on the organization of a disciplined labor movement. Its methods may include a recourse to a general strike which will not merely serve as a defense against Fascist counter-revolution but will carry the revolutionary struggle into the camp of the enemy.
>
> . . . .
>
> Capitalism is doomed. If it can be superseded by majority vote, the Socialist Party will rejoice. If the crisis comes through the denial of majority rights after the electorate has given us a mandate we shall not hesitate to crush by our labor solidarity the reckless forces of reaction and to consolidate the Socialist state. If the capitalist system should collapse in a general chaos and confusion . . . the Socialist Party . . . will not shrink from the responsibility of organizing and maintaining a government under the workers' rule.[19]

The old guard bitterly assailed this part of the *Declaration of Principles*. It was "Communist, Anarchist and illegal," said Louis Waldman, Socialist candidate for governor of New York in 1932. Some pacifists, too, were alarmed. Even John Haynes Holmes, an old friend of Norman Thomas, wrote that "the Detroit Declaration of Principles is Communism, pure and simple."[20] Thomas denied it. He professed to see no departure from historic socialism except that the 1934 declaration was more specific than previous ones in naming the general strike as the weapon of the workers, and in announcing their intention to survive chaos, as their German friends had not done. "In the event of a complete collapse we will not try to carry out a nose-counting election in a lunatic asylum," he said, "but if we have power we will establish the kind of rule which will make order and true democracy possible."[21] Allen appealed directly to pacifists who had endured a similar crisis in the F.O.R.:

200

The organization of a government will require the maintenance of that government, and for this task there will be necessitated a police force as in any state .... To that police force we shall have to give the sanctions of some violence. Not to do so would inevitably usher in brutal reaction and plunge the world backward, as Hitler has plunged it backward in Central Europe. On that issue I know where I stand. I believe that all but a few pacifists will share that stand, and if they are not now members of the Socialist Party, they speedily will be.[22]

The *Declaration* was adopted by a large majority in the convention, but upon a petition of over 25 per cent of the delegates it was submitted to a referendum of the membership at large, where it engendered bitter animosity and a pamphlet war. It finally carried the party by a vote of 5,993 to 4,872.[23] Most party members on both sides of the issue probably voted against revolutionary violence, although the majority were more militant.

J. B. Matthews's Revolutionary Policy Committee denounced the *Declaration of Principles* for not sanctioning violent revolution. It complained, too, that the *Declaration* was "based on an idealistic evaluation as opposed to a materialistic, empirical analysis of society."[24] To put it another way, Thomas and Allen did believe in the democratic idea, and they held also that it must condition the strategy of socialism: "socialism must be shaped according to the ideals as well as the objective, materialistic experience of America."[25]

Revolutionary Policy Committee members doubted that either the middle class ideals or the experiences of Americans were relevant to the achievement of a socialistic state. Even a general strike is an inadequate alternative to liberal parliamentarism, wrote Irving Brown. Reformism had failed in England, Germany, and France, he continued, whereas revolutionary seizure of power had placed the working class in control of Russia. The proletariat has only one road to power, he concluded—revolution and a workers' dictatorship. Brown, like other members of the committee, based his criticism of militant and progressive Socialists on these absolute Marxist doctrines. However wrong he was, he perceptively characterized his opponents. "Standing between 'revolution' and 'reformism,' " he wrote, "they offer the way out by combining both on the basis of the promise that argues that 'circumstances,' 'specific conditions' and 'expedience' are the determinants in deciding upon the methods and instruments to be used in the social revolution."[26]

In other words, according to the radicals, Devere Allen's adherence to "peaceful and orderly means" of social change was based upon the pragmatic consideration that violence was poor strategy for the workers, and would compromise the democratic ideal of their movement.

With Thomas he believed that power was distributed in American society, as in the labor movement itself, even though it was not distributed equitably. Violence was likely to precipitate a further concentration of power to the disadvantage of labor. The Revolutionary Policy Committee was quite correct in its analysis of these pacifists, but it was inconsistent in attacking Thomas for the idealism of his view of democracy while at the same time criticizing Allen for the pragmatism of his version of pacifism (its own strategy was "empirically" arrived at, as it thought, by the application of absolutist Marxist dogmas to experience).

The pacifism of Norman Thomas, Devere Allen, and other Christian Socialists was, indeed, rooted in ideals, as was that of nonreligious Socialists. In many respects the same humanitarianism motivated both groups. But each found that translating social ideals into action required making pragmatic decisions. The ethical distinction between violence and nonviolence was tenuous, especially in dealing with groups of people seeking justice. The line between that coercion which was justifiable (or redemptive, as the Christians said) and that which was not seemed thin. The attempt to put these distinctions into words was the occasion for a bitter debate from which Socialists never fully recovered. The *Declaration of Principles* was essentially an abstract statement of policy, but to the Socialist Party of 1934, factionalized, intensely conscious of its social responsibility, and imagining imminent political opportunity, the *Declaration* seemed to pose a very real choice of directions which might result in either leadership or impotence.

Their work in the labor movement and the Socialist Party led some pacifists to accept the apparent necessity of some forms of coercion. It also forced them to evaluate the use of force in terms of both pragmatic realities and ethical principles, explicitly to relate peace and justice. Reforming pacifists increasingly distinguished between violent and nonviolent coercion. They originally had viewed pacifism as a way of living; they learned to think of pacifism also as a technique of social action. However, they were handicapped in left-wing controversy because they had not formulated, or systematized, those principles of nonviolent action which they affirmed.

> What I like about Gandhi's method of non-violent resistance is that it is a method of generating *power*. And I'm blessed if I can see that Socialism or mere organization of the workers does that.

> So even though we cannot always draw a sharp line between violent and non-violent coercion, and between coercion and persuasion, or between persuasion and education, or between education and propaganda, nevertheless we can strive to make such distinctions as clear as possible in each case, and we can always advocate methods which are distinctly less violent . . . than those which are frequently practiced. The encouragement of constant thinking, discussion and action in the direction of non-violence will give us steadily more power and more understanding of how to solve social problems in the direction of increasing social justice. Gandhi's program involves a constant search for social truth.
>
> —RICHARD GREGG[27]

American pacifists endowed Mohandas K. Gandhi with a mystique born of their need for a political model and enhanced by distance. John Haynes Holmes first heard of him in 1917, and he formed an emotional attachment to the Indian's ideas even before reading them first hand. Throughout the war the New York preacher defended pacifism against charges of being ascetic and irrelevant, but he could marshal few precedents for its successful use by large groups of people. Gandhi became the text for sermons and articles saying that men could follow Jesus and still be politically effective. He was the subject of a whole issue of the *World Tomorrow* in 1924. His spiritual autobiography was serialized in *Unity* by Holmes, whose frequent comparisons of Gandhi and Jesus led Reinhold Niebuhr to say that "his one absolute is Gandhi's perfection."[28] Indeed, pacifism was an essentially religious commitment for Holmes, an eternal moral principle which almost conveniently was relevant to the quest for social justice. Viewing the Indian from that context, Holmes absolutized Gandhi's way. He emphasized its universal applicability, but he failed to examine it as a social technique limited in time and circumstance.

Other pacifists followed Gandhi's progress, looking for nonviolent techniques. They hailed his noncooperation campaign and march to the sea of 1930. Through Roger Baldwin and J. B. Matthews the F.O.R. helped to organize an American League for India's Freedom and raised a fund in Gandhi's support. The Fellowship resolved that his "rejection of the method of war and his valiant attempt to displace it with methods of non-violence mark an epoch in the social advance of humanity."[29] Dorothy Detzer and Jane Addams believed that young pacifists ought to be "pouring" into India to learn from Gandhi. Kirby Page wrote an

203

account of the Indian leader's life, ideals, and crusade for independence, and thus contributed to a growing body of pacifist literature on the Indian approach to conflict.[30] Gandhi's influence grew as American pacifists used his example to formulate the assumptions they already held. After World War II he would be studied intensively by pacifists, scholars, including William Stuart Nelson and Joan Bondurant, and civil-rights leaders such as James Farmer and Martin Luther King, Jr. But the first extensive gloss on Gandhi was *The Power of Non-Violence* by Richard Gregg, and it became virtually a manual of style for pacifist action.[31]

Gregg had practiced law in Boston after graduating from Harvard College and Harvard Law School. He interrupted his career in Boston to take a position with his brother-in-law, who had interests in India, and together they spent three months there. After his return to America, between 1915 and 1920, Gregg was a labor consultant, and then for three years he did statistical, legal, and publicity work for the Federation of Railway Shop Employees. In the midst of a major strike of the federation he came across an article about Mohandas Gandhi. Impressed by a few excerpts of the Indian's writing, Gregg read more. After taking some courses in agriculture at the University of Wisconsin and working for a season on a farm, he sailed for India in January, 1925. There he stayed for four years, spending a total of seven months at Gandhi's *ashram*, or spiritual retreat. Shortly afterward he wrote *The Psychology and Strategy of Gandhi's Non-Violent Resistance*, which he expanded into his more famous book.[32]

The Power of Non-Violence was infused with the concept of *Satyagraha*, the philosophy of social action which Gandhi was molding into a powerful force for Indian independence. Gregg's book was not couched in the language of the Indian seer, though. It used the vocabulary of social psychologists and even militarists to argue that violence inevitably is self-defeating, and that the principle of nonviolence is in accord with Western notions of human nature and political strategy. Gregg shared the ambiguity of the F.O.R. regarding the ethical limits of coercion; he minimized the problem of its use because he shared also the widely held pacifist assumptions of the unity and plasticity of human nature. He emphasized, therefore, the persuasive possibilities of nonviolent resistance. Nevertheless, his main contribution was his treatment of coercion *as a step* in the process of attaining reconciliation of opposing groups or persons. This view, which he derived from Gandhian *Satyagraha*, made a realistic approach to some conflict situations plausible.

Gregg was not concerned with the dilemmas traditionally used to embarrass pacifists—what would you do if a man assaulted your wife, or, what would you do if a thief threatened to kill your children? Gregg was dealing, instead, with resistance to social injustice or aggression. He assumed, therefore, that there would exist a clash of interests or issues which might be resolved by both parties, and he expected that conflict would be prolonged. Time would favor the resister, he thought, since it would give the oppressor a chance to feel the pressure of public opinion, to develop respect for his victim, and to consider nonviolent alternatives. Gregg's difficulty was that he explained the mechanism of social action in terms of an attack by one individual on another. He did this, no doubt, in order to simplify his explanation and to avoid the complications of group dynamics. But simplification made his illustration transferable to the traditional dilemmas of a thief in the night or an assault on one's wife, cases with which he did not intend to deal.

In the first place, nonviolent resistance puts an aggressor off balance. He is surprised by the fact that his victim does not return his blows but, in fact, holds a different scale of values than he does. He loses his poise, self-confidence and "moral balance." Gregg called this "moral jiu-jitsu." Initiative passes to the nonviolent resister, along with other advantages. The attacker is exhausted by prolonged anger. Part of his energy is even directed against himself, since the victim's behavior arouses his "more decent and kindly motives" and puts them in conflict with his fighting, aggressive drives. Finally, in the presence of onlookers the assailant dramatizes the difference between himself and his victim to his own disadvantage so that his own need for social approval works against him. Nonviolence thus tends to throw the aggressor off balance, according to Gregg.[33]

What is more important, he added, it makes the opponent receptive to new ideas. His growing respect for his victim removes any basis for fear, anger, or foreboding. He is susceptible to suggestion because he is excited and surprised, so that his attention is "spontaneously concentrated on new ideas." His intention is to reduce the other person to subservience, but the victim's behavior suggests that it is not necessary. Gregg cited psychologists who held that "imagination and suggestion together are much stronger than conscious will power," and he concluded that nonviolent resistance might create an impulse too strong for the previous intention so that the assailant will entertain a wholly new solution for the issue over which he was so ready to fight.[34]

Underlying Gregg's discussion of the mechanism of nonviolence were the assumptions that (1) there are latent moral sensibilities in all hu-

205

man beings, that (2) all people have similar ultimate desires, that (3) human nature is in some respects plastic, and that (4) therefore, nonviolence could be used as a method of social action.

Gregg supposed that all men are morally sensible: "These human traits of love, faith, courage, honesty, and humility exist in greater or less strength in *every* person," he wrote.[35] For this reason every assailant is vulnerable to the pressure of his own "decent and kindly motives" when they are aroused. Nonviolence as a means of persuasion is largely a matter of tapping the subconscious moral attitudes of men. Gregg neglected the real possibility of antagonisms in the subconscious; bigotry and racial pride are examples of largely nonrational emotions which may even be suppressed by the will. He might well have replied that these are universal fears which nonviolence could dispel, but it is nevertheless true that any resistance would probably tap latent antagonisms as well as moral values, and it is a moot point which are more likely to prevail in any given oppressor.

Onlookers will probably sympathize with the nonviolent resister, Gregg said, because they respond to universal moral values. The history of recent racial, labor, and antiwar struggles in America suggests that his observation of the public was correct, but for the wrong reason. When third parties to a social conflict are inclined to intervene in favor of the apparent victim of violence it may well be that they are interested in order more than in justice. Gregg himself conceded this with regard to labor disputes.[36] This does not invalidate the effectiveness with which nonviolent resisters might appeal to neutral parties, but it does qualify the operation of latent moral values in a social struggle.

Reinhold Niebuhr underlined that point in the very title of his *Moral Man and Immoral Society*. Whereas individuals may sacrifice their advantages, groups always operate in their own interests. He quoted David Hume to the effect that whatever is the real nature of human beings, their political nature is egoistic.[37] He rejected violent revolution in 1932, but only on practical grounds, and he opposed the Fellowship's repudiation of any violence in 1933 because he took it to be arbitrary. He developed a strategy of social action which reflected Gandhi and anticipated Gregg. It would be frankly coercive, but not violent. It would have important strategic advantages, and one of these would be to rob an opponent of his traditional identification of the *status quo* with peace and order. That was a political, not a moral consequence, he insisted, although it might make possible an equitable settlement.

A second assumption of *The Power of Non-Violence* was that all people share at least the desire for security and fulfillment. Apprehension for one's security or a misunderstanding about the way life is fulfilled is responsible for the emotions of anger, fear, pride, and greed which divide men, said Gregg. The nonviolent resister refuses to acknowledge the reality of these divisive emotions, and he thereby modifies their force. More important, his fundamental object is not "to injure or crush and humiliate his opponent," although these things may happen incidentally. He seeks, instead

> to convert the opponent, to change his understanding and his sense of values so that he will join wholeheartedly with the resister in seeking a settlement truly amicable and truly satisfying to both sides. The nonviolent resister seeks a solution under which both parties can have complete self-respect and mutual respect; a settlement that will implement the new desires and full energies of both parties.[38]

In this sense only nonviolent resistance provides the grounds for the fulfillment and security of both parties to a conflict.

Gregg put in moral terms what others would state politically: that all parties to a dispute have interests in an approximation of justice. Reinhold Niebuhr defined justice in political terms as the relatively equal distribution of power in society. Power is the object of all groups of persons, he insisted—nations, classes, or races. The genius of the Marxists was their understanding that a "disproportion of power in society is the real root of social injustice."[39] The romantic flaw of Marxism was its failure to deal realistically with the strong centers of political power that would replace private ownership. Niebuhr, like Norman Thomas, advocated democratic socialism because it would distribute power and thus approximate justice. He, like Devere Allen, Kirby Page, and A. J. Muste, preferred nonviolent action to revolution. Nonviolence permits a maximum of objectivity on both sides and makes understanding and accord possible, although not inevitable, he said. It may lead also to a discrimination "between the evils of a social system and the individuals who are involved in it."[40] Moreover, he agreed that in this country violence would split the labor movement. It would preclude labor solidarity, the very prerequisite of attaining power. It would unite the middle class against the workers. Political organization and unionization could unite labor, gain the support of the middle class, and force capital to come to terms with a stronger proletariat. Nonviolence might contribute to a more equitable distribution of power; violence would create only a new inequity.

Underlying Gregg's whole argument was the assumption that human nature is in some respects plastic, that social habits and beliefs can be changed. Under some circumstances antagonism and aggressiveness can be transmuted into respect and cooperation. If the opponent's nature can be changed, the resister's can be molded and disciplined. In Gandhian fashion, Gregg believed that discipline would spring from inner qualities: from creative insight into people which is "akin to love"; from an abiding faith "in the ultimate possibilities of human nature; a courage based upon a . . . realization of the underlying unity of all life . . . ," and "a strong and deep desire for and love of truth . . . ."[41] Truth is relative, he said, and if one cannot attain an understanding which eliminates anger or enmity toward others he should be forthright and courageous rather than hypocritical and cowardly:

> Courageous violence, to try to prevent or stop a wrong, is better than cowardly acquiescence. . . . The inner attitude is more important than the outer act, though it is vitally important . . . to make one's outer conduct a true reflection and expression of one's inner state. Fear develops out of an assumption of relative weakness. Since all men have the innate possibility of moral strength, to be afraid is really a denial of one's moral potential powers and is therefore very harmful. Violence and anger at least show faith in one's own moral powers and thus provide at least a basis for further growth . . . . If one has not the special courage or discipline or conviction to resist wrong or violence without counter-violence, then I agree with Gandhi that it is better to be violent than to be cowardly. But he who has the courage to fight and yet refrains, is the true non-violent resister.[42]

His sense of the plasticity of human nature is strong in this passage, but he applied it more originally to demonstrate the possibility of disciplining groups of people to fight and yet refrain from violence.

Psychology and war itself provided evidence that this discipline could be accomplished. John B. Watson had shown that all fears besides those of falling and of a sudden loud noise are conditioned, and he had confirmed the work of Ivan Petrovich Pavlov which showed that conditioned responses could be reconditioned. To put it another way, a person usually reacts to threatened danger in terms of fear and anger, Gregg explained, and these emotions are expressed in flight and pugnacity, respectively. He concluded,

> We know that the elemental instinct of flight and emotion of fear can be controlled and disciplined by military training. Ages of war have taught us that this control and discipline are practical and effective. Since that is possible, it is equally possible to control and discipline the parallel and equally elemental instinct of pugnacity and emotion of anger.[43]

Group discipline, rather than saintliness, is required for nonviolence to become a useful form of social action.

208

A nonviolent-resistance movement is parallel to a military venture in many ways, Gregg wrote: it requires disciplined emotion and action; it has a psychological and moral aim; it operates against the morale of the opponents; and it requires "courage, dynamic energy, capacity to endure fatigue and suffering, self-sacrifice, self-control, chivalry, action."[44] Like warfare, nonviolent resistance requires also principles of strategy which would be determined by circumstance. It might involve protests, demonstrations, and publicity, or it might require voluntary suffering. It might resort to a strike or boycott. It would keep the opponent off balance, surprise him by its frankness and fair play. It would seek to engage him in negotiations at every turn, but never to compromise its sense of justice. The nonviolent movement would be like an army in emphasizing unity and utter devotion to its cause and in training disciplined groups.[45] Gregg held that the very fact that military virtues and even principles of military strategy apply to the technique of nonviolent resistance indicates that as a mode of settling disputes the Gandhian method does not entirely reverse Western experience.

Gregg's emphasis on individual and group discipline and on character building reflected the influence of Gandhi. In a sense, the book was inconclusive precisely because of that influence. His experience in India helped Gregg to organize his defense of the realism, potential, and requirements of nonviolent resistance as a technique of social action. But he was not entirely clear about what it might be *used for* in America. He expressly suggested using the method in labor disputes, sanctioning coercion by strikes and boycotts, and that was the one specific Western conflict situation in the book. He did not anticipate the use of the technique in the American struggle for racial equality. He did not suggest how it might be used against military aggression. For the most part his writing was theoretical and his examples, except for Gandhi, were hypothetical. Consequently, he minimized the use of coercion. He implied that nonviolence is largely a method of persuasion. It is a kind of language, he wrote. His book was an exposition of the power of that language. In this sense it exposed an optimistic faith in the rationality, plasticity, and goodness of man. It was apparently open to the criticism of Reinhold Niebuhr that pacifism ignored universal sin in individuals and inevitable conflict among institutions.

To rest with this criticism, however, would be to miss the historical significance of the book. If it presumed a sort of natural theology of pacifism, it was valued more for its theory and exposition of a social-action method. It was the model for many handbooks on training and action techniques, some of them written by Gregg himself. It was studied by the founders of the modern civil-rights movements in their youth. After considerable experience in that movement, the authors of a detailed *Manual for Direct Action* in 1964 still accounted *The Power of Non-Violence* "the best general discussion of the concept and its ramifications."[46] The book endured because Gregg treated coercion as one step in the process of nonviolent action. That is to say, coercion might be regarded as a part of the technique of redistributing power so as to reach a mutually satisfactory approximation of justice.

The world is ever changing, Gregg believed, and the very differences among people mean that the adjustments involved in social change result in further conflict. The nonviolent resister should "not confuse peace with the absence of conflict"; he should seek to resolve specific issues, not to eliminate struggle.[47] Gandhi taught that a man should use force in the fight for social justice, rather than sink into inaction. But it was better still, he said, to seek justice by some nonviolent means because the manner of dealing with a conflict is inseparable from the solution sought. Pacifists had said often that the means determines the ends. But even that dictum is not the full implication of Gregg and Gandhi, for, according to them, it is equally true that the goal determines the means used. Implicit in their thinking, then, was their repudiation of a disjunction between means and ends.[48]

The convertibility of ends and means was apparent in Gregg's treatment of suffering and of coercion. He followed all Christian pacifists in saying that "voluntary suffering is always necessary to the accomplishment of any desirable change in an economic, political or personal situation." Suffering is not good in itself, however; the martyr is virtuous because he values something, not because he suffers. Voluntary suffering may be necessary to persuade an opponent of one's sincerity and to maintain one's own discipline and integrity, but it is, after all, "the incidental and secondary aspect of the matter if one's object is to accomplish an improvement in conditions."[49]

Similarly, coercion is necessary if the attachments to the *status quo* are extremely strong, but it is not valuable in itself. Gregg preferred "moral pressure" to coercion, and he sanctioned economic or political pressure only as a last resort. Nevertheless, he was willing to employ them when necessary in order to force an oppressor to seek a just settlement. These actions would be coercive, since they would compel an opponent to choose between conceding to the resister or suffering economic or political loss, neither of which he wished to do. As means, the methods of coercion must be evaluated according to their effects, and violent coercion must be distinguished from nonviolent action.

210

Violence—severe and often uncontrolled force, injurious or destructive action—invariably impedes the attainment of social justice, pacifists argued. They returned to the issue that disrupted the F.O.R. and the Socialist Party. Gregg noted that violent acts divide men from one another and prevent the reconciliation of their interests. Relying on physical force presumes separateness, he wrote; it also confirms disunity. Echoing Reinhold Niebuhr, Devere Allen, and Norman Thomas, he said that laborers could not attain power through violence in America because its use would mobilize the middle class against them. Even if they could get power, the use of violence would alter their own movement from a crusade for economic justice to a power struggle. Most important, violence in any specific labor dispute would tend to confirm the basis of injustice, which is the very division of society. Liberal pacifists limited coercive force because of their analysis of society: violence *creates* a false social setting for justice. Consequently, they said, whatever use is made of economic and political pressure, violent force must be abjured because "the end as actually achieved always partakes of the nature of the means employed."[50]

Violence impedes international justice, too, according to pacifists. Over and over they wrote that fighting settles nothing. "The first of the political causes of war is war itself," wrote Aldous Huxley.[51] Fighting merely creates a new imbalance of power. It shakes the fundamental customs, habits, and values of each participating nation, and therefore it disrupts the very conditions of stability and justice. He agreed with numerous American pacifists that modern war as well as its preparation centralizes power, suppresses responsible self-government, and results in new forms of injustice and conflict. The notion of war as a social process stretched back among pacifists to at least Kirby Page. The idea of peace as process embraced most of the interwar peace movement. The effective limits of coercion depended largely upon one's analysis of the relationships of power, and the development of committed neutralism among liberal pacifists early in the thirties reflected their assessment of the international scene as much as their arbitrary repudiation of force.

Richard Gregg, like many of his American friends and like Gandhi himself, emphasized the self-defeating nature of violence and minimized the coercive aspects of nonviolent direct action. And yet both men interpreted nonviolence, or *Satyagraha*, as a means of achieving social change, and they thus distinguished it from the personal doctrine of nonresistance that characterized virtually all absolute pacifists before World War I and numerous pacifists afterwards. Five years after Gregg

211

published *The Power of Non-Violence*, Krishnalal Shridharani analyzed Gregg's doctrine specifically as a social technique, and he frankly acknowledged the element of compulsion in the method.[52] He said, in fact, that its distinctive *form* of compulsion made nonviolence effective in contrast to violence. It might be necessary to force an opponent to make a moral decision; it might be necessary even to compel him to break with tradition in order to make mutual justice possible. If force is of a kind which negates the essence of the process and the goal, as physical violence was presumed to be, then it must be rejected.

This view appealed to John Haynes Holmes and Kirby Page, who had required that social action be redemptive in a religious sense. It underlay Reinhold Niebuhr's defense of nonviolence in *Moral Man and Immoral Society*, although not his subsequent sanctions of class and international war. It appealed to Norman Thomas and Devere Allen, who were convinced that social action was necessary and were sure, too, that violence would defeat all hope for a new order. It provided a pragmatically based ethic with an absolute injunction against violence. It was consonant with the reorientation of the Fellowship of Reconciliation in 1934.

 True reconciliation recognizes that if injustice is to be overcome, religious radicals must plunge into the organization of pressures. This involves the unpleasant business of bargaining, maneuvering for advantage, forcing the political and economic pace. This involves the development of a powerful labor movement, the organization of farmers and tenants, the encouragement of cooperatives, the building of a strong political instrument of justice and the use of each of these to whittle down privilege, to cajole, coerce and eventually absorb all business affected with a public interest and to control it through machinery set up and directed by society. In this way we attack the roots of violence in the injustices of a social order which subsidizes inequalities and rewards those who exploit the weakest and neediest.

—HAROLD FEY[53]

The Fellowship put the concept of nonviolent action into practice wherever possible, confirming its faith in that possibility of social reform which had been called into question during the crisis of 1933–34, and which soon would be challenged by the approach of war. When Howard Kester resigned as secretary for the South, he was replaced by Claud D. Nelson who continued the work in southern labor and race relations.* He published a pamphlet criticizing the use of martial law to break up strikes, and for this document he was bitterly denounced by the textile industry. He also convened about forty leaders in religion, education, and labor who formed the Southern Council in Religion and Economics late in 1936 in order to promote the civil liberties of workers among local churches.[54]

Other F.O.R. members sought to relieve the plight of southern tenant farmers. Norman Thomas appealed directly to President Roosevelt to remedy defects in agricultural policy which, Thomas said, accentuated the hardships of sharecroppers. Howard Kester, Powers Hapgood, Claud Williams, and Ward Rogers helped to organize Arkansas farmers. On one occasion Hapgood and Kester were driven out of Mississippi County, Arkansas, by the Ku Klux Klan. Rogers, a young graduate of Vanderbilt School of Religion and Boston University and a member of the executive committee of the Southern Tenant Farmers' Union, was arrested and convicted of anarchy because he had advocated joint organization by blacks and whites. Williams, an ordained minister, was held for twenty days in a Ft. Smith jail because he had led a strike of Federal Emergency Relief workers protesting a wage reduction.[55]

The F.O.R. supported labor on the national level, too. In 1936, A. J. Muste returned to the Christian and pacifist fold from the Trotskyist movement and was appointed chairman of the Committee on Industrial Relations of the Fellowship to succeed Edmund B. Chaffee, who had died that September. Muste sought to develop techniques which could be used on the community level to avoid outbursts in case of strikes, methods which would emphasize persuasion, with nonviolent coercion as a last resort. In 1937 he was appointed full-time industrial secretary. He must have sensed the fulfillment of years of devotion to the labor movement as workers organized lie-down and sit-down strikes, and as basic industries such as United States Steel and General Motors signed collective-bargaining contracts.† Muste and the F.O.R. council defended

---

* Nelson was a native of Arkansas and a graduate of Hendricks College who had worked with the foreign division of the Y.M.C.A. during World War I and with its student division afterwards.

† The lie-down strike was claimed as the contribution of two pacifists who were members of the American Federation of Full Fashioned Hosiery Workers, on strike beginning Oct. 1, 1936, at the Berkshire Knitting Mills at Reading, Pa. In December a small but determined committee planned and publicized a campaign in which over 135 pickets lay down at a plant entrance in order to deter

213

labor's right to organize and commended the nonviolent character of the strikes and the discipline of strikers, although they warned that the "physical possession of property and physical coercion of non-strikers" implied latent threats of violence.[56]

The strike won acceptance as a legitimate tool of labor after 1937, unions gained strength, and prosperity rose. The problems of industrial injustice paled before the threat of a second world war. Numerous pacifists found it possible to transfer their commitment to nonviolence from the domestic to the international scene. The radicals had been wrong, they pointed out; social reform was being achieved without class war. For a few years they were tempted to believe that their faith in constructive nonviolence might prove to be as realistic in foreign affairs as it seemed to have been in the labor movement. Meanwhile, a few pacifists found another field of action.

It was ironic that race relations, the very area in which nonviolent direct action became widely used, was neglected in pacifist discussions of nonviolence before World War II. Economic struggle seemed much more immediate, especially in the early thirties when the questions of coercion and violence were most fully debated, and when Richard Gregg was writing about *The Power of Non-Violence*. Pacifists were not unmindful of racial injustice; they bracketed it with economic wrong and gave it much attention in the *World Tomorrow*, but they did not generally regard it as an urgent social *struggle*. It did not seem to involve the question of a minority's use of violence, as did the labor question. The race-relations work of the Fellowship was originally conceived of as educational, to bring individuals into contact with persons of another race, to leaven the sum of prejudice with understanding. There must be a new white man, wrote Devere Allen, a man who will break the bonds of ignorance, superstition, fear, and economic dependency on cheap labor, in order to escape his confining heritage of caste.[57]

George Collins, youth secretary of the F.O.R. in the early twenties, made the first organizing trip into the South in 1924. He was struck by the needs of the region. The next fall he and Juliette Derricotte, the Negro dean of women at Fisk University, represented the F.O.R. at the

---

strike-breakers from entering. Even tear gas failed to move them, and they had to be arrested and jailed. Their action did not close the mills, but it did lead the national conference of their union to appoint a standing committee to study the use of nonviolent techniques in labor disputes. Herbert B. Bohn, "We Tried Non-Violence," *Fellowship*, III (Jan., 1937), 7–8, an account which Harold Fey vouched for on the basis of personal investigation; and Muste, "Sit Downs and Lie Downs," *ibid.*, (Mar., 1937), p. 5.

National Interracial Conference, sponsored by about twelve organizations. Their attendance helped to promote subsequent conferences. Collins interested Howard Kester and his wife in southern race-relations work, meanwhile; and late in 1929 at Memphis, Kester organized the first of many interracial conferences.* His meetings often were sponsored with the Friends Service Committee. One at Birmingham, Alabama, prompted Ira DeA. Reid of the National Urban League to write that the F.O.R. appeared to be in a better position than anyone else to advance understanding.[58] Kester's responsibilities included also promoting internationalism and industrial justice in the South. He became increasingly involved in economic issues, and after the 1933 crisis he resigned from the council in order to devote himself to the cause of organized labor and tenant farmers. His successor, Claud Nelson, continued to hold interracial conferences, but he devoted more and more attention to the peace emphasis of the Fellowship, especially after 1936 when he gave half of his time to the Emergency Peace Campaign.

Peace became the preeminent concern of the Fellowship in the next half-decade. As Europeans went to war, Americans began to pull out of the economic depression which had precipitated the social struggles of the early thirties. Labor had won legal recognition and was gaining strength, and the question of violence in class war became academic. Pacifists launched a concerted drive for neutrality; organized local, youth, and denominational groups; and lobbied for exemption from military service for conscientious objectors. The impulse toward direct social action continued to exist in the Fellowship, however, although it was temporarily overshadowed by peace work. When the antiwar crusade abated during World War II, it became apparent that the concept of nonviolent action had taken root among a number of pacifists concerned to go beyond educational work with race relations.

In the spring of 1941 the national council of the F.O.R. appointed a committee on nonviolence, headed by J. Holmes Smith, a former missionary to India. Searching for ways to apply the Gandhian approach, the committee experimented with a spiritual center in Harlem, promoted relief for European refugees, and cooperated with Friends who were interested in forming an all-pacifist research committee to study nonviolent action. Smith, in his committee report for 1941, said that the youth conference of the Fellowship had decided to explore non-

* Kester suggested establishing a southern office in 1929. Fearing that the F.O.R. would be regarded as a northern interloper, the council delayed until in Oct., 1930, when an indigenous Southern Advisory Committee was appointed. The following year, Kester was employed as full-time secretary with headquarters in Nashville.

violent action in connection with race-relations issues.[59] An incident in Cleveland that summer epitomized the conjunction of pacifism and the civil-rights movement: young pacifists who had Quaker backgrounds or had studied nonviolence in the abstract were unexpectedly given a chance to test their traditions and theories in experience; young blacks, bent on gaining their rights under the law, happened upon an effective technique.

Seven former Antioch College students had established "Ahimsa Farm," a cooperative about thirty miles from Cleveland which they modeled along the lines of a Gandhian training center for nonviolent living. They studied Shridharani's *War Without Violence* and Gregg's *The Power of Non-Violence*, among other pacifist works. One of them, Lee Stern, was a member of a Young Friends Group in the city. These Quakers had met occasionally with some Negro young people from an Abyssinian Baptist Church in an effort to reach better understanding, the traditional approach to race relations. Upon learning that some of the blacks were determined to get into a customarily segregated swimming pool at Garfield Park, and that they would meet violence with force, the Friends persuaded them to attend a special meeting to discuss the Gandhian approach to conflict. Thus, in the summer of 1941 these young Friends inadvertently found themselves involved in an action project in order to prevent violence from occurring.[60]

They had not made any special study of nonviolence, however, and so Lee Stern brought the situation to the attention of the members of Ahimsa Farm, most of whom belonged also to the F.O.R. They welcomed the project. Stern and one other member went to the special meeting and presented the concept of nonviolence to about thirty Negroes. Although they were very skeptical of the method, the blacks agreed to try it with only those who could remain nonviolent when provoked. Four of them felt that they could qualify.

After another planning session, four blacks and twelve white men (from Ahimsa Farm, the Young Friends, and the local F.O.R.) did get into the pool. The water was crowded with Sunday swimmers seeking relief from the extreme heat of the day. Nevertheless, when the racially mixed group entered the pool everyone else got out and stood around the edge. After a few minutes of swimming the young people left the water, rested a bit on some nearby grass, and then walked slowly to the dressing rooms. For a time they were surrounded by the crowd and narrowly avoided violence.

A new strategy was devised for a second demonstration a few weeks later which was aimed at integration of, not mere entrance to, the pool. Before the interracial group arrived at the park, white young people from a Congregational work camp entered and mixed with the crowd. When their black and white friends got into the water, and agitators urged people to get out as before, the work-campers stayed in. Others followed their example, the crowd became disorganized, and eventually the pool was fully integrated.

Lee Stern and Byron Clark, another Ahimsa Farm member, recounted their successful encounter to a discussion group at the annual conference of the F.O.R. in the fall. The chairman, James Farmer, was elated. Here, it seemed, was proof of a conviction he had held for some time, that nonviolence could be applied profitably to the American civil-rights struggle. In memoranda to A. J. Muste, Farmer proposed organizing an interracial, nonviolent-action movement on a national basis. The F.O.R. concurred in principle, but left the initiative with a group of young Chicago pacifists who founded the Congress of Racial Equality (CORE).[61]

Among the prominent young pacifists in 1941 were James Farmer, secretary of the F.O.R. for the Mid-Atlantic area and then a field worker with youth and on race relations; George Houser, youth secretary of the Chicago F.O.R. and subsequently chairman for F.O.R. action projects in Cleveland; and Bayard Rustin, F.O.R. youth secretary for New York State and, after October, 1942, youth secretary for the Fellowship. Each young man experimented with direct nonviolent resistance in race relations. George Houser led a futile attempt to integrate a Cleveland, Ohio, roller-skating rink in 1942, for example. That same year Rustin, a Negro, defied the Jim Crow rule on an interstate bus going to Nashville, Tennessee, won service in previously discriminatory restaurants, and broke segregation on a Cape May, New Jersey, public swimming beach.[62]

With friends in Chicago they established a Men's Interracial Fellowship House in January, 1924, breaking a restrictive covenant to do so. White members signed the lease, and then the Negroes moved in and successfully resisted eviction. The lease ran out after six months and was not renewed, but a second project was opened in July and lasted at least seven years. An interracial women's residence was founded, too, although it lasted only two years. The Chicago group organized into a Committee of Racial Equality, whose abbreviated name, CORE, suggested its intention "to get at the roots of the problem of discrimination."[63] The committee sponsored a nonviolent demonstration against segregation in the (appropriately named) White City Roller Rink on the city's south side.* It used the sit-in method to integrate small eating places and a downtown restaurant.

Its leaders called a conference for June, 1943, with the endorsement of the Fellowship and brought local groups from seven cities into a National Federation of Committees of Racial Equality.† The next year the national conference at Detroit changed the name to the Congress of Racial Equality. Although CORE was an independent organization for which the F.O.R. took no official responsibility, nonetheless "in practically every instance" it was the F.O.R. members in a locality who took "the initiative in forming the CORE groups and in carrying forward the CORE work."[64] James Farmer was at the same time the national chairman of the Congress of Racial Equality and the race-relations secretary of the Fellowship (1941–45); George Houser was both executive secretary of CORE (1945–57) and race-relations, projects secretary of the F.O.R. (1944–55); Bayard Rustin was an F.O.R. youth and college secretary (1941–52) and active in the War Resisters League and civil-rights movement—he would coordinate the 1963 March on Washington. Thus, the leading staff members of the early CORE were on the payroll of the Fellowship. Until 1957, indeed, the office of CORE was at the F.O.R. headquarters; and the two organizations cooperated closely.

Farmer and Rustin urged through *Fellowship* that the logic of pacifism issues in nonviolent action for civil rights.[65] This conviction and the determination to make progress underlay A. Philip Randolph's March on Washington Movement which was largely responsible for President Roosevelt's appointment of the first Fair Employment Practices Commission in 1941. Two years later, Randolph, head of the Brotherhood of Sleeping-Car Porters, explicitly called for a national "program of non-violent civil disobedience and non-cooperation [which] should include refusal of Negroes to obey any law which violates their basic citizenship rights . . . ."[66]

Nonviolent resisters were not all absolute pacifists in the sense of abjuring international war, nor were all war resisters motivated by an absolute ethic. Many pacifists had serious reservations about the ag-

---

* When persuasion failed to end segregation there, CORE took the case to court under Illinois civil rights law, but when the case came to trial eight months later only three of the original twenty-four participants were still in Chicago, and it was lost.

† The first national chairman was James Farmer and the secretary-treasurer was Bernice Fisher, another F.O.R. member and the first secretary of the Chicago Council Against Racial and Religious Discrimination.

218

gressiveness of direct action; and some objected even to coercion, holding, instead, a nonresistant position. Nevertheless, Farmer, Rustin, and Houser expressed the direction in which the Fellowship of Reconciliation had tended for two decades. They had the faith of Gandhi and Gregg in nonviolent resistance as a method of action which would accept the inevitability of conflict and would seek to resolve it by forcing an opponent to choose a new approximation of justice. They rejected violence because it seemed to defeat the possibility of mutual justice or respect. They found in this view of pacifism an answer to the problems of social action where political power is controlled in the interests of the *status quo*. The necessity of ending racial injustice soon, the inflexibility of democratic institutions, and the danger of violence and counteraction, all seemed as real to them as the imminence of class war had seemed to radical Socialists in 1934.

The line of development from the crisis over the road to Socialist power, through Richard Gregg's articulation of a theory of nonviolent action, to the organization of direct action projects in civil rights pointed beyond World War II. Activists then would be tempted to ignore the fact that CORE's ideological background was:

> interest in pacifism, trade unionism and cooperative communities; inspiration derived from Gandhi's example in India; opposition to the capitalist system; and criticism of legalism as a major strategy in the struggle for civil rights.[67]

Militant leaders of the sixties who doubted the capacity of a predominantly white society to make an equitable and honorable place for its black minority could find, if they wanted to, religious pacifists alongside radicals in the thirties wrestling with the possibilities of a capitalistic system adjusting to real power in the hands of labor. As briefly during World War I and more fully in the sixties, so then during the depression peace and justice were linked not only in the affirmations but also in the dilemmas of the pacifist Fellowship. Nonviolence was interpreted as an alternative to violent change as well as a moral obligation.

This view of pacifism underlay the commitment of liberal pacifists to neutralism. The two notions were analogous to the extent that action-oriented pacifists accepted the clash of economic interests as a model of conflict, and yet repudiated violence as an instrument of either maintaining or overthrowing the *status quo*. Neutralism and nonviolent action were parallel developments of pacifist thought in the thirties, and each reinforced the other. Civil disobedience was not then linked to neutralism, as it would be during the cold war, because in the neu-

219

trality controversy pacifists cultivated popular majorities; direct action was political work. Not all neutralists were pacifists, nor did all pacifists view neutrality as a positive program. Many of them were merely convinced that war was futile or that America was secure in isolation. Nevertheless, leading pacifists came to believe that neutrality was consonant with internationalism and change. They campaigned to keep America both out of war and responsible to the world.

PART FOUR

Before the Next

"Come on in, I'll Treat You Right,
I Used to Know Your Daddy."

Clarence D. Batchelor, of the New York *Daily
News,* won the Pulitzer prize for this cartoon
in 1937.

A Pacifist Rationale for Neutralism

Again I have become the child of an aching heart,
  Carrying the burden of Japan's crime,
Begging the pardon of China and of the world,
  With a shattered soul;
I have become a child of sadness.

—Toyohiko Kagawa[1]

In the last analysis, the test of pacifism was the problem of war. Pacifists derived much of their missionary zeal from their reaction to one world war and their apprehension of a second. They increasingly regarded pacifism as a technique with which to challenge social and economic injustice; but what had it to do with international conflict?

There were, of course, many agencies of international mediation: the League of Nations, the World Court, arbitration, and traditional diplomacy. None of these avenues prevented disputes from arising, however, or replaced war as a court of last resort, while at the same time the world was ripped by forces which seemed to be irreconcilable. Whatever optimism lingered after Versailles was crushed early in the depression years by economic crises, totalitarian regimes, and a mounting arms race. Events in Manchuria and Germany, in Ethiopia and Spain, impelled the American peace movement to unify in order to influence foreign-policy making. The same events unified pacifists behind a program of strict neutrality, however, and therefore spelled the eventual division of the national peace movement as internationalists articulated alternative theories: neutralism and collective security. World peace and order were first challenged in the Far East.

The pacifist editors of the *World Tomorrow* watched the rim of the Pacific for a decade before the Manchurian crisis. They were in close touch with Y.M.C.A. and missionary people in the Orient. They hailed the rise of Chinese nationalism and supported demands for the abroga-

223

tion of European privileges. In Japan, they reported, a conservative military faction anxious to rival Western imperialism was contending with middle-class leaders eager to emulate Western liberalism. The pacifist editors were aware of the economic and population problems of Japan, and they criticized American policies on immigration restriction, naval armaments, continued occupation of the Philippines, and commercial rivalry which were used by Japanese militants to symbolize Western animosity. During the twenties the editors expected that the militarist and conservative party of Japan would be overthrown, and they largely ignored China as an issue in Japanese-American relations, but they were prepared to grasp the significance of aggression in Manchuria in September, 1931.

Sherwood Eddy was in Mukden when Japanese troops occupied it on the pretext of protecting the Southern Manchurian Railroad. As soon as he could get to Tientsin he cabled Kirby Page, asking him to inform Senator Borah and Secretary of State Henry L. Stimson that local evidence pointed to a carefully premeditated attack by the Japanese army. The situation was critical, he wired:

ALL ORIENT LOOKING TO KELLOGG PACT SIGNATORIES AND LEAGUE OF NATIONS FOR ACTION STOP ASIA BELIEVES PACT AND LEAGUE ARE ON TRIAL AS WELL AS JAPAN AND CHINA[2]

The League was on trial in the minds of many pacifists, too, as Japanese forces captured the eastern provinces of Manchuria, landed at Shanghai, and drove back the Chinese army. By February, Japan had established Manchukuo as a virtual protectorate, and the sensitive pacifist, Toyohiko Kagawa, asked his people, "What will you do with the whole world's hate? Shall you not awaken until you have been beaten down and crushed like Germany?"[3]

The editors of the *World Tomorrow* also interpreted the Japanese attack as the continued threat of militarism. That it was a pathway "deeply grooved" by Western imperialists and that Japan was economically dependent on Manchuria did not seem to them to mitigate the enormity of her criminal effort to capitalize on world confusion and Chinese weakness. Her aggression would stimulate further Chinese resistance, they predicted, and would threaten world peace.[4] The editors called upon the League of Nations and the United States government to "demand the cessation of armed fighting and to set in operation the processes of pacific settlements of this controversy." The League should assure Japan that property and life in Manchuria would be protected, they said; it should insist that Japanese troops be recalled to the Southern Manchurian Railroad zone within a specified time. It should back this demand with the warning that its members would break diplomatic relations if Japan remained recalcitrant, and as a last resort, they would institute an economic boycott of certain Japanese goods. A total blockade should not be effected, though, since it would threaten millions of innocent people with starvation and would be a kind of warfare.[5]

The peace movement as a whole was "far more sensitive to Manchuria than was the rest of the nation," as one historian has concluded, and at first the pacifist wing was especially militant.[6] In fact, James G. McDonald, chairman of the Foreign Policy Association and the Interorganization Council on Disarmament, was "shocked and horrified by the willingness of so-called radicals and pacifists to jump into the use of sanctions almost without thinking."[7] A number of them wanted the United States to recall its ambassador from Japan, and Dorothy Detzer called for the withdrawal of all Western ambassadors. The Women's International League would not endorse her plan, but it did urge vigorous diplomatic action and direct consultation with other powers. Miss Detzer conferred often with State Department officials during the fall, but they could not assuage her apprehension—born perhaps of her flair for the dramatic—of a covert understanding to treat Japan with moderation in order to further American national interests. Insistently, she demanded the publication of diplomatic correspondence and urged that the Kellogg-Briand Pact and the Nine Power Treaty of 1922 be invoked against the Japanese. The pacifist-oriented Emergency Peace Committee also wanted the Kellogg-Briand and Nine Power agreements employed, and it would have sent a delegation to Stimson except that the larger Interorganization Council agreed on September 29 to do so.[8]

Peace advocates were as nearly united as they ever became in favor of cooperation with the League of Nations in vigorous diplomatic sanctions. Early in November the Interorganization Council on Disarmament unanimously endorsed collaboration with the League, asked that the United States be represented at the council meeting of the world organization, and proposed an "investigation by an international commission of inquiry."[9] The League of Nations Association naturally viewed the crisis as proof of the League's importance, but even the national board of the W.I.L.P.F. called for American cooperation in any peaceful (diplomatic) venture, relying upon the League to contain the Far Eastern conflict. Pacifist Frederick Libby wrote that the State Department's "confused" quibbling about seating arrangements at

225

Geneva and its semi-independent activities there were not enough to produce the strong antiwar measures so obviously required.[10] The Secretary of State was necessarily more cautious than the peace advocates; the hesitant consultation in Geneva which he authorized won their endorsement without satisfying them. Accordingly, the Stimson Doctrine of January 7, 1932, that the United States would not recognize any territorial change made in violation of treaties to which it was a party—the Kellogg-Briand and Nine Power treaties, for example—was a popular one. A few pacifists demurred, fearing that the statement would exacerbate rather than reconcile the Japanese, but the Emergency Peace Committee, the National Council for Prevention of War, the Interorganization Council, and most other peace groups were enthusiastic about the doctrine.

They were all the more dismayed, therefore, when Japanese units attacked Shanghai at the end of January, indiscriminately bombing and strafing civilians. The consensus behind the Stimson Doctrine broke down in view of the apparent failure of nonrecognition to do more than preserve American integrity. Pressure mounted for direct action in the form of economic sanctions. In February, President A. Lawrence Lowell of Harvard University drafted and circulated a petition to the President and the Congress advocating American cooperation with any sanctions the League might employ. In March an American Boycott Association began to promote a consumer's boycott of Japanese goods which would second the boycott already initiated in China. Influential pacifists divided over the use of economic coercion.

A number of pacifists—Kirby Page, for one, Norman Thomas, Sherwood Eddy, and Reinhold Niebuhr—advocated some sort of economic coercion to force Japan to arbitrate. Page argued that nonviolent pressure was the only alternative to increasing exploitation: "In an imperfect and developing world suffering is inescapable. The policy is to use that method which involves a minimum of suffering with a maximum of redemption."[11] The F.O.R. had agreed in November that the United States should "not obstruct" the League's application of economic sanctions, and after the bombing of Shanghai it approved a consumer's boycott of Japanese goods.[12] The pacifist Emergency Peace Committee called upon Secretary Stimson to extend his policies to include cooperation with the League in an embargo on military goods, restrictions on loans and credits to Japan, and "as ultimate measures," refusal to clear Japanese imports or shipments destined for Japan, excepting foods.[13] The W.I.L.P.F. concurred in principle, although as

226

an organization it refused to endorse the boycott. Dorothy Detzer and Ray Newton personally commended these measures to the State Department. Indeed, for a time in February, the peace movement thought the administration was drifting toward the collective use of economic sanctions against Japan, and an influential group of pacifists seemed to be in the vanguard of this movement.

Other pacifists—John Haynes Holmes, for example, Emily Greene Balch, William I. Hull, John Nevin Sayre and most Quaker groups— feared that even the veiled threat implied by nonrecognition had only hardened Japanese militarism. Their inherent distrust of coercion confirmed by the event, as they thought, they henceforth approached international conflict in "the spirit of persuasion, conciliation, and mutual understanding."[14] One student of the period concluded that "those peace leaders who saw the world primarily in terms of inescapable struggle [whether influenced by Marxist theories of social conflict or by theological doctrines of total depravity] looked with far greater favor upon certain types of coercion than those individuals who viewed the historical process as invariably leading towards greater cooperation."[15]

There is a measure of truth in this division of pacifist opinion, and it was exploited by critics such as Reinhold Niebuhr, who subsequently accused pacifists of being naïve idealists. But it is inadequate as an explanation of pacifist support for neutrality legislation. Some of those most influenced by Marxist analysis became increasingly suspicious of economic coercion, as Devere Allen did. Some others who were most predisposed to persuasion objected to a discriminatory boycott for very practical reasons. Nevin Sayre, for one, had sponsored in the Interorganizational Council a resolution for an "economic boycott against Japan" in cooperation with the League.[16] He gave up the idea in November, 1931, when Secretary Stimson told him that economic sanctions could easily lead to war, that he counted on public opinion and wise diplomacy, and that if a boycott were employed he would feel as though he "had lost his battle." Thereafter, Sayre advocated measures applied equally against both belligerents.[17] In any case, as leading pacifists evaluated the economic boycott they articulated a *political* point of view that would underlie their promotion of neutrality legislation.

For one thing, they found the public unwilling to venture abroad in the interest of international justice. From a friend in Shanghai, Kirby Page received an urgent appeal to awake the American conscience to the necessity of direct action against Japan. He replied, sadly, "We have been moving heaven and earth to arouse a public opinion, but with distressing lack of success."[18] Frederick Libby, who had urged strong measures in the fall, wavered in the spring. Official sanctions would divide the country politically, he said, and a voluntary consumer's boycott which he rather favored would be effective only if accompanied by a campaign of hate, which he deplored. Nevin Sayre felt that pacifists were pitted against "militarists" for control of public opinion on naval expansion and imperialism. He implied that a boycott could too easily become an instrument of distinctly national interest.[19] Perhaps pacifists sensed the seed of isolation underlying national antiwar sentiment. Had they failed to inculcate transnational values in the popular mind? If so, then pressure for coercive economic sanctions could divide the peace movement and even contribute to militant nationalism.

More important, the Manchurian crisis seemed to reveal the futility of relying on the League of Nations as a force for international justice. A few voices—the *Nation* and the *New Republic,* for instance—had been skeptical from the first, but the majority of pacifists who had rallied to the League also became disenchanted with it. Sherwood Eddy wrote from Shanghai even before the bombing that the League had raised hopes by voting for Japan to evacuate, and then had dashed them by crawling "completely down."[20] Paul Porter, a field secretary for the League for Industrial Democracy, came back from Manchuria and said flatly that the "league of imperialist powers" would be unable to avert war.[21] Japan appeared to defy world opinion by ruthlessly attacking Shanghai, and she did defy the League by withdrawing from it after its Lytton Report branded her an aggressor. The League of Nations, more cautious than even the State Department all along, was virtually powerless. Pacifists increasingly lost hope in it, and followed Kirby Page's analysis that it was little more than an alliance for its members' interests. Years later, when Nazi warplanes multiplied Shanghai's horror in Warsaw, Charles Clayton Morrison recalled that the principle of collective security had broken down in Manchuria. In the absence of a working international system, he said, a discriminatory embargo or anything else but strict neutrality was clearly an alliance in war.[22]

If the Manchurian crisis led articulate pacifists to reappraise the American antiwar public and the League of Nations, it stimulated them also to look more closely into the developing totalitarian state. Nevin Sayre received a constant flow of information from Japan, principally from an astute Presbyterian minister, Theodore Walser. By January 6, 1932, Walser had concluded, "there seems no hope now of blunting the edge of the sword, so to speak. The military have taken control of things." He agreed with the position taken by the F.O.R. and the Inter-organization Council in trying to get the United States to act decisively in the fall, but he added:

> I feel that the USA has done enough. At times, I have felt that the pressure from the USA exerted to influence the Japanese Government has stiffened the opposition here and strengthened the forces of militarism. The reason for this has been, I think, that the record of the USA in the same "dirty business" of economic imperialism is so bad that pressure against Japanese imperialism is not received with very good grace.[23]

Walser's letters reached numerous pacifist leaders—Nevin Sayre, Frederick Libby, Kirby Page, Raymond Wilson, and others—and they gradually unfolded a picture of Japanese military figures manipulating international affairs, including the imperialist image of the United States, in order to secure domestic power. He sent his notes through friends because the mail was censored. Freedom of speech was curtailed. He and the Japanese pacifists were living "in more or less of a 'Reign of Terror.' "[24] They heard rumors of pacifists being killed or imprisoned. Police kept them under surveillance, questioned them, and caused them to lose their jobs. There was no excuse for illusion.

Meanwhile, Walser and Japanese F.O.R. members supplied their American friends with detailed, confidential accounts of the political struggle of the military for control of civil government in Japan. Long documents described the dispute. In the spring of 1932, when the outcome was still in doubt, Walser enthusiastically welcomed the prospect of a peace commission from the American F.O.R. Its position of opposition to American imperialism and militarism was well known, he wrote, and if it came repentantly but fortified with facts, its witness might be used by the rapidly waning liberal faction. No other American group, including the church, would be as welcome. The F.O.R. was unable to finance the project, and friends of peace in Japan found themselves "losing ground rapidly." By the end of the year, Walser reported, "Military control is almost complete." Student military training was being taken seriously, he wrote; every excuse was used to excite the popular mind; a thoroughly fascist government seemed to be in the wind; and both militarism and communism were growing in China. "I am convinced that nothing short of world wide (League plus the USA plus the USSR) non-violent coercion of Japan (through diplomatic and economic sanctions), animated by a spirit of love and sacrifice, will save the situation," he concluded.[25] Those who read his letters had reason by then to doubt that either public opinion or international organization was capable of such a solution.

 . . . the problems of American neutrality which confronted Woodrow Wilson at the beginning of the World War were very much like the problems which face the Administration today . . . .

—FRANKLIN D. ROOSEVELT

. . . many factors [are] being taken into consideration especially the factor of public opinion in this country . . . . the United States is definitely committed to a policy of not becoming entangled and of avoiding being drawn into any orbit of hostilities . . . .

—CORDELL HULL[26]

The Far Eastern crisis eroded American diplomacy of some of the moral rhetoric that stamped the Kellogg-Briand Pact and even the Stimson Doctrine. It exposed a bedrock of isolationism, a pervasive reluctance to make commitments abroad. Applying that principle in a world again at war led to the divisive issue of neutrality and revealed the fault line of American foreign policy. The traditional view of neutrality was that America had a right as a neutral to trade freely on the seas (at least she had insisted that Germany grant that right, and she went to war partly in defense of it). That doctrine weathered almost beyond recognition after World War I. It was upheld in the thirties by a resolute few, notably Professors Edwin Borchard and John Bassett Moore, but most American leaders abandoned it for one of two new approaches.

Many advocated strict, or impartial, neutrality. The right to trade freely could not be guaranteed under the conditions of modern warfare, they argued. A nation which desired to remain at peace in the midst of total war must abnegate its chance to profit from the conflict and must maintain a strictly neutral, uninvolved stance. Secretary of State William Jennings Bryan had taken this position until at least March, 1915, of course; in the thirties it was clearly enunciated by Charles Warren, an international lawyer and former attorney general (1914–18); and it was championed in the Senate by Gerald P. Nye, among others. An alternative policy was gradually articulated by a number of leaders including James Shotwell and Norman Davis (a close friend and adviser of Cordell Hull and chairman of the American delegation to the Geneva Disarmament Conference). By cooperating with other nations in the use of diplomatic and economic sanctions against aggressor states, they claimed, neutral parties might halt or at least contain conflict. This policy was set off as an alternative to strict neutrality in the Far Eastern crisis, and it came to be known as collective security.

No one of these three alternatives was entirely satisfactory. Traditional neutrality had the virtue of preserving national sovereignty and the right to trade, but it was almost certain to be violated and to lead to war. Strict neutrality had the advantage of keeping the nation out of conflict altogether, but it did so at the double price of surrendering both the right to trade with belligerents and the privilege of influencing world affairs by restraining an aggressor nation. The policy of employing discriminatory embargoes in pursuit of collective security had the advantage of allowing the government to oppose aggression elsewhere in concert with other nations and without fighting, but it was decidedly unneutral in fact, and the attempt to make economic sanctions effective might well lead to military ones. In order to remain strictly neutral, it seemed, the nation would have to surrender its influence until in a general war it might have to fight in self-defense. But in order to prevent a war from becoming general, the country would have to run the risk of fighting in disputes to which it was not a party.

The neutrality controversy raised another question related to the issue of impartial versus discriminatory embargoes: should policy be mandatory or discretionary—how far should foreign policy be prescribed by law and how much left in the hands of the administration? There was in the thirties a powerful mistrust of executive initiative in making foreign policy. It was a suspicion born of the widespread feeling that Wilson had drifted into an unnecessary First World War; it was compounded by the experience of successful assertions of congressional authority in opposition to American entry into the League of Nations and the World Court; and it was strengthened by the reticence of Republican Presidents and even Roosevelt himself, at first, to exert leadership in foreign affairs. In the crucial years of 1937–39 this distrust was increased by the resentment harbored by many legislators for Roosevelt's domestic policies, his attempt to pack the Supreme Court, and his interference in congressional elections. Much of the State Department's time was spent in trying to mollify Congress, and much of

231

Roosevelt's hesitation in foreign policy can be attributed to his fear of losing domestic programs.

Disagreement over impartial versus discriminatory embargoes, reluctance to trust the administration with discretionary authority, and Roosevelt's refusal to be bound by Congress—all combined with hesitancy in the State Department—forestalled the passage of neutrality legislation until 1935, when the peace groups assumed the initiative on behalf of strict neutrality.

The peace movement broke with traditional neutral rights and supported legislation permitting discretionary embargoes which was introduced in 1929 by Senator Arthur Capper of Kansas and Congressman Hamilton Fish of New York. Their resolutions deployed restrictions on trade in arms (already widely regarded as a source of involvement) in support of collective action against aggressors. James Shotwell spoke for the League of Nations Non-Partisan Association and indicated the future direction of the Carnegie-supported societies when he wrote that "the fundamental problem is surely just what it has always been, namely, to orient the United States with the League."[27] That orientation was a basic objective of pacifists, too, but no more so than preventing American involvement in a future war. The negative sanction embodied in the Capper resolution appeared to meet both objectives, and so it was supported by the Fellowship of Reconciliation and the Women's International League. Senator Borah introduced a resolution in 1931 which would have empowered the President to embargo any nation, provided only that other arms-producing countries agreed. His bill was given its most effective support by the peace movement, including the W.I.L.P.F., F.O.R., and N.C.P.W., which viewed it as a measure of American cooperation to prevent war and suppress traffic in munitions. According to historian Robert Divine, its defeat was owing largely to the combination of the munitions lobby and the isolationist bloc in Congress.[28]

In the last months of his tenure in office, Secretary of State Stimson mounted another campaign for discretionary neutrality, legislation which would permit the President to lay an arms embargo upon one or another nation. Hoover gave him only limited support, but the peace societies were enthusiastic lobbyists. Legislation was blocked in the Senate by Hiram Bingham of Connecticut and an alert munitions lobby, but Stimson secured a parallel resolution in the House from Congressman Samuel D. McReynolds of Tennessee. The State Department supported the bill there, insisting that it was directed solely toward the

232

undeclared Chaco war between Bolivia and Paraguay which had broken out in the summer of 1932, but a number of congressmen became convinced that it was actually directed toward Japan. McReynolds got a favorable committee report only after an amendment limiting the legislation to the Western Hemisphere had been wrung from him by Hamilton Fish, who had reversed his position on neutrality. Even then, the House failed to act on the measure. Stimson's chagrin was the greater because he had hoped, in fact, to have the embargo in the executive department's limited arsenal of measures applicable to the Far East.

His successor, Cordell Hull, was reluctant to become committed to a discretionary embargo. There were domestic issues far more important to the administration, he knew; and if presidential discretion had to be sacrificed in an overt test of strength, the instruments of foreign policy would be restricted still further. A new resolution by McReynolds was accepted by the Democratic majority of his committee, though, and Hull gave it public support with which it passed the House by a large and partisan majority.

Meanwhile, and as consideration passed to the Senate, Norman Davis won permission from Hull and Roosevelt to make a policy statement at the Geneva Disarmament Conference that the United States would promise to consult with other powers in the event of international conflict and, further, to refrain from obstructing collective sanctions if it agreed upon the aggressor party. Some such pledge was necessary to reassure the French and to revive the conference, and anyway it accorded with the inclinations of Davis and his friends in the League of Nations Non-Partisan Association. He liked to call it a negative declaration which would preserve American unilateral sovereignty; but isolationists saw in it the genesis of collective security and involvement. On May 24, two days after Davis committed the administration to this policy, Senator Hiram W. Johnson of California undermined it by amending the original neutrality resolution so that any embargo would have to apply equally to all belligerents. Unaccountably, and without even talking to Hull, the President concurred. The Foreign Relations Committee favorably reported the amended resolution to the Senate.

Confronted with a potential diplomatic explosion, Hull pulled back and the President agreed to drop the matter altogether. The State Department was not really agreed upon what neutrality legislation it desired, but it was perfectly clear that it could not allow the Davis

233

statement to be explicitly repudiated or its own power to be defined in advance by Congress. It postponed the issue in order to retain a modicum of initiative, and in so doing it disappointed the peace movement.

Frederick Libby and the National Council, among others, wanted the new administration to support both the World Court and the Disarmament Conference. He and his staff were in close touch with Capitol Hill and the State Department, and were lining up legislative support on both issues. Libby agreed with Joseph Greene, who had written the original embargo resolution sponsored by Borah, that the Johnson Amendment would undermine Norman Davis and the Disarmament Conference. He preferred the Borah resolution and urged the public to give the President "the power to embargo shipments of war materials to any country when and if it is deemed advisable to do so" and in cooperation with other nations.[29] Privately, Libby admitted that the progress made thus far had been "worth working for."[30] If genuine disarmament could not be obtained, then strict neutrality seemed all the more important. He got neither that year. On June 5 he phoned Undersecretary of State William Phillips. "Any progress on the World Court?" he asked. "I would rather not answer." Libby pursued: "Will the arms embargo come up for passage in this session?" Phillips replied, "I doubt if [we] hear any more of it, but please do not quote me." A week later he told Libby frankly that both the Court and the embargo were out for the session.[31]

For a time it looked as though the State Department would have to go through its retrieval act again the following year, when on February 28, 1934, the Senate adopted the strict, or impartial, arms embargo that had been on its calendar for nine months. Hull secured McReynolds's promise to block it in the House, although he was under increasing pressure from League of Nations members to support a proposed embargo of Paraguay and Bolivia. At length, both houses were persuaded to pass legislation which was impartial, empowering the President to embargo arms to all belligerents, but was limited to the Chaco war.

Now acutely aware of the pitfalls in treating neutrality on an ad hoc basis, the State Department set out to write definitive legislation. The committee which Hull created for that purpose commissioned an exhaustive study by Charles Warren. In his report, Warren recalled World War I and recommended that upon the outbreak of future conflicts an impartial embargo of arms be placed upon all belligerents, and he added a number of detailed recommendations designed to protect the strict neutrality of the United States. The Warren report was submitted to the President and summarized by R. Walton Moore, who himself had worked for a strict embargo in the House when he was a congressman and in the State Department when he joined it in the summer of 1933. Moore suggested an alteration in the Warren report which became the basis for later battles with isolationists: he proposed that the legislation should be permissive; it should give the President the authority to apply it at his discretion.[32] Otherwise, the legislation that was evolved in the State Department in the fall of 1934 was largely a refined version of the Warren memorandum, and it provided that:

> Whenever, during any war in which the United States is neutral, the President finds that the public interest requires . . . he may, in his discretion, make proclamation thereof, and it shall thereafter be unlawful to export . . . to such country or countries he may designate . . . .
>
> Provided, however, that any prohibition of exports, or of sale for export, shall apply equally to all belligerents . . . .[33]

The State Department was still wavering when Congress convened in 1935, however. Its draft legislation had been criticized by the navy on several grounds (for one thing, the navy objected to prohibiting the use of the American flag on belligerent vessels on the grounds that "any artifice to deceive an enemy, not amounting to perfidy" had been considered "legitimate" for hundreds of years, and that the United States had "often" used the flags of neutrals for deception).[34] Perhaps more important, strict neutrality was criticized within the circle of State Department advisers, particularly by Norman Davis who was still firmly committed to nonobstruction of collective security, even though he disclaimed any desire to "get mixed in or take sides on any European political questions."[35] Thus, Hull entered the legislative year without a consensus. He could not give the President firm leadership, nor could he expect it from Roosevelt. The President identified pacifists as isolationists, and he distrusted their "wild-eyed measures to keep us out of war."[36] He was aware of a "large and increasing" pressure for neutrality legislation, though, and was not clear about the turn he wanted to take. Most of all he wanted executive freedom, but he was prepared to compromise even that in 1935. The administration was prepared only to dodge the question of neutrality. The situation was ripe for aggressive congressional initiative at just the time that pacifist-oriented groups became virtually unanimous in pressing for strict and mandatory neutrality legislation.

The F.O.R. had just emerged from a crisis over the use of force in the social struggle, and its leaders had a renewed dedication to nonviolence. The W.I.L.P.F. had expended great energies in the now futile

235

disarmament campaign. The N.C.P.W. was still divided over neutrality, but its Washington staff increasingly favored impartial and mandatory legislation. The revelations of the Nye committee (itself so largely a product of pacifist efforts), the failure of the Geneva Disarmament Conference, defeat on the World Court issue, the collapse of collective security in the Far East and then in Ethiopia and Spain, the rise of Hitler, and the haunting specter of another European war—all these things strengthened the case for neutrality, in the opinion of pacifists. The time when concerted action might prevent war was rapidly passing, they concluded. They began to speak freely of the likelihood of another war, and they set to work to keep America out of it. Their most effective program was the formulation and popularization of neutrality legislation.

The bills which Senators Gerald P. Nye and Bennett Champ Clark and Congressmen Maury Maverick and Frank Kloeb introduced in the spring of 1935 included a ban on Americans traveling in war zones or in enemy vessels; prohibition of loans or credits to belligerents; and a discretionary, limited embargo on other goods. The Nye-Clark resolutions stemmed directly from the considerations of the Nye committee. The President, again without consulting Hull, had encouraged the committee to extend its considerations to neutrality, but Senator Key Pittman's Foreign Relations Committee insisted on its own prerogative. Nye acquiesced willingly. His committee would gladly "wash its hands of the whole question," he said, but that did not mean he wanted the issue itself dropped.[37] Indeed, he and Clark introduced resolutions which were sent to Pittman's committee, and then with Maverick he spearheaded months of adroit political maneuvering to bring the legislation onto the floor for decision. The President and the State Department found themselves on the defensive in the face of clever leadership in Congress which was fully coordinated with the mobilization of public opinion.

Staff members of the National Council for Prevention of War planned much of the campaign. They gathered material, wrote speeches, and sponsored radio talks by members of Congress. They flooded the press with neutrality propaganda through *Peace Action* and special releases (and Libby even won limited encouragement from Arthur Sulzberger of the not-too-friendly New York *Times*). They largely arranged the June 18 congressional hearing on the Maverick resolution. They used contacts with labor and civic groups built up in successive disarmament drives. With the F.O.R. and W.I.L.P.F. the National Council urged members of its constituent groups to write, wire, and speak for the bills. These three organizations dominated a fledgling coalition of pacifist and nonpacifist groups, the National Peace Conference. Although its member groups were divided on the question of impartial embargoes, the Peace Conference was persuaded to sponsor a mass meeting at Carnegie Hall in New York City at which perhaps 2,500 persons listened to Nye, Clark, and Maverick warn of impending war and insist on legislating America out of it.[38] Even the Federal Council of Churches resolved in favor of withholding material from all belligerents in future wars. A vocal part of the public was aroused on the neutrality issue. Its influence was felt in Congress, and its impact was not weakened, as it had been in the World Court campaign, by a division between isolationists and internationalists.

The problem was to bring the legislation to a vote, where public opinion would count. Toward the end of the session twenty senators threatened to filibuster in order to get consideration of neutrality. They actually began on August 20, but after about three hours Senator Pittman arrived with a comprehensive bill which the Foreign Relations Committee had approved. It passed the next day. Meanwhile, the N.C.P.W. was lobbying in the House. Jeanette Rankin of the N.C.P.W. wrote personal letters to 175 congressmen, imploring them not to adjourn without settling American policy regarding foreign war. About 35 replied promptly that they would not. With this encouragement, she and Warren Mullin stationed themselves at the door to the chamber, spoke to congressmen as they went in and out for roll call votes, and suggested that they go directly to McReynolds about the Pittman bill.[39] Maury Maverick and Fred Sisson led a 10-man delegation which sought an interview with the President. Rebuffed at first, they got 100 congressmen to sign a petition pledging not to adjourn until mandatory legislation was passed, and won their interview. The Pittman bill would pass, they told Roosevelt, if it were not held up in committee, and they were determined to have it. At length the President withdrew his opposition on the condition that the embargo feature of the legislation should extend only to February 29, 1936. On that basis neutrality legislation was accepted by the House without a recorded vote.

The Neutrality Act of 1935 provided that upon the outbreak of war the President should proclaim the fact, and that then an embargo on arms and implements of war should be applied to all belligerents. The President was allowed discretion in defining war, arms, and implements of war, and in applying the embargo to other states entering a conflict.

The act created a National Munitions Control Board, headed by the Secretary of State, to license and supervise the munitions trade. The act prohibited the carrying of munitions in American ships to belligerents or to neutral ports for transshipment to belligerents. It gave the President discretionary power to warn citizens that they would travel on belligerent ships at their own risk.[40]

This act of 1935 was a fundamental revision of American neutrality policy. It abnegated traditional rights to trade in arms with warring powers in favor of strict neutrality and keeping out of war. Still, it gave the President much discretionary authority. Several neutrality measures were introduced in 1936, but the very diversity of plans seemed to divide both the peace movement and the State Department. As a result, the 1935 legislation was extended to May 1, 1937, with a few amendments which made it somewhat more mandatory and impartial.* Even though American neutralism had been basically altered, therefore, pacifists were far from complacent. They faced a three-fold challenge: they would have to counteract those peace societies which, like the League of Nations Association, were promoting a limited and discretionary embargo that could be used for concerted action with other nations; they expected to face an administration bent on winning more independence for itself, if not outright repeal of the embargo; and they were determined to extend the mandatory embargo to include raw materials. Like their opponents, they were responding to events abroad.

> Our quarrel with the use of economic sanctions now is not a theoretical one, but is based on a belief that the use of economic sanctions suggests a world which we have in no sense as yet approached.
>
> ... there is no way as yet, under the present organization of the world, to make economic sanctions effective, or indeed to bring forward any plan that is effective in stopping a war once it has started . . . . What governments seem to be doing is to proceed along lines that are almost certain to

* The 1936 amendments prohibited granting loans or credits to belligerents, denied the President the authority to restrict shipments of raw materials, made mandatory the previously discretionary power to embargo states entering a war in progress, and protected the Monroe Doctrine by exempting from embargo American republics at war with non-American states unless "cooperating with a non-American state or states in such a war." See Divine, *Illusion of Neutrality*, pp. 122–59, for detailed treatment of the 1936 legislation.

238

> make peace impossible, and then to put their peoples in the
> hole, when trouble does break out, of trying to reverse the
> process at the time when it is least possible to do so.
>
> —DEVERE ALLEN, 1937[41]

As Ethiopia fell before mechanized Roman legions beginning in the
fall of 1935, as Spain was rent by civil war the following year, and as
Austria and Czechoslovakia were absorbed into the Nazi empire in
1938, pacifist leaders considered their impressions of the international
scene confirmed. In each case the operation of power politics was revealed in both aggression and the world response to it. The League of
Nations and the idea of collective security to prevent war seemed to
fail each successive test. Even more disturbing than these individual
failures was the over-all trend of affairs: from a simple case of imperialism in Africa, conflict broadened to an ideological contest in the
Iberian Peninsula and culminated in a fascist threat to both democracy
and the Western alliance system in central Europe.

A pacifist rationale for American neutralism emerged in response
to those events. It was articulated largely by a few individuals, including Kirby Page, Devere Allen, Harold Fey, Frederick Libby, Dorothy Detzer, A. J. Muste, John Nevin Sayre, Reinhold Niebuhr, Charles
Clayton Morrison, and Norman Thomas.* Their views were widely
disseminated through articles, books, pamphlets, and the official statements of their organizations. Most rank-and-file pacifists probably
cannot be said to have had a systematic interpretation of international
affairs, but they do seem to have appropriated many of the ideas and
catch phrases of their leaders. So, too, did critics of pacifism; and for
this reason criticisms often bore little relevance to systematic pacifist
thought.

Articulate pacifists held that the semineutrality of the Western powers was predictable because of the operation of economic interests and
power politics. They found pious professions of neutrality and national
righteousness insufferable. They sensed that in fact the great powers
were making world war more nearly inevitable by rejecting explicit

---

* Niebuhr contributed to the analysis of Germany in the early thirties when
he could not conceive of supporting a war; he subsequently swung to collective
security and proved to be the pacifists' sharpest critic after 1939. Thomas was
not an absolute pacifist, at least not after the Spanish Civil War, but he was
adamantly against American participation in any war and against violent class
revolution. His political leadership and his ideas won for him an audience
beyond his party.

239

but nonviolent aid to the victims of fascist aggression. So-called collective security without a commitment to transnational values was nothing but a synonym for alliance, they said. Their neutralism was reinforced by their futile search for ways to strengthen democracy in nonfascist nations without committing the world to war.

In this respect the Italian invasion of Ethiopia raised again the question of using economic sanctions against an aggressor, an issue which had been broached in the Manchurian affair. About 300 pacifists discussed it at the twentieth annual conference of the Fellowship of Reconciliation in Bound Brook, New Jersey, about two months after the Italian offensive began. A considerable majority of members there opposed the use of economic policy as a coercive instrument of diplomacy. Some favored the use of economic but not military sanctions, arguing that one did not necessitate the other. Sherwood Eddy supported an economic boycott even if it should lead to war, but Eddy was drifting away from pacifism. More representative was the statement of an unofficial committee which repudiated military sanctions, objected to a League police force, and questioned the wisdom of economic reprisals. It held that an embargo would not be supported with unanimity, would have to be backed up by military force, and if effective would be an act of war. There was no quick cure for aggression, the committee admitted.[42]

The Fellowship did urge that neutrality legislation be invoked, and that if the flow of munitions were cut off from the belligerents, exports of subsidiary materials such as oil and steel should be stopped, too. Otherwise neutrality would favor Italy. The Women's International League and the National Council took similar positions, and as a matter of fact, the State Department would have preferred to do so. It advised only a "moral" embargo on war materials. The fact that full economic sanctions were not invoked even after the League of Nations Council declared that Italy was an aggressor confirmed Norman Thomas, Devere Allen, and Kirby Page in their view that the foreign policy of all the major powers was profoundly influenced by their own economic interests. Since imposition of economic sanctions under ARTICLE XVI of the League Covenant implied a willingness to back them with military support, Page concluded that the whole system was inoperable unless the vested interests of the most powerful members were directly threatened. That is to say, the League was necessarily ineffective in preserving peace; at most, it could unite nations in a defensive war.[43] A pacifist wrote early in 1937:

240

The European sky has been deeply overcast the last few months. The defeat of the League and the triumph of militarism in Abyssinia was a harder blow to peace-workers than the tragedy of Manchuria. It exposed the hollow unreality of the "collective system," and proved, like Hitler's remilitarization of the Rhineland, the success of diplomacy by the *fait accompli*.[44]

Many pacifists were profoundly shaken by civil war in Spain. That conflict seemed even more tragic than the Ethiopian one because it represented a more explicit attack on democracy and a repudiation of peaceful change. Aggression was broadened from imperialism into an ideological struggle. But the failure of the Western powers to support democratic Spain seemed to be as predictable as their failure to thwart Italian expansion. Pacifists across the country were disturbed. "How do you analyze the Spanish situation?" they asked. "Is it possible to hold to a philosophy of non-violence . . . where a duly constituted government representing a progressive tendency is attacked by counter-revolutionaries?"[45] It was a question that demanded an answer.

A number of leaders, like Devere Allen, A. J. Muste, and Norman Thomas, felt especially close to the Spanish scene because of their labor and socialist connections. Allen even had been in Madrid during the 1931 revolution. General Francisco Franco's attack on the Republic presaged Adolf Hitler's absorption of Czechoslovakia, and pacifists did not feel neutral in either case, even though they did not countenance armed resistance.

According to some of them, the trouble with the Spanish revolution was that it had never been completed. The revolutionaries had not reorganized the army nor liberated the Moors; they had lost peasant support because of their failure to effect land reform; they had won the bitter opposition of the church. More important, they had not been able to close their own ranks. They succumbed to the Nationalists because they could not govern, because democracy was not yet strong in Spain. A. J. Muste concluded that the revolutionaries should not have taken the field against Franco, but rather let him come to power. They might have refused any cooperation, challenged him to make good on the problems of the Spanish masses, and agitated his regime. The pacifist leader argued that Franco might have been toppled, as several previous rightist regimes had been, and that at least the country would not have been plunged into fratricidal civil war. Moreover, he continued, it would have been difficult for Franco to bring the Moorish army into Spain or to secure overt support from Hitler and Benito Mussolini.

241

Finally, Spain could hardly have been made such a helpless victim of the international power struggle as she had become.[46] H. Runham Brown, Jessie Wallace Hughan, Kirby Page, John Haynes Holmes, and Devere Allen tended to agree with Muste, although Allen was not sanguine about the frailty of a rightist dictatorship. Norman Thomas denied that there was any background in Spain for a "Ghandi-like resistance to fascism."[47]

In the light of this analysis, and in view of the Loyalists' prosecution of the war, some pacifists sought ways to strengthen the Spanish Republic without involving other nations in war. On the one hand, they contributed to and administered funds for Spanish relief. On the other, they urged that neutrality laws be applied to Germany and Italy as well as to the Loyalists and Nationalists. They assumed that the Spanish government could put down the rebellion if it were not for outside help that Franco received. They complained that Allied "nonintervention" was hypocritical and pathetic, that America's pseudoneutrality actually benefited the Nationalists. They asserted that in the Spanish Civil War, as in the Ethiopian crisis, the Western democracies elevated their own national interests and called them principles. They sadly concluded that social change sanctioned by democracy in the Iberian Peninsula had been reversed while the West piously looked on.[48]

Meanwhile, the New York local of the Socialist Party encouraged Socialists to volunteer for military service with Loyalist Spain under the name of the Eugene V. Debs Column. It acted without authorization from the national party, presenting Norman Thomas with "something of a fait accompli."[49] The national executive committee approved the action, although it censored the local for its procedure, and set up an independent committee both in order to prevent the column from becoming a pawn of the factions still dividing the party, and to avoid official association with what could be construed as an illegal project.[50] Pacifists objected to the Debs Column because it sanctioned warfare and also on several tactical grounds. They complained, for instance, that a few hundred men would be of little help; they warned that American reactionaries could use the Debs Column as an excuse to arm Franco; they feared that it would be a blow to the peace movement and neutrality legislation. Perhaps most important, the F.O.R. charged that the Spanish Civil War was a battle between "two groups of European nations . . . jockeying for position in 'the next war.' "[51] The question was not fighting to save the Spanish Republic, John Haynes Holmes wrote to Thomas, "but rather do we want to participate in a war between Italy-and-Germany and Russia."[52]

242

The national executive committee asked Thomas to reply to this criticism because of his position of leadership and because of his pacifist connections. He denied being an absolute pacifist but reiterated his opposition to war. He rejected the Fellowship's charges of tactical errors, and concluded that "the Socialist Party position is that it will use to the uttermost non-violent methods consistent with true democracy. But . . . it will not yield to fascism anywhere without a struggle and . . . nonviolence is not its first and last commandment."[53] He insisted on freedom of debate within the party in order to retain both war resisters and freedom fighters. Until 1938 he did not reply directly to the F.O.R. charge that the civil war was but a facade for an international war. Then, speaking for himself and not the party, he acknowledged that civil and international wars were entwined.

Thomas was careful not to jeopardize neutralism in the light of the Spanish crisis. No legislation could guarantee peace in a world of international capitalism, he said, but he preferred the relative insulation of strict neutrality legislation which would be mandatory on the President. The problem was "how to make an effective case for official neutrality and an embargo on the means of war and yet not have it apply to the Spanish government," particularly since "there might be civil wars in which we should not want the governments to buy arms in America"—in Latin America, for example.[54] Working with national executive committee members Max Delson and Devere Allen, Thomas hit on a formula which he incorporated in a statement to Congressman Sam McReynolds, who was conducting hearings on neutrality. The Socialists advocated mandatory neutrality legislation which would prohibit loans and the sale of war materials to all belligerents, but would exempt "armed rebellion against a *democratically elected* government."[55] Congress had discriminated against the duly constituted Spanish government by applying the embargo there, they held, and that legislation should be repealed.

It was not, and so in the spring socialists joined numerous pacifists to demand that if the embargo were retained it should at least be applied to Germany and Italy, where Franco was getting important supplies. The public was aroused, too, by the vicious bombing of Guernica by rebels using German and Italian planes. President Roosevelt felt the mounting pressure of antifascist opinion. As early as May 22 he was exploring ways of applying the Neutrality Act to Germany, and one month later he asked Secretary of State Hull to establish the extent of fascist participation in the civil war. If Hitler or Mussolini admitted it, he thought, the Neutrality Act would have to be invoked against them;

he could not "compound a ridiculous situation" if the English and French continued to deny the existence of fighting once it was established.[56] Hull inquired into the facts and also into European reaction to possible extension of the embargo. He reported to the President that it would be regarded as "a gratuitous interference in continental affairs."[57] American policy remained unchanged, therefore, and Roosevelt defended it on the high ground of the peace movement: supplying arms to one party in the conflict or extending the embargo to other nations would be "involving ourselves directly in that European strife from which our people desire so deeply to remain aloof."[58]

The Socialist Party itself was surprisingly aloof from the throes of European socialism. After a lively debate in January, 1937, Spain became little more than a symbol in the factional warfare within the party. Even the Debs Column amounted to little.* The Spanish Civil War fleshed out the torturous conflict of values represented in the crisis of 1934, but for many Socialists the conflict remained abstract. Thomas felt it more acutely than most, for it faced him with the waning of his religious pacifism, although he remained close to his pacifist friends on neutrality policy.[59] Nor did they protest the Debs Column too vociferously. Their sympathies were with the Loyalists, and besides (as Thomas reminded them), they had not taken advantage of the peaceful Spanish revolution of 1931 to educate workers and peasants in nonviolent defense.

Devere Allen had urged just that course of action. He had wanted the F.O.R. to introduce pacifism into Spain as it was trying to do in Latin America through Charles Thomson. A number of things were in the Fellowship's favor in Spain, Allen wrote: its anti-imperialism, the strong strain of Spanish mystical idealism, and the revolutionary movement for social and economic justice. But the opportunity to proselytize Spain was also a three-fold challenge to American pacifism, according to Allen. First, Spanish religion was identified with reactionism, and so exclusively religious pacifism would be repugnant to the Loyalists. Second, no one of prominence in the Spanish labor movement would have any patience with a pacifism which disavowed all force, although several leaders there were working closely with the War Resisters Inter-

---

* By midsummer, 1937, the Socialists in charge of Debs Column work successfully recommended abandoning it, and one of its consistent supporters complained that volunteers had been sold out to Stalinist-controlled units in Spain —virtual death for Trotskyists. Felix Morrow claimed that the true number of volunteers under the Column was six. Morrow to Sub-committee on Spain of the national executive committee of the Socialist Party, July 12, 1937, Thomas papers.

244

national. Third, pacifists who wanted to be fully effective in the search for peace and justice would have to ally themselves "openly, zestfully, with the great world movement for economic change," while seeking to win labor to a pacifist philosophy.[60] Spain was a land of great opportunity for the Fellowship, Allen concluded. Antimonarchist and working-class groups there had effected a revolution with discipline and without hatred or violence.

The F.O.R. could not meet the challenge. It had not resolved the questions of its own religious emphasis, its relationship to the labor movement, or its position on the use of force to accomplish social change. It had weathered the 1929–31 crisis over religion by remaining ambivalent; it was just becoming seriously involved in social issues; and the crisis over force and violence lay two years in the future. The ideas of the Fellowship were being molded by the very situations in which, if any, pacifism as a technique for social change might have been tried. By 1936, when the rationale of nonviolence had become clear, Spain at least seemed to be beyond pacifism.

Reactions to the subsequent disarmament of Czechoslovakia were mixed. They were restrained by a general presentiment that some sort of conflict was bound to occur there. Some pacifists criticized the Allies for vacillating. Others, like English author Vera Brittain, defended "conciliation" as the sole alternative to "an ever-darkening night of hatred, suspicion and fear," leading to a war which would annihilate the Czechs along with other Europeans.[61] It seemed apparent to numerous pacifists, in any case, that the Czech people, like the Spaniards and the Ethiopians, had fallen prey to European power politics. They had been crushed by the policies of French caution, British conservatism and suspicion of Russia, American capitalism, and German and Italian expansionism. "Anyone who knows the nature of fascism, knows that fascism must expand and Hitler has obligingly laid out his plans for all to read in *Mein Kampf*," wrote Dorothy Detzer.[62] The European powers had failed to halt his aggression. They had not defended European democracy because they were protecting their own interests; the causes of war and the game of power politics had not changed in the generation following World War I, as far as pacifists could see.

 The tragedy of the present hour is that again the nations satisfied with the dominant position which they think victory will give them, are insisting on "unconditional surrender" to obtain recognition from their enemies that they alone have the right to determine the future. There are no indications that they are thinking in terms different from those which governed the victors at Versailles. If this game of power politics continues unchecked, the world will move inexorably toward a third world war.

—*War, Transition and Peace*[63]

In this view the European war, when it came, was not merely like World War I, but it was a continuation of it. The Great War had been a power struggle, a test of rival empires driven into conflict by an armaments race, militant nationalism, and fear of one another. No single nation had been solely to blame. Allied victory was written into a peace treaty which humiliated Germany, weakened her economically, and isolated her by excluding her from the League of Nations. The League, in this view, had become essentially the guarantor of the *status quo* created by the war, including both the power relationships on the European continent and the empires in Africa and the Middle and Far East. Accordingly, in the opinion of liberal pacifists, the approaching war had many characteristics of the earlier one. It came as the climax of an international arms race and the organizing of rival alliances (the Axis versus the League). It was the product of heightened nationalism and suspicion. All the belligerents shared responsibility for it; even though Germany clearly was an aggressor, the Allies had been in a measure oppressors.

Continuation of the "old policies" by the Allies led inexorably to the rise of military despotism in Germany: "Hitler is to be regarded as the child of the World War, the subsequent diplomacy, and the economic anarchy which has prevailed in the world," pacifists concluded.[64] Richard Gregg spoke for many of them when he argued that even in the case of the Nazi government a foreign policy based on a "personal devil theory" is superficial. Liquidating Hitler would not put an end to military totalitarianism or war, said Gregg, because he was a product, not a cause of them.[65] The same power struggle that resulted in the First World War and was continued afterwards by the victorious nations would culminate in a second European conflict. "I remember too well the 'War to end War,' and to 'make the world safe for democracy,' " said Professor George Collins of LeMoyne College:

I cannot believe that this present war is a war of democracy against dictatorship. It is rather a war of one imperial system . . . against a nation determined to build a like system in a like manner. Ask the natives of India and Uganda their opinion of British democracy.[66]

246

Similar statements scattered through pacifist literature led to a widespread charge that pacifists made no distinction between Nazism and Western democracy. They were willing to compromise with totalitarianism, wrote journalist Aurel Kolnai, in one attack. Blindness to the real struggle between Nazism and liberal civilization was leading to disaster, he warned. "In a word, it is not war but peace which seals the doom of liberal civilization."[67] Kolnai's complaint was somewhat justified. Pacifists had overemphasized the universal responsibility for war and the inadequacies of the Allies. Their economic interpretation of war did mask differences between belligerents. Their theological interpretation, assigning both sin and potential goodness to all men, had a similar effect.

Pacifists generally recognized the differences between the dictatorships and the Western nations. Kirby Page referred to Hitler's policies as "aggressive, atrocious and suicidal."[63] John Haynes Holmes described Nazism as "savagery," "barbarianism," and "tyranny," and urged Christians to rebuke Hitler's "base cruelty."[69] Nevin Sayre was in painfully close touch with the suffering of Germans who were persecuted because of their peace witness, close friends such as the exiled Friedrich Siegmund-Schultze, a leading light in the ecumenical, peace, and social-settlement movements. Other exiles also were well known to selected pacifists. Nevertheless, in their attempt to sell neutralism pacifists undoubtedly stressed the universal guilt of nations so much that they obscured their political premises.

The editors of the *World Tomorrow*, especially Kirby Page, Reinhold Niebuhr, and Devere Allen, followed German history as closely as they did Japanese. At the outset of the decade they were apprehensive of the Republic's fate, despite the temporary stability indicated by the elections of September 14, 1930. They judged that moderate Social Democrats were combining with middle-class parties to support the government of Chancellor Otto Bruening instead of taking the offensive in a drive for socialization. The success of the coalition was contingent upon a rise in prosperity and upon a decrease in commodity prices and consequent labor support, they said. Instead, Germany seemed to slide into an economic malaise like the postwar depression. This decline intensified the desperation of reactionaries and the strength of the radical Right and Left. Moreover, pacifists concluded that ultranationalism was more attractive to voters than class war, inasmuch as elections showed that the Nazis were gaining at the expense of the Communists.[70] The German people were being "ground between the millstones of economic distress and international

247

indignity," Devere Allen wrote, and all that the Socialists had to offer was "the same flabby acquiescence in liberal policies, chiefly illusory, that paved the way for Italian fascism . . . ."[71]

On the basis of this analysis, leading pacifists concluded that success for either the Socialist-conservative coalition or a Nazi government depended upon economic prosperity and nationalistic fervor, both of which were largely dependent upon conditions outside of Germany. Economic conditions were all the more critical for the Social Democrats because nationalism was the binding force of the opposing Nazi party.[72] Accordingly, representative government in Germany could be saved by nothing less than a drastic reduction in reparations, wrote the pacifist observers.[73] When the vicious circle of economic nationalism tightened as currency supplies contracted during the depression, German tensions were screwed to the breaking point.

Pacifists who read the *World Tomorrow* faithfully were not deluded into a sense of false security by the reelection of old Paul von Hindenberg in May, 1932. The editors did not predict the exact sequence of events in Germany, but they expected that a dictatorship of the Left or Right would emerge, and they felt that the militant Right would probably seize power first. They did not expect that Hitler's regime would be permanent; it would fall to a revolution of the Left whether from within the Nazi party or from outside, they thought. Hitler would talk defiantly to the world at first, they added, but he would not dare to take a divided nation into war. Within a few months of his seizure of power they had revised their estimate of the Nazi movement and its impact on world affairs. Behind its nationalistic and reactionary leadership they thought they saw a broad, radical rank and file. Hitler would greatly intensify France's "fear psychosis" and lead to a new arms race, they warned. He might well turn to international aggression to compensate for domestic failures, just as he had used the tool of anti-Semitism to ward off criticism. Pacifists sadly concluded that "a world situation is created in which war becomes once more a dangerous possibility."[74] Granted that there had been nonviolent alternatives to Nazism in Germany, were there any alternatives to war after Hitler had totalitarian power?

In dealing with this question, articulate pacifists assumed that the threat to world peace resulted from two characteristics common to totalitarian states: first, fascist nations and Japan compensated for their internal problems by aggressive foreign policies that increased international tension; second, the totalitarian powers differed from

248

others not only because they were not democratic, but also because they were have-not nations. It is important to understand these two assumptions. They underlay the conviction that there were possible alternatives to world war. Coupled with the pacifists' analysis of war itself, these assumptions formed the basis for their response to successive crises in the Far East, Ethiopia, Spain, Austria, and Czechoslovakia.

According to pacifist theory as developed in the *World Tomorrow*, fascist Germany and Italy and militaristic Japan faced serious internal weaknesses, and the means by which these countries dealt with their own problems increased the danger of war. This result was to be expected because totalitarianism itself was largely the product of violence and a strained social and economic order. The very milieu of the economic distress which spawned dictators like Mussolini and Hitler impelled them to provide some measure of economic security, if not prosperity. But fundamental problems such as the unequal distribution of land and wealth, the burden of foreign debts, and trade barriers made recovery impossible without extraordinary measures.[75] Such steps were taken when Hitler repudiated German reparation debts and began a massive rearmament program.

Economic weakness was not the only vulnerability of military dictatorships. Authority there rested superficially on military power, but it was actually based on an insecure and temporary acquiescence of the people. To secure control, therefore, dictators had to propagate such myths as Aryanism; the conspiracy of other states against the homeland; communism (in Stalin's case) or fascism; and above all, nationalism. Pacifists had long held that extreme nationalism had been a major cause of World War I. They feared that a second world war was likely because nationalism was coupled again with militant and aggressive foreign policy, hatred, suspicion, and blinding fear. Hitler and Mussolini had risen to power partly because these sentiments had been engendered by the Treaty of Versailles and subsequent Allied policy. Once in power, the dictators identified themselves with their nationalistic creeds, which they fashioned into elements of state cohesion and party loyalty. In order to remain in power they seemed bound to intensify militant nationalism still further.

Pacifists' policy was dictated also by their belief that the aggressor states of Japan, Italy, and Germany were the great have-not nations of the industrialized world. The Western powers were like two robbers, Kirby Page said. The thieves went out early and returned about midnight with money and jewels. A third thief went out later, but he

249

found that the valuables had been taken from the houses that he visited. Upon going to the home of the two early robbers he learned that they had repented and signed an agreement not to steal any more. When he suggested that they divide their plunder with him, they refused: indeed, they warned him never to steal again![76]

The Western democracies had divided up the markets, resources, and underdeveloped territories of the world, Page explained. These nations had won and maintained their holdings through economic imperialism and military might. They had even divided up the properties of the former German Empire. Then they had piously agreed that imperialism should be brought to an end. They had condemned Japan for using in Manchuria the very techniques that they had used in China, Africa, the Near East, and Latin America. They had disarmed Germany, but in violation of their own agreements they had increased their military forces.[77]

The British and French empires, Soviet Russia, and the United States produced within their boundaries large amounts of the most important minerals and strategic materials, Page noted. Japan, Italy, and Germany did not. The major producers controlled even more resources than they extracted, and they restricted the availability of these materials by means of credit controls and trade barriers. They also built high-tariff walls around the world's richest markets. The most favored nations thus perpetuated the *status quo* which benefited them and which they alone could change peaceably. Kirby Page warned that the governments of Germany, Italy, and Japan would resort to war rather than continue the *status quo*. A conflict between democratic and totalitarian states would be a struggle between the House of Have and the House of Have Not, as Norman Thomas said—a clash of what Page called "the self-righteousness of the surfeited with the self-assertion of the frustrated."[78]

Their analysis of the threat to world peace apparently posed by both the internal instability and the international disadvantage of totalitarian states led some pacifists to react to fascist aggression in terms of two principles: to strengthen democracy in nonfascist countries, and to alleviate the differences between have and have-not nations through peaceful means. Pacifists, in adopting these principles, did not assume that Nazi demands were just or that Hitler was altruistic. They accepted the idea that, as Evan Thomas wrote, "Italy and later Germany decided to sacrifice even the pretense of justice and freedom in the interests of straightforward power politics."[79]

They added, though, that the crux of the peace problem was not

250

totalitarianism per se, but also the inflexibility of political and economic arrangements. They proposed drastic economic changes, not because they trusted Hitler, but rather because they believed that Nazi power and programs were based largely on economic nationalism, a view shared in some measure by Cordell Hull, among others.[80] They promoted a world economic conference because it seemed to be the only peaceful way of changing the *status quo*, and not because they thought it would guarantee peace, an observation made also by nonpacifist James Shotwell. They believed that the origins of Nazism were important precisely because they regarded it as a grotesque form of the struggle for power. As Kirby Page wrote, the forces that produced National Socialism were the very pressures which impelled the Axis powers to challenge the international *status quo*. Stephen Raushenbush added that if Americans overlooked that fact they would easily be enlisted in the preservation of the existing order against inexorable forces of change. This analysis of the relationship of international politics and war to the preservation of the *status quo* and to the necessity of peaceful change elicited the approval of perceptive nonpacifists, including John Foster Dulles, an expert in international and corporate law and future Secretary of State.[81]

The liberal pacifist assumed that nonviolent measures of securing just changes in the international order existed. He consequently viewed attempts to preserve the *status quo* through the threat of war as both futile and wrong: they were wrong because the existing order ought not to be wholly preserved; they were futile because they merely shifted the grounds of the power struggle without abetting the pressures for change. A number of pacifists had hesitantly supported the use of non-military sanctions until about 1935. After that time they insisted upon strict neutrality because they believed that the European nations would stand by their pledges to enforce peace only when their direct interests were at stake. They concluded that collective security had become a winsome name for an alliance in defense of the *status quo*.* Pacifists became known as isolationists (and collective security became the test of internationalism) largely because they defended neutralism on the grounds that the war was distinctly European:

---

* Richard Current suggests that the term "collective security" came into use in the United States about 1934, at least partly as a way of circumventing widespread apprehension of becoming involved in alliance while promoting the idea of mutual international interests. "The United States and 'Collective Security,' " in Alexander Deconde, ed., *Isolation and Security* (Durham: Duke University Press, 1957), especially pp. 44–45.

> The same power politics, the same imperialist rivalries, the same spoils, the same ruling classes and cliques . . . it is the same war, after a brief pause for breath, continued afresh. It represents an attempt on the part of the victors to hold onto their spoils, and of the defeated to revise the verdict of the harsh Treaty of Versailles.

. . . .

THIS IS NOT OUR WAR![82]

For some time after the autumn of 1939 the public seemed to agree that the war was an essentially European affair. The "phony war" would erupt in the *blitzkriegs* of the spring of 1940, however, and an ever increasing majority of Americans would conclude that the Allies deserved aid and, hesitantly, would repudiate their neutralist posture.

In any case, the liberal pacifists' political analysis was hardly heard beside their repetitious cry that war is futile. On the one hand, they said, there is no real victory in modern war; there is only cessation of fighting. They could quote James Shotwell's conclusion that war can no longer be contained by diplomatic objectives. They added that differences between belligerents are modified by war itself: total war imposes some form of totalitarianism on all combatants, invades every facet of national life, shackles even the victors with new vested interests and new elites, breaches every rule of war. "I do not believe it is possible to humanize war," said John Nevin Sayre.[83]

The First World War was invoked to demonstrate the futility of war, as it was for every argument favoring strict neutrality. "To an unprecedented degree Americans were prisoners of memory," recalled journalists Harold Lavine and James Wechsler.[84] Pacifists especially were bound by ideas which they themselves had helped to fashion. The very approach of a new war proved the tragic futility of the previous one, according to the F.O.R. Oswald Garrison Villard wrote bitterly, "The pity of it all is that many persons in Washington in and out of government, really believe that we shall have to repeat the stupidity of Woodrow Wilson in the near future."[85]

The contention that modern war is futile was the earliest, strongest, and most popular argument wielded by pacifists. As the European war developed, though, the American public would distinguish between the belligerents and increasingly favor the Allies. When aid from the United States proved useful in the Battle of Britain and elsewhere, the war would seem to be less futile and more purposeful.

By contrast, as the decade closed liberal pacifists continued to defend neutralism as a constructive alternative to involvement with the Allies in at least three respects. Strict neutrality would enable the government to lead in mediating the conflict and reconstructing the postwar world, they said; it would allow Americans to aid all victims of war; and through it the nation could "save civilization by maintaining an island of peace and sanity in a world gone mad."[86] Numerous nonpacifists would share that sentiment. It had roots deep in the American past, in the notion of a city set upon a hill. The torch of civilization had passed from Europe to the United States, the editor of the *Atlantic Monthly* would write in November, 1939, and "it must be preserved by people who are not . . . stumbling in a blackout."[87]

More important to the people than the art, literature, and sense of humor which the *Atlantic Monthly* promised to keep alive was democracy itself. The generation of Americans, pacifist leaders included, who faced the prospect of warfare in 1939 had endured a decade of social dislocation. They had been threatened by political extremists from the Right and Left. As socialists, some of them had felt keenly the menace of fascism because of their affinity with European politics. Everyone had watched the march of dictatorships across Europe. Added to all this were memories, especially painful for radicals, of the intolerance of the First World War, the reaction of the Red Scare, and the conservatism of succeeding generations. It was not surprising, then, that some liberals feared that war would usher in another period of reaction. It would "inevitably end all social and political progress," wrote Oswald Garrison Villard. It would "lower still further the standard of living, enslave labor, and, if persisted in, impose a dictatorship and turn us into a totalitarian state."[88] Convinced that the editors of the *Nation* were advocating a course of collective security that would have just such results, Villard resigned from the magazine with which he had been associated for nearly half a century.

Neutrality was valued, too, for the opportunity to help the victims of war on both sides. The F.O.R. formed a committee on refugees to bring exiles to the United States. It worked with the larger American Friends Service Committee for Christian Refugees, and with the Inter-Collegiate Committee to Aid Student Refugees. Pacifists appealed for public support of voluntary agencies, and for federal programs to aid the victims of war by sending food and medical aid to people on both sides. They argued that if the nation became a belligerent it would be unable to aid innocent war victims among the enemy, and might even have to cooperate in blockading and starving civilians.

Some pacifists interpreted strict neutrality also as offering an avenue of peace action. Until September, 1939, they urged Roosevelt to initiate mediation between the Axis and Allied powers, chiefly through a world

253

economic conference. Upon the outbreak of hostilities the F.O.R. asked the President to join other neutrals in a commission standing ready to mediate between the belligerents.

> The only hope that . . . peace can come out of the war depends on having a significant bloc of nations not involved in the war. It is for this reason, and not the ground of a dream of isolation or a desire to save our own skins, that we urge redoubled efforts to keep the United States out of war . . . .[89]

This proposal is one more instance of the enduring example of World War I, since it clearly was derived from the Woman's Peace Party plan for a Conference of Continuous Mediation. It also illustrates the way in which pacifists would become isolated from the American public, for it would be acceptable neither to isolationists, with the fear of foreign involvement, nor to advocates of collective security, with their support of an Allied coalition against the fascists.

The plan for a commission of neutrals reflects the emphasis on constructive action that had invigorated pacifism when its leaders were preoccupied with social problems. The whole idea of constructive neutralism—the extension of democracy and social justice, humanitarian relief work, aggressive but nonviolent action in conflict situations—mirrors the concept of pacifism as a technique for social action. In advocating neutrality, pacifists implicitly invested foreign policy with the attributes of their own social philosophy.

None of the approaches they suggested was tried: neither war resistance, nor nonmilitary sanctions, nor strict embargoes of belligerents, nor economic internationalism, nor an alliance of neutrals for mediation. Accordingly, they did not feel that the failure of peace implied the failure of pacifism. Perhaps their suggestions were inoperable or useless, but they could and would argue that there had been reasonable alternatives to war which had not been tried.

The European war when it came served, in fact, to confirm them in their social assumptions. It seemed to dramatize with tragic finality the truth of their contention that violence breeds more violence, that World War I led to national intransigence which produced a new war. Politics seemed to have been but an extension of war, to paraphrase and invert Karl von Clausewitz's famous dictum. The causes of war were horribly exaggerated by totalitarianism, liberal pacifists said, but otherwise they remained the same: nationalism and chauvinism, economic imperialism, the alliance system and secret diplomacy, economic and political pressures, and fear. Hitler was plainly an aggressor and Mussolini an accomplice. But their aggrandizement had become general war because

254

Allied policy, too, was dictated by national self-interest. The democracies' struggle for survival was real enough, but the notion that they were fighting for "one world" was an illusion. Ideas similar to these were expressed by A. J. Muste, Kirby Page, and others during World War II. They were consonant with the tenets of "the international mind" of the First World War and with the pacifist interpretation of the cold war when it developed.

Meanwhile, their ideas of war apparently confirmed, pacifists opposed both isolationist apathy and war-idealism in America. Those who interpreted pacifism as social action drew closer to those who viewed it as a personal and religious obligation; pacifists who were internationalists found themselves supporting isolationist programs; pacifists who had divided over the alternatives to a Far Eastern war united to promote American neutrality.

X

The Emergency Peace Campaign

> The chief obstacle to the peace movement in this country—
> and for that matter throughout the world—is . . . its own
> confusion as to the program to be worked out at any given
> time.
>
> —JAMES SHOTWELL, 1930[1]

For a brief time the strongest peace societies cooperated through the
Interorganization Council on Disarmament, but by 1932 it was dis-
integrating because of differences over its function and the nation's
policy in the Far East. In its wake there appeared the elements of three
distinct antiwar coalitions: a radical united front including Communists; a grouping of conservative, largely informational societies dedicated to international organization and including those related to the
Carnegie Endowment; and a body of political-action societies with
largely pacifist leadership. In December, 1935, the latter two groups
joined forces through an association in which pacifists gained considerable leverage which they applied for two years in the Emergency
Peace Campaign. Their campaign only accentuated differences within
the pacifist and internationalist coalition, however, and provided a
dramatic setting for the polarization of peace advocates over the issue
of strict neutrality versus collective security. After 1937 the chief ob-
stacle to the peace movement was not confusion but rather a sharp
competition for alternative programs of foreign policy.

The half-million-dollar Emergency Peace Campaign of 1936–37
was the greatest unified effort made by peace advocates until at least
the Vietnamese war. Although it encompassed the whole range of peace
societies and had an internationalist program, it undoubtedly was "a
leading cause of the wave of isolationist sentiment which swept the
country . . . and produced the demand for strict neutrality legislation."[2]
Pacifists originated and administered the campaign, but they could not
contain it.

256

War and fascism seemed to be concomitant threats in Europe in 1932. Henri Barbusse and Romain Rolland, prominent French pacifists and authors, initiated a World Congress Against War at Amsterdam which culminated one year later in an American united front for peace. In response to a request from the Second International and in a desperate attempt to find friends for the Soviet Union, the Comintern had announced its policy of supporting a united front. Consequently, at Amsterdam, Communists united with Socialists, free thinkers cooperated with Christians, agitators joined war resisters—all against fascists.[3] Together these disparate elements advocated mass war-resistance, and denounced Japanese aggression in China, military preparations, "capitalist imperialism," the Treaty of Versailles, and the League of Nations. Significantly, in light of subsequent Communist influence in the united front, the congress pleaded for a cessation of attacks on the Soviet Union. An American Committee for Struggle Against War was formed to support the manifesto of the congress, and to build a "broad, powerful anti-war movement in the United States."[4] The committee represented intellectuals rather than workers. Although it was radical, it was not then a Communist organization.

In September, 1933, the American League Against War and Fascism was organized at a United States Congress Against War. Russian Commissar for Foreign Affairs Maxim Litvinov's proposal at Geneva for total disarmament had paved the way for accord between some liberal peace advocates and Communists in America. The American League drew individual members from the American Federation of Labor (A. F. of L.) Trade Union Committee for Unemployment Relief as well as from the Fellowship of Reconciliation. The arrangements committee of the league in 1933 included Communists Oscar Ameringer and William Z. Foster, and also Fellowship members Devere Allen, A. J. Muste, Ray Newton, and Tucker Smith. Allen concluded:

> The presence of almost every important pacifist organization and every leader of pacifism who could get there clearly shows that pacifists have decided that silly accusations are worth nothing more than their face value and that it is inconsistent to cooperate regularly with capitalists who believe in international war but disbelieve in class war, while refusing cooperation with workers who believe in class war though detesting international war.[5]

He exaggerated. Important leaders, most notably Kirby Page, stayed out on principle and not just because they could not get to the meeting. The F.O.R. itself refused to affiliate. Nevin Sayre was one of the League's delegates to President Roosevelt to protest war appropriations, and this

257

cooperation raised the question of the Fellowship's role in the united front. The executive committee agreed to cooperate on specific projects, but insisted that "the Fellowship of Reconciliation is not at present affiliated with the American League Against War and Fascism, and the Fellowship's name must not be used with such implication."[6]

The American League lost its appeal for most peace advocates as the obstructionist tactics of the Communists became more apparent. In February, 1934, Communists broke up a Socialist demonstration at a league meeting in New York City. Both the League for Industrial Democracy and the National Association for the Advancement of Colored People withdrew from the united front. In an effort to salvage its prestige the American League chose as its new president Professor Harry Ward of Union Theological Seminary, influential in the Methodist Federation for Social Service and chairman of the American Civil Liberties Union. He had welcomed the Comintern's united-front policy from the beginning, and had invited Kirby Page to bring the *World Tomorrow* into it.[7] Instead, Page engaged in a spirited and increasingly public contest with Ward.

Their debate was significant because each man had advocated radical social and economic changes for more than a decade, each had defended the civil liberties of even Communists, each had a following among Christian young people, and each held positions of influence in the organized movement for peace and justice. Their dispute symbolized the issues dividing the F.O.R. and the Socialist Party and also extended the controversy to international affairs. It is hard to escape the conclusion that Page unconsciously assumed an insincerity or impropriety of motive which Ward probably did not then harbor. That assumption was altogether exceptional in the record of Page's relationship with opponents, but his reaction against communism was emotional, largely because he objected to its latent premise rather than its explicit program. Its cooperation in antiwar ventures was dangerous because its ultimate goal was revolution, not peace, he believed. It did not advocate violence, but it presumed the ultimate necessity of violence. Page concluded that anyone accepting that premise contributed to the Communists' underlying objective: "Their reason for desiring a united front is for the purpose of transforming an international war for the purpose of the seizure of power."[8] To unite with Communist-dominated groups would weaken the public effectiveness of pacifists and threaten their organizational integrity, he insisted.

That position became the view of liberal peace advocates. The Fellowship went on record as opposing affiliation with "communistic, fas-

258

cist and other organizations" sanctioning "the use of armed violence in international, racial and class war."⁹ Did Communists dominate the American League Against War and Fascism? By 1934 even Devere Allen concluded that they did. Aware of the need for cooperation among peace groups, and alarmed by the prospect of war in Europe as the result of totalitarian expansion, Allen had tried earnestly to work with Communists on international issues (although he had no use for their doctrines). He gave up, bitterly, and resigned from the American League. He wrote:

> I take this course of action with considerable regret, partly because of my friendship with many of those associated with the League in the past, but chiefly of course because of my disappointment that certain events have made it impossible, in my judgment, for those who desire to struggle against war and fascism to do so through the medium of the League . . . it is no longer possible to conceal the fact that the Communist Party, so far as its official leadership is concerned, considers the League as an opportunity, primarily, to disrupt and attack the various other participating organizations . . . .
>
> It seems clear to me that the ineptitude of the Communist Party not only renders useless anything it may desire to do for the struggle against war and fascism in general, but even jeopardizes, in its fanatical disloyalty to the principles of mass action, the safety of the Soviet Union, to the protection of which . . . it has considered itself especially devoted.¹⁰

In the national executive committee of the Socialist Party, Allen sponsored a separate antiwar committee to work through party channels and organize labor.¹¹

Competition of Socialists and pacifists with Communists was most obvious in their attempt to organize young people. In the twenties peace and war did not evoke much excitement outside the halls of debating clubs. A few young people went on peace caravans for the Friends each summer, but their trips were pretty banal affairs when compared with the antiwar crusades of the thirties.

Between 1929 and 1934 student opinion seems to have shifted markedly. More conscious of international developments than they had been in the twenties, students were also more isolationist with respect to war and empire. Polls indicated that the large percentage of young people interviewed favored government control of the munitions industry and denied that a strong military establishment would ensure American neutrality. About 81 per cent of 65,000 college students polled by the *Literary Digest* in 1935 indicated that they would not bear arms for the United States if American forces invaded another country, and 16.5

per cent said that they would refuse to fight even if their nation were invaded.[12]

Since probably not more than 0.30 of 1 per cent of the 34 million men who registered for the draft in World War II were conscientious objectors, it is clear that the pacifism indicated by these polls was not very deep seated or absolutist.[13] As a matter of fact, the only thing that remained constant about student opinion in the thirties was the intense involvement of thousands of young people in questions of war and peace.

Their interest took many forms. Often it was expressed in scattered protests. Students occasionally boycotted Hearst Metrotone newsreels on the grounds that they were blatantly militaristic, with the result that the movies were actually discontinued by a few theaters. Sometimes the introduction of an R.O.T.C. unit on a campus elicited student protest. Much more important than isolated incidents such as these, however, were the annual nationally coordinated antiwar drives which began in 1934. They illustrated both the changeable character of the student antiwar movement and the controversy within it.

To a great extent the position of youth groups in the American peace movement was defined in terms of their attitude toward the famous Oxford Pledge. In February, 1933, undergraduates of the Oxford (University) Union voted 275 to 153 that "this House will not fight for King and country in any war." The resolution was adopted by student groups in other English universities and was publicized widely. It was bitterly attacked in some quarters, but when it was brought to a vote again in the Oxford Union, it carried by an even larger majority than before.[14]

The Oxford Pledge, as it was now known, received much attention in the United States, too, and was adopted by the Socialist Student League for Industrial Democracy and the Communist-controlled National Student League. These two left-wing groups sponsored an "antiwar strike" in 1934. Some 25,000 students, mainly in New York City, left their classes on April 13. They held rallies and many repeated the Oxford Pledge. A year later the antiwar strike was repeated on a nationwide scale with the additional cooperation of the National Council of Methodist Youth, the Inter-Seminary Movement (Middle Atlantic Division), and the communist American Youth Congress and Youth Section of the American League Against War and Fascism. About 175,000 students participated, and again many of them accepted the Oxford Pledge.[15]

The coalition masked intense competition for leadership on local campuses. The Young People's Socialist League (Y.P.S.L.) issued detailed instructions for protests against R.O.T.C. in Chicago, for example, and specified that Communist groups such as the National Student League or the American League Against War and Fascism should not be listed as sponsors. Kirby Page consulted with strike committees on several campuses. On some he found true coalitions. At the University of Oregon the strike committee had even disavowed violence in class war. On other campuses, notably the University of California and the University of Washington, Communist groups were so dominant that he felt unable to cooperate. Even innocuous Communist support could weaken the antiwar thrust of a demonstration. A young Socialist wrote from Iowa City of a meeting sponsored by the American League. Two bearded old men came out with a red banner and the full support of the students, he wrote. "Since then the strike has been branded as Communist on the campus, even among liberals."[16]

By 1936 most pacifists had left the American League Against War and Fascism, both because of its effect on public opinion and because of its disruptive influence in their organizations and demonstrations. They believed that extreme left-wing peace sentiment was a tenuous thing, subject to sudden shifts with every wind that blew from Europe. They were right: Ward's group was renamed the American League for Peace and Democracy in November, 1937, and it abandoned the Oxford Pledge and promoted collective security until the German-Russian nonaggression pact of 1939; then it became the isolationist American Peace Mobilization until the German invasion of Russia, June 22, 1941; and it finally agitated for American intervention.

Liberal pacifists founded, therefore, an organization of their own and secured the participation of conservative peace bodies in a coordinated effort to stave off war, the Emergency Peace Campaign.

This coalition was possible because nonpacifist peace societies themselves had been stimulated to new activity and cooperation. Shortly after the Amsterdam congress which initiated the left-wing common front, Clark Eichelberger wrote to James Shotwell, warning of the imminent dissolution of the Interorganization Council on Disarmament. Eichelberger was the charming and resourceful director of the Chicago branch of the League of Nations Association. He was said to be doing more in Chicago than was the national office in New York, and on a sixth of its budget.[17] He brought new drive into the right wing of the peace movement, and he hoped to find a basis on which it might work with pacifist-oriented groups in order to form a wide-ranging, powerful public force. Shotwell, with whom Eichelberger would work closely throughout the thirties, had become impatient of that tactic. It was

261

futile, he said. It was necessary to go instead directly to chambers of commerce, businessmen, and professional people. He implied, too, that it was necessary to go on their own terms, which were negotiated disarmament and economic cooperation both coupled to strengthening the League of Nations.[18]

Similar discussions of strategy took place in the World Peace Foundation where Raymond Rich had advocated a more energetic program since 1927, when he became general secretary. In May, 1933, he analyzed the needs of his organization, the Foreign Policy Association, and the League of Nations Association in the context of the depression, and he concluded that an exchange of staff and services would benefit everyone. A conference in June brought together leaders from these groups, the Carnegie Endowment, and several other societies interested in popularizing the concept of international organization and in fashioning instruments for the adjustment of international disputes. Eventually, they formed a temporary committee on cooperation and were advised that the Carnegie Corporation would contribute $65,000 on a matching basis for a cooperative program of international education. In March, 1934, the World Peace Foundation, Foreign Policy Association, League of Nations Associations, and Woodrow Wilson Memorial Foundation occupied common office space in New York City. For the time being they concentrated on familiar programs.[19]

Then, on January 29, 1935, the Senate failed to muster the necessary two-thirds majority for adherence to the World Court. Conservative peace advocates were dismayed. The tide was running "swiftly and strongly" against them, Rich reported to his trustees. "The peace forces, having for the most part disregarded the popular, are losing the populace," he said. "Our opponents know the ends they want and are achieving them. The peace forces desire a score of different objectives and are in grave danger of attaining none."[20] Newton D. Baker joined him in urging Nicholas Murray Butler, "as dean of the whole peace movement," to convene a dozen or so key men to fashion a fresh approach to the peace movement.[21] Office work and educational programs were not enough to stem the waves of nationalism and isolation, he seemed to say. Shotwell agreed, although for the moment he was more concerned about revamping the League of Nations for action than again trying to coordinate peace organizations.

The party at President Butler's home on April 13 was distinguished almost to a fault. These men, in their dinner jackets and black ties, were educators, editors, lawyers, or political figures. They typified conservative internationalists,

262

Anglophiles who believed that the United States had inherited England's role as arbiter of world affairs. As representatives of a social class that had taken on many characteristics of a caste, they showed little sympathy for the plight of colonial peoples. The world they wanted to save was limited to Europe and its overseas possessions; they took Latin America for granted and neglected the Orient . . . . Mingling so much with each other and so rarely with the man on the street, the internationalists were never able to comprehend prevailing public attitudes on foreign affairs . . . . They failed to realize that most Americans were neither intensely isolationist nor internationalist, but confused and uncertain about the complexities of foreign policy. Mistaking this confusion for indifference, the internationalists continued to preach the Wilsonian abstractions which they alone understood.[22]

They had confined themselves largely to informational rather than political programs partly because they could not overcome the factional loyalties of peace advocates, and partly because they belonged to the elites who by and large determined policy anyway. But there set Colonel Edward House, who, with Baker, could remember being overruled politically on the League issue; and Norman Davis, who, more recently, had been frustrated by the Senate in his attempt to cooperate in applying collective sanctions. The defeat of the World Court bill and the disintegration of the European order dramatized how serious political ineffectiveness could be and also left these men almost without a policy. They needed both a viable program and a surer organizational base, and they empowered James Shotwell, Roland Morris, and Senator John Pope as a committee to find both.[23]

The object of the committee members was to find a program upon which all peace forces could unite, and also which could gain the "substantial financial backing" of President Butler and the Carnegie Endowment which was essential for effective organization.[24] It was a delicate task. They had to reconcile the various foreign policy priorities of their friends. They had to bring in Butler without letting him dominate the program. They had to attract the "professional peace societies," which some of them distrusted as negative and irrelevant, if not practically communistic. They worked out a statement that included world economic cooperation (expressly noting that the *status quo* must be changed), American association with the League (without any obligation involving the use of armed force), and an oblique reference to negative cooperation with collective sanctions. It included also matters much in the public mind—control of arms traffic, war profits, and disarmament. As Senator Pope said, their object was not to "stem the tide but . . . swerve it into the true channel of international cooperation."[25]

On May 11, Butler approved their statement and agreed to call a representative conference in October.

Meanwhile, another peace platform was being drafted by a committee of the National Peace Conference. Hardly an organization at all, the N.P.C. had succeeded the Interorganization Council as a clearing house for peace work and was largely the instrument of liberal pacifists and other action-oriented peace advocates. James Shotwell participated in some of its meetings, dissenting from its clear preference for neutrality, and Clark Eichelberger was appointed to its committee on a statement of principles.

He sent Pope a copy of the National Peace Conference statement almost immediately after it was written, and the Senator was surprised to find it "very well prepared."[26] It covered the same ground as the one his committee had written, including an endorsement of his resolution to adhere to the League, but it also referred to debts, tariffs, and the naturalization of foreigners refusing to take an oath of military service. Despite some differences in the phrasing of neutrality policy, the two statements constituted a basis for bringing pacifists and non-pacifists together and for resting the new coalition on a reconstituted National Peace Conference.

Nonetheless, when forty-four persons gathered at Columbia University on October 3 to consider the future of the peace movement, those who were oriented to the Carnegie Endowment, World Peace Foundation, and League of Nations Association clearly predominated.* President Butler was empowered to create a committee and to arrange a program of action, and he appointed Newton Baker as chairman. Nevin Sayre was the only pacifist named to the committee, but then Baker and Shotwell were not thinking in terms of parity with the pacifists.† They had in mind something more than a cooperative venture. They were thinking of a body representative of its constituent members, together with an administrator who would coordinate peace efforts in consultation with executive heads of various agencies, and a council of perhaps 100 elder statesmen (like themselves) who would give the movement thoughtful leadership. Provision should be made for groups to make reservations to the national program, Shotwell conceded:

* The prominent pacifists attending were Hannah Clothier Hull (W.I.L.P.F.), Frederick Libby (N.C.P.W.), Nevin Sayre (F.O.R.), Estelle Sternberger (World Peaceways), and their colleague, in a special sense, Norman Thomas.

† The committee was composed of Nicholas Murray Butler, Thomas J. Watson, Newton Baker, Roland Morris, James P. Pope, Henry L. Stimson, Josephine Schain, William T. Stone, Walter Van Kirk, James Shotwell, Clark Eichelberger, and Nevin Sayre.

The extreme left wing, the non-resistant pacifist section of the peace movement, cannot accept the same kind of provision for ensuring peace which the average citizen demands both in domestic and international affairs. *A peace movement without the pacifists would be an absurdity, but a peace movement based upon pure pacifist doctrine can never achieve its aim.*[27]

He wanted the pacifists, but not their programs. He would let them dissent from the application of sanctions through the League, but he did not want them to offer disarmament and neutrality as substitutes for collective security.

In such a venture leadership was critically important, and at Shotwell's suggestion, Baker recommended Walter Van Kirk as director. Secretary of the Department of International Justice and Goodwill of the Federal Council of Churches since 1925, able administrator, radio news commentator, and author of books including *Religion Renounces War*, Van Kirk was well known and respected by the organizational executives with whom he would have to work. He was not an absolute pacifist; but he had demonstrated his understanding of pacifists, and as president of the National Peace Conference, his ability to work with them. Indeed, Shotwell wrote that naming Van Kirk as executive head of the new organization would make it possible to give "recognition" to the National Peace Conference "while subordinating it to the broader plan."[28]

Shotwell's expectations were not realized. Instead of being brought into line through the "subordination" of the National Peace Conference, pacifists wielded increased leverage in the new organization. There were at least three reasons for this unexpected strength.

The first was financial. Baker had thought in terms of a $50,000 budget as he developed a program of action that fall. He approached Van Kirk on that basis, thinking he was "authorized" to do so.[29] After prolonged negotiations, the Carnegie Corporation finally granted $7,500 until June 30, 1936, with the possibility of renewal. The Carnegie Endowment granted a similar amount for 1936. The uncertainty of support was as important as the amount. With this sum the Peace Conference was expected to launch a national program of peace education, sponsor mass meetings and issue press releases, build a peace movement on both local and national levels, create a master file of key persons interested in it, and prepare policy recommendations for reference to its members. Van Kirk was supposed to work through the constituent organizations, of course, but with minimal funds he became dependent upon the resources of the action-oriented groups of the left wing. These groups had developed personnel, techniques, and a disposition to organize public opinion on specific issues.

Their leverage was all the greater, in the second place, as a result of the three days of intense discussion, December 16–18, during which the National Peace Conference was reconstituted. Twenty-nine organizations were represented, and pacifists were about as numerous as nonpacifists. The plan of organization and the activities of the conference were left substantially as they had been defined between Van Kirk, Baker, and the officers of the Carnegie Endowment one month before.[30] The idea of a consultative body of experts was retained, but the director, president, and a select steering committee determined the conference program, including its use of experts. Walter Van Kirk was accepted as director, of course. Nicholas Murray Butler was proposed for president and chairman of the steering committee, but after Oswald Garrison Villard made a scathing denunciation of Butler's peace record, someone nominated Nevin Sayre. Much to Sayre's surprise, he was elected. Like the officers, the steering committee was balanced numerically between pacifists and nonpacifists. Already more involved in political activity, pacifist leaders obtained considerable initiative in the committee.*

The third reason for the pacifists' substantial influence in the peace movement after its reorganization was that by December 18 they had fashioned a "broader plan" of their own to which the National Peace Conference itself was temporarily subordinated—the Emergency Peace Campaign "to keep the United States from going to war," to promote "such political and economic changes as are essential to a just and peaceable world order," and to enlist pacifist organizations and individuals in this common cause.[31]

Ray Newton broached the plan to eight or ten people after the Friday evening meeting of the annual conference of the F.O.R. on October 12, 1935. During the day they had weighed various strategies for cooperation with other peace groups, including the proposals being made in President Butler's name. How could they take part in a nationwide peace movement without sacrificing their essentially pacifist program? Newton reminded them that the United States might be drawn into world war in six months to three years. It was not inevitable, he said, but he saw nothing to prevent it. He recalled how rapidly sentiment

---

* The minutes of 1937 show that the persons most active in introducing resolutions and influencing the program were Walter Van Kirk, John Nevin Sayre, Clark Eichelberger, Dorothy Detzer, Frederick Libby, and Jesse MacKnight (of the N.C.P.W.).

had shifted in favor of the last war effort, and how the peace movement had been caught almost unaware. He proposed that they themselves initiate a much intensified peace campaign. He wanted between half a million and one million dollars for a united effort of prominent peace advocates, foreign-affairs experts, clergymen, and hundreds of students.[32]

The little group was excited at the prospect, and its enthusiasm spread. The next day the F.O.R. set its priorities as keeping the nation out of war, using the crisis to extend pacifism and attack the roots of war, and preparing to withstand "the tempest in case it breaks upon us."[33] On November 8 the A.F.S.C. gave its official support. The Service Committee largely sponsored the plan for the next two months and then paid Newton's salary and put many of its staff at his service. Frederick Libby endorsed the idea when it was presented to his National Council in mid-November. Shortly, Newton enlisted Kirby Page so that, with Libby and Nevin Sayre, the campaign had the backing of the only four pacifists capable of raising the sums it would require. On November 20 about forty persons met in Philadelphia and planned a three-day conference of over one hundred pacifists early in December at Buck Hills Falls, Pennsylvania.* There the essential features of the campaign were confirmed. Ray Newton and Devere Allen presented the plan to an even larger gathering at Cambridge, Massachusetts, at the year's end. On January 4, 1936, an executive committee began detailed planning, already assured of twice as much money as Newton Baker had ever dreamed of procuring for the new National Peace Conference, and more than six times as much as its yearly budget. Initiative had passed to the pacifists.

The policy-making body of the campaign was an autonomous council. Its members were chosen for their capacities and contacts and were not delegated by the organizations which they nonetheless represented. The nucleus of the council was an executive committee. At first it included only Newton, Clarence E. Pickett (A.F.S.C.), John Nevin Sayre (F.O.R.), and Mildred Scott Olmsted (W.I.L.P.F.), but soon it was increased by the addition of key staff members and others representative of a broadening pacifist coalition. During three months

---

* The Buck Hills conference was held Dec. 4–6, 1935. The November planning conference included those who would guide the campaign for its two years' duration, notably Ray Newton, Kirby Page, Nevin Sayre, Devere Allen, Frederick Libby, Dorothy Detzer, Mildred Olmsted, and Harold Fey; and also Rabbi Sidney E. Goldstein, Rufus D. Bowman (representing the Brethren), Roswell Barnes (secretary of the Federal Council of Churches), and Quakers Richard Wood and Hannah and William Hull.

of planning the executive committee played a significant role in shaping the campaign by selecting staff, identifying priority projects, and outlining general policy; but once the campaign was launched, in April, it acquired its tone and character largely from its leading staff members, particularly Ray Newton and Kirby Page.

The genial Newton was both executive director and co-chairman of the finance department. His influence in the campaign came from his own dedication to it and from his fund-raising and administrative abilities. He attended to detail well before committee meetings, and elicited great efforts from able colleagues. Page, too, had influence as a fund-raiser. He could tap sources not usually available to the peace movement as a result of his connections in the churches and the Y.M.C.A. and his experience on the speaker's circuit. Page was in his prime in these years. He was a tall man, whose penetrating blue eyes, kindly manner, and gentle speech disposed several of his acquaintances to speak of him as "saintly." He held firm opinions of men and issues, though, and was most comfortable in free-lance work. He traveled widely (although he never learned to drive a car, relying instead upon public transportation or the help of his wife, Mary Alma) and was adept at running public meetings. Chairmanship of the speakers' bureau of the E.P.C. gave him the widest possible scope for his energies, particularly since he secured the executive director of the Adult Education Council of Chicago, Fred Atkins Moore, to handle administration. Mass meetings with well-known speakers and smaller meetings for which local people had to be provided with material were the most visible aspects of the Emergency Peace Campaign. They gave Page a platform from which to reach the public on behalf of peace as he understood it and from which to preach coalition to the peace movement.

Other departments also had considerable freedom to develop programs. The committee on legislation, for example, included Frederick Libby, Jesse MacKnight, Jeanette Rankin of the National Council for Prevention of War, William T. Stone of the Foreign Policy Association, and was chaired by Dorothy Detzer. She was authorized to send the campaign director any policy recommendations upon which she could secure agreement among her colleagues, and Newton could then issue them as official campaign plans if he felt they were in accord with E.P.C. policies. If he was in doubt, he was to submit them to the executive committee for consideration.[34] Essentially the same people served as legislative representatives for both the Emergency Peace Campaign and the National Peace Conference, but they had direct access to the

268

public through the campaign that was denied them by the formal procedures of the conference.

The two organizations were affiliated in March when the E.P.C. became a member of the National Peace Conference with a commitment to popularize the "various approaches" to peace of member organizations, and with the promise of more access to members' facilities.[85] The pacifist leaders had intended from the beginning "to coordinate as effectively as possible the right and left wing groups."[36] Even the name of their new organization represented a deliberate attempt to broaden their appeal from what they had originally called a No-War Movement.* They were clear that membership in the National Peace Conference did not mean any change of "the main pacifist emphasis" of their campaign, but they could launch it in the mantle of the whole peace movement.[37]

KEEP THE UNITED STATES OUT OF WAR AND PROMOTE WORLD PEACE!

This crusade is being launched because of the serious possibility that within the near future a general war will break out in Europe and Asia. The signs of the times are more disquieting than during the years preceding the outbreak of the World War.

The peace sentiment of the nation must be adequately organized if peace legislation is to be adhered to during the hysteria of crisis. Mass pressure from citizens is required both for the enactment and the maintenance of a pacific foreign policy.

—No-Foreign-War Crusade[38]

On April 20, Adolph Hitler unveiled his military machine in Berlin, a birthday gift to himself. Scarcely twenty-four hours later his Air Minister conferred on him the title Supreme War Lord. The same day a salty old English pacifist, member of Parliament, and former leader of the British Labour party, opened the Emergency Peace Campaign by calling for appeasement through removal of the causes of war.

Septuagenarian George Lansbury did not anticipate the pace of his travel when he acceded to Kirby Page's request for a month's tour on behalf of the Peace Campaign. No sooner had his liner put in at the

* The name Emergency Peace Campaign was adopted on Jan. 8, 1936.

269

quarantine station in New York than he was specially ferried to the harbor dock and a waiting taxi, whisked to the old Pennsylvania Station, and entrained for Washington.[39] His party arrived in the capital about eight o'clock and was hurried to a hotel where a dinner sponsored by the National Peace Conference was already in progress. There he gave a forty-minute speech, only to be taken to another room for a radio broadcast. Listeners across the country and in England heard the mayor of Philadelphia tap the Liberty Bell as the broadcast opened, heard a short message from Eleanor Roosevelt, and the main address by Lansbury. It was past midnight before the guest got to bed.

He did not rest long because he had to return to New York the next day for both a luncheon and an evening meeting in Carnegie Hall. There, before a huge audience, he received some of the 3,000 carrier pigeons released at the Washington Monument that morning bearing messages from Mrs. Roosevelt and others to himself and the mayors of many cities in which the campaign would hold meetings. He listened to scores of telegrams and letters from civic and church organizations supporting the campaign. He heard many speeches and was especially impressed with student antiwar activity. His turn came about ten o'clock and was followed by another radio broadcast. The regimen was repeated the next day in Philadelphia—another train ride, a luncheon for peace workers and donors, an evening address before about 4,000 people, a train for another city—and in nearly a score of cities in the East and Middle West for one month. He was frequently accompanied and often overworked by Kirby Page, but he remembered the association as exhilarating.

Lansbury had only fleeting glimpses of the unfolding campaign between April 21 and May 18. In the Far West another English pacifist, Quaker physician and Member of Parliament Alfred Salter, was touring another twenty cities and sharing podiums with American peace advocates. Page's bureau had organized one- and two-day study conferences and public meetings in a total of 278 cities. Some two hundred ministers, educators, and peace leaders responded to an appeal by Harry Emerson Fosdick, and grouped in twos and threes, toured every state but Wyoming. Moreover, 3,500 ministers each promised to give five talks on peace during the two months and to assist the campaign in other ways.[40] Staff members participated in denominational meetings and cultivated the religious press.

Speakers at each meeting and conference developed the same theme: the United States must not under any circumstances become involved in a European war, but it must attempt to avert war by removing its causes, particularly the inequitable distribution of economic power. The legislative department of the campaign formulated a program for governmental action which pointed the spring meetings toward the fall elections: a defense policy limited to American soil rather than national interests abroad, continuation of reciprocal trade agreements and stabilization of currency through international action, participation in the International Labor Organization, membership in the World Court, cooperation with the League of Nations on nonpolitical activities, control of the munitions industry, and extension of the neutrality embargo to include supplementary war material. The department furnished copies of bills, hearings, and reports to local committees. It compiled and distributed voting records on peace issues together with a questionnaire for interviewing candidates. It encouraged public meetings to pass resolutions on political issues.

A farm department operating in conjunction with the National Council claimed to have put peace propaganda in practically all the local units of the Grange, Farmers Union, and Farm Bureau Federation; and it brought thirty-six farm organization leaders to various institutes on international relations. Tucker Smith, director of Brookwood Labor College, directed the labor department which sponsored three troupes of players presenting antiwar skits to 120 labor audiences in 24 states, operated three-week summer training schools and institutes of shorter duration for labor leaders (in conjunction with the A.F.S.C.), and developed a labor press servicing 420 papers. Special staff members were added to work with Negro and Jewish minorities. Never had the peace movement been so united or so closely in touch with the people as it was during the Emergency Peace Campaign.

Perhaps the most striking innovations came from young people. Students at Princeton University organized the Veterans of Future Wars in order to satirize the demands of war veterans for bonuses, and even of war itself. They demanded "an adjusted service compensation" of one thousand dollars for every male citizen between eighteen and thirty-six, the bonus to be paid June 1, 1965. Because their study of history demonstrated that it is customary "to pay all bonuses before they are due," the students demanded immediate cash payment, plus 3 per cent interest compounded annually and retroactively from 1965 to 1935 so that those to be killed or wounded in the next war might have "the full benefit of their country's gratitude" while living.[41] By the opening of the Peace Campaign the students claimed to have 375 college posts and over 30,000 members. Ladies' auxiliaries sprang up to demand immediate pensions for future war widows and a trip to Europe

271

"in holy pilgrimage" for all mothers of future soldiers.[42] Students in Charleston, South Carolina, organized an International Order of Diplomats, asking that all diplomats be designated for front-line trench service in the event of war. Congressman Maury Maverick joined in the fun, praised the new organization, and recommended that it internationalize and "hold a convention in the Polish Corridor."[43] At least one local council of the Veterans of Foreign Wars was not so sanguine. It accused the youths of a travesty on "things sacred," and promised bodily punishment to any future veterans found in the vicinity of a past veteran.[44]

The student strike against war for 1936 was planned for the opening week of the Emergency Peace Campaign. Indeed, the E.P.C. appropriated one thousand dollars for the strike, and it voted to cooperate with the sponsoring left-wing American Student Union which had officially adopted the Oxford Pledge. The council explicitly refused to cooperate with Communists in the strike.[45] About half a million high school and college students were reported to have left their classrooms and to have participated in demonstrations. Sometimes college administrations cooperated with the strike, as they did at Amherst College, Rutgers University, and the universities of Pennsylvania, Idaho, and Oklahoma, among others. Classes were cancelled at Cornell University, where 2,200 students and faculty gathered in a peace meeting.

University of Kansas students were dispersed by a tear-gas bomb, and this treatment led to a fight in which some 300 young people participated. Oswald Garrison Villard and other speakers at a large peace meeting at Temple University were heckled and pelted with over-ripe tomatoes and bags of flour. In the ensuing melee the speakers' stand was overturned. At Wayne University an American Student Union group administered the Oxford Pledge to about 1,000 strikers, despite the opposition of both the school administration and the Detroit Board of Education. The largest single demonstration was probably the meeting of 5,500 people at Borough Hall, Brooklyn. The most spectacular one, according to the New York *Times*, took place at Columbia University. It began with a parade of 200 members of the "William Randolph Hearst Post No. 1, Veterans of Future Wars," including 20 musicians from the university band who were led by a student using a crutch for a baton. Then about 3,000 students from Columbia University, Barnard College, Teachers College, and Union and Jewish Theological seminaries assembled in South Field and took the Oxford Pledge.[46]

Youth work formed the principal activity of the campaign in the summer months. At Duke University, Grinnell College, and Whittier College 223 young volunteers were trained during the month of June for peace-education work. They raised about $12,000 toward their own expenses (which averaged about $5.00 per week per person). Some of them worked as individuals in settlement houses, church gatherings, and boys camps; but most were organized into forty-five teams, including three equipped with sound trucks and talking pictures, one using marionettes, and a Negro debating team. Ten of them spent the summer visiting youth conferences, but most of the teams were sent into politically strategic rural communities upon which the legislative department wanted to focus attention.

Legislation became an increasingly central concern as the fall elections approached. During the spring peace advocates had conferences with the President in which they objected to increases in military spending. Roosevelt replied politely that arms increases were minimal.[47] Peace workers got no more decisive a response from Congress. The 1936 Neutrality Act was an extension of the compromise package of the previous year.

The legislative program of the Emergency Peace Campaign was itself a compromise designed to attract political support. It included even an antilynching law, a deliberate bid for the black minority. Its very breadth may have weakened its impact. Several pacifists thought so. Despite the fact that the campaign had originated partly from frustration with the compromising line on neutrality of the National Peace Conference and had given first priority to mandatory neutrality, including embargoes on credits and loans, it had to some extent substituted the slogan of "No-Foreign-War" and the program of international cooperation for strict neutrality legislation. From the outset the pacifists had agreed that "the movement was not to be isolationist. No member of the policy making council was an isolationist."[48] Their reluctance to concentrate on strict neutrality probably reflected their awareness of the leverage they could wield in an internationalist peace coalition; it suggested also, perhaps, anxiety that they might cease to be identified with that internationalism which had nourished their pacifist commitment. The political reality is suggested, in retrospect, by a remarkable exchange between Dorothy Detzer and Senator Borah at the 1936 Republican convention.

Peace advocates lobbied at both conventions that summer. During the Democratic convention, flyers containing the peace program were distributed from the air. "Put the Peace People Into Power," they said. Walter Van Kirk testified at each convention on behalf of about twenty-

273

five organizations. The Republicans gave him only seven minutes and then "utterly ignored" him.[49]

The reason, apparently, was William Borah. Peace workers relied upon the platform committee, where they had friends representing Herbert Hoover and Governor Alf Landon, the expected presidential nominee. Landon knew that there was an Atlantic and a Pacific Ocean, the pacifists were told, because he had seen the blue spots on the map. His representative, William Allen White, had all the more freedom, but his authority was illusory because Senator Borah was writing the foreign policy for the party. On that ground even Senator Nye had a resolution turned down in committee, as he later told Dorothy Detzer.

No one was more persistent than Miss Detzer, and the day the platform was to be presented she finally got into the room where Borah had closeted himself. He admitted that he was writing all the foreign policy planks. He acknowledged that one of them would repudiate the League and the World Court.* He could not leave that part out, he said, because it was "a matter of principle."

"Then, Senator," said Dorothy Detzer, "may I ask what you are suggesting on neutrality?"

There was a blank look on the senator's face, and then he replied, "I have written in the platform that all disputes must be settled by pacific means."†

"But, Senator, that is not neutrality. Is there nothing in the platform about forbidding the shipment of munitions in case of war, or the extension of loans or credits, or the shipment of basic raw materials?"

She recalled a second blank look before he said, "No."

"Anything on disarmament?"

"No."

"Anything on the control of munitions?"

"No."

She rose to go. "I am not a Republican," she said, "and this doesn't matter to me, but I cannot understand the Republican Party. You might at least have divided the peace vote by being consistently isolationist and offering a strong neutrality plank. . . . this will wash us up on the Republican Party."

---

* The platform read: "Obedient to the traditional foreign policy of America and to the repeatedly expressed will of the American people, we pledge that America shall not become a member of the League of Nations nor of the World Court nor shall America take on any entangling alliances in foreign affairs."

† The platform read: "We shall promote, as the best means of securing and maintaining peace by the pacific settlement of disputes, the great cause of international arbitration through . . . independent tribunals. . . ."

Borah was very nervous, now. "Sit down again," he urged. "There is a mistake about the neutrality. That was just an oversight!" He asked her to find Senator Nye, adding that he would accept anything the senator might write as a neutrality plank. She left and found Nye in less than an hour. He went to Borah and worked out a resolution on neutrality at the last minute but for one reason or another, the committee would not then accept it.[50] The Republican party neither attracted nor split the peace movement.*

The significance of the incident lies in Dorothy Detzer's own perception of the power of strict neutrality to divide the peace movement. The broad peace coalition rested upon truly common goals, such as the formation of international institutions and the redistribution of economic power. During the year and a half following the Detzer-Borah encounter pacifists increasingly gave priority to mandatory neutrality, however, and they thereby prepared the way for an opposition movement of other internationalists and for their own uneasy alignment with nationalistic isolationists.

Speakers were scheduled at well over one thousand events in the fall, in almost two-thirds of the cities reached before, and in 256 new ones.[51] But even before the fall meetings were held, E.P.C. staff members began to plan their political programs for the winter and spring of 1937. They expected to follow the wide-ranging discussions which had been sponsored so far by putting pressure upon the new Congress for "an adequate neutrality measure," with attention also to international economic cooperation and defense policy. They planned a spring No-Foreign-War Crusade which would unite all citizens opposed to war on foreign soil (even if they were not uncompromising war resisters) to demand strict, mandatory neutrality legislation and a defense policy "restricted to the protection of continental United States against invasion."[52] The crusade was formulated by Kirby Page. It reflected his and Newton's ambition for a broad peace coalition which would reach even beyond the established organizations and become a powerful national movement. Thus, they secured World War I veteran and attorney Charles P. Taft, II, as chairman of the winter neutrality campaign and Admiral Richard E. Byrd as chairman of the No-Foreign-War Crusade.

The national staff was expanded in order to handle the 1937 pro-

* The Democratic platform read, in part: "We reaffirm our opposition to war as an instrument of national policy. . . . We shall continue to observe a true neutrality in the disputes of others; to be prepared, resolutely to resist aggression against ourselves; to work for peace and to take the profits out of war; to guard against being drawn, by political commitments, international banking or private trading, into any war which may develop anywhere."

gram. It grew to include 150 members, as many as 84 serving in the 33-room Philadelphia headquarters. Ninety-one persons served in 20 area offices which were opened early in January. They formed local "peace committees" in some 1,200 cities, and claimed to have working contacts in 600 more. Special attention was given to farm and labor groups. Kirby Page and Fred Atkins Moore staged a new series of public meetings featuring British preacher and pacifist Maude Royden, novelist Kathleen Norris, Sherwood Eddy, and others, and drawing larger attendance than the Lansbury meetings of the previous year.

Dorothy Detzer worked with the staff of the National Council for Prevention of War in order to exploit every avenue to public opinion. They sent out instructions on how to produce political resolutions from public meetings. They prepared and distributed comparisons of pending legislation and analyses of voting records. They kept in touch with E.P.C. contacts through their own *Legislative Letter*, the National Council's *Peace Action* newsletter, and the facilities of constituent organizations. They tried to direct letters and telegrams to specific political figures (Warren Mullin and Jeanette Rankin had even campaigned in Congressman Sam McReynolds's Tennessee district). They phoned friendly newspapers asking them to press Roosevelt to clarify his views. They distributed their own point of view through press releases and Devere Allen's No-Frontier News Service, which had greatly expanded in conjunction with the campaign. They lobbied on the Hill. They provided information, air time, and even whole speeches to congressmen supporting mandatory neutrality. The State Department found itself spending much time on a matter it would like to have deferred except that, as Herbert Feis said, "the opinion of the public and of Congress was vehement in the demand for action."[53]

Neutrality legislation was still pending in the House on the twentieth anniversary of American entrance into World War I when the Emergency Peace Campaign reached its climax. The cycle of public meetings in its No-Foreign-War Crusade was grander than ever before. It was inaugurated by a national broadcast on April 6 featuring Richard Byrd, Eleanor Roosevelt, and Harry Emerson Fosdick. The cultivation of local communities was more intensive; there were now workers and committees in some 2,000 towns and cities, on 500 college campuses, and in farm and labor organizations. The list of national sponsors was more impressive; it suggested that the campaign had the blessing of the liberal establishment. The literature was more ingenious. Participants received a 52-page illustrated handbook describing the goals of the

276

crusade and ways of bringing legislative pressure for their realization. On its cover was a color reproduction of a Liberty Bond poster, a soldier with drawn bayonet, and the captions,

Stop This From Happening Again!
Protect Your Dollars and Save Your Sons!
Keep the United States Out of War and Work for World Peace![54]

A 25-page *Speakers' Outline* prepared by Kirby Page was sent with other materials to the 643 prominent men and women who gave their time without payment to address public meetings, and to the labor officials, housewives, and college students who led small discussion groups. The importance of all this talking was that the views of the directors of the campaign were widely disseminated by its speakers and sponsors whom they supplied with information. Their message was carefully framed to encompass the peace movement on their own terms: the experiences of 1914–17 might be repeated unless new neutrality legislation were passed, defense policy were limited to national territory only, economic advantages were redistributed by lower trade barriers, and the United States helped to transform international agencies from tools for the preservation of the *status quo* into instruments of international justice.

The 1937 Neutrality Act was passed in the midst of the No-Foreign-War Crusade. It was drawn from the welter of fifty-one bills proposed to replace the 1936 act, and it represented groups of concessions. Instead of a selective embargo suitable for collective security, the act provided that when the President should proclaim a state of war to exist an embargo on arms and implements of war should be applied equally to all belligerents.* But Congress did not satisfy neutralists, either, for instead of extending the embargo to war trade, it adopted the "cash and carry" formula. Americans could sell materials to belligerents if the goods were titled over to foreign hands and carried in foreign ships. The President was given the discretion to invoke this provision, and his authority was strengthened elsewhere in the act also. R. Walton Moore had advised Roosevelt while the legislation was still pending that it was not too restrictive. He said, in fact, that its object was more to keep the nation from involvement in war than to maintain

* The act also prohibited Americans from traveling on ships of warring powers, prohibited loans (except short-term credits) to belligerents, and required that American merchant ships trading with powers at war should not be armed. The act, a Joint Resolution of Congress, was enacted into law on May 1, 1937. U.S., *Statutes at Large*, Vol. L, 212.

neutrality.[55] Pacifists thought as much. They were "distressed" that the bill gave "such wide discretionary power to the President."[56] They welcomed an opportunity to reduce it.

Even though the major pacifist organizations had supported the campaign, they worried that its umbrella-like program would jeopardize their distinctively pacifist emphases. Their initial reservation had resulted in a two-year limitation on campaign activities. Even after several months, Harold Fey wrote to Kirby Page that

> the number of pacifists must be increased and the pacifists we now have organized, instructed and disciplined in the uses of non-violent techniques . . . . It isn't a matter of institutional imperialism . . . . It is simply that until there is something else which does the job the FOR is attempting to do, the FOR must keep at its job.[57]

One answer to Fey was the enrollment program of the campaign. Cards on which persons might pledge not to participate in war were distributed at various meetings, collected, and filed. Twenty-three thousand names of pacifists were eventually collected in this way, and the campaign staff argued that "the enrollment is thus laying the basis for F.O.R. work as well as work for the other organizations co-operating with the E.P.C."[58] Pacifists had insisted on this registration. Indeed, they had specified from the outset that strengthening pacifism should be a main emphasis of the Emergency Peace Campaign.

When Admiral Byrd was chosen honorary chairman of the No-Foreign-War Crusade in November, 1936, and minor changes were made in the statement of purpose to broaden its appeal, John Nevin Sayre reacted strongly, his objections exposing his apprehensions rather than any overt threat to pacifism.* "The E.P.C. was planned and organized as centrally a pacifist movement," he reminded Ray Newton. To select a nonpacifist and admiral as figurehead of its most important cycle of meetings and to weaken its stated objectives was virtually to "haul down the pacifist flag," he said.[59] It was a serious diversion of pacifist personnel and money to a job more suited to middle-of-the-road

---

* The October statement opposing war outside the continental territory was changed to wars waged "in Europe and Asia," and the former demand for defense policy limited to the continental United States was changed to read simply "the United States." Minutes of the Council, Oct. 13 and Nov. 13, 1936, E.P.C. papers, box 2.

Military figures besides the admiral were placed in the campaign, including Maj. Gen. Smedley D. Butler, U.S. Marine Corps, Retired, and Sgt. Alvin C. York. Nonmilitary, nonpacifist sponsors regarded by some pacifists as right-wing included publishers Frank Gannet, William Allen White, Marshal Field, Cecil B. DeMille, and Charles P. Taft.

peace groups. Ray Newton insisted that pacifists were still at the core of the program, guiding it, giving it a distinctive antiwar bias, and incidentally reaping audiences for pacifism. For him, as for Kirby Page, Frederick Libby, and Devere Allen, the times demanded a political response. The objective of the campaign had been and was essentially to keep the nation out of war.[60]

Sayre was persuaded that pacifism still had a central place in the campaign, and so the disagreement did not become serious. Pacifist groups were guarded in their cooperation nonetheless. Only the fact that the campaign would definitely terminate after 1937 prevented the W.I.L.P.F. from pressing its feeling that the coalition was competing with it for funds and was weakening its left-wing, pacifist witness. These apprehensions became operative during discussions of the future of the movement.

Nonpacifists also were restive in the coalition. According to Sherwood Eddy, many believed that the campaign "began its first meetings to keep us out of war, ending up with an appeal for absolute pacifism, which was the goal of the whole undertaking."[61] There were reports of a prevalent fear that support of mandatory neutrality legislation implied an "isolationist philosophy" in the national headquarters.[62] Because of qualms such as these the smallest phrases used in the campaign occasioned lengthy discussion. The directors spent several hours deciding that the expression, "to keep the United States from going to war," was better than "to keep the United States out of war!" The latter sounded to some too isolationist, too pacifist.[63]

Perhaps Admiral Byrd best illustrated the dilemma of well-meaning peace advocates. In the icy solitude of the Antarctic it had seemed crystal clear that he should use the remainder of his life for peace. In the company of peace advocates during the fall of 1936, clarity escaped him. He was disturbed by the enrollment of pacifists through pledge cards, even though he respected their position. "It seems to me that the chairman himself should be able to sign whatever card is sponsored by the movement," he wrote, "and since I am subject to call to duty by the government at any time, I would have to resign my commission as an Admiral in order to be able to sign such a card." Byrd was perplexed, also, by the Emergency Peace Campaign resolution favoring revision of the government's military and naval policy. Pacifists held that large armaments for any purpose enhanced the danger of war, and they believed that restriction of defense to the continental territory would be an effective step in reducing military power. They could not spell this out to the admiral and retain him. "I don't see just what revision can be made in this policy," Byrd wrote. "It is already the policy of the government to arm for defense only."[64]

Clark Eichelberger, director of the League of Nations Association, objected strongly that the stated goals of the Peace Campaign included mandatory neutrality legislation which his organization could not support. They were so weak on the League that he was inclined to think "he had been taken in by a number of people who really were opposed" to it.[65] Eichelberger insisted that League of Nations Association views on neutrality should be distributed along with other campaign literature. Privately, he rued the popular strength of the campaign with which he increasingly disagreed. National Peace Conference meetings which brought him into contact with pacifists were kept harmonious "by frankly avoiding the 'permissive' controversy," as Frederick Libby put it.[66] The director of the conference tried to straddle the widening gap caused by what many of its constituents regarded as the campaign's "isolationist emphasis." They, even more than the W.I.L.P.F. and F.O.R., were "heartened" to learn that the Emergency Peace Campaign would definitely terminate in January, 1938.[67]

How then could the resources, contacts, and impetus of the campaign be conserved? Kirby Page and Ray Newton worked out an elaborate plan for a unified peace movement to keep the nation out of war. They would have the National Peace Conference continue to operate through its affiliated national organizations, together with newly established local peace councils, but they would associate with it an action agency in which the left-wing groups were merged into an expanded N.C.P.W.[68] The more they talked of consolidation, though, the stronger was the insistence that the National Peace Conference itself should be the coalition. Pacifist groups, such as the F.O.R. and the W.I.L.P.F., were afraid of losing their identities and bases of support in an amalgamation. Conservative peace societies were afraid of another left-wing coalition, and were eager to use the local contacts developed during the campaign. At length, a joint meeting of the Emergency Peace Campaign council and the National Peace Conference on April 19, 1927, agreed that the N.P.C. should be given stronger administrative and coordinative functions so that it could formulate and promote a definite peace program instead of being just another clearing house for the programs of its member agencies.

Page was elated; a real coalition for peace seemed imminent. He was mistaken. He did not appreciate the strength of the forces resisting consolidation, at least not until reorganization was completed in May. Discussion then revealed the general assumption that the N.P.C.

would continue to be a clearing house, only on a larger scale. Its functions would be "direction finding," conferring, distributing information, and sponsoring "occasional united efforts to influence legislation."[69] The one special effort it undertook was the Campaign for World Economic Cooperation, originally projected as the last cycle of the Peace Campaign. It was expanded into a fifteen-month program, beginning October 1, and it was directed by Clark Eichelberger.* Pacifist groups began to return to familiar grooves of action. Page's coveted united front for peace was in disarray. In the last quarter of the year it was shattered.

> Except in the event of an invasion of the United States or its Territorial possessions and attack upon its citizens residing therein, the authority of Congress to declare war shall not become effective until confirmed by a majority of all votes cast therein in a Nation-wide referendum. Congress may by law provide for the enforcement of this section.
>
> —Louis Ludlow[70]

Pacifists continued to seek exclusively mandatory neutrality after passage of the 1937 Neutrality Act, but they insisted as well that the President should implement existing legislation in the Far East, particularly after large-scale fighting erupted in northern China in July. They demanded, also, that American forces be withdrawn and that American citizens remain only at their own risk. The F.O.R., W.I.L.P.F., N.C.P.W., and the Peace Section of the Friends Service Committee worked together in their now customary fashion. The National Council staff got twenty-four congressmen to sign a letter urging the President to invoke the law and wrote a radio speech for Senator Nye along the same line. The Women's International League attached a note on the Far East to every communication from its office, sent 5,000 special letters to key contacts, and made at least one phone call to each branch urging that pressure be brought upon the President. By September the pacifists were gearing their political program to the Far Eastern crisis.

* On June 7, 1937, Ray Newton was made nominal co-director "with the understanding that Mr. Eichelberger shall assume full responsibility for the administrative direction of the campaign." Minutes of the steering committee of the N.P.C., E.P.C. papers, box 18.

Clark Eichelberger had challenged Senator Nye and neutrality on the popular radio program Town Meeting of the Air in July, and he rapidly emerged as the pacifists' most formidable opponent on the Far Eastern question, an anomalous situation because at the same time they worked together on the economic campaign. In the National Peace Conference, Eichelberger frustrated pacifist efforts to get a strong neutrality resolution, calling instead for "collective action" against aggressors.[71] With several other nonpacifists he wrote Secretary of State Cordell Hull that neutrality should not be invoked, that it should be revised to permit discriminatory embargoes.

When Roosevelt, in a speech of October 5, 1937, urged that an international "quarantine" of aggressors was necessary to preserve peace, pacifists reacted both in anger at his failure to invoke neutrality and in fear of his use of concerted action. Dorothy Detzer complained, "The President's Chicago speech appalled most peace-minded people in America. Citizens are baffled to find him condemning nations for breaking international law while at the same time he himself does not carry out a national law now on the statute books, passed by an overwhelming will of the people in order to meet just such a crisis as has come in the Far East."[72]

That speech contained both striking phrases and ambiguities. Its intention was not clear, but it effectively crystallized opposing tendencies in the peace movement.[73] People *thought* they understood it. Eichelberger wrote the President of the warm support of those who believed in world cooperation. He pledged to mobilize public opinion for what he took to be the administration's clear orientation toward collective sanctions.[74] The League of Nations Association distributed 100,000 copies of the speech, and the World Peace Foundation trustees endorsed what they assumed was its reference to the use of sanctions to uphold treaties and prevent wars. Oswald Garrison Villard, on the other hand, saw nothing inconsistent in telling the President it was his greatest speech and at the same time encouraging him to enforce neutrality.[75]

Staff members of the National Council for Prevention of War regarded the speech as a direct challenge to neutrality, and they altered their congressional strategy to meet it. Now they believed that pacifists could neither persuade nor force the President to accept their neutralist position. They therefore resumed the campaign to check his executive discretion. They turned to the most extreme measure in their arsenal of plans to keep America out of war, the constitutional amendment to require a national referendum before Congress could declare war,

282

except in the case of an invasion of the United States. This resolution, sponsored by Congressman Louis Ludlow of Indiana since 1935, provoked one of the most intense battles of the neutrality controversy, one which the administration only narrowly won.

The National Council spent much time, effort, and money on the Ludlow Amendment before it came to the floor of the House on January 10, 1938.* It helped to organize a hearing on the bill before a subcommittee of the Judiciary Committee of the House in June, 1935. In the winter of 1936–37 the council paid for the publication of Ludlow's book, *Hell or Heaven*, which argued the case for the amendment. On April 8, 1937, Ludlow informed the House that he was circulating a petition to discharge his resolution from the Judiciary Committee for consideration by a Committee of the Whole. In his quest for the required 218 signatures he had the full-time help of Jesse MacKnight and Stephen Raushenbush whose work was financed by a special fund of $4,000. In addition, the council brought pressure to bear locally on recalcitrant congressmen, occasionally with success.[73]

The pacifists were able to capitalize on popular and congressional fears of war when Japanese planes bombed and sank the U. S. river gunboat, *Panay*, on December 16. The next day, Libby had his whole staff at the Capitol together with lobbyists from the Women's International League. Action was imperative, not only because antiwar feeling was at a temporary high, but also because the House Judiciary Committee was rumored to be meeting on the fifteenth to sidetrack the Ludlow Amendment. By midafternoon only three more signatures were needed. Congressional signers were helping, now, and Congressmen Francis Case and Hamilton Fish found two other congressmen who promised to sign if they could get a third. Case heard of a likely prospect, but the House was moving to adjournment and there seemed to be no way of contacting him. Suddenly the congressman appeared in the lobby with his coat and hat on. Case persuaded him to sign on the spot and then collected on the two remaining promises. By four o'clock the required number of signatures had been obtained. Ludlow spoke on the N.C.P.W. radio program that night, "a happy man."[77]

A Gallup poll taken in October had shown 73 per cent of those questioned supporting the amendment, and the pacifists tried to turn opinions into votes. Late in December prominent friends of the Na-

---

* Ironically, Clark Eichelberger had moved to have the N.P.C. encourage Ludlow to bring his bill to discussion on the floor of the House in April, and Dorothy Detzer had successfully deferred consideration of the motion. Minutes of the N.P.C., Apr. 19, 1937, Carnegie Endowment Archives, IV A141:70395.

tional Council, including William Allen White, organized a National Committee for the War Referendum. Once more the country was canvassed. The first week in January, Libby's staff reported a flood of supporting letters to congressmen.[78]

The administration was fully aroused to the seriousness of the Ludlow Amendment, and was adamantly opposed to it. According to Cordell Hull, the executive branch marshaled its whole force to defeat the proposal.[79] Roosevelt and Hull spoke out against it. Postmaster General James Farley applied the pressure of patronage to congressmen who threatened to support it, personally phoning every Democrat in the House that he could reach. Moreover, Clark Eichelberger made good his October promise to mobilize public opinion by organizing a Committee for Concerted Peace Efforts which counteracted the pacifist war referendum committee.

Several of Eichelberger's friends and colleagues had met weekly in November and December.* They were looking for an alternative to the despair implied by R. Walton Moore:

> I am rather hopeless of anything being done by our Government that will check the predatory activities of some other nations. If it can be said that we have any definite foreign policy, I think it consists of complete political isolation, coupled with an effort to extend our foreign trade, which means, I suppose, that the enormous power we possess is not to be used to make a really more peaceful world.[80]

Early in December, Eichelberger reported to Hull that his group was about ready to sponsor a bill amending the Neutrality Act to enable the President "to apply the provisions of the Act to aggressor nations but not to their victims."[81] While the National Council solicited signers for Ludlow's petition on December 14, the new committee issued a "Statement on Behalf of Concerted Peace Efforts," which opposed isolation and neutrality and called for international cooperation against aggressors.[82] In opposition to the Ludlow Amendment it enlisted the support of over one thousand prominent figures and important peace societies including the League of Nations Association and the National Committee on the Cause and Cure of War.

---

* The group included Josephine Schain and Henrietta Roelofs of the National Committee on the Cause and Cure of War, Marian Miller of the National Council of Jewish Women, Henry Atkinson of the Church Peace Union, Charles Fenwick of the Catholic Association for International Peace, Emily Hickman of the National Board of the Y.W.C.A., Edgar J. Fisher of the Institute for International Education, William Hinkley of the Union Student Peace Committee, and others. Margaret Olson (secretary to Eichelberger) to "Dear Secretary," Dec. 16, 1937, Baker papers, box 145.

284

When the petition to discharge the Ludlow resolution from the Judiciary Committee came to the floor of the House for a vote, Speaker William Bankhead of Alabama, in an unprecedented action, stepped down from the rostrum to read a brief letter from the President. Roosevelt insisted that the proposed amendment was not practicable, that it was incompatible with representative government, and that it would cripple the executive's conduct of foreign policy. After about twenty minutes of spirited debate the House voted 209 to 188 against consideration of what majority leader Sam Rayburn called "the most tremendous blunder since the formation of our government under the Constitution."[83]

Cordell Hull interpreted the vote as evidence of powerful isolationist sentiment in the country. He and the President were acutely sensitive to public opinion, and perhaps his political adviser was correct in attributing to them both a tendency "to pay too much attention to vociferous minorities."[84] But considering the pressure exerted by the administration, so persuasive that Ludlow himself reportedly advised some proponents of referendum that the time was not propitious for its consideration, the fact that the Ludlow Amendment failed by only twenty-one votes to come before the House is striking evidence of the influence which its supporters wielded in the Congress.[85]

That influence was not grounded in unanimity on any foreign policy, isolationist or not. It was based on a popular desire to stay out of war which was shared by the advocates of collective sanctions. It was based also on the intention of many legislators to check the President's prerogative in foreign affairs. The substance of referendum was not really at issue as much as was confidence in the executive branch, a fact lost on neither Cordell Hull nor the perceptive commentator of the Foreign Policy Association, William T. Stone. The incident typified the role of pacifists between the wars. They translated an inchoate antiwar feeling into political issues, and they thereby helped to bring foreign policy into the realm of domestic politics. The episode was historically unique, however, because although it created a strong alignment of pacifists with isolationists and neutralists, it also was the occasion of their first clear defeat. Some pacifists continued to agitate for war referendum (it continued to be a popular idea), but there was never again any serious hope of passing it.

The vote was significant in another respect. The peace groups which placed highest priority on international organization and concerted action had been aligned behind a pressure group, the Committee for Concerted Peace Efforts, and forced to make their position clear. Shot-

285

well claimed that Clark Eichelberger had "won all but the extreme pacifist wing to the support of collective security."[86] His claim was hastily made, but nonetheless important, for it acknowledged the commitment of nonpacifist peace advocates to a strategy of public action that they had long abjured. A. Lawrence Lowell less than one year before had interpreted the State Department's preference to be that "we should keep on inquiring, but not take action that was calculated to stir up the people."[87] Shotwell himself had helped to plan a reorganized peace movement without securing political leverage within it. Now he recognized that "good generalship in the strategy of the peace movement" was represented by the aggressive director of the League of Nations Association who, with his staff, would organize a series of committees to make successive assaults on American neutrality.

The National Council for Prevention of War could no longer presume to speak to Congress for a peace coalition. Along with other strongly pacifist groups (the Women's International League, the Fellowship of Reconciliation, and World Peaceways), the National Council became isolated from the rest of the peace movement. Pacifists, long accepted as leaders, had cooperated with the isolationist bloc in Congress to seek strict and mandatory neutrality legislation. These pacifists were isolationists only in the limited sense of wanting to stay out of war. They had coupled their support of neutralism with demands for international cooperation on many lines. It was the very fact that they were not really isolationists which made them important, for they brought the sanction of internationalism to the concept of strict neutrality, and their examples helped church and civic groups to do likewise. Only after 1937, when pacifists lost a measure of leadership among internationalists, could the rest of the peace movement begin its slow and often confused reorientation in the direction of collective security and executive leadership.

If the rupture of the peace movement was significant for peace advocates and for American foreign policy, it was not less important for pacifists themselves. They continued to affect national policy through at least 1939, and they sought to influence public opinion after that, but their greatest political efforts were behind them. The leadership of the neutrality drive gradually passed into other hands.

Signs of War

Who is in charge of the clattering train?
The axles creak and the couplings strain;
And the pace is hot, and the points are near,
And Sleep has deadened the driver's ear;
And the signals flash through the night in vain,
For Death is in charge of the clattering train.[1]

On Monday, January 17, 1938, an anxious Oswald Garrison Villard lunched with the upper echelon of pacifist leaders.* He told them he had recently attended a lengthy dinner meeting where twenty-four prominent men drawn from the State, War, and Navy departments, from corporation law and publishing, had discussed ways of breaking down the nation's antiwar sentiment and building support for a strong foreign policy directed against aggressors. They would proceed under the slogans "Protect Our Rights" and "Protect the Sanctity of Treaties," Villard said. Norman Davis had presided and was said to have seen the President shortly afterward.[2]

The dinner meeting was described to the staff of the National Council for Prevention of War on Wednesday and to a larger group of pacifists on Saturday.† By this time it was interpreted as an effort of "the President and his advisors," and was coupled with rumors of a projected alliance with Great Britain and plans to operate jointly with the

---

* The luncheon group included Frederick Libby, Dorothy Detzer, Emily Balch, John Nevin Sayre, Harold Fey, Ray Newton, and Walter Van Kirk.

† Largely because of their cooperation with nonpacifists, as in the National Peace Conference, and because of their contacts on the Hill, Washington pacifists had considerable access to the thinking of certain State Department officials. Frederick Libby recorded on Dec. 20, 1938, for example, a discussion with Norman Davis which mirrored Davis's confidential talks with Anthony Eden at Brussels, but when Davis bandied Eden's phrase "risk of war" in connection with sanctions, he threw pacifists into a panic. Understandably, they assumed that he spoke the private wishes of the administration.

British navy to break the Japanese blockade of China.[3] Thoroughly alarmed, pacifists committed themselves to yet another antiwar campaign and appointed a steering committee chaired by Frederick Libby. Before the month was out Norman Thomas invited the group to coordinate its work with an antiwar drive being planned by the Socialist Party.[4]

Thomas had defined the terms of the drive in a radio address: "Collective Security Means War." The League of Nations liberals still believed "after the failure of the League in every major crisis" that the world could be policed on *status quo* terms which divide nations into haves and have-nots, he said. The trouble was that states do not act disinterestedly. An effective embargo could not be applied because it would threaten the interests of those who applied it. A genuinely effective embargo, as of oil against Japan, would provoke the aggressive have-not nations to fight. Thomas concluded, almost presciently, "The tragedy is that the advocates of collective security while far from powerful enough to bring about genuine collective security or to guide governmental policy in war will be an important force in making the American people accept the war."[5] His party planned to launch its antiwar drive with a mass meeting at New York's Hippodrome theater on March 6.

Early in February pacifists cemented their coalition with Socialists, agreed to an initial six-month campaign, and accepted Norman Thomas's slogan: "Keep America Out of War."[6] The Fellowship of Reconciliation voted to cooperate "but not carry the main load or be deflected from its principal work," which was to promote pacifism. As Quaker author and teacher Douglas Steere said, "Our main job is to recruit pacifists and get them ready for whatever may be ahead and what emergencies may come."[7] With this reservation pacifists helped to plan and conduct the Hippodrome meeting. Perhaps 4,500 persons heard Norman Thomas, Dorothy Detzer, and Senator Robert La Follette, Jr., in person, while thousands more listened by radio. Oswald Garrison Villard presided over the coalition his report had so largely provoked.

Meanwhile, pacifists still working in the National Peace Conference with Clark Eichelberger and others were planning the joint Campaign for World Economic Cooperation. Their program reached its scheduled midpoint when some 650 delegates enrolled at a conference in Washington, March 24–26, in order to consider the report of a committee of experts chaired by James Shotwell. The experts offered specific proposals to revive international trade, which they regarded

288

as "the most potent instrument of peaceful change."[8] They admitted
that the success of their program was "predicated upon a peaceful international society"; but the world was virtually at war, and so the deliberations of the conference turned on how to restore international
order.[9] Walter Van Kirk, director of the National Peace Conference,
surprised the delegates by going beyond the detailed report and calling
for a world conference on economic relations which the United States
should convoke in order to undo the injustices bred by the last world
war and to forestall another one.[10]

The idea of an international peace conference on economic questions was not new in 1938. Fruitless meetings had been held in 1922,
1927, and in 1933. Nevertheless, the idea persisted. In September,
1935, Sir Samuel Hoare, the British foreign secretary, declared at
Geneva that his government would gladly explore the possibility of
equalizing the national resources of discontented nations. Five months
later, however, his government defeated a motion in the House of
Commons by George Lansbury, leader of the Labour party, that
England should immediately call a conference to deal with economic
and territorial problems. Lansbury had the support of 137 members of
Parliament, including the venerable David Lloyd George.[11]

When Lansbury arrived in the United States to help inaugurate the
Emergency Peace Campaign the following April, he insisted that "the
causes of war are economic and territorial," and that the only remedy
for conflict was a conference to revise the Treaty of Versailles and provide free access to raw materials and markets.[12] His general sentiment
found a ready response in the State Department. Assistant Secretary of
State Francis B. Sayre, in whom Secretary Hull had vested economic
and commercial policy, said simply, "If goods cannot cross frontiers,
armies will."[13] Lansbury's specific solution won a response from peace
advocates who called for an international conference. Nevin Sayre,
brother of the assistant secretary, insisted that nations must "voluntarily make those readjustments of economic privilege and power
needed to lessen the likelihood of war."[14] Before returning to England
the Englishman tried to interest the President in his plan. Roosevelt
was noncommittal, arguing the need for careful preparation and some
sign of serious interest from the dictators. Lansbury promised to send
him some "peg" across the ocean, some gesture that might warrant "a
meeting of chiefs."[15] He fashioned his peg with the help of the International Fellowship of Reconciliation, of which he had been a founder.

At a joint conference of the I.F.O.R. and the British F.O.R. that
summer, Nevin Sayre proposed creating some sort of peace embassy

that could carry the Fellowship's message to the governments. Canon Charles E. Raven made the suggestion more concrete, and immediately after the conference the Embassies of Reconciliation was organized in order to send out pacifists who would appeal for peace and propose an international conference directly to national leaders. The venture was primarily British, although Americans John Nevin Sayre, Rufus Jones, and Harry Emerson Fosdick were associated with it.*

Lansbury was the first "ambassador of reconciliation" appointed. In August and September he visited the premiers or prime ministers of the Scandinavian countries, Premier Leon Blum of France, and former Prime Minister Paul Van Zeeland of Belgium. In April, 1937, he had a two-hour conference with Hitler. Lansbury reported—with Hitler's approval—that "Germany will be very willing to attend a conference and take part in a united effort to establish economic cooperation and mutual understanding between the nations of the world if President Roosevelt or the head of another great country will take the lead in calling such a conference."[16] Lansbury had, or thought he had, the peg he had promised Roosevelt. He got similar assurance from Mussolini in July, and at the end of the year he was encouraged by the response of other chiefs of state in Europe.

The movement for a world economic conference which Lansbury had promoted throughout 1937 received impetus from a distinguished nonpacifist, Paul Van Zeeland of Belgium, who in April was commissioned by Great Britain and France to study international economic conditions. He had no illusions about Hitler's government and no intention to promote an international conference unless it could serve a demonstrably useful purpose. In the course of his investigations he uncovered some evidence that Germany was ready to abandon autarchy and increasing evidence that Britain would not be enthusiastic about a general freeing of trade. Van Zeeland's final report, issued on January 26, 1938, included many recommendations of a technical nature which were designed to make world markets and resources more available to all states. The Prime Minister urged the United States, Great Britain,

* Percy W. Bartlett, of London, resigned as general secretary of the British F.O.R. in order to devote full time to the Embassy project. Sayre served as co-treasurer, Fosdick was a sponsor, and Rufus Jones was chosen to be an "ambassador" to the Far East. In addition to Sayre and Bartlett, the executive board included the British pacifists Canon Raven, chairman; Barrow Cadbury, co-treasurer; H. Runham Brown; Henry Carter; and the prominent German pacifist, Friederich Siegmund-Schultze. In addition to Jones, Bartlett, and Lansbury, the "ambassadors" included Henry Carter, general secretary of the Social Service Department of the Methodist Church in England; Muriel Lester, prominent in the British F.O.R.; Ruth Fry, an English Quaker; and Siegmund-Schultze.

France, Germany, and Italy to join in a Pact of Economic Collaboration on specific items which "would impart to the world the impetus which it is awaiting in order to recover confidence in the pacific destiny of nations."[17] He had little hope that his modest proposals would be accepted.

Their significance was not lost on peace advocates. Coinciding with Lansbury's visits to European capitals in December, Van Zeeland's conclusions focused unimpeachable attention on projects for economic cooperation. Clark Eichelberger had urged the President in July to initiate a world-wide movement. The Women's International League petitioned Roosevelt in August and October. The conservative National Committee on the Cause and Cure of War followed suit in January, 1938. Van Zeeland's analysis became a basic point of departure for the National Peace Conference committee of experts, and in England the director of the Embassies of Reconciliation concluded that the report justified calling a conference for "international economic cooperation."[18]

President Roosevelt was already and unhappily familiar with the idea of a world conference on economic questions. In the spring of 1937, Secretary Hull had urged the British to make a concerted effort to restore international order and to initiate economic reform. Support by the democracies would be immediately forthcoming, he said, and even if the dictators resisted pressure to join such a program, its moral and economic influence would exert tremendous pressure on them.[19] At that time, Hull could do no more than make suggestions. An American initiative in Europe was discouraged even within his department. The idea was resurrected at the time of the "quarantine" speech in a detailed memorandum by Under Secretary of State Sumner Welles, who proposed that the President should dramatically challenge the world diplomatic corps to attend a comprehensive peace conference. As Roosevelt considered the Welles plan he gave economic problems and treaty revisions more emphasis, although he still coupled them with the principles of international law, neutrality, and the rules of war.[20] The plan was shelved in the fall on the advice of the Secretary of State, who feared that it would accomplish nothing concrete, would lull isolationist sentiment and weaken rearmament programs, and should not in any case be undertaken without prior agreement from the French and British.[21]

In January, 1938, Roosevelt revived the plan to take dramatic initiative in peace-making now in the context of closer cooperation with the English on Far Eastern policy. Hull still insisted on prior agreement with the British government; and after a series of confused negotiations it became clear that Prime Minister Neville Chamberlain intended to keep the initiative in his own hands, and that he would not encourage a multilateral, open-end conference.[22] Like some American peace advocates, he believed that a satisfied Germany and Italy were the only hope for peace. Unlike them, he hoped to satiate fascist ambitions without a general or drastic alteration of world economic, political, or colonial conditions. The American proposal largely precipitated a split in his cabinet that resulted shortly in the resignation of Anthony Eden as foreign secretary. Eden welcomed the intervention of the United States on any basis. He expected no more of Roosevelt's general efforts at appeasement than of Chamberlain's specific ones, but he was convinced that even failure would ultimately draw the democracies into the firmer alliance which he believed might contain Italy and Germany. He assumed that Welles and Roosevelt had the same objectives in mind, that they were putting obstacles in the way of aggression by the only method open to them and were shrewdly capitalizing on prevailing sentiment for military and economic disarmament.[23] At any rate, since Britain would not surrender the initiative, and since Americans would not permit their government to become involved upon any but independent terms—if at all—Roosevelt abandoned his plan for a world conference. Hull declined even to comment publicly on the Van Zeeland report at the end of January. After the British rebuff, after German annexation of Austria in March, and well before Munich, Roosevelt and Hull doubted the possibility of any peaceful change at all.

Pacifist leaders apparently did not know of Roosevelt's plan or the reasons for its failure. They continued to agitate for a world economic conference. As late as August even Shotwell favored extensive economic reorganization in central Europe, and Eichelberger conveyed an appeal from former Premier Leon Blum to the President to seize the initiative.[24] The F.O.R. and the W.I.L.P.F. made similar pleas, and the National Peace Conference began to build public support for the program. On September 12 and December 28, Nevin Sayre led N.P.C. delegations to the White House on behalf of a world peace conference. Roosevelt explained that he had continually explored the possibilities for several years, that the machinery was all ready, and that he could start it "by pressing a button" the moment he saw a ray of light. He regretted that the situation looked dark indeed.[25] Pressure for a conference continued into 1939, and when the President did not call one, some peace advocates became suspicious of his true intentions.

Roosevelt had faced, in fact, what pacifists learned only after September, 1939—that a conference to redress international grievances was not a realistic alternative to European war because such a conference could not be convened. Whether the economic program of pacifists could have staved off war if it had been effected is problematical. The fact that Germany was not satisfied with piecemeal acquisitions does not prove conclusively that she would have accepted a general revision of the *status quo*, as Lansbury believed. The fact that Eden and Winston Churchill criticized Chamberlain for deciding "to wave away the proferred hand stretched out across the Atlantic" does not prove that they could have made more of it than an alliance against the fascists.[26] Even a limited conference such as Roosevelt proposed would have had to bring about fundamental economic and territorial changes in order to have relaxed international tensions—drastic changes which Lansbury, the Labour party, and the peace movement, but not the Conservatives, desired. It is improbable that even Churchill would have accepted a hand stretched across the Atlantic if it had held economic internationalism or loosening of the empire.

A comparison of the Van Zeeland report with the Hull trade agreements programs illustrates the fundamentally different assumptions available to leaders in the British government, the State Department, and the peace movement. The Belgian had urged economic *rapprochement* between the democratic and totalitarian states in order to modify political and ideological rivalry, whereas the State Department appeared to be providing for economic solidarity among the democracies alone. The more he observed foreign policy in this light the more William T. Stone became convinced that it was the product of compromise between two emerging emphases:

> To one section of opinion, it was—and is—essential for the democratic nations to unite against the menace of fascist aggression, to uphold "orderly processes" and to defend the security of treaties. To the other group, which has never liked the attempt to line up the "peace loving" democracies against the "bandit" dictatorships, the best hope of preserving peace lies in preventing the alignment of the world into two ideological camps each armed to the teeth.[27]

It is at least possible that American foreign policy after Eden's resignation represented not compromise between these two positions, but rather the inapplicability of either of them. In any case, Stone's characterization did apply to the peace movement.

At the Conference on World Economic Cooperation at the end of March the committee of experts recommended full support and exten-

293

sion of Hull's reciprocal-trade-agreements program and also endorsed many aspects of Van Zeeland's report, including a Pact of Economic Collaboration open to all who would accept its conditions. Moreover, it recommended equal access for all nations to the resources and markets of nonself-governing areas, the liquidation of colonies, and the negotiation of German colonial claims as a political issue. It encouraged using international organizations to facilitate economic interdependence. All of these recommendations were accepted unanimously by the conference. But the committee included also a long section linking economic cooperation to collective political action, recommending:

> . . . should any revision of our Neutrality Law be undertaken which would extend it to cover raw materials, the new provisions should be framed flexibly enough to allow a distinction to be made in clear cases . . . between victims of aggression and aggressors.[28]

The New York *Times* assumed that there was "practical unanimity of insistence on collective security," until pacifists made it clear that they regarded inclusion of the political section as a breach of faith.[29] Attempts by the neutrality bloc to win a compromise failed in executive session. Substitute motions, including Van Kirk's proposal for an international conference, were narrowly defeated in the public meeting. Eichelberger finally proposed that both versions be printed.

That suggestion seemed fair to pacifists, but it fixed the division among internationalists between those who wanted collective action to contain aggression on the grounds that political order was a prerequisite for economic cooperation and those who opposed the further alignment of the world into armed ideological camps on the grounds that basic economic change was a prerequisite for political order. Clark Eichelberger had proposed the economic campaign less than one year earlier on the assumption that establishing international economic cooperation was the "one overwhelming issue" on which peace advocates could unite, and that "agreement upon a united program [would] simplify the problem of *a coordination of* all organizations."[30] Even this program, like that for disarmament, neutrality, and the Emergency Peace Campaign before it, yielded division. There was nowhere to go but apart. About one week after the disruptive conference, Eichelberger resigned as director of the Campaign for World Economic Cooperation.

He and Shotwell continued to advocate its program—the division was never as clear cut as it might seem in retrospect—and the N.P.C. continued to act as a clearing house for common concerns. As these

concerns became fewer it became less important The world was entrained for war, the signals were obvious, but no one was in command.
Not sleep, but a cacophony of advice and interests deadened the driver's ears. Neither heads of states nor peace leaders could make common
cause.

 All the signs show that we are again in 1916. If it is not to
become 1917, we must act without delay.

—"Call to the National Anti-War Congress"[31]

There were frequent meetings of the Keep America Out of War Committee at Norman Thomas's home that spring. Thomas hoped to build
a noncommunist united front against war; and he needed the contacts,
resources, and legislative know-how of the pacifists. Clarence Senior
became executive secretary, and the committee agreed to concentrate
on farm, labor, and youth groups. Frederick Libby was left to operate
independently on the Hill. His staff concentrated on Roosevelt's naval
program, more in the hope of tying it to continental defense than of
reducing it. They testified at hearings, wrote speeches for senators, and
prepared to campaign that summer for friends such as Senator Gerald
P. Nye and Congressman Maury Maverick. They even got an extended
memorandum onto the President's night table with the help of Mrs.
Roosevelt. Frederick Libby traveled incessantly along the North Atlantic seaboard soliciting funds and public support. In April he spoke
to 29 meetings and perhaps 19,000 persons from Washington to South
Dakota. Probably there was some basis for the suspicion of Clarence
Senior and others that Libby wanted to use the new committee to increase farm and labor contacts. So did they. The National Convention
of the Socialist Party endorsed the committee and its call for a National
Anti-War Congress in May.[32]

Socialists extended the united front to young people who were becoming divided along the same lines as adults. Late in 1937 the major
pacifist youth groups joined with the Young People's Socialist League
in a Youth Committee for the Oxford Pledge. As Norman Thomas
said, Socialists would do anything to prevent the "wholesale conscription of our youth in a new war under the old capitalist and nationalist
auspices."[33] Shortly after that alliance was formed, the American Stu-

295

dent Union abruptly changed its position and repudiated the Oxford Pledge. If it seemed ironic that pacifists often were paired with isolationists in supporting neutrality, it was equally paradoxical that the conservative League of Nations Association and Youth Committee for Concerted Peace Action found themselves allied in a collective security bloc with the left-wing American Student Union, American Youth Congress, Young Communist League, and American League for Peace and Democracy.*

This division among young people weakened their April 27 antiwar demonstrations. It prevented the formulation of a general-strike appeal by the broadly representative United Student Peace Committee, which had conducted the affair the previous year. Consequently, the nature of the strike depended on local leadership. The youth committee of the Keep America Out of War Committee issued suggestions for campuses where the American Student Union or Communists might compete for control. Elaborate maneuvering for position preceded demonstrations in Boston, Chicago, and other academic centers where Socialist organizers and young Socialists led the neutralist antiwar forces. At several universities there were two strikes representing, respectively, neutrality and collective security groups. Some students took the pacifist Oxford Pledge, but others took a new pledge against the fascist powers. The Young People's Socialist League estimated that as many as 25,000 students took part in the strike, fewer than in previous years, it admitted, "due to the division of ranks, and the increasing drive toward war."[34]

The issue was clearly joined at Vassar College in August during a World Youth Congress. European delegates openly favored economic aid and, if necessary, military sanctions against aggressor states. Americans split on the question of concerted action, with a majority favoring it. The Congress was a "discouraging experience" for those young pacifists who were present.[35] They had held positions of leadership, even though they were in the minority. They reacted to their increasing isolation from other idealistic young people much as their elders responded in a similar situation: they formed a stronger coalition of pacifists and Socialists, and they developed more local pacifist fellowships.

Convinced that the internationalists who advocated collective security in the thirties were playing a role like that of those who had supported preparedness before World War I, the Keep America Out of War

* The American League for Peace and Democracy was the successor to the communist-dominated League Against War and Fascism.

leaders renewed their efforts. They scheduled their national antiwar congress for Memorial Day weekend in order to underline the parallel threat to American neutrality from two European wars, but they could not sustain the campaign it launched. Representatives of labor outnumbered those of adult peace groups. They formed a separate antiwar council, but its work gradually was eclipsed by domestic labor issues and was preempted by the parent Keep America Out of War Congress (K.A.O.W.C.). By August there was an advisory committee of prominent peace advocates, labor leaders, Socialists, and isolationist political figures, but the congress remained largely a paper organization. It was nearly $4,000 in debt in December. Libby's staff declined to continue raising funds for it, but took over some functions when its Washington office was closed.[36] Despite sporadic attempts to invigorate it, the organization remained little more than a clearing house for the neutralist bloc in the National Peace Conference. In April, 1939, Socialist Party executives were advised that with the exception of the Youth Committee Against War,

> The Keep America Out of War Congress, as a whole, has been largely moribund nationally and without strong local work outside of New York and a few scattered communities . . . partly because of physical difficulties and basically, probably, because of its failure to form the actual federation of anti-war forces that was originally conceived as being, and its own tendency to become an anti-war movement (a weak one) . . . .[37]

Noninterventionist peace groups were still very much on their own.

Convinced that preparations for defense presaged a shift to collective security like that preceding World War I, the National Council for Prevention of War lobbied vigorously against the administration's supplementary naval appropriation of 1938 (in which it lost) and the attempt to fortify Guam the following year (in which it won). But the council faced a declining constituency. Its eleven Jewish organizations resigned, together with other societies such as the American Association of University Women. Even the Y.M.C.A. and the Y.W.C.A. were divided over collective security. The council lost staff members, too. Its able representative in Geneva, Laura Puffer Morgan, resigned at the end of November, 1937, because she could not accept the council's adamant neutralism.* Two directors of branch offices left in the next

---

* Mrs. Morgan was made the Geneva representative of the National Peace Conference on Libby's recommendation and on the condition that funds for her salary could be found. Libby secured them from his own National Council and from Clark Eichelberger and the League of Nations Association. Libby diary, Nov. 29, 1937, Jan. 3, 17, and 18, 1938, and *Fighting for Peace,* p. 222.

few months, as did Mrs. Louis D. Brandeis and others. Contributions declined. By June, 1939, the council was nearly $70,000 in debt—almost its annual budget—and it had to cut back its staff to a skeleton force on reduced salaries. Some even suggested that it abandon the legislative program for a less controversial educational one: the council's very reason for existence was at stake. Things were so bad that the ever-optimistic Libby reflected, "Now we have struck bottom and from here on we will be moving up."[38]

Convinced that bills for national mobilization would soon inaugurate a draft like that of World War I, the peace churches and the F.O.R. made every effort to secure liberal provisions for conscientious objectors. Convinced that Far Eastern policy was framed for American interests rather than for neutrality, and that the President was seeking increased discretion in order to carry out his own judgment rather than the will of the people, the leaders of the Women's International League also were struck by the parallel with the prewar situation in 1916 as they remembered it. They planned to organize a vital local branch in every congressional district; they tried to increase their membership by almost one-third; they distributed detailed accounts of pending legislation and voting records through *Fellowship* magazine; they passed resolutions and lobbied against naval increases, industrial mobilization, and conscription. With the Fellowship of Reconciliation they promoted asylum for political and religious refugees, aid to victims of war, inter-American cooperation, and entrance into the World Court and the League of Nations. Their membership campaign failed by far to reach its goals, however.* Funds dwindled alarmingly. The league could not even afford to send *Fellowship* to its members after 1938, and the magazine lost a large measure of its political content.

In truth, the very notion of a deadly parallel with World War I—the conviction that Europe was again on the eve of war and that America was again on the verge of involvement—which prompted pacifists to keep the United States out of war also encouraged them to turn inward and cultivate their own constituency. The international crisis and the consequent dissolution of the coalition of internationalists in the peace movement raised again the question of priorities: what relative emphasis should be given to pacifism as an expression of social conscience and as a form of social action? The issue was raised in a new context, but it was as familiar as conscientious objection in World War I, the debate on the F.O.R. statement of principles, and the attempt to define

* The American branch of the W.I.L.P.F. claimed to have about 14,000 members at the end of 1938; it had hoped to reach at least 20,000.

the role of force in the labor movement. The discussion was labeled "crisis strategy," and it began in the national council of the Fellowship in 1935.

Crisis strategy was, the minutes explicitly noted, the result of "the growth of war psychology and the intensification of the international crisis."[39] It was based upon real memories of the First World War, an awareness of the growth of dictatorships and the total nature of modern war, and the anticipation of being persecuted. That this fear was largely unfounded in view of what actually happened does not detract from its importance. On the other hand, it was not the only factor which shaped pacifist considerations at the time. There were present, also, a tradition of personal and religious conscientious objection to war and an emphasis on nonviolent social action—two fundamentals of pacifist belief.

The discussion centered on a document written by the executive secretary, Harold Fey, which defined the goals of the Fellowship for many years afterward.

> History clearly shows that the only opposition to war which is likely to continue after the war actually begins is the pacifist opposition. This is probably the reason why governments usually ignore other peace groups, but concentrate on raising public opinion against those who refuse to sanction or support the wars . . . presented to us as *fait accompli*. Since the strength of pacifism is in direct proportion to its organization, the first effort of government in time of war will be to isolate the war resister by breaking his communications with others of like mind.
>
> . . . .
>
> What the pacifist faces when war breaks out is an ever-increasing pressure of fascist terrorism designed to short-circuit his influence and break his morale . . . . If a man is sure that his friends know of his plight he can endure torture or even death itself in the knowledge that his actions are of significance to the cause. But isolation tends to rob both living and dying of significance.[40]

Fey did not explain how the pacifist witness in wartime would prevent another war, but he did describe two lines of organization which the Fellowship finally pursued, the creation of both community and denominational groups.

Within a year of Fey's report there were over sixty local fellowships. Local and regional activities were increasingly reported, and a news bulletin to be called "Love in Action" was planned for community groups.[41] The emphasis on local organization received fresh impetus from a conference called by the F.O.R. in January, 1937, at Pendle Hill, Pennsylvania. The conference endorsed the policy of forming community groups, called "pacifist teams." They should consist of five to twelve members each, should have officers and keep records, but should levy no dues. They should be coordinated with other teams and "cut across the lines of national pacifist organizations."[42]

The stated purposes of the teams represented the pacifist belief in the possibility of nonviolent conflict-solving. They were to organize pacifists for more effective social action, to "prepare pacifist measures adequate for security . . . to assist in the development of an efficient and reliable pacifist technique . . . to give a worthy demonstration in case the day of war arrives . . . and, above all, point the way for preventing later wars."[43]

In a sense, however, the stress on pacifist-action teams represented also the disillusionment with peace action that was beginning to affect pacifists gripped by the notion that history was being repeated. Once again, it seemed, political activity had divided the peace movement without winning administration support for active neutralism. Again, antiwar slogans had an unintended isolationist ring that contrasted with the values that pacifists cherished. The drift toward war which they assumed led many pacifists to anticipate their wartime role as a minority and to prepare for it: "in time of peace the pacifists are spending too much energy in helping the work of the peace forces generally," the members of the Pendle Hill conference agreed. "Today the differences between the pacifists and the peace forces begin to stand out more clearly . . . ."[44] Only the former remained adamantly against war itself on ethical as well as political grounds, and they clung more tenaciously to those convictions which made them ever more distinctive. By 1937 pacifists had developed a theology and political theory of nonviolent social action, and they had defended it in conflict over strategy in the social struggle. At the same time they had become aware that they had not developed a body of experience which would demonstrate their theory. The concept of pacifist teams was, therefore, at once an expression of confidence in the power of nonviolent action and a confession of the failure of pacifists to apply that power to social problems.

The reasons given for organizing pacifist teams revealed another basic pacifist conviction, the obligation of individuals to abstain from violence and war. That was why pacifists were to be recruited, converted, and strengthened. That was the civil liberty which would have to be defended. That was the reason for asserting the essentially religious quality of pacifism. "It is not an accident that the majority of absolute pacifists stem from religion . . . ," the conference reported. "Indeed we believe that in its highest revelations religion discovers the

300

spirit and the method by which God himself successfully deals with the stubborn sons of man."[45] The nation was drifting to war, they feared, and local pacifist groups might contribute to the antiwar spirit. They would at least be "islands of sanity" where pacifists might witness their faith in the time of trial and persecution which nearly all of them expected to come.

Pacifist teams were basically study groups whose members met to discuss the basis of their common faith, to clarify their views, and to hear speakers inspire them to new zeal. They often worshipped together and participated in work projects such as helping refugees and repairing toys for a settlement house. This was intended to express humanitarian love, to keep members sensitive to human needs, and to knit the small fellowships together more closely; but it was small compensation for the pacifists' weakening influence on national policy.

Community groups grew in number and activity At least one full page of *Fellowship* was devoted to them each month. By 1939 the Philadelphia F.O.R. was employing a full-time secretary and had formed eleven neighborhood groups. Other large cities had several pacifist teams each. A distinctly regional pattern of organization emerged in the F.O.R., in contrast to the functional pattern that had developed from attention to international affairs and industrial and interracial relations.* The regional pattern did not signify a conscious rejection of social action, but it did reflect the rapidly growing membership, organized in local groups and facing the challenges of wartime. It reflected, too, an unconscious change of emphasis among the leaders of the F.O.R. They were developing forms of "love in action" which were especially suited to pacifism on the defensive—social service, self-study, and the discipline of group worship. For the present at least, the F.O.R. and most of its members found strength and fellowship in the religious basis of pacifism with its emphasis on the personal obligation to abstain from war.

In the years just before the Second World War the F.O.R. sought to identify, recruit, and organize pacifists also along denominational lines. National churches began to define their roles in wartime and their obligations to the conscientious objectors among their members.

---

* Besides the executive secretary, Harold Fey; the chairman, John Nevin Sayre; and the office secretaries; these was a secretary for each of four areas: the Pacific Coast (Harold Stone Hull), the South (Constance Rumbough), New England (John M. Swomley), and the Midwest (Don E. Smucker). Fey resigned in Apr., 1940, to become an editor of the *Christian Century*, and A. J. Muste eventually became co-secretary with Sayre. There were other shifts in the staff, but the regional emphasis remained.

301

Conscious of their isolation from the collective security bloc of the peace movement, proneutrality groups met in Atlantic City in April, 1939, to discuss their strategy. One of their recommendations was that the F.O.R. should begin a major drive to promote a religious pacifism. The executive committee of the Fellowship agreed to carry out the Atlantic City recommendations if they could be financed independently of its regular budget. Harry Emerson Fosdick served as chairman of the special campaign and helped to raise funds. He and Allan Knight Chalmers drew up an "Affirmation of Christian Pacifist Faith" which they circularized through their Covenant of Peace Group.* One hundred ministers sponsored a nationwide series of Christian Pacifist Conferences from September, 1939, through 1940. The series was intended to promote antiwar sentiment and to extend and strengthen the pacifist witness of the Christian churches. It was assumed that there were possibly one million people who were conscientiously opposed to war and who could be drawn together.[46] That estimate was far too generous, but what pacifists there were in the churches did congregate more closely than before.

The peace churches officially maintained their historic positions. The Mennonite Brethren Church of North America explicitly renewed its pledge of nonresistance. Seven branches of Mennonites united to form a Peace Committee which, like the Church of the Brethren Peace Committee, was largely a fellowship of absolute pacifists and nonresisters. The peace churches jointly tried to make arrangements for conscientious objectors. Objectors formed small fellowships among the Disciples of Christ, Protestant Episcopal, Baptist, Lutheran, Christian Science, and Unitarian churches.† These groups were affiliated with the F.O.R. They devised pacifist pledges which were acceptable to the Fellowship, and some of them set up bureaus to register objectors in their churches.[47] Within the Catholic Church there was a small,

---

* The Covenant of Peace Group was formed in 1934 by Allan Knight Chalmers and about 20 other leading ministers who sponsored a Consecration Meeting in Riverside Church, New York City, in May, 1935, where 274 ministers formally renounced support of all wars.

† The Disciples Peace Fellowship was formed in 1935 and affiliated with the F.O.R. in 1942; the Baptist Pacifist Fellowship was first reported June 11, 1940; the Episcopal Pacifist Fellowship was formed and affiliated with the F.O.R. in the fall of 1939; the Lutheran Pacifist Fellowship was formed in Minneapolis, May 12, 1941; the Unitarian Pacifist Fellowship was formed in 1940, but was reorganized and affiliated with the F.O.R. in the summer of 1942; the Christian Science Fellowship was formed by Feb., 1942. The membership of these groups varied from a score to the 538 in the Episcopal Fellowship in the summer of 1941.

but determined, band of people who held that no modern war could be just. They dominated the staff of the *Catholic Worker* and organized a group called Pax, for Catholic pacifists.

Pacifists had repeatedly insisted that the rival of Christianity was war itself. The two were mutually exclusive, they said, and the churches could not ethically be neutral on the question of the war effort. They posed an either-or choice, only to find that most Christians did not accept their statement of the problem. Religious pacifists were faced with the dilemma of either cooperating in the churches at the expense of their own consistency or criticizing the churches with the consequent loss of their source of organizational strength and their greatest field for witnessing.

One solution was advanced before the war. "We believe that God leads his church into new life through obedience of the individual believer in refusing war for Christ's sake," said the signers of the "Affirmation of Christian Pacifist Faith."[48] The question of participating in war was a matter for individual consciences, and the witness of pacifists within the church would help lead it to their uncompromising position. Writing late in the war, A. J. Muste explained:

> It is already quite generally felt that the church as such cannot "bless" or participate in war and that what a man as citizen under the scourge of "an unnecessary necessity" may have to do, he must still as a Christian abhor and repent of. This seems obviously a transitional position in a progress from glorification of war or uncritical acceptance to a recognition that what the church cannot bless it must repudiate as sin and that when the Christian man finds that he cannot reconcile the claims of Caesar and Christ, his allegiance is to Christ alone.[49]

Muste had said all along that it would be a grave error of strategy for Christian pacifists to disrupt the church; moreover, it would be a denial of the very pacifist way of life. The church must maintain "full fellowship." It must not assume that "it is the normal thing for its young men to go to war . . . . It must compel each volunteer or selectee to make his own conscientious decision. If the soldier does that in the spirit that 'I can do no other,' the church may bless him equally with the conscientious objector."[50]

Nonpacifist leaders in the churches agreed on the relationship of the church to individuals and the war effort. F. Ernest Johnson stated the prevailing attitude in 1940 when he wrote that the individual conscience has rights which the church must defend, since everyone must determine for himself the limits of ethical accommodation to that which is practical.[51] For the most part, on the national level at least, the churches would remain above the battle and would defend the rights of pacifists in World War II. Prominent churchmen would continue to affirm the pacifist position throughout the war, and contrary to their expectations, the F.O.R. and similar groups would be allowed to continue and expand their work. The Protestant churches generally maintained that war was evil, even if it was necessary.

Upon the outbreak of the European war in 1939 the Federal Council of Churches called upon fellow Christians to repent, since every land shared the responsibility for war; to maintain spiritual bonds with Christians throughout the world; to defend the liberties of speech and conscience; to acknowledge that war is incompatible with Christian doctrine, that it is evil even to those who feel called upon to fight; to seek peace; to cast out evil while defending tolerance and truth; and to pray without ceasing. It added:

> To those who for conscience's sake cannot fight, this war is anathema. To those who fight for conscience's sake, war is still evil, though they believe it an inescapable choice in the present evil world. From the baleful wind of the last war we now reap the whirlwind. Thought and conscience will be cleared if we brand it as evil.[52]

Sustained emphasis on religious commitment and on the last war affected the tenor of the F.O.R. Its leaders stressed the personal obligations of Christian pacifism in their organization of local and youth groups and in their drive to win the churches. Their emphasis was illustrated and powerfully reinforced through their efforts to make adequate provisions for conscientious objectors to war.

Serious consideration of the alternatives under conscription began at a time when war resisters were still opposing selective service itself. In the spring of 1936 the Church of the Brethren appointed a committee of its younger leaders to evaluate what services would be consistent with the historic position of the church. The committee suggested that any kind of constructive service or relief work "under church or civilian direction in and outside of the war zone" seemed to be inconsistent with the historical position at the church.[53] Young men were urged to resist military service, and pastors were asked to accompany objectors if they went before local draft boards. The committee cautioned the church, though, that its plan presupposed that the denomination would make its position clear to all levels of government before the introduction of a draft.

The peace committees of the historic peace churches were working closely together. Their representatives acted jointly upon the recommendations of the Brethren committee, and went to the White House on February 12, 1937. There they noted the drift toward another war and recounted the pacifist witness of their churches based "on the Christian way of life . . . and on the conviction that love is the greatest power in the world."[54] Although they spoke on behalf of objectors for *either* "religious or conscientious reasons," the men who talked to President Roosevelt represented church groups and they based their pleas for exemption from military service on religious grounds. Although they earnestly defended the interests of the nonreligious war resister, they did not actually represent him. This fact became increasingly clear in the subsequent struggle to win rights for conscientious objectors to war.

In 1939 representatives of the three peace churches tried to write a statement which they might present to the President "indicating their willingness to engage in relief and reconstruction work, but also presenting a plan for the absolute pacifist." There was some disagreement over including absolutists—those who objected to noncombatant or alternative service. "The Peace Section, however, was very clear," according to its minutes, that any statement which the Friends should sign should include provision for the absolutist, and expressed the hope that whatever benefits might be given to members of the historic peace churches should be given to *"religious* pacifists of other affiliations."[55]

Between January and September, 1940, pacifist organizations sought to influence the provisions of legislation on conscription. They were most active in the summer, when the military affairs committees of the House and Senate began hearings on the Burke-Wadsworth Bill. SECTION 7(d) of that bill provided exemption for only members of a "well-recognized religious sect whose creed or principles forbid its members to participate in war in any form . . . ."[56] The bill exempted these persons only from combat service as the President might define it, virtually repeating the provisions of the 1917 law on conscientious objection, as if to underline the parallel between the wars. Pacifists objected that it failed to provide for (1) religious objectors other than members of the historic peace churches, (2) nonreligious objectors, (3) those who would refuse both combatant and noncombatant service, and (4) those who would object even to alternative service. Moreover, they complained that (5) the act did not provide for civilian administration of C.O. service. They pointed out that the army had recognized only traditional nonresistance, and they predicted correctly that this restricted view would cause trouble from those who conscientiously objected to military service as well as to killing.

305

In July and August pacifists, led by the Friends, sought to modify the Burke-Wadsworth Bill in two main respects: they asked for provision for all objectors, whether members of peace churches, other denominations, or no church at all; and they sought recognition of the whole range of pacifist positions—noncombatant service, alternative civilian service, or absolute noncooperation. Pacifists proposed that American legislation should be modeled on liberal British law, which accepted all bases and kinds of conscientious objection.[57] They were only partly successful in changing the Burke-Wadsworth Bill.

The Selective Training and Service Act of 1940, which was signed into law on September 16, assigned conscientious objector (C.O.) status to any person

> who, by reason of religious training and belief, is conscientiously opposed to participation in war in any form.[58]

Nonreligious objectors were excluded from the provisions of the law for another generation, although all religious pacifists were covered. Interpretation of the act was largely a matter for local Selective Service boards, and practice would vary from place to place. The struggle to broaden the coverage shifted from the legislative halls to the offices of the Selective Service System.[59]

The act provided that objectors could elect to take noncombatant service or to do "work of national importance under civilian direction."[60] It did not meet the demands of those who absolutely objected to conscription of any kind, but it encouraged pacifists to expect civilian administration of it. Efforts to arrange for this arrangement were hobbled at the outset by the 1940 act which made the local draft board the agency through which objectors were classified instead of creating an independent organization with which they might register. Civilian administration was impeded also by division within pacifist ranks between those who wanted civilian direction under church auspices and those who wanted government administration of alternate service. Recognizing the great variety of C.O. positions, pacifists proposed a dual scheme of administration by both government and private agencies.

At the end of September, 1940, Colonel Lewis E. Hershey of the Selective Service asked the historic peace churches to suggest a concrete program of service and to indicate how much responsibility for it they would accept. The National Service Board for Religious Objectors (N.S.B.R.O.) was formed in order to take joint action in response to Hershey's request. Led by its executive secretary, Paul Comly French, the National Service Board became the coordinating agency for the private agencies administering the Civilian Public Service (C.P.S.) projects of conscientious objectors during World War II, and it was immediately recognized by Selective Service officials as the spokesmen for the pacifists.* The National Service Board acted, in fact, "much like a bureau of the Federal Government."[61]

Pacifists responded to Colonel Hershey's request for a concrete program by proposing that each objector be given the alternatives of working for a government agency with pay or under privately financed agencies such as the peace churches. A plan for dual administration and optional service was approved by the Selective Service Administration, the historic peace churches, the F.O.R., and representatives of the larger religious denominations. It was vetoed at the end of November by the President, who was hostile to the idea of government-financed alternative service.[62]

No appropriation had been made for Civilian Public Service; and the first director of Selective Service, Clarence A. Dykstra, president of the University of Wisconsin, doubted that Congress would finance the work unless, considering the President's attitude, the government fully controlled and directed the program. Accordingly, Dykstra asked the religious agencies if they would administer all projects and pay the cost except for transportation and equipment. He pointed out that the alternative to this procedure would be for every objector to work without pay on government-administered projects.[63] The national council of the F.O.R. already had concluded that "it is a matter of great importance that there be some Alternative Service available under strictly private and/or religious auspices for those C.O.'s who cannot take it under Government agency control."[64] Friends and other members of the N.S.B.R.O. felt the same way, and so they agreed to finance the costs of administration and maintenance of all camps for objectors for an experimental period of six months, beginning January 1, 1941. The experiment could not be abandoned easily, once it was launched.

Most pacifists in 1941 did not anticipate the extent to which the government would control alternative service. A few who feared the

---

* Member organizations included the F.O.R., A.F.S.C., Brethren Service Committee, Committee on World Peace of the Methodist Church, the Disciples of Christ Department of Social Welfare, the Mennonite Central Committee, and the Molokan Advisory Committee. The Committee on the Conscientious Objector of the Federal Council of Churches was a consulting member. The War Resisters League was represented through the F.O.R. Paul Comly French was the dominant influence in the development of the N.S.B.R.O. He had been a newspaperman and the director of the Federal Writers Project in Pennsylvania. After resigning from the N.S.B.R.O. in 1946 he was executive director of CARE and president of a publishing firm.

worst refused even to register. They had no intention of "cooperating with the government in making their [sic] draft act run as smoothly as possible," as Evan Thomas said.[65] A vigorous minority in the Fellowship, including Richard Gregg and co-secretary A. J. Muste, objected to registration for much the same reason. The service did not exempt absolutists or nonreligious pacifists, Gregg complained. Registered objectors who were found by their local draft boards to be insincere because they lacked religious training and belief or who refused to accept alternative service were subject to unpredictable military discipline, whereas those who refused to register at all were subject to clearly defined civil law and jail sentences. As long as this situation existed, Gregg said, he could not by his example sanction registration.[66]

The partnership between the church agencies and the government was unique in American history. It was initially a sincere attempt to maintain tolerance of diversity, but it brought together two different conceptions of the conscientious objectors. The Selective Service Administration viewed them as a special class of drafted men; it looked upon the church groups as agents of the government. Participants in the N.S.B.R.O. believed that the objectors had a moral right to exemption from military service, and that the church groups were independent agencies. Indeed, many of those who originally entered the experiment had a more special vision for the Civilian Public Service camps: they should become havens where pacifists could work out the moral equivalents of war.

The Brethren had hoped to develop forms of nonviolent and democratic community life. Mennonites expected to learn to live as a brotherhood. Clarence Pickett, executive secretary of the A.F.S.C., and Thomas Jones, president of Fisk University and first director of Quaker C.P.S. units, looked forward to developing a corps of men trained in the pacifist way of life and in techniques of nonviolent action. All the peace churches expected to train their pacifist members for postwar reconstruction work. The example of the Friends Service Committee during and after World War I was fresh in their minds. "Cooperative Pacifist Service Colleges," read an advertisement in *Fellowship,* "that is what we can make C.P.S.C. stand for, training schools in pacifist principles."[67] As historians Mulford Q. Sibley and Philip E. Jacob explained,

> The fundamental conception of C.P.S. was . . . that of a religious order whose members, though under legal compulsion, were moved primarily by their personal ideals to perform a sacrificial service. The

308

c.o. was expected to demonstrate by the superior quality of his work the integrity and constructive nature of his faith.[68]

No such religious order would emerge. On the contrary, the Selective Service Administration would progressively extend its control over the program, thwarting its independent development. It would become ever more clear that Civilian Public Service was an adjunct of the military establishment. Private agencies would become involved in the politics of administration. They would become embroiled in internal disagreement over their political roles. The debate over participation in c.p.s. would be most virulent in the Fellowship of Reconciliation, which would finally get out of the administrative program. Even the Friends Service Committee would turn over its responsibilities to the government after the war. But in the course of providing for objectors through at least 1941 the major pacifist organizations increasingly emphasized the religious and individualistic basis of conscientious objection.

Religious pacifists after the dissolution of the liberal peace coalition continued to sponsor social action, although they gave it a lower priority. They participated in the anti-interventionist coalition until in 1941 its program narrowed to the concept of a fortress America. They helped to create the Congress of Racial Equality in order to pioneer new techniques of reform. These approaches were not only direct and nonviolent, but they relied almost entirely upon pacifists. In a sense, they were the methods of a minority unable to mobilize the public by conventional means. Even in their work for social justice, therefore, pacifists increasingly emphasized personal commitment and a limited constituency. This was more dramatically suggested in their responses to foreign affairs, particularly after the failure of the campaign for world economic cooperation. International order was shattered, and with it the American peace movement. Again all the signs pointed to war. Many pacifists thought they recognized the signals, and they cultivated a pacifist constituency, building stronger local and denominational units and providing for conscientious objectors. The personal obligation of war resistance and of Christian pacifism became the dominant motif of the War Resisters League, the Fellowship of Reconciliation, and the Peace Section of the American Friends Service Committee.

Mildred Scott Olmsted wrote from Geneva in the fall of 1939 that the international executives of the w.i.l.p.f. had parted believing that Hitler meant war and knowing that some of them would never meet again. She looked up the street past fountains and flowered parks to the old *Maison Internationale* which had been a peace center for nearly two decades. It faced the mountains across the sparkling lake, "an island of peace, intelligence, dignity and tolerance in a crazy world of violence."[69] Pacifism would have to be like that, she thought. John Nevin Sayre, in America, urged the President to convene a peace conference even as he confessed, "It is not within my personal power to halt the flood of persecution that rushes on its devastating course through Germany, Austria and Czechoslovakia. Though I denounce Hitler with all my soul, that accomplishes nothing."[70] It was in his power only to save individual refugees and to affirm his uncompromising refusal of the war method. Even as he worked to keep America out of war, his perception of the historical parallel yielded a greater determination to prepare in pacifism a refuge from the floodtide of violence.

310

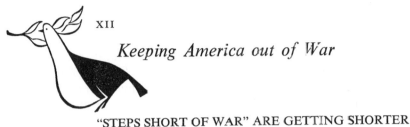

XII

Keeping America out of War

"STEPS SHORT OF WAR" ARE GETTING SHORTER
—Youth Committee Against War[1]

Reinhold Niebuhr was in England when war came on September 3, 1939. The holocaust had been foreshadowed a week before by the announcement of the German-Russian nonaggression pact. That had been "stunning and sickening" news for the American professor both because it suggested Hitler's imminent invasion of Poland and because it illumined the "complete hollowness of both nazi and communist ideological pretensions." This realization, above all, made it clear to Niebuhr that where integrity or even rational goals are lacking, force must be met by force, aggressive tyranny by war. He was not yet prepared to say that America should quit her neutral stance to join the Allies, but he bitterly resented the arguments of those pacifists "who equated American neutrality with the Sermon on the Mount."[2]

Niebuhr returned to America filled with admiration for the courage of the British. Having seen at first hand the idealism and fortitude of English men and women, and having contrasted this with the intellectual and moral vacuity of German and Russian radio broadcasts during the fall crisis, he wrote all the more caustically of American pacifism. He respected individual nonresisters, he said, whose asceticism was politically irrelevant as a matter of principle; but he castigated those who tried to commit Americans to neutrality on religious grounds. "The Christian Church of America has never been upon a lower level of spiritual insight and moral sensitivity than in this tragic age of world conflict," he wrote. "Living in a suffering world with its ears assailed by the cries of the miserable victims of tyranny and conflict, it has chosen to identify the slogan 'Keep America out of war,' with the Christian gospel."[3] One year after experiencing his first air raid in

311

England, Niebuhr wrote that if America became involved he would support the war effort without hesitation.[4]

The conversion of peace advocates to collective security significantly influenced American foreign policy. According to journalists Harold Lavine and James Wechsler, "the most effective presentations of the Allied cause did not come from those who had been identified with the earlier crusade; they were suspect. They came from the recantations of those who had most effectively debunked the last war": from historian Walter Millis, who regretted that his revisionist *The Road To War* had made such a great impact; from publicist Dorothy Thompson, who in 1939 warned that civilization itself was threatened by the Nazis, although a decade earlier she had written that no one could win another war; from attorney Charles P. Taft, who wrote that he still respected the pacifists with whom he had worked in the Emergency Peace Campaign but added, "I am glad there are not too many . . . ."[5] They included Sherwood Eddy, who was apprehensive of the war and the peace to follow it, but saw no alternative to fighting, and Rabbi Judah L. Magnes, who renounced pacifism to support the war even though he believed he was transgressing God's word: "We do not know what else to do."[6] No former pacifist was more influential in winning support for the Allies than was Reinhold Niebuhr. Every peace advocate was both pawn and product of intense competition for the public.

War in Europe fixed Roosevelt's objectives but not his course. He called Congress into special session September 21, asking for outright repeal of the arms embargo, and took personal command of the legislative campaign. Sailor that he was, he tacked before the prevailing winds of antiwar sentiment which accompanied popular sympathy for the democracies. The embargo itself was unneutral, he argued; it favored the dictatorships, and repeal was necessary to keep their war from America. This was the line taken by the State Department earlier, in the spring, and by Eichelberger's group the year before. It placed neutrality revision on the high ground of the restoration of international law without conceding that the addition of broad presidential discretion made it possible to convert policy under the old law into collective security. The official position was spelled out to Libby when he complained that even before the German invasion administration personnel were attacking the embargo as a breeder of war. "The speeches to which you refer were carefully considered before they were delivered," Roosevelt replied. "They express this Government's policy to keep from involvement in foreign wars and, with that end in view, to secure

312

a revision of existing neutrality legislation."[7] If the administration's objective was to aid the Allies, it was veiled in antiwar rhetoric.

Neutrality revision had failed in the spring on largely partisan grounds, a campaign year was in the offing, and so the President applied pressure wherever he could do it discreetly. In the middle drawer of his desk he kept the voting record of Democrats on the Vorys Amendment, which had scuttled his previous attempt to repeal the embargo. He avoided any public display on which his opposition might draw political lines, however, and suggested that the State Department might cultivate popular opinion through Clark Eichelberger. With Hull's approval, Eichelberger formed a new citizens' group, the Non-Partisan Committee for Peace through Revision of the Neutrality Act, and obtained as chairman William Allen White, a Republican who had been a member of Libby's board of directors and an advocate of strict neutrality. The committee was a function of the League of Nations Association staff. It put prominent Americans on record in favor of repealing the embargo and popularized them through press and radio in order to counteract the neutralist campaign.

Libby had begun planning that campaign while still in bed September 1, awakened at four-thirty in the morning by the war news hawked in the street below. The National Council came to life. It laid away differences over naval spending with Senator David Walsh and sent out thousands of copies of his antiwar speech. It welcomed a radio program by its erstwhile foe on the World Court issue, Father Charles E. Coughlin. It helped a lobbyist sent by advertising executive Chester Bowles, who would become a leader of the American First Committee. It fielded several staff members to work with labor unions. It organized a large public meeting in Washington for the Keep America Out of War Congress and pacifist groups, securing Norman Thomas and Senators Nye, Clark, and Capper to speak. In short, it made common cause with everyone who worked to retain the impartial embargo. Many people did. The neutrality bloc in the Senate asked for research men. The Women's International League and the Fellowship of Reconciliation mobilized their contacts and sent out speakers. Hundreds of those who attended the Washington rally visited their congressmen on behalf of neutrality. About thirteen thousand volunteers answered a mailed appeal to help during the "emergency" and received specific directions throughout the fall. Farm, labor, and church groups responded to pleas to write their legislators. At the end of September, Congress was inundated with proembargo mail.[8]

The neutralists lost their edge in the following month owing to Eichelberger's contending committee, the shift of some prominent Republicans, Roosevelt's astute political management, and the pro-Allied sympathies of the public. The Neutrality Act of 1939 was billed as an act to keep the United States out of war, although it extended cash-and-carry provisions to the sale of arms and munitions to belligerents. It passed both houses of Congress by substantial majorities.* Libby was assured by Senator La Follette and others that his effort had increased the antiwar forces of the country and was a great victory, but the $20,000 campaign had failed, and his organization was again poor. His staff joined the Keep America Out of War Congress and pacifist leaders in a program which was less ambitious financially but even more aspiring, a campaign for neutral mediation to end the war in Europe.

The idea of having the United States initiate a commission of neutrals to mediate won unanimous endorsement from the National Peace Conference in September.† The proposal was held in abeyance while the two major wings of the N.P.C. battled over repeal of the arms embargo, but military inactivity on the western front in the fall encouraged the Peace Conference to believe that mediation might be possible, and appeals from certain small neutrals made some sort of peace move seem imperative. On November 16 a delegation from the Federal Council of Churches discussed this possibility with the President, who said that the public was not prepared for it. Early in December the Peace Conference corresponded with leaders of public opinion in anticipation of issuing a manifesto for a neutral conference for mediation, and Professor Philip Jessup of Columbia University prepared a memorandum in support of it. No public call was issued, but in January, 1940, the organization again urged Roosevelt to initiate immediate and continuing mediation. It sent a delegation to discuss the program with Secretary Hull. Early in February the President announced that he was sending Under Secretary

---

* Similar bills passed the Senate on Oct. 27 by 63:30 and the House on Nov. 2 by 243:181, and the final bill was passed on Nov. 3 by votes of 55:24 and 243:172, respectively.

† On Sept. 6, 1939, the N.P.C. adopted a program prepared by Walter Van Kirk and Henrietta Roelofs: "1. keep the United States out of war; 2. initiate a continuous conference of neutral nations to procure a just peace; 3. work for permanent world government as the basis of peace and security; 4. prevent exploitation of war for private gain; 5. recognize and analyze propaganda to prevent warped judgments and unjust animosities; 6. strengthen American democracy through solving pressing domestic problems and vigorously safeguarding civil liberties." Seventy-seven thousand copies of this program were distributed, and it was presented on national radio Sept. 20. *The National Peace Conference and the European Crisis: An American Peace Program* (N.P.C., n.d. [1939]).

314

Sumner Welles to Europe for exploratory, informational talks with belligerents. When the director of the National Peace Conference reviewed the year, therefore, he concluded that the Welles mission indicated "that the Administration felt that the public had come to support such a policy. The Conference feels that it had a share in this process."[9] Far from being the example of constructive unanimity the report implied, however, the idea of mediation, like that of an economic conference, carried the seeds of division.

The annual conference of the Fellowship of Reconciliation in September, 1939, sent the President a letter which expanded upon the N.P.C. recommendation. It said that criteria for negotiation should include peace conferences "democratically set up and under civilian and not military control," a peace addressed to basic economic problems such as tariffs, access to raw materials, internationalization of colonies, and steps toward world government based upon economic and social justice.[10] Clearly, pacifists had extended the notion of a world economic conference into the war period. They coupled it with their notions of constructive neutrality.

They noted the existence of two great groups of neutrals: the inter-American states, and the Oslo powers—the small nations of northern Europe.* As German pressure had mounted on Poland the Oslo powers had been called together hurriedly by King Leopold of Belgium (acting on the suggestion of George Lansbury, according to Harold Fey). They issued a joint statement on August 23 which appealed to the great powers to keep negotiations open. No agency of mediation was named, but five days later, Belgium and Holland offered their services. In October, King Leopold requested that Roosevelt initiate a peace move. The United States politely declined, distrusting German peace feelers and knowing that any suggestion of further appeasement would be opposed by Britain and France.[11] Quite alone and afraid of imminent invasion, the Belgian king with Queen Wilhelmina of The Netherlands offered again to mediate between the great powers in November. American pacifists took their cue from the repeated Belgium-Dutch appeals: only the United States could unite the Oslo powers and American states into a significant world force independent of the European power struggle.

* Belgium, Luxembourg, Holland, Denmark, Norway, and Sweden had signed mutual trade agreements at Oslo in 1930 and 1932. Finland was included when the agreements were renewed in 1937. The grouping of states took on a political cast in July, 1938, when it was agreed that they should cooperate on security and international problems and should pursue a neutral course.

Harold Fey hoped that the President might secure an armistice—
Hitler had offered as much—and begin negotiations. He thought that
a tentative settlement of European problems might be effected by organizing the Poles into a separate nation (presumably acquiescing in the
Russian-German partition of Poland) and federating the Balkans. Ma-
ture colonies like India should be freed and others placed under international jurisdiction. He added that since "there has been a great deal
of lying on both sides" two tests of the negotiators' good faith could be
applied: progressive multilateral disarmament, and liberal economic
measures such as tariff reductions and stabilization of currencies. Extensive financial help from America should be extended in order "to
make possible a shift from an armament economy to a peacetime economy." Some beginning should be made "to organize the world" for
peace.[12] Nevin Sayre dismissed the argument that the time was not ripe
for negotiations between the belligerents by arguing that time was of the
essence for the neutrals in their own interests. He reminded Secretary
Hull that only persistent efforts had overcome initial reluctance to negotiate the Chaco war, and he concluded, "The epitaph which the years
have written over many efforts for peace since 1913 is that they come
too late."[13]

Pacifists passed on what information they could to prod the State
Department. Sayre sent the Secretary reports of conversations held by
Corder Catchpool and Percy Bartlett with high-ranking Dutch and Belgian officials who told them what Hull already knew: that they were
ready to act for the Oslo powers if there was any possibility of neutral
success, but that they dared do nothing to further alienate France and
Britain.[14] European contacts reported also that the German government
was divided over the war, but that the division could not be exploited
from the outside. Devere Allen was operating his No-Frontier News
Service from Brussels, and he sent word of emphatic support for
American-initiated mediation from leading labor officials with whom
he was in contact.[15]

Pacifists like Sayre and Allen were filled with urgency; no step
seemed too small to take toward peace. They also were confirmed in
their view that there was a third side to the war, the cause of the noncombatant nations which were committed to liberal trade policies, disarmament, world organization, and internationalism—the conditions of
lasting peace. There was nothing artificial about the gap between the
Axis and Allied powers. It was real enough to destroy civilization. But
for liberal pacifists the gap was not absolute and it might therefore be
resolved into a larger view, or settlement. The loss of the neutrals would

316

obscure that fact, they believed. It would be one more step toward a world war in which neither side would accept anything but victory. And they had drawn the lesson for twenty years that one-sided victory would preclude justice and order.

The plan was never feasible. The American public would have rejected it for mixed reasons. The Allies had already indicated that they were through with appeasement, and the Germans made it clear in February that they were interested only in a victorious peace. In the forlorn hope of the low countries was etched the pathos of all neutralists. In the plan of mediation lay the frustrated international bias of all liberal pacifists. The idea perfectly illustrated the way in which they became isolated from the American public, for it was acceptable neither to isolationists, with their fear of foreign involvement, nor to the advocates of collective security, who trusted in a military coalition against the fascists to establish a just order for peace.

Nonpacifist internationalists considered the organization of neutrals mainly in connection with the formation of a postwar world. When war broke out, James Shotwell organized a Commission to Study the Organization of Peace, of which he was president and Eichelberger was director. Other groups sponsored by the Council on Foreign Relations and the Federal Council of Churches began to study postwar issues, and on December 27, Cordell Hull established a similar committee within the Department of State with Sumner Welles as chairman.[16] There was much interaction between the public and private study groups. Early the following year, Welles won Roosevelt's endorsement of a special mission to the European belligerents to explore the prospects for peace. What exactly they had in mind is not clear, but the Secretary of State managed to temper the trip to information-gathering and to couple it with departmental consultations with neutral powers about postwar settlements with particular respect to international economics and armaments. Problems "arising from the war" were specifically excluded from these conversations with neutrals.[17] The Allies were apprehensive of a separate settlement with the Axis; the neutrals were disappointed at the lack of concrete peace terms and viewed the scheme as quixotic. American isolationists denounced the idea of involvement abroad; and pacifists complained that the President's good intentions lacked relevance to the existing conflict. Historians William Langer and Everett Gleason concluded that the scheme was a "remarkably picturesque manifestation of American indecision in the face of a war which the people and Government of the United States could neither wholly ignore nor resolutely embrace."[18]

317

In fact, both the Shotwell-Eichelberger group and the State Department were convinced that there was no longer any just basis on which Nazi ambitions could be accommodated. Cordell Hull made this point clear to the National Peace Conference delegation which discussed mediation with him for an hour in January. He was already working with foreign governments to prevent the mistakes of Versailles, he said, but he doubted that the belligerents would brook "interference in their war"; the world was faced with "ruthless aggression on the part of lawless states which have outlined vast plans of conquest."[19] Hull was determined to give as much succor to the Allies as he could without involving America in war; anything else would lull people into a false sense of well-being. Similar assumptions guided Shotwell's commission as it studied the organization of peace. Its report, published on Armistice Day, 1940, argued for collective force under a new league of nations: "law can be enforced only if the power of the community, overwhelmingly greater that the power of any of its members, is brought to bear when and where lawlessness begins."[20]

Precisely those assumptions distinguished the Shotwell study from the pacifists' plan and worried neutralists when Roosevelt announced the Welles mission. Norman Thomas told Socialist executives that he favored an American initiative to end the war but felt it would be "an enormous tragedy if the well-meant efforts of Roosevelt and Sumner Wells [sic] do as much to put us into this war as did the well-meant peace efforts of Wilson and Colonel House during the first world war."[21] The Young People's Socialist League, Youth Committee Against War, and some denominational pacifist groups were divided over the question of governmental mediation. Some opposed it "on the ground that the United States government would attempt to make a settlement which was favorable to the Allies and which would tend to draw us into the war."[22] The Keep America Out of War Congress was worried even about the weekly radio programs of the Commission to Study the Organization of Peace; it seemed to hear "all aid to the Allies" in every one of Shotwell's supposedly objective interviews. That suspicion, born of the neutrality controversy, would be carried into wartime discussions of the United Nations. It did not have time to congeal around the issue of mediation. Shortly after Welles returned from Europe the Germans moved into Denmark, Norway, Holland, and Belgium, and demolished the neutral bloc.

The end of Hitler's "phoney war" stimulated the advocates of collective security to reorganize. In May, Clark Eichelberger and William A. White set up a Committee to Defend America by Aiding the Allies on

318

the foundation of their old committee for neutrality revision. There was no longer any pretense of neutrality, but Eichelberger still maintained that collective defense was an alternative to war. Others began to agitate for outright participation. These persons were known for a long time simply as the Group because they worked covertly, except for a premature "Summons to Speak Out" for involvement which they released on June 10. They were men and women of accomplishment in journalism, publishing, business, and communications, mostly from the Northeast and many with experience in military or government service.[23] They believed that the logic of collective security predicated a wartime alliance, and they were impatient with well-intentioned attempts to obscure that fact. They operated privately through their considerable access to public media and political leadership. The Group was a transmission belt for English needs, and it greatly facilitated the exchange of destroyers for bases in September. In that effort it developed close relations with the Committee to Defend America by Aiding the Allies.

The Keep America Out of War Congress was the only national antiwar coalition when German troops rolled out across the low countries. It was essentially a pacifist-Socialist coalition, although it attracted also prominent isolationists such as Chester Bowles and John T. Flynn.* Its governing council represented most pacifist groups and finally took over the political functions of their coordinating "general staff." The more than fifty local K.A.O.W.C. groups in the summer of 1940 had been formed out of old N.C.P.W. peace councils or created anew by local Socialists. The Chicago group had its own office, bulletin, and full-time secretary (a Socialist). The Maine group was headed by the state secretary of the Socialist Party. K.A.O.W.C. mailings went regularly to all state secretaries of the party, many secretaries and presidents of the W.I.L.P.F., some regional F.O.R. leaders, and the three regional offices of the National Council. Socialists valued the coalition for the left-wing political emphasis it gave the antiwar movement; pacifists valued it for its contacts with labor and young people.

There were some weaknesses in the coalition. Pacifist groups supported specific projects better than the organization itself, which they suspected of becoming a separate and competitive entity dominated by

---

* Bowles, an advertising executive, was on the governing committee of the K.A.O.W.C. Flynn was its national chairman in 1940. He had been economic adviser to the Nye committee in 1934–35, was a bitter critic of Roosevelt on personal, domestic, and international grounds, and became very influential in the America First Committee.

319

Socialists. The Socialist Party was divided over the war question. Its national convention enacted a strong, Marxist, antiwar plank and opposed pending armament bills, conscription, military training, and any form of aid to the Allies. The day after the convention, German troops invaded Denmark and Norway, and some Socialists urged a policy of national defense and aid to the Allies. They would live no longer in the image of the "Saints of 1914–19."[24] The most serious break in party ranks came from the well-organized Jewish section. The Yiddish organ of the party, *Stimme,* printed material opposing the platform on war, and another Jewish journal even reported that Norman Thomas had endorsed Wendell Willkie for President! After prolonged wrangling, the Jewish section agreed to suspend *Stimme* temporarily and to work directly with its members.[25]

A more serious threat to the left-wing coalition came from the Communists who, since the Russion-German nonaggression pact, were as eager as the Nazis were to keep the United States out of war. They parlayed the catchy slogan, "The Yanks Are Not Coming," into a song and a movement:

> Let us voice the Yankee promise
> Let us forge the hearts of men
> In the firm determination
> We will never go again.

> Let the bugler keep on blowing,
> Let the drummer beat his drum;
> They are in for disappointment
> For the Yanks will never come.[26]

The Communists operated through existing organizations, especially unions, and tried to infiltrate the K.A.O.W.C. Its leaders felt threatened because deep-rooted antiwar sentiment was being rallied "behind a program which is not truly anti-war and which conceivably might become pro-war if Stalinist policy so dictated."[27] There was also the danger of public reaction against imagined Communist ties. The Keep America Out of War Congress required local groups to condemn Soviet as well as German aggression. With the F.O.R. and the W.I.L.P.F. it made every effort to expose the source of Communist front movements and events and to dissociate itself from them.

If there was a threat from the Left in the winter of 1940, there was a void on the Right. On the theory that "blood profits put business in the Red," the K.A.O.W.C. set up a businessmen's committee.[28] A luncheon with John T. Flynn as speaker netted over $125 in contributions from some of the businessmen, but little more was accomplished. Con-

320

servative isolationists organized independently in the summer when Princeton law student R. Douglas Stuart, Jr., won the backing of General Leonard Wood, William H. Regnery, Philip F. La Follette, and others.* On September 4 he was able to produce an impressive list of men and financial resources sponsoring the new America First Committee. They were pledged to build an "impregnable defense for America" and to oppose "aid short of war" in Europe.[29] In the following months the America First Committee not only filled a gap in antiwar organization, but even overshadowed the Socialist-pacifist coalition of the Left. Norman Thomas admitted just before Pearl Harbor that America First, not the Keep America Out of War Congress, was "the nearest to a mass organization against war."[30]

Thomas originally was critical of America First. It was obviously conservative and apparently anti-Semitic, he thought, and it tended toward an "armed isolationism and hemispheric imperialism."[31] During the presidential campaign Socialists stayed clear of conservative isolationists. Thomas knew that America First leaders, including his friend John Flynn, were trying to control its extremist hangers-on, though, and he became impressed with its importance. By January, 1941, the Keep America Out of War Congress admitted that America First was attracting "moral and financial support" it had been unable to reach. It could have cooperated informally with the conservatives, since Flynn and Sidney Hertzberg were then in the national councils of both organizations.† Instead, it resolved formally to join in a concerted campaign to keep out of war, and it deputized Frederick Libby to work out the details with America First. The conservatives apparently valued the church, labor, farm, and peace contacts of the left-wing coalition, because they made substantial grants of money to it.‡ The organizations vainly fought the Lend-Lease Act, with Libby and Dorothy Detzer in the pivotal roles of lobbying for both of them. They then supported together a plan for an advisory referendum of the people on peace or war.

---

* Wood was chairman of the board of Sears Roebuck and Company, Regnery was a publisher and major contributor to the N.C.P.W., and La Follette was the former governor of Wisconsin. Their organization was first called the Emergency Committee to Defend America First, an obvious retort to the Committee to Defend America by Aiding the Allies.

† Hertzberg had been director of the Writers Anti-War Bureau of the K.A.O.W.C., was editor of the noninterventionist but liberal *Uncensored,* and was publicity director for America First until he resigned in March, 1941.

‡ According to Wayne Cole, the A.F.C. gave in the first quarter of 1941: $1,000 to the N.C.P.W., $500 apiece to the Youth Committee Against War, the K.A.O.W.C., and the W.I.L.P.F., and channeled at least $2,500 to the Ministers No War Committee. *America First,* p. 227.

The N.C.P.W. sent out thousands of copies of a supporting speech by Senator Burton K. Wheeler. America First reportedly raised $10,000 for cross-country tours by the senators, and pushed the idea in its own branches. K.A.O.W.C. co-sponsored public meetings on the plan and allocated $1,000 for work on it through the youth committee.[32]

Association with America First eventually weakened the left-wing coalition and precipitated its decline. Cooperation was possible only on strictly isolationist grounds. Having vigorously opposed any increases in military spending in 1940, the K.A.O.W.C. now acquiesced in the fortress concept of America First and meekly inveighed against something called "armaments economics and imperialism."[33] The F.O.R. anticipated this trend and on January 28 voted to withdraw because of it.[34] The W.I.L.P.F. and the W.R.L. noted important differences with the antiwar Congress, but they stayed in awhile longer in order to preserve the united front. The A.F.S.C. decided to leave the coalition.

The organization was increasingly dominated by antiwar Socialists. In February a vigorous Socialist, Mary Hillyer, was named executive director, and a new executive committee took over active control. It included no representative of any pacifist organization.* In March the K.A.O.W.C. elected to become a separate membership organization. It expected to continue cooperating with pacifists through the "general staff" of leaders which had been revived to determine pacifist strategy, especially regarding conscientious objectors, but the organizational dynamics of the peace movement were such that the K.A.O.W.C. also competed with pacifist groups for funds and members. Few pacifists besides Frederick Libby helped shape the decisions of the organization that spring. By June only Abraham Kaufman of the War Resisters League was attending the governing committee, and his group withdrew in August because it opposed continued association with the America First Committee.[35]

The people who reorganized the Keep America Out of War Congress had the future in mind, or so they thought. "With the possibility of . . . getting into war more imminent," they proposed to create "something like the People's Council for Peace and Democracy" of World War I.[36] Such was the tyranny of memory. So strong was their notion of a historical parallel that they could not anticipate the difference that Hitler and a decade of totalitarianism had made. So fresh was their disillusionment with war that they could not appreciate the fresher disillusionment with peace. So obvious was popular antiwar sentiment that

* The executive committee included Lenore G. Marshall, John T. Flynn, Norman Thomas, Bertrand D. Wolfe, and Dorothy Dunbar Bromley.

they misjudged the public willingness to risk collective security. So well organized were noninterventionists that they could not appreciate the forces setting them apart from one another. So keen was their memory of progressives and radicals encountering war and discovering a common aversion to it that they could not grasp the import of progressive internationalists discovering the acceptability of war—living with conflict. Socialists thought for the moment that they were more radical than they were in fact. The noninterventionist peace movement appeared to be a stronger force than it actually was.

Its apparent power worried the advocates of collective security. Shortly after the opening of a concerted drive for intervention, the Fight for Freedom, Clark Eichelberger went to Secretary of the Interior Harold Ickes in despair of getting any encouragement from Roosevelt. "He proceeded to weep on the corner of my desk," Ickes told the President's secretary, "as I had shed briny tears on yours. If anything, he was more lugubrious than I had been." Eichelberger had tried in vain to get administration senators to stump for the pending defense bill and aid to the Allies. "He felt, as I have already expressed it to you, that Lindbergh is gaining and that people are becoming confused and anxious in increasing numbers."[37] Roosevelt was taking only the surest steps to get only the measures he deemed most essential in the winter and spring of 1941. For whatever motives, he confronted the isolationists obliquely. The men around him grew impatient. Stephen Early held back letters complaining that Ickes and other administration figures were accusing isolationists of playing into the hands of the dictators. Those people were well-intentioned appeasers, Early said, and they deserved to be deprecated "in the strongest terms."[38]

The Fight for Freedom was designed to take the case for intervention out of the administration's hands and also to take the initiative from the Committee to Defend America, which was torn between those who advocated all aid short of war and those who would go further. Even after the moderate William A. White resigned at the end of 1940, the committee was unable to pull together for outright intervention, and so a separate interventionist campaign was launched on April 19 after months of careful planning. It sought to unify all advocates of collective security and to take their case to the people and, through them, to the President. Structurally, it resembled the Emergency Peace Campaign. It was replete with impressive sponsors, cooperating organizations, a speakers' bureau, an independent news service, and specialized appeals to labor and minorities. Its greatest asset was contact with the publishing trade, whereas that of the E.P.C. had been the clergy. It had an

323

independent policy-making executive committee which promoted successively militant programs: repairing British warships in American shipyards, embargoing Japan, conveying goods to Britain, patrolling the Atlantic, and repealing neutrality legislation. As the Fight for Freedom gathered momentum, it pulled the older Committee to Defend America along with it until the two all but merged. By midsummer, Eichelberger was saying that American involvement would be inevitable and welcome.[39]

Even the church was rent by the nation's choice. A new journal, *Christianity and Crisis*, appeared February 10, 1941, as a direct challenge to Christian pacifists with political ideas. The editorial and sponsoring boards included clergymen who were members of the Group, which even then was planning the Fight for Freedom.* The editor, Reinhold Niebuhr, did not advocate declaring war, pleading instead that religion be kept within its proper sphere, which was not foreign policy. His theological arguments more than any others prepared churchmen to reject neutralism presented as a Christian duty and to accept intervention as a necessary political alternative. Henry P. Van Dusen actively lined up clerical support for direct aid to the British war effort on this pragmatic basis, but ministers such as Episcopal Bishop Henry Hobson and Methodist Bishop James Cannon called for a distinctly Christian crusade against the Axis.[40] Christian pacifists countered through the Covenant of Peace Group with a new affirmation signed by over 2,000 Protestant clergymen. The pledge not to sanction another war was taken both "as a Christian" unable to reconcile war with the central teachings of Jesus and "as a loyal citizen" opposed to the belligerency of the nation.[41] A Ministers No War Committee issued bulletins highlighting political action. By October it claimed 2,200 members and admitted having had one resignation.

The lines between military intervention and armed isolation grew taut, and the tactics of allegation, name-calling, and smear appeared. The K.A.O.W.C. resisted a temptation to print an exposé of the financial backgrounds of Committee to Defend America sponsors, but Socialists often followed a Marxist line ascribing intervention to the profit motive. Advocates of collective security were branded as British sympathizers and, after Soviet Russia was drawn into the war, even as fellow travelers with the Communists. Roosevelt partisans were accused of hypocritical trickery, of maneuvering the country into war while talking peace. Isolationists, on the other hand, were called fascist dupes,

* They were Francis Miller, Henry P. Van Dusen, and Henry Sloane Coffin.

charged with abetting the dictators, and accused of anti-Semitism. They paid dearly for the incaution of Hamilton Fish and others who let themselves be exploited by neo-fascists and subversives. They never recovered from the effects of Charles A. Lindbergh's tactless speech in Des Moines, September 11, in which he accused the Jews of pressing the country toward war. Virtually everyone who had cooperated with America First protested with little effect. As historian Wayne Cole concluded, the speech dealt the America First Committee a "staggering blow."[42] Thomas and the K.A.O.W.C. tried in vain to dissociate themselves from it.

By then the Keep America Out of War Congress was bankrupt. It was nearly $1,000 in debt, with no money in sight. Faithful contributors of the past did not respond. Libby suggested making a more positive approach; "people are weary of contributing to the negative cause of simply keeping out of war," he said.[43] Nothing was done but to cut back on staff and operations. In November the landlord was advised that the office probably would be vacated after 1941. Toward the end of the month, Norman Thomas confessed to Senator Wheeler that certain of "the more aggressive opponents of war" had come to feel that Congress was helpless to prevent it.[44]

Pearl Harbor for all its shock was almost an anticlimax in the history of the Keep America Out of War movement, already weak and beaten in its most important political objectives. Roosevelt had won congressional approval for a series of steps that had extended American military and economic goods to the Allies, had accepted an anti-German naval commitment in the Atlantic, and had removed most of the fetters from neutrality legislation. The notion of a historical parallel with World War I predicated that limited intervention and extensive executive power were inevitably a prelude to fighting. Whether or not the country would have taken additional steps into European war had it not been attacked in the Pacific, the President had legal power and public support to give all aid short of war to the Allies. That, and not war itself, was the essential political defeat for the neutralists.

America First disbanded in favor of victory. The Keep America Out of War Congress dissolved, since its articles of incorporation designated its sole purpose as opposing war. Most members of its governing committee reconvened to form a Provisional Committee Toward a Democratic Peace. They thought they might promote civil rights, equal distribution of the costs of war, and a just peace. They took no position on war itself. They hoped to regroup "progressive, pro-democratic, anti-imperialist forces," and to "attract former interventionists."[45]

325

But where were such forces to be found in 1941? Former interventionists were already organized into a variety of internationalist groups, including the Committee to Study the Organization of Peace. The "anti-imperialist" forces presumably meant the Socialist Party, but the few Socialists who were left mainly followed Norman Thomas in giving "highly critical support" to the war, and they lost their last measure of political identity.[46] "Pro-democratic" apparently referred to the defense of civil liberties, but except in the case of Japanese-Americans these rights were not as flagrantly violated as they had been in World War I; and the American Civil Liberties Union was, on the one hand, more specialized in their defense and, on the other, weakened by factionalism. It could not contribute much to a movement for peace and justice. Indeed, progressive ideals were diffused throughout society and were not as identifiable with pressure groups as they had been in 1917. There was neither an ideological nor an organizational base for a broadly progressive antiwar coalition in World War II, and it remained provisional.

Pacifists were a separate and well-organized constituency with a larger membership and a smaller public than at any time since they formed the nucleus of the progressive antiwar movement of the First World War. They were not specifically invited into the proposed 1941 coalition. They came to terms with the war independently. The American Friends Service Committee concentrated on war-relief work and on its new role in the administration of Civilian Public Service camps. The half-dozen remaining staff members of the National Council for Prevention of War pledged not to obstruct the war effort but rather to work for an early and just peace by negotiation. The executive committee of the War Resisters League reaffirmed its faith in pacifism and increased its services to conscientious objectors; but it hastened to add that it respected also the point of view of those "to whom war presents itself as a patriotic duty," and it promised not to obstruct civil or military authorities in "carrying out the will of the government."[47]

The American Section of the Women's International League tried to encompass pacifism without being committed to it, and it lost about half its membership from both its patriot and its pacifist wings. Emily Balch felt torn by "irresistible motives pulling in opposite directions."[48] She loathed war and appreciated the moral courage of her pacifist friends as keenly as ever. In a sense she leaned on them. But in the absence of alternatives, in view of the horrors to which the victims of fascism were fated, and in contact with European women who defended brute resistance without consciously abandoning the pacifist spirit, she could not bring herself to oppose this war. "If she found in the Women's International League an abiding and congenial home, it was because the League stood, as she conceived it, not so much for pacifism, absolute or otherwise, as for liberation from all that divides and separates men, for reaching out to one another, for building up together."[49]

Three days after the attack upon Pearl Harbor the executive committee of the F.O.R. declared:

> Trusting in God, we meet this hour without dismay. Despite the human foolishness and sin which mark us all and which have sundered us into warring nations we are all children of the one Father who is eternal God and whose name is Love. His Kingdom will come and His will be done on earth as it is in heaven.[50]

The committee reiterated its conviction of the futility and evilness of war. It acknowledged the gravity and complexity of the problems facing the nation, and with the War Resisters League it pledged neither to support nor to obstruct the war effort. It outlined several concrete tasks for pacifists interested in constructive action, and it concluded, "remembering in gratitude and affection those who bore witness to this Fellowship of Reconciliation faith in the last war, we dedicate ourselves now to the daily practice of this faith in repentance, humility, love and joy."

The leaders of the Fellowship had tried to strengthen that faith as the steps toward war grew shorter after the dissolution of the broad coalition of internationalists in 1938. At the same time that they cooperated with the anti-interventionist bloc, they built up local and denominational groups and provided for conscientious objectors. Indeed, membership in the F.O.R. satisfied the religious requirements of the Selective Service, and the Fellowship officially represented the War Resisters League in the National Service Board, which administered Civilian Public Service. The F.O.R. and the W.R.L. acquired new members with the addition of young people whose initial awareness of war came when they were threatened with the draft or were active in the Keep America Out of War Congress, and of older pacifists who had not been active in the movement between the wars. In 1938 the Fellowship had about 5,000 active members. When the Selective Service Act was signed into law, on September 16, 1940, the active membership was estimated to be 6,700. A sharp increase followed immediately and carried into the war years: there were 9,000 active members in August, 1941 (out of a total of 11,500); 10,500 active members in October, 1942 (out of a total of 13,000); and altogether slightly less than 15,000 members at the war's end. The income of the F.O.R. rose dramatically from $29,721 in 1938 to $60,084 in 1941 and $100,000 in 1945. The W.R.L. grew from 900 active members and an income of less than $5,000 in 1939 to 2,300 members and an income of $20,000 in 1945.[51] Thus, the war accentuated the development of a substantial pacifist constituency rather isolated from the public.

As in World War I, the principles of liberal pacifism and the existence of central organizations ensured a national program. Inevitably, this program acquired political ramifications as it came into contact with or criticized the government. But once again those who rejected the war effort gave their highest priority to the religious and individual aspects of pacifism as they accepted the role of a wartime minority.

"If I Should Die Before I Wake . . ."

Jacob Burck was a cartoonist for the Chicago *Times* when he won the Pulitzer prize for this cartoon in 1941.

328

Conclusion

The Fellowship of Reconciliation persisted despite the collapse of the political antiwar movement because it was not formed around projects, but rather around values. For this reason it is difficult to assess the achievements and failures of liberal pacifists between the wars. Doubtless there were men and women who thought of pacifism only in terms of warfare; they helped to swell the membership of the F.O.R. in the years just before World War II. But for the leaders pacifism was not a self-contained motivating doctrine distinct from other assumptions. It was an attitude that resulted from their holding a particular set of values and ideas which were defined in response to specific situations. It did not produce a set of accomplishments which could be labeled "pacifist" precisely because it operated only in relation to their experiences. Consequently, different aspects of the pacifist rationale were manifested at different times in varying historical circumstances. Typologies which seek to cut across the movement horizontally or sociologically without relating to its development in time are artificial and illusory. It is possible, though, to survey pacifism between the wars in terms of assumptions which underlay it, and see changes in them.

One set of assumptions involved religious ideas, which had emerged in the writings of liberal Protestant pacifists by 1941. Fundamentally, these men viewed God as active in history, but bound by the very moral laws he created. They rejected violence on the grounds that it is absolutely inconsistent with love and the moral order of the universe, with the Fatherhood and kingdom of God, the authority of Jesus' experience, and the historic and social role of the church. This religious rhetoric permeated expressions of the pacifist faith in nonviolence: that war is the apotheosis of violence and authoritarianism, leading only to new forms of injustice and exploitation and to new struggles for power; that peace requires the spirit as well as the instruments of justice. John

329

Nevin Sayre and his friends had insisted that for all its social and political involvement, the Fellowship should not outgrow that pacifist faith which brought transnational values into the purview of each individual conscience. "Some rule of birds kills off the song in any that begins to grow much larger than a fist or so" (the poet John Ciardi has written). The very commitment to peace and justice that had thrust liberal pacifists into events and issues had to be preserved against the time when conscience necessarily would be a private thing: "bird music is the tremolo of the tremulous. Birds let us know the songsters never are the strong."[1]

Although liberal pacifists held a constant religious commitment between the world wars, they changed their ideas in two important respects: they consistently repudiated violence, but in contrast to traditional nonresistants, they increasingly sanctioned some forms of coercion; and their definition of nonviolent force became relative to the demands of time and place. Consequently, their ethical decisions tended to reflect political judgments.

These changes reflected, in turn, the development of a relativistic Christian ethics in the thirties, particularly by Reinhold Niebuhr, and also modifications of the optimistic and rationalistic social gospel in favor of historical categories. For liberal pacifists the authority of the Bible derived from its effect on history as well as its insight into contemporary experience. They rejected the doctrine of inevitable progress. They understood Jesus as a historical revelation of the nature of God and man. By Fatherhood of God they meant the self-denying Creator and Redeemer, active in history. Man, they felt, is potentially good or evil; his development is influenced by his social and physical environment and ideals. Because he is essentially a child of God, however, he has latent goodness, will, and responsibility. Pacifists concluded that it is the responsibility of Christians to choose the kingdom of God, an ideal which was antithetical to the existing economic and international order. In this sense, Christianity implies pacifism, they urged. To a remarkable degree they made that view respectable among churchmen, and John C. Bennett, president of Union Theological Seminary, has said even that in many Christian circles between the wars "the burden of proof . . . shifted to the non-pacifist."[2]

Viewing "the way of Christ" as a historical precedent, pacifists argued its social utility even as they conceded the relative and ambiguous character of every judgment about it. Consequently, Kirby Page could greet 1942 with virtually the same creed he had fashioned in 1917:

330

I believe that the way of the cross is God's way, Christ's way, and therefore the right way to live, even in wartime . . . .

I believe that love is more powerful than hate, that mercy is mightier than vengeance, and that evil can be overcome with good.

I believe that war can be abolished through allegiance to Christ, and through the creation of an international mind, an international heart, and appropriate agencies of international justice and friendship.

I believe that the method of war with its bombing planes and starvation blockade is irreconcilable with the way of Christ, and therefore I cannot approve of any war or engage in its destruction and decimation.[3]

This historical point of view was critically important to wartime pacifists if they were to affirm the instrumental value of their faith without resting their case on its social effectiveness. As Evan Thomas wrote, the social aim of Christianity was "not utopia but to keep the dynamic struggle for spiritual values alive."[4]

The religious understanding of pacifists had broader implications in the context of their search for political realism, however. The relative ethics of some and the historical approach of others led many liberal pacifists to conclude that they could apply pragmatic criteria to alternative forms of social action and still remain within a religious ethic. This notion lay at the root of Christian nonviolence, which was advocated on the grounds of both prudence and Christian duty. It was the basis, also, for two different emphases which competed for the Fellowship's resources. Devere Allen, Roger Baldwin, and others who stressed the ethical side of pacifism sought to deemphasize its theological cast in order to pave the way for coalitions with non-Christian reformers and war resisters. Nevin Sayre, above all, believed that Christians must cooperate with others in the cause of peace and justice without denying their essentially religious basis.

Both emphases derived from the pacifist commitment to social action and organizational strength as well as from its humanitarian values. A. J. Muste recognized this in 1936 when he returned from St. Sulpice and his radical odyssey: "The F.O.R. must be and become revolutionary," he wrote to Sayre, "but out of *religious* experience and in a religious sense, or else it has no function and will wither away."[5] In his work and writings as secretary of the Fellowship from 1940 to 1953 Muste would blend political radicalism and religion into a personal style.* Early in the 1950's he would lead in almost counterpoint fashion

---

* From 1940 to 1946 he and Nevin Sayre were co-secretaries of the F.O.R.

both the radical Peacemakers, which advocated noncooperation with the draft and nonpayment of "war taxes," and the Church Peace Mission, which was designed to place pacifism before the churches on theological grounds. Muste kept religious faith and political effectiveness in a distinctive balance.

Nevertheless, the emphases on broadly ethical considerations, on the one hand, and Christian commitment, on the other, were presented to the F.O.R. as alternatives when its statement of principles was debated in 1929–30. They were reconciled then by the expedient of writing a descriptive statement of the organization's Christian origin and position. They would signal a choice of directions for the Fellowship in the 1960's and would result in a still more inclusive description in 1965.[6] They would confront the International Fellowship of Reconciliation as alternatives in 1967–69. This continuing debate over a statement of principles reflected changes in the language and understanding of religion, but it was not only theological. It involved questions of strategy as well. Allen and Baldwin, among others, saw opportunities to create political leverage out of left-wing alliances. Sayre, who was no less committed to social action than they were, saw the importance of creating a strong constituency in the Christian community both as a source of political leverage and as a refuge when political action was impossible, as during war. Each emphasis was defended by interpreting Christian ethics as a matter of personal judgment dependent upon historical circumstances, and this interpretation meant that ethical decisions rested upon social ideas and political analysis.

Pacifists shared with most of their fellow Americans liberal assumptions which were constant between the wars—the primary value of the individual, the efficacy of the democratic process, and a pragmatic approach to choices—while they, like others of their generation, reassessed their ideas about the process of realizing those values. They never questioned the importance of peace and freedom, for example, but they found it hard to reconcile freedom with order, and peace in change. War and a renewed emphasis on religion interrupted the development of a systematic political theory in support of nonviolence, but at least four important elements characterized pacifism between 1914 and 1941 and had an enduring influence on the movement afterwards. They were: (1) the ultimate value of the individual, (2) a distrust of centralized economic and political power, (3) a view of social conflict in terms of the struggle for power, and (4) an emphasis on the relationship of ends and means. These elements, scattered throughout

332

the writings of numerous pacifist leaders, were all characteristic of the thought of A. J. Muste.

Muste's belief in the absolute value of the individual, for example, came from his religious background; he had been reared in the Dutch Reformed Church and had been trained in its ministry, although by 1920 he had moved to the Society of Friends. Long after he had rejected formal and doctrinal religion in the early twenties, he remained committed to the importance of the individual, and in this respect he was like many of his contemporary reformers and writers. When he returned to the church, in 1936, it was because he had concluded that "it was shallow to think that a 'good system' under which men should automatically become good could be achieved, and still more shallow to think that the character of the men who worked for the new system and the means they employed were matters of no importance."[7] The Fellowship of Reconciliation had held from its beginning that reverence for personality was a fundamental value in social relationships. Muste spoke for it in 1940 when he said:

> The problem of democracy which concerns so many in this country today is likewise in the last analysis a problem of the nature of the human being, the quality of the individual. If human beings are essentially animals, even if they be very complicated and clever animals, then every society . . . will be essentially a wolf-pack . . . and then the distant as well as the immediate future will be with the dictators, since they are in that case building on the realities of human nature. Only if the human being is a creation of spirit, a being capable of making moral decisions and therefore of governing himself, is the dream of a free democratic society capable of fulfillment.[8]

Muste added, as did other Christian pacifists, that the concept of human dignity is essentially a religious one. Human responsibility is dependent on the existence of a creative and loving God and an orderly moral universe.

Although the person is of ultimate worth, however, individual freedom itself is contingent upon social justice, pacifists acknowledged. Therefore, some forms of compulsion are necessary to protect and extend personal values in society. And some forms of society are preferable to others—democracy is better than tyranny. Numerous pacifists added to their high valuation of the individual an intense distrust of concentrated political power.

Evan Thomas, for one, had learned such a distrust in the camps and prisons of World War I. Twenty years later he returned to the peace movement as chairman of the War Resisters League and the New York

333

Metropolitan Board for Conscientious Objectors in order to help younger objectors. Whatever absolute meaning reality might have, he wrote, it takes on practical meaning only as it is applied relatively: "we are forced to act as if all values are relative." The greatest foe of intellectual freedom is absolutism, if personal freedom is totalitarianism, and "it is war and the fear of war which alone make dictatorships possible, even necessary."[9] Pacifists cannot eliminate war and dictatorship, he confessed, both because they have not enough political power and because political solutions are compromises which always will be threatened by the principles of authoritarianism and violence, to which conflict tends. As in World War I, he believed that the pacifist could only refuse to submit to the military requirements of the state for the sake of individual worth and freedom. Conscientious objectors in both wars made that minimal assertion.

In peacetime their distrust of centralized political control was revealed in their resistance to compulsory R.O.T.C. and universal conscription. Pacifists John Nevin Sayre, Oswald Garrison Villard, and Edwin C. Johnson largely sponsored the Committee on Militarism in Education, which opposed compulsory military training in public high schools and colleges. All pacifists opposed the draft, which was adopted on the eve of World War II, and universal military training, which was defeated after each world war. Led by John M. Swomley, they would mount a strong but futile campaign against the reintroduction of conscription in 1948.* During the Vietnamese war they would give important support to the largely spontaneous draft-resistance movement, and would continue to work for the abolition of conscription altogether.

Pacifists in each war broadened their distrust of concentrated power to include the economic and industrial. That position had been characteristic of their original progressive antiwar coalition. It was a movement for peace and justice, and so it found an aggressive role after the war. In Lawrence, Massachusettts, Muste himself had discovered that the conditions of poverty, insecurity, and bondage were being created for workers by virtually unrestrained textile manufacturers. Subsequently, as secretary and organizer of the Amalgamated Textile Workers Union and as leader of the American Workers party (1933), he sought to organize laborers to break the absolute power of the owners. Similarly, young Reinhold Niebuhr was concerned about the depersonalization of economic and social relationships in the years when he

---

* John M. Swomley, professor of social ethics at St. Paul Seminary, Kansas, was youth secretary of the F.O.R. from 1940–53, and executive secretary from 1953–60.

was first formulating his ideas on nonviolence. In his maturing view social power had both economic and political bases, and the totalitarian concentration of power was as dangerous and self-defeating as anarchy was foolish. This was not a distinctly pacifist interpretation, of course, but it was one which profoundly influenced the pacifists who shared it, and who supported Norman Thomas in the Socialist Party.

Leaders such as Devere Allen, Kirby Page, A. J. Muste, Edmund B. Chaffee, and Harold Fey generally agreed with Thomas's analysis of the relationship of violence and injustice. The crux of his assessment of capitalism was that it denied power to the workers and concentrated it, instead, in the hands of those who profited from the concentration of industry. Thomas emphasized what he called "industrial democracy." He insisted that power must be democratically dispersed in a socialistic state, a point at which he differed sharply from Communists and even radical Socialists who wanted to concentrate the power of the state, at least temporarily.

His analysis of capitalism in terms of the concentration of power led Thomas to assume the reality and necessity of class struggle, which is why the question of the road to Socialist power loomed so large in the early thirties. Liberal pacifists were faced with that question because they, like A. J. Muste, had become involved in social reform. Increasingly, their criticism of society became sharper, and they became active partisans of underprivileged groups—labor and ethnic minorities. Like numerous other reformers, they became convinced that some forms of coercion might be necessary to establish social justice, so that their experience in reform movements made them reexamine some of the traditional tenets of pacifism. They came to distinguish between violence and nonviolence, as well as between coercion and persuasion. This distinction produced tension within pacifist organizations, since some pacifists believed that coercion of any kind violates the spirit of reconciliation and love, while others rejected all absolute distinctions and regarded even the use of violence as ethical in some cases. In the crisis of 1933–34 the Fellowship officially repudiated violence and sanctioned nonviolent coercion. During the dispute the organization had been virtually a microcosm of left-wing America, for it was debating the question of the road to power that divided Socialists, Communists, and even labor leaders among themselves in these years. The significant point is that their distrust of centralized economic control (under capitalists, at least) had as its corollary the view of *social conflict as a struggle for power*, and this view was reinforced by all their experience in social reform.

335

The same view characterized their understanding of international relations. Pacifist leaders had supported virtually every effort to convince the public of the futility of war and to make America responsible to the world. They created numerous educational programs, including peace caravans and conferences. They published a large amount of literature and organized an independent news service. They lobbied for disarmament, the World Court, the League of Nations, and the internationalization of economic power. They learned to mobilize public opinion in these campaigns, and they sought to coordinate the peace effort. They organized the greatest single effort of the interwar years, the Emergency Peace Campaign, and they cooperated with groups abroad, such as the Embassies of Reconciliation.

They opposed both the tyranny of European dictatorships and the American participation in the war against them. This apparent paradox is explained partly in terms of the pacifists' traditional aversion to war, and partly by their distrust of centralized control. Devere Allen and Oswald Garrison Villard, for example, may have been rationalizing their opposition to war in forecasting an eclipse of democracy if war were declared. But even if that were so, they were revealing a fundamental element of pacifist thought, the distrust of the concentrated power. Moreover, as the League of Nations proved incapable of stemming the rush to war from Manchuria onward, pacifists were encouraged to draw the conclusion that international relations, like economic competition, were essentially a matter of power struggles. The balance of power among nations is constantly shifting, they observed, and wars arise largely from the attempt to maintain the *status quo*, just as the balance of power among economic groups is constantly changing, and revolutions occur when privileged groups prevent orderly and continuous change. This point of view emerged exactly as the international order was shattered, successively in Manchuria, Ethiopia, Spain, and Czechoslovakia, and with it the American peace movement. Politically active pacifists found that responsibility to the world and the futility of war—both corollaries of the transnational values they held—were being interpreted as alternative courses for America. Internationalism was described by some as a commitment to the Allied democracies, the sole hope for justice with world order. The futility of war was used by others to justify strict neutrality.

Pacifists saw clearly that collective sanctions would only further divide the nations into rival alliances, and they mounted an impressive campaign to maintain American neutrality, but that insight and that campaign cost them their initiative and leadership in the broad coalition

336

of internationalist peace advocates. They did not see as clearly that the 1937 Neutrality Act was defined in the national interest, and that nationalistic values would predominate in the defense of neutralism. That lack of foresight, or their helplessness in the neutrality campaign, caused them to lose initiative in the antiwar movement to Socialists and nationalistic isolationists. After war broke upon Pacific shores pacifists were left almost alone of that progressive and internationalistic coalition which in World War I had opposed equally war and injustice.

By that time the essential tenets of a theory of nonviolence had been expressed, although its political analysis remained incomplete. Richard Gregg and Krishnalal Schridharani had argued that nonviolent action is consistent with both human behavior and political order because of the integral relationship of ends and means in all human endeavors. They both had treated coercion as one step in the process of persuading an opponent to come to a reasonable approximation of justice. They both had opposed the use of violence because, they said, it is inconsistent with the objects of mutual justice.

Pacifists long had asserted that the means determine the ends; Kirby Page and Evan Thomas had reached that conclusion in World War I. But they were slow to see the implication that the goal also determines the means, that both are parts of a single experience, as Gandhi might have said. Upon the outbreak of World War II the executive committee of the War Resisters League said that "religion, art and science rest upon truth, made alive in men who are truthful, and in an abiding faith that *the methods chosen determine the ends attained.*"[10] This assertion was repeated very often in pacifist literature. "It is already apparent that the ends of the methods of coercion and intolerance are stagnation and death," wrote Evan Thomas. "The ends of the methods of truthfulness and good will are limitless in possibilities and are still shrouded in mystery."[11] Violence invariably destroys personal worth and democratic procedures, he said; nonviolent action is appropriate to human nature not because men are naturally good, but rather because they are potentially good.

A. J. Muste added that nonviolent action was relevant to the political order. It could challenge the balance of power in a way which would be consistent with its goal of justice. Success in a violent revolution or a large-scale war, for example, depends on the organization of a tightly knit, well-organized party. It requires regimentation and repression. New inequalities are created out of the old ones. The trouble is that conformism and party control, once established, prove exceedingly hard to break, as the cases of Russia, Germany, and Italy seemed to show. The very existence of social democracy depends upon voluntarism and diversity, and nonviolent action stimulates these because it challenges the convictions and assumptions as well as the power of the established order. According to Muste, nonviolence also avoids the disorganization of economic and political life which often characterizes violent revolution and war. This is because the nonviolent resisters organize around a program of social justice and can succeed only as far as they can put their program into effect. Nonviolence is a revolutionary method, then, because in the first place it employs direct social action such as education, persuasion, demonstration, boycott, civil disobedience, and nonviolent resistance. It is revolutionary, too, because in repudiating the use of violence it is consistent with the political ends it seeks to bring about.

During and after World War II, Muste would urge that nonviolent, direct action be applied on a wider scale than ever before. He would encourage its use in the field of race relations and civil rights where his friends in CORE would inaugurate sit-ins and freedom rides in the 1940's. He would welcome its application to conscription during the war in the form of walk-outs from Civilian Public Service camps and work stoppages in the prisons, and afterwards in nonpayment of taxes, nonregistration for the draft, and even draft-card burning. He and his friends would apply it during the cold war to create pressure for disarmament and an end to nuclear testing: they would be found climbing fences into restricted military reservations, picketing biological warfare centers, swimming out to Polaris missile submarines, refusing to cooperate in civil defense exercises, and trying to sail into nuclear testing zones. They would walk from San Francisco to Moscow and from Quebec to Guantanamo, Cuba, in an effort to call attention to the arbitrary division of the world into two blocs of world powers. But well before nonviolent, direct action would be applied on a significant scale to civil rights or foreign affairs, it was girded with the pacifist assumption that it is consistent with the integral relationship of ends and means, with human nature and the democratic political process, and with a view of social conflict in terms of a struggle for power. The premise has remained constant since the thirties: nonviolence is a philosophy of life expressed in a method of action which accepts conflict as a problem calling for resolution rather than as something to be eliminated or ignored.

Even so, pacifist political thought in 1941 was weakened by vagueness. Richard Gregg and A. J. Muste, the very men who were writing of nonviolence as a technique, left their distinction between persuasion and coercion hazy. They implicitly relied on stimulating moral responses in opponents. Having astutely evaluated European power politics and the origins of World War II as the failure of militant nationalism, pacifists offered only neutrality as a public alternative, although that was an ever more obviously nationalistic program. Having failed to keep America out of war, they offered young men a private morality that looked like noninvolvement. Having made room within the Christian ethic for pragmatic criteria for ethical and social decisions, pacifists were slow to articulate an explicitly political theory of nonviolence. To this extent they earned Krishnalal Shridharani's criticism that:

> The shortcomings of pacifism . . . are the direct result of an inadequate understanding of the nature of *social change*. The pacifists fail because they regard peace as an end in itself. As a result, they minimize the significance of other human values, though they may be subjective, such as freedom and justice, which rile people's blood and cause great social and political upheavals.[12]

To the extent that they rely on persuasion alone, Shridharani continued, "The pacifists dream is just a pious wish with underpinnings of mere 'good will.' . . . When their hope of peace is frustrated in the process of social change, as often happens, they are in a dilemma." They are left with the choice of "upholding the violent method or maintaining the *status quo*."[13] He argued that "there is an element of *compulsion* in Satyagraha as it is worked out in India" which made Gandhi's method realistic and distinguished it from previous pacifism, he concluded.[14]

There was an element of compulsion in American pacifism, too, as it was applied to the problem of social change. It was evident in the liberal pacifists' view of social conflict in terms of power relationships. It was a product of the association of their social action with their repudiation of violence. It was reflected in the increasingly pragmatic orientation of the social-gospel movement. The element of compulsion was not carefully integrated with pacifist religious assumptions, however. It was not clearly defined in relation to the idea of nonviolent action. The vagueness of the distinctions between persuasion and coercion, and between violence and nonviolence as well, was the greatest weakness of pacifist theory on the eve of World War II.

But the very existence of such a distinction at all set pacifist thought in 1941 apart from that in 1914, and presaged the postwar development of nonviolence into a significant social force. Gandhi would become an important symbol for leaders in the Negro struggle for social justice—for Martin Luther King, Jr., James Farmer, and Bayard Rustin—because of his effectiveness as well as for his spiritual teachings. Nonviolence would attract activists in the antiwar and civil rights move-

339

ment because it promised direct action as well as peace and justice. Liberal pacifists had struggled with the ethics of conflict and with the dilemma of seeking far-reaching reform without sanctioning violence since World War I. Why, then, did they not more clearly articulate the coercive aspects of pacifism in relation to its philosophy?

One reason was the religious orientation of traditional pacifism, with its stress on persuasion, individual commitment, and inward change. Pacifism had its deepest roots in liberal Protestantism and its best organized constituency in the Protestant ministry. The coming of the Second World War renewed its religious emphasis and retarded the systematization of a pragmatic political theory of nonviolence. Indeed, leaders like John Haynes Holmes could not conceive of an authentic statement of nonviolence except one couched in religious terms. In *Out of Darkness*, Holmes slipped innocently from political analysis into religious affirmation, just as he had done twenty years earlier in *New Wars for Old*.[15] Even Muste described pacifism as "a way of life, not merely a tool or device." It was "the political strategy of the prophets, including Jesus," he wrote.[16] Holmes and numerous others, although not Muste, imbued nonviolence with an almost mystical authority which prevented them from evaluating nonviolent alternatives within the full range of political actions.

A second reason that the political implications of nonviolence were not clarified earlier was that the development of pacifism from individual nonresistance to social nonviolence required not only a modification of the social gospel, but of political liberalism as well. Liberal thought, as it was formulated in the eighteenth century, was concerned with the absolute worth of human personality—the spiritual equality, inalienable rights, autonomy, and freedom of individuals. It also included a belief in the essential rationality and goodness of man. It involved, too, the belief that the state governs only by consent and that "when the terms of the contract are violated individuals have not only the right but the responsibility to revolt and establish a new government."[17] Until the end of the nineteenth century liberals minimized the role of the state and stressed the value of tolerance and diversity, and the superiority of voluntarism over force. Historically, liberalism was characterized by the development of political machinery to accommodate social change. As Joan Bondurant has observed:

> Liberal Democratic theory emphasizes devices, machinery, instruments; it slights concern for social action techniques. Liberal Democracy is first of all a system to operate within a social situation where there already exists extensive, fundamental agreement. Within this

340

situation the most prominent device for regulative action is majority
decision. The one technique for adjusting conflicting interests is the
unrefined method of compromise . . . . Beyond these elements lies
tacit reliance upon violence. For sanctions characterized by violent force support the majority decision. Should the representative,
majority system be subverted, the ultimate right lies with violent
revolution.[18]

Pacifism was historically oriented to liberal values—the primacy of
the individual, the distrust of economic and political concentrations,
the value of voluntary association, the appeal to experience and reason.
Long before 1914 peace advocates had been concerned to develop machinery for establishing peace—world courts, arbitration treaties, and
international organizations. But in the twentieth century many pacifists
became convinced that liberal conventions did not always apply in their
social systems. They were faced with the apparent fact of a class struggle in an economic system where, they maintained, the instruments of
political control were in the hands of a class which opposed change.
Some of them were challenged by racial injustice where, again, political
machinery seemed to be ineffective. Their nation was increasingly involved in international power struggles which the League of Nations,
and subsequently the United Nations, proved incapable of solving.
They were faced, in short, with the challenges of their generation. Believing that the traditional political avenues of redress were closed to
them, some pacifists resorted to direct action, supporting strikes and
initiating sit-ins; believing that modern war was futile and unwarranted,
they refused to participate in it. In both cases they modified political
liberalism by challenging the majority consensus and by-passing political machinery while at the same time repudiating the ultimate sanction
of violent revolution. It is likely that pacifists were unable to assess
their modification of political liberalism for the very reason that they
were acting on the basis of liberal values.

There was a third reason that no distinct program of nonviolent
action emerged by World War II: pacifists put their major efforts
into securing a majority consensus for their policies. They developed
a remarkably effective lobbying organization, considering their resources, and they became adept at manipulating the support of other
civic organizations. They learned techniques of mass education. They
conducted political campaigns. Even with respect to labor, where the
issue of violent revolution was presented, they tended to support the
Socialist Party and traditional political activity. Throughout most of
the interwar period their assertions that war is futile and the Americans

341

must accept world responsibility and transnational values were not seriously contested. They were often ignored and their implications were disputed, but until the height of the neutrality controversy pacifists operated comfortably within the loose majority consensus on foreign affairs, trying to manipulate prevailing antiwar sentiment in support of specific programs. This situation did not characterize pacifists in civil-rights work, where nonviolent action had its greatest political development, and it changed radically after Pearl Harbor.

The liberal pacifists' essential quest then would be for a distinctive role in wartime. That had been their problem in World War I, too, but now they lived in a nation fighting in defense of itself as well as its perceived ideals, in a world where the only alternatives to victory appeared to be totalitarian regimes no longer bearable. Pacifists went on the defensive again, not because they were attacked as subversive, but rather because they were tolerated as irrelevant. Certain things were conceded to be within their purview—religious services, humanitarian programs, provision for conscientious objectors—but everything they touched seemed to acquire political ramifications. The war itself demanded interpretation because they expected to help frame policies of peaceful reconstruction at its end. Their quest for a wartime role would extend far beyond World War II into the cold war, however, because *it was characteristic of wartime that the nation had a near-ultimate commitment to one side in a polarized world*, a position which the pacifist could not share. A new generation of peace advocates would grow up trying to understand and live beyond that fact.

After the Second World War pacifists would find themselves still in a role of a minority with little access to the public. They would not share the anticommunist ideology of the nation, even though they would have few illusions of Soviet good will. They would be unable to acquiesce in a policy of militant containment, nuclear deterrence, or calculated limited warfare, but they would be almost without means to affect public policy. Consequently, they would turn to forms of direct action with which, under Muste's leadership, they would challenge the prevailing consensus on foreign policy. With the death of Stalin in 1956 and an apparent thaw in the cold war they would organize a new liberal coalition for a SANE nuclear policy and operate it in deliberate counterpoint to a radical Committee for Nonviolent Direct Action (C.N.V.D.A.) for unilateral disarmament.

As late as 1960, Muste would argue that "radical pacifism is the only substantial element in the non-Communist 'Left,' " but he would perceive even then that pacifism was entering a "new phase."[19] He could

342

see potentially new antiwar constituencies among theologians and scientists opposed to nuclear warfare and in the widespread civil-rights movement, itself utilizing techniques of nonviolent direct action. Within a few years he would encourage cooperation also with the rejuvenated antiwar movement focusing on the Vietnamese war and with militant youth groups. Pacifists would seek to reach these mass movements and engage in political action by using the methods of direct action forged when they had a limited constituency and a hostile public. Younger pacifists would honor the progenitors of radical nonviolence, and would be tempted to discount the importance of those who had employed traditional political forms between the wars.

That attitude would be ironical, for liberal pacifists played a significant role in the American peace movement then. They developed political techniques with which they broadened the basis of decision-making in foreign policy. They contributed both to an increasing understanding and acceptance of national responsibility in the world and to a powerful conviction that war is futile and that the United States should keep out of it. They led and, to a large extent, coordinated peace organizations until internationalism and neutralism became widely accepted as exclusive alternatives. Even then, they retarded the shift toward collective security and forced its advocates to adopt their own techniques of mobilizing popular support. They did not keep America out of war, but they developed an interpretation of the war as the continuation of a power struggle having its origins in World War I. They relied on traditional techniques of pressure politics, but they experimented with the ideas and methods of direct action. They not only laid the basis for radical nonviolence, therefore, but they also developed forms of action that would be required when pacifists would once more have access to a broadly antiwar coalition, as in the sixties.

A. J. Muste died on February 11, 1967, half a century after the war that made him a liberal pacifist. His passing was quiet, and he communicated no presentiment that the old arguments over which he had travailed thirty years earlier would accompany the ferment in the movement for peace and justice within two years of his death. He was memorialized, of course, and the tributes were singularly personal, as his life had been. Everyone who recorded his influence recalled that coherent impression of life which he had carried away from St. Sulpice. Many of his younger colleagues were puzzled by it. "Foxy Grampa's gone. We've got to do our *own* homework now," wrote one. "Hare Krishna, A. J. HARE KRSNA, HARE KRSNA . . ."[20] That remark symbolized a gap that was only partly generational which Muste had

343

bridged. The life style of the young radical tended toward absolutizing the relative choices that confronted all Americans: the individual in society, change with order, justice for peace, the frustrations of being unable to realize the very values that gave American culture coherence. In large measure the reformers of Muste's generation had reacted against arbitrary authority in religion and thought, in economic and political life. They had been committed to no one formula for peace and no single tactic for effectiveness. If they arbitrarily rejected war it was because they believed that warfare was the apotheosis of violence and authoritarianism which threatened their every liberal value. If their tactics changed with their perceptions of their world, their values remained as constant as their purpose. They conceived that their task was, in a phrase that Muste liked to quote from Martin Buber, "to drive the plowshare of the normative principle into the hard soil of political reality."[21] In that sense the rationale of liberal pacifists and their role in the peace movement were one: it was theirs to put foreign policy under the judgment of the same values that lifted them into the controversies of their time, and theirs, at last, to pit themselves "in Holy Disobedience" against what they believed to be the social instruments of war and authoritarianism.

344

Bibliographical Notes

These notes are confined to selected sources for the
study of pacifism and its role in the peace movement to
World War II. Bibliographies useful in broadening the
subject include the carefully annotated edition of *To
End War,* by Robert Pickus and Robert Woito (San Francisco: World
Without War Council, 1970); the *Bibliography of Books on War, Pacifism, Nonviolence and Related Studies,* by William Robert Miller (Nyack, N.Y.: Fellowship of Reconciliation, 1960); and the *Bibliography
on Peace Research in History,* by Blanche W. Cook (Santa Barbara:
ABC-Clio, 1969). A list of signed articles is appended to the dissertation by Vernon Howard Holloway, "American Pacifism Between
Two Wars, 1919–1941" (Yale University, 1949). The Swarthmore
College Peace Collection is preparing a comprehensive index to this
pamphlet literature. Although ephemeral, it is a fruitful source of antiwar thought because pamphlets incorporate relatively concentrated
arguments and often have the sanction of the groups which distribute
them.

Manuscript Sources

The richest repository of material on the pacifist wings of the peace
movement is the Swarthmore College Peace Collection. The largest
and most important personal collections housed there are the Jane Addams, Devere Allen, Edwin and Lucia Mead, William I. and Hannah
Clothier Hull, and Emily Greene Balch papers; but there are important
gleanings also in the Henry Wadsworth Longfellow Dana, Richard
Gregg, Jessie Wallace Hughan, and especially the A. J. Muste papers.
The SCPC is the official repository for several peace organizations, and
has large holdings for the Fellowship of Reconciliation, the Committee
on Militarism in Education, the Emergency Peace Campaign, the Wom-

en's International League for Peace and Freedom, and the National Council for Prevention of War. Important smaller collections include among others the American Union Against Militarism, the American League Against War and Fascism and related groups, the Woman's Peace Party, the War Resisters League, and the People's Council of America for Peace and Democracy. There are a few papers of the Congress of Racial Equality, although most of its records are housed at the University of Wisconsin. Several large and virtually unexplored groups of collections deal with conscientious objectors in World War II; these include the papers of Julien Cornell, a prominent lawyer, the New York Metropolitan Board for Conscientious Objectors, the National Service Board for Religious Objectors, and Paul Comly French, director of Civilian Public Service; most of these documents are restricted, but they reward selective research when permission is secured. Most of the pacifists groups active during the cold war are well represented at Swarthmore, although the University of Wisconsin also holds a body of Committee for Nonviolent Direct Action papers. The SCPC also holds important papers of the international peace movement, periodicals, and pamphlets. See the *Guide* to the collection.

As invaluable as are the SCPC holdings, they must be supplemented by several other collections. The Norman Thomas papers at the New York Public Library document the emerging pacifism of both Norman and Evan Thomas during World War I, but should be used in connection with the papers of Lillian Wald, also at the New York Public Library; David Starr Jordan, at Stanford University; Paul Kellogg, at the Social Welfare History Archives Center of the University of Minnesota; and the Louis P. Lochner papers, at the State Historical Society of Wisconsin, among others. Three important organizations not represented in the SCPC are the records of the papers of the League for Industrial Democracy in the scattered collection of the Tamiment Institute Library, N.Y., the American Civil Liberties Union Archives at Princeton University, and the large collection of Socialist Party of America papers at Duke University. The latter is particularly useful, in conjunction with the Thomas papers and the papers of the Keep America Out of War Congress in the SCPC, in documenting the left-wing antiwar movement prior to World War II.

The John Nevin Sayre papers are housed at his home and office in Nyack, N.Y., and include subject-matter files, correspondence, and otherwise unavailable records of the F.O.R. and the I.F.O.R. The Kirby Page papers at the Southern California School of Theology, Claremont,

346

contain a wide-ranging correspondence and an unpublished autobiography. Frederick Libby's detailed diaries, used by permission, date from World War I and eventually will be deposited in the Library of Congress. There are some American Friends Service Committee papers in the SCPC, but the large primary collection is deposited at Haverford College and includes the important files of the Peace Committee.

Several groups of papers are particularly important in evaluating the influence of pacifists within the larger peace movement and the interaction of peace groups. The Carnegie Endowment for International Peace Archives and the papers of James T. Shotwell at Columbia University include the papers of affiliated organizations, notably the League of Nations Non-Partisan Association. Selected files from the Newton D. Baker papers, the William Borah manuscripts, and the Norman Davis papers in the Library of Congress yield glimpses of the developing collective-security wing in the thirties, and hints of its informal relationship with the State Department. The Department of State records of the National Archives are not rewarding in proportion to their mass, except for the neutrality file (811.04418); the well-organized Franklin Delano Roosevelt papers in the Franklin D. Roosevelt Library at Hyde Park, N.Y., are far more useful in regard to both policy-formulation and contact with peace groups.

INTERVIEWS AND ORAL MEMOIRS

The Columbia Oral History Project in Butler Library includes valuable reminiscences by Roger Baldwin, Tracy Mygatt, Frances Witherspoon, Norman Thomas, and others active in the First World War period. Personal interviews with peace leaders proved to be as important for checking interpretations as for collecting information, however; historians have otherwise limited tools for verification.

The most important of some thirty interviews with American peace advocates included a visit with Mary Alma Page, wife of pacifist author and speaker, Kirby Page, in 1960; conversations with Marie H. Allen, wife of Devere Allen, editor and founder of the Worldover Press news service, throughout the summer of 1961; a visit with Harold Gray, prominent C.O. in World War I, in 1963; interviews with Dorothy Detzer Denny, legislative representative for the W.I.L.P.F., Alfred Hassler, executive director of the F.O.R., George M. Houser, an executive director of CORE, A. J. Muste, executive secretary of the F.O.R., Claud Nelson, secretary for the South with the F.O.R., Ray Newton, secretary of the Peace Section of the A.F.S.C., Clarence Pickett, executive secretary emeritus of the A.F.S.C., Norman Thomas, Socialist Party leader, and Evan W. Thomas, chairman of the New York Metropolitan Board for Conscientious Objectors and of the War Resisters League, all in the summer of 1964; visits with Frederick J. Libby, secretary of the N.C.P.W. in 1966–67; and interviews with Clark Eichelberger, director of the League of Nations Association, Dr. Harry Laidler, secretary of the League for Industrial Democracy, and E. Raymond Wilson, executive secretary emeritus of the Friends Committee on National Legislation, in 1968–69.

A series of interviews in 1968–69 were of considerable help for understanding the period since World War II. They included among others: visits with Stewart Meacham, peace education secretary of the A.F.S.C.; Robert Gilmore, a founder of SANE, the Committee for Non-violent Action (C.N.V.A.), and Turn Toward Peace; Lawrence Scott, a founder of C.N.V.A. and executive director of A Quaker Action Group, and Charles Walker, an officer in numerous pacifist groups including the C.N.V.A., the F.O.R., the A.F.S.C., and *Liberation*. Occasional long conversations since 1964 with John Nevin and Kathleen Sayre in their home in Nyack, N.Y., and among some of their old friends in Europe have been the most valuable oral resource of all.

PERIODICALS AND ANNUAL REPORTS

The New York *Times* is a useful index to organizational sequences and activities, but not to internal development of pacifist groups. The most important periodical sources in this regard are *Christian Century* (1920–41), which under Charles C. Morrison was sympathetic to absolute pacifism between the two world wars, each of which it reluctantly supported, and the *World Tomorrow* (1918–34). The latter was the unofficial spokesman for liberal pacifists in the Fellowship of Reconciliation. Most of the peace groups had their own house organs, of which the most useful have been: *News Letter* and *News Sheet*, published by the F.O.R. irregularly from 1916–35, and *Fellowship* magazine (1935–   ), which succeeded them and largely took the place of the *World Tomorrow*; the *Bulletin* of the People's Council of America (Aug., 1917–Aug., 1919); *Pax International* (1925–40), the journal of the Women's International League for Peace and Freedom; the *War Resister* (1923–41), of the War Resisters League; *Peace Action* (1934–41), published by the National Council for Prevention of War; and *World Events* (1933–39), the principal organ of Devere Allen's

348

news service. Other pacifist periodicals are of selective use and should be studied in connection with the individuals or groups they represent.

Annual reports are usually included in archival records, but those of the A.F.S.C. were published as the *Annual Report* (1924–). Addressed to an interested public instead of a limited membership, they suggest the range of Quaker action projects. The *Peace Year Book* (1910–), published by the National Peace Council, London, is an annual compilation of world-wide organizations for peace, officers, and official periodicals.

MEMOIRS AND AUTOBIOGRAPHIES

The First World War period is rich in autobiographical accounts. Jane Addams, *The Second Twenty Years at Hull House, September, 1909 to September, 1929* (New York: Macmillan Co., 1930), should be supplemented with her *Peace and Bread in Time of War* (New York: King's Crown Press, 1945 [1st ed., 1922]),which deals specifically with the organization of women's peace work. The 1945 edition of this work is particularly interesting, since it includes an introduction by John Dewey, who had supported the First World War. Jane Addams, Emily Greene Balch and Alice Hamilton, *Women at The Hague: The International Congress of Women and Its Results* (New York: Macmillan, 1915), includes descriptions of the congress by participants and also a text of the Julia Grace Wales Plan. Lillian D. Wald, *Windows on Henry Street* (Boston: Little, Brown & Co., 1934), is useful for the progressive American Union Against Militarism, and Morris Hillquit, *Loose Leaves from a Busy Life* (New York: Macmillan Co., 1934), contains valuable chapters on the Socialist Party and the People's Council of America. Max Eastman, *Love and Revolution; My Journey Through an Epoch* (New York: Random House, 1964), opens with an account of the life and thoughts of the literary radicals among whom Eastman moved, and it can be supplemented with Floyd Dell, *Homecoming; An Autobiography* (New York: Farrar & Rinehart, 1933), and the wartime numbers of *Masses* and *Liberator*. David Starr Jordan, *Days of a Man,* 2 vols. (New York: World Book Co., 1922), John Haynes Holmes, *I Speak for Myself* (New York: Harper & Bros., 1959), and Stephen Wise, *Challenging Years* (New York: Putnam's Sons, 1949), are important accounts of general use; Vida D. Scudder, *On Journey* (New York: E. P. Dutton & Co., 1937), provides glimpses of a progressive who was attracted to pacifism as she perceived its radical implications; and Ammon Hennacy, *Autobiography of a Catho-*

lic Anarchist (New York: Catholic Worker Books, 1954), describes the conversion of a socialist who was imprisoned for essentially political reasons. Lella Secor Florence recalled some internal details of "The Ford Peace Ship and After" in a chapter of Julian Bell, ed., *We Did Not Fight: 1914–1918 Experiences of War Resisters* (London: Cobden-Sanderson, 1935).

The rationale and treatment of conscientious objectors in World War I are documented in Kenneth I. Brown, ed., *Character "Bad": The Story of a Conscientious Objector as Told in the Letters of Harold Studley Gray* (New York: Harper & Bros., 1934), Ernest L. Meyer, *"HEY! YELLOWBACKS!": The War Diary of a Conscientious Objector* (New York: John Day Co., 1930), and Arle Brooks and Robert J. Leach, *Help Wanted! The Experiences of Some Quaker Conscientious Objectors* (Philadelphia: Pendle Hill, 1940). The repudiation of warfare by men who had supported it is recounted in Harry Emerson Fosdick, *The Living of These Days: An Autobiography* (New York: Harper & Bros., 1956), and Sherwood Eddy, *A Pilgrimage of Ideas, or, the Re-education of Sherwood Eddy* (New York: Farrar & Rinehart, 1934), and *Eighty Adventurous Years, an Autobiography* (New York: Harper & Bros., 1955). Kirby Page helped to write both of Eddy's books, even as he had helped to reshape Eddy's thinking. Page's own autobiography, "My Cup Runneth Over," was written in the fifties and is held with his papers. "Sketches for an Autobiography" by A. J. Muste was published serially in *Liberation* (1957–60) and is brought together in Nat Hentoff, ed., *The Essays of A. J. Muste* (Indianapolis: Bobbs-Merrill, 1967), but they should be supplemented by the autobiographical notes incorporated in a series of lectures by Muste in his papers (SCPC).

Threescore: The Autobiography of Sarah N. Cleghorn (New York: Harrison Smith & Robert Haas, 1936), provides useful glimpses of the pacifist experiment at Brookwood Labor College in the twenties, and Joseph B. Matthews, *The Odyssey of a Fellow Traveler* (New York: Mount Vernon Publ., Inc., 1938), describes his movement through social-gospel reform, pacifism, socialism, to communism. Matthews's work appears to be factually accurate, but it must be read with care because it is subtly colored by his subsequent bias against radicalism. The broadly ranging work of the A.F.S.C. is revealed in Clarence E. Pickett, *For More Than Bread, An Autobiographical Account of Twenty-Two Years' Work with the American Friends Service Committee* (Boston: Little, Brown & Co., 1953), and the personal diplomacy of the Emergency Peace Campaign is described in George Lansbury,

My Pilgrimage for Peace (New York: Henry Holt & Co., 1938). The operation of a pacifist-oriented peace lobby between the wars is recounted in Dorothy Detzer, *Appointment on the Hill* (New York: Henry Holt & Co., 1948), and in Frederick J. Libby, *To End War* (Nyack, N.Y.: Fellowship Publications, 1969). These books should be supplemented by *The Autobiography of James T. Shotwell* (New York: Bobbs-Merrill Co., Inc., 1961), and the partly autobiographical *On the Rim of the Abyss* (New York: Macmillan Co., 1936), by Shotwell, a nonpacifist peace advocate with significant connections in the State Department. Cordell Hull was outspoken in recalling the influence of neutralist peace groups in his *Memoirs,* 2 vols. (New York: Macmillan Co., 1948). Anthony Eden, *Facing the Dictators; The Memoirs of Anthony Eden, Earl of Avon* (Boston: Houghton Mifflin Co., 1962), and Winston Churchill, *The Second World War: The Gathering Storm* (Boston: Houghton Mifflin Co., 1948), are important in framing the story of the negotiations for a world economic conference.

PACIFIST WRITINGS

Contemporary peace activity has created a public for anthologies of writings on pacifism and nonviolence. Mulford Q. Sibley, ed., *The Quiet Battle; Writings on the Theory and Practice of Non-Violent Resistance* (New York: Doubleday & Co., 1963), groups examples drawn from throughout history in such a way as to suggest the increasingly self-conscious and political use of nonviolent action. Arthur and Lila Weinberg, eds., *Instead of Violence; Writings by the Great Advocates of Peace and Nonviolence Throughout History* (New York: Grossman Publishers, 1963), artfully arrange representative thinking on the subject from the present to ancient times. The presentation and selection are more humanistic than political, and a sense of coherent tradition emerges from the book. Staughton Lynd, *Nonviolence in America; A Documentary History* (Indianapolis: Bobbs-Merrill, 1966), arranges selections from colonial writers to recent civil rights and antiwar activists in order to establish the existence of an "indigenous American tradition of nonviolent resistance to social evil." The author's position is more effectively defined than is the tradition itself. The strongest sections are the most recent, whereas the interwar period is completely ignored. Peter Mayer, *The Pacifist Conscience* (Chicago: Henry Regnery Co., 1967), intentionally develops the pacifist position by drawing upon representative selections in a chronological sequence

351

from ancient to contemporary times. The book is more reflective in mood than Lynd's; it joins nonviolence to social reform, but with emphasis upon principle more than on technique. It is apparent that anthologies of pacifist writing reflect in their organization the very dilemmas and differences of emphasis that characterized pacifists themselves.

In World War I, John Haynes Holmes published *New Wars for Old* (New York: Dodd, Mead & Co., 1916), and also many sermons, among which the most direct statements were *The International Mind* (1916), *A Statement to My People on the Eve of War* (1917), *The Church in War Time* (1917), *The Spiritual Conditions of An Enduring Peace* (1918–19), and *The Price of Peace* (1918–19). See also his *Patriotism Is Not Enough* (New York: Greenberg Publ., Inc., 1925). Jane Addams, whose prewar internationalism was indicated in *Newer Ideals of Peace* (New York: Macmillan Co., 1907), put her wartime feelings into later autobiographical accounts after being frustrated in attempts at public explanation early in the war. Other pacifists who valued a variety of international approaches included Randolph Bourne, who edited *Towards an Enduring Peace; A Symposium of Peace Proposals and Programs, 1914–1916* (New York: American Association for International Conciliation, 1916), and Emily Greene Balch, who edited *Approaches to the Great Settlement* (New York: B. W. Huebsch, 1918). Publication of her book was the last achievement of the rapidly dissolving American Union Against Militarism and a futile bid for rapprochement with traditional internationalists.

The position of the F.O.R. was presented in its journal and in pamphlets, notably W. Fearon Halliday, *Personality and War* (1916), and Norman Thomas, *et al., The Conquest of War* (1917). That of antiwar socialists was developed in Alexander Trachtenberg, *The American Socialists and the War* (New York: Rand School of Social Science, 1917), and in periodicals that survived censorship, including the moderate *Intercollegiate Socialist*.

The wartime essays of Randolph Bourne are collected in James Oppenheim, ed., *Untimely Papers* (New York: B. W. Huebsch, 1919), Carl Resek, ed., *War and the Intellectuals; Essays by Randolph S. Bourne, 1915–1919* (New York: Harper & Row, 1964), and are brought together with selected correspondence in Lillian Schlissel, *The World of Randolph Bourne* (New York: E. P. Dutton, 1965).

Devere Allen's thinking may be traced in the periodicals he edited, *World Tomorrow* and *World Events,* in many pamphlets, and particu-

352

larly in two books: *Pacifism in the Modern World* (New York: Doubleday, Doran & Co., 1929), a collection of essays by leading liberals who addressed themselves to nonviolent forms of social change in a variety of contexts; and *The Fight for Peace* (New York: Macmillan Co., 1930), a comprehensive history of the peace movement which was also an extended tract for war resistance. Those pamphlets which most clearly suggest Allen's distinctively activist approach are *A War-Time Credo,* a flyer reprinted from *The Oberlin College Literary Magazine* (Feb., 1917), written while he was a student at Oberlin College, *War Resistance as War Prevention* (1929), and *Will Socialism End the Evil of War?* (1931). They should be supplemented by his "Bring the Peace Movement to Socialism!" in *The Eighteenth Convention of the Socialist Party of America* (1934), and "Pacifism and Its Critics," in the *American Socialist Monthly,* IX (Feb., 1937), 25–31.

Kirby Page was the most influential single pacifist author and speaker of the interwar period. Pacifist and socialist notions infuse ten books on religious living which he wrote between 1929 and 1950. His social views are most fully articulated in *A New Economic Order* (New York: Harcourt & Brace, 1930), and *Individualism and Socialism; An Ethical Survey of Economic and Political Forces* (New York: Farrar & Rinehart, 1933). His interpretation of war is developed in *The Abolition of War* (New York: George H. Doran Co., 1924), and *What Shall We Do About War?* (New York: Eddy & Page, 1935), which he wrote with Sherwood Eddy, and in *War; Its Causes, Consequences and Cure* (New York: George H. Doran Co., 1923), *National Defense; A Study of the Origins, Results and Prevention of War* (New York: Farrar & Rinehart, 1931), and *Must We Go To War?* (New York: Farrar & Rinehart, 1937). Page also was the author of numerous pamphlets and of editorials in *World Tomorrow*. His analysis of war and world order was closely paralleled by that of Norman Thomas, although the Socialist leader gradually lost his absolute pacifist commitment in the thirties. Thomas's thinking on war is most explicit in sections of *As I See It* (New York: Macmillan Co., 1932), *The Choice Before Us; Mankind at the Crossroads* (New York: Macmillan Co., 1934), *Socialism on the Defensive* (New York: Harper & Bros., 1938), and *Keep America Out of War; A Program* (New York: Frederick A. Stokes Co., 1939), but see also his pamphlet, *The Challenge of War; An Economic Interpretation* (New York: League for Industrial Democracy, 1924). Thomas never wavered in his defense of conscientious objectors. See, in addition to his history of objection in World War I, especially the pamphlets,

War's Heretics; A Plea for the Conscientious Objector (New York: Civil Liberties Bureau of the A.U.A.M., 1917), and *The Christian Patriot* (Philadelphia: W. H. Jenkins, 1917).

The pacifist thought of A. J. Muste is most fully articulated in writings dating from his "return to pacifism" in 1936 to his death in 1967, but his works after World War II incorporate a revolutionary perspective characteristic of his activity in the twenties and early thirties. Accordingly, his articles in *Fellowship* and *Liberation* during the cold war should supplement his other writing. They are well represented in Nat Hentoff, *The Essays of A. J. Muste*. See Muste's *Non-Violence in an Aggressive World* (New York: Harper & Bros., 1940), and *Not By Might* (New York: Harper & Bros., 1947), and particularly three of his pamphlets, *The World Task of Pacifism* (Wallingford, Pa.: Pendle Hill, 1941), *War Is The Enemy* (Wallingford, Pa.: Pendle Hill, 1942), and *What Would Pacifists Have Done About Hitler?* (New York: Fellowship of Reconciliation, 1949). Muste's attempt to yoke nonviolent action with social revolution reflects a position developed also in Europe and most fully presented by a Dutch sociologist, Barthélmy DeLigt, in *The Conquest of Violence; An Essay on War and Revolution* (New York: E. P. Dutton, 1938).

Muste, Thomas, and Page represented a still more generalized desire, to demonstrate the realism of nonviolent forms of resistance to evil, especially war. Particularly clear presentations of this intention in religious terms are: Leyton Richards, *Realistic Pacifism; The Ethics of War and the Politics of Peace* (New York: Willett, Clark & Co., 1935); Paul Hutchinson, *World Revolution and Religion* (New York: Abingdon Press, 1931); and Luman Jay Shafer, *The Christian Alternative to World Chaos* (New York: Round Table Press, Inc., 1940).

A thin shade of emphasis distinguishes these works from those which stress the injunction of religious ethics against war or participation in war. A major intellectual edifice was reared for this position by studies in Biblical criticism and church history, deriving mainly from England. These books include Charles E. Raven, *War and the Christian* (New York: Macmillan Co., 1938), and *The Theological Basis of Christian Pacifism* (New York: Fellowship Publications, 1950); and George H. C. Macgregor, *The New Testament Basis of Pacifism* (London: James Clarke & Co., Ltd., 1936). The last named book was very helpful in buttressing the pacifist inclinations of American and British Christians, and a more recent work by Jean Lasserre, *War and the Gospel* (English trans., Scottdale, Pa.: Herald Press, 1962), appears to have played a similar role among French-speaking Christian pacifists.

354

Studies of historical precedents for Christian pacifism were important both because they indicated the persistence of the dissenting tradition and because they fed the modern pacifist movement within the churches. Adolf Harnack documented the rejection of military service by the early church in his *Milita Christi: Die Christliche Religion und der Soldatenstand in den ersten drei Jahrunderten* (Tübingen: T. C. B. Mohr, 1905), a work of profound importance in Europe and America among churchmen who followed Harnack's Biblical interpretation of the social gospel. Cecil John Cadoux, *The Early Christian Church and the World* (Edinburgh: T. & T. Clark, 1925), was the standard scholarly English work in the field, and see Cadoux, *Christian Pacifism Reexamined* (Oxford, England: Blackwell, 1940). G. J. Heering's *The Fall of Christianity* (1928 [English trans. London: George Allen & Unwin, 1930]) has been much used by subsequent writers, although it is probably supplanted for Americans by Roland Bainton, *Christian Attitudes Toward War and Peace; A Historical Survey and Critical Re-evaluation* (Nashville: Abingdon Press, 1960). Catholic pacifism was anticipated by the critical work of a German, Franziskus Stratmann, *The Church and War, A Catholic Study* (Engl. trans. New York: J. P. Kennedy, 1931).

The notion of distinctly Christian obligation to eschew violence, or at least of a religious tradition of nonviolence, prompted numerous books and pamphlets of the interwar period. Henry Hitt Crane, *Pacifism— A Way of Life* (1939–40), and Charles F. Boss, *The Case for Methodist Conscientious Objectors* (n.d., ca. 1936) and *Epitome of Peace* (n.d.), were pamphlets written for the Commission on World Peace of the Methodist Episcopal Church. The Department of Social Education and Social Action of the United Christian Missionary Society sponsored A. T. DeGroot, *Christianity Is Pacifism* (n.d. [ca. 1935]). The Episcopal Pacifist Fellowship distributed Elmore McNeill McKee, *Why Pacifism in These Times?* (n.d.). The F.O.R. sponsored innumerable pamphlets along this line. Individual examples of religious appeals include Kirby Page, *If War Is Sin* (New York: Fellowship of Reconciliation, n.d. [ca. 1935]), Theodore Ainsworth Greene, *What Can Christians Do for Peace?* (Boston: Pilgrim Press, 1935), John Nevin Sayre, *What Christian Pacifism Proposes* (New York: Fellowship of Reconciliation, n.d.) and *War is Unchristian, But—* (1924), and three books: E. Stanley Jones, *The Choice Before Us* (Nashville: Abingdon-Cokesbury, 1937), Albert R. H. Miller, *The Church and War* (St. Louis: Bethany Press, 1931), and Rev. J. A. Boord, *Christianity and War: Can They Co-exist?* (Burlington, Iowa: Lutheran

355

Literary Board, Inc., 1938). The latter, written by a Lutheran minister, is an example of the unsophisticated and somewhat simplistic level to which the language of religious obligation can turn. Far more careful are the statements in Charles W. Gilkey, *Jesus and Our Generation* (Chicago: University of Chicago Press, 1925), and Charles C. Morrison, *The Social Gospel and the Christian Cultus* (New York: Harper & Bros., 1933). The man who more than any other epitomized the acceptance of Christian duty to forsake war was Harry Emerson Fosdick, and his example was all the more dramatic because he had supported the First World War. In a series of pamphlets he developed an increasingly absolute and applied pacifism: *Shall We End War?* (New York: Clearing House for Limitation of Armament, 1921), *A Christian Crusade Against War* (New York: n.p., 1923), *A Christian Conscience About War* (n.p., 1925), *The Unknown Soldier* (Washington, D.C.: Government Printing Office, 1934), and *Jesus' Ethical Message Confronts the World* (New York: the author, 1939).

Fosdick's 1939 pamphlet, *Dare We Break the Vicious Circle of Fighting Evil with Evil!* [*sic*] (New York: Riverside Church), approached the ethical side of pacifism which had been developed partly in response to the image of Gandhi. John Haynes Holmes popularized Gandhi from 1917 to 1926, when he ran the Indian's spiritual biography in *Unity* magazine. Kirby Page made a brief but serious attempt at interpretation in his *Mahatma Gandhi and His Significance* (New York: Eddy & Page, 1930), but Gandhi's example was appropriated most fully by Richard Gregg in a series of books: *The Psychology and Strategy of Gandhi's Non-violent Resistance* (Triplicane, Madras: S. Ganesan, 1929), *Gandhiji's Satyagraha or Non-violent Resistance* (Triplicane, Madras: S. Ganesan, 1930), and *The Power of Non-Violence* (Philadelphia: J. B. Lippincott Co., 1934). The last title was published in a revised and condensed version in 1944 by the F.O.R., and a second printing was done in 1951; a second revised edition was published in 1959 by the F.O.R. and in 1966 by Schocken Books. Overseas editions include English and Indian versions in 1934 and 1935, an abbreviated version by M. M. Temple in Lusaka, Zambia, subsequently translated into Portugese, a Spanish, and a German edition. Gregg followed this book with a series of training manuals, including *Training for Peace: A Program for Peace Workers* (Philadelphia: J. B. Lippincott Co., 1937), and *A Discipline for Non-Violence* (Philadelphia: Pendle Hill, n.d.), and these have been updated for the contemporary peace and civil-rights movements. The convertible relationship of means and ends which Gregg introduced through Gandhi was developed by Aldous Huxley, *Ends and Means; An Enquiry Into the Nature of Ideals and Into the Methods Employed for their Realization* (New York: Harper & Bros., 1937), and this publication led into discussions of pacifist ethics such as that of Harold Fey in "Ends and Means," *Fellowship,* IV (Feb., 1938), 2. The political aspects of nonviolence were further analyzed in *War Without Violence* (New York: Harcourt, Brace & Co., 1939), by Krishnalal Shridharani, a former participant in Gandhi's *Satyagraha* campaigns.

Some pacifists coupled their total rejection of war with traditional approaches to peace and internationalism. International law is promoted in Lucia Ames Mead, *Law or War* (New York: Doubleday, Doran & Co., 1928), and Charles C. Morrison, *The Outlawry of War; A Constructive Policy for World Peace* (Chicago: Willett, Clark & Colby, 1927). It is coupled with the World Court notion in Kirby Page, *An American Peace Policy* (New York: George H. Doran Co., 1925). Pacifist attempts to approach the war question from an analytical, rather than an ethical-religious, point of view include: William I. Hull, *The War-Method and the Peace-Method; An Historical Contrast* (New York: Fleming H. Revell Co., 1929), George A. Coe, *War Mind-Habits* (New York: Fellowship of Youth for Peace, n.d.), Lola Maverick Lloyd and Rosika Schwimmer, *Chaos, War, or a New World Order?* (New York: Campaign for World Government, 1938), Jessie Wallace Hughan, *A Study of International Government* (New York: Thomas Y. Crowell Co., 1923), and August Claessens, *Social Attitudes Towards War and Peace* (New York: Rand School Press, 1934). These few books should be supplemented with the periodical and pamphlet literature created by pacifists in each campaign for disarmament, economic internationalism, world order, and neutralism.

The most distinctive peace strategy devised by pacifists was war resistance. It had a limited development during the interwar period, by comparison with the sixties, but already its theory and connection with social radicalism were suggested. The best treatments of the international and largely English movement are pamphlets by William J. Chamberlain, *Fighting for Peace: The Story of the War Resistance Movement* (London: No More War Movement, 1928), and Grace M. Beaton, *Twenty Years' Work in the War Resisters' International* (New York: War Resisters League, 1945). The best account of efforts in the United States is still the pamphlet by Jessie Wallace Hughan, *Three Decades of War Resistance* (New York: War Resisters League, 1942). Two important supplements to it are William Floyd, *War Resistance* (New York: Arbitrator Press, n.d. [*ca.* 1932]), a pamphlet, and Otto

357

Nathan and Heinz Norden, eds., *Einstein on Peace* (New York: Simon & Schuster, 1960). Einstein's image bolstered the little war-resister movement in the thirties somewhat as Gandhi's example encouraged the advocates of nonviolent action.

Some of Reinhold Niebuhr's writings should be grouped with pacifist writings. These include *Does Civilization Need Religion?* (New York: Macmillan Co., 1927), and *Moral Man and Immoral Society* (New York: Charles Scribner's Sons, 1932), and also a large number of articles and book reviews. Niebuhr's trenchant criticism of pacifism in the late thirties evoked responses of which George H. C. Macgregor, *The Relevance of an Impossible Ideal* (London: James Clarke & Co., Ltd., 1941), was the most closely reasoned. The example of Reinhold Niebuhr illustrates a general principle, of which the thought of John Nevin Sayre and A. J. Muste are even better instances, that the range and development of pacifist thinking can be appreciated only with due regard for the periodical literature and intraorganizational memoranda which related underlying assumptions to specific historical situations.

Secondary Sources

The boundaries of this book have been set by Lawrence Wittner, *Rebels Against War; The American Peace Movement, 1941–1960* (New York: Columbia University Press, 1969), and Peter Brock, *Pacifism in the United States; From the Colonial Era to the First World War* (Princeton, New Jersey: Princeton University Press, 1968). Brock's massive work is the definitive study of American pacifism before the twentieth century. It illumines the inner drives and dilemmas of peace sects, conscientious objectors, and Garrisonian nonresisters and relates them to their historical contexts. The dissipation of nonresistance late in the nineteenth century is not adequately set in the matrix of an expanding peace movement, however. An important part of that story is discussed in Robert Beisner, *Twelve Against Empire: The Anti-Imperialists, 1898–1900* (New York: McGraw-Hill, 1968). Another part, the idea and modern organization of internationalization in America, is thoroughly developed in Warren F. Kuehl, *Seeking World Order; The United States and International Organization to 1920* (Nashville: Vanderbilt University Press, 1969). Detailed treatments of the prewar peace movement are David S. Patterson, "The Travail of the American Peace Movement, 1887–1914" (Ph.D. dissertation, University of California, Berkeley, 1968), and Michael A. Lutzker, "The 'Practical' Peace Advocates: An Interpretation of the

American Peace Movement, 1898–1917" (Ph.D. dissertation, Rutgers University, 1969). These and other studies supplement the long standard works on pacifism and the peace movement: Merle Curti, *The American Peace Crusade: 1815–1860* (Durham: Duke University Press, 1929), and *Peace or War; The American Struggle, 1636–1936* (New York: W. W. Norton & Co., 1936); Devere Allen, *The Fight for Peace;* and A. C. F. Beales, *The History of Peace* (New York: Dial Press, 1931). Curti's books are balanced, chronological narratives; Allen's is partly topical and is strongly biased to war resistance; and Beales's puts American programs into the summary context of European peace movements through the First World War.

The First World War

The standard treatment of the antiwar movement is Horace C. Peterson and Gilbert C. Fite, *Opponents of War, 1917–1918* (Madison: University of Wisconsin Press, 1957), but see Sondra R. Herman, *Eleven Against War* (Stanford: Hoover Institution Press, 1969), for a stimulating interpretation of the assumptions underlying and dividing the internationalist movement, 1898–1921. Several of the organizations formed in the oppressive milieu which Peterson and Fite describe have been studied in detail. The American Civil Liberties Union has been presented with clarity and thoroughness in Donald Johnson, *The Challenge to American Freedoms; World War I and the Rise of the American Civil Liberties Union* (Lexington: University of Kentucky Press, 1963). The relationship of the People's Council of America to the labor movement was established in an excellent monograph, Frank L. Grubbs, Jr., *The Struggle for Labor Loyalty: Gompers, the A.F. of L., and the Pacifists, 1917–1920* (Durham: Duke University Press, 1968). *The History of the Women's Peace Party*, by Marie Louise Degen (Baltimore: Johns Hopkins Press, 1939), has been followed by a narrative history, Gertrude Bussey and Margaret Tims, *The Women's International League for Peace and Freedom, 1915–1965; A Record of Fifty Years' Work* (London, England: George Allen & Unwin, Ltd., 1965). Unfortunately, it is rather dominated by the record of meetings and resolutions, as are parts of Vera Brittain's history of the International Fellowship of Reconciliation, *The Rebel Passion; A Short History of Some Pioneer Peace-Makers* (New York: Fellowship Publications, 1964). Most of *The Rebel Passion* consists of sketches of European peace leaders. There is no adequate history of the American branch of the W.I.L.P.F., although an honors' thesis from Harvard University, David A. Swope, "The Women's International

League for Peace and Freedom, United States Section, 1919–1941" (1963), is a useful beginning. The A.U.A.M. is well developed in Blanche Cook, "Woodrow Wilson and the Anti-Militarists, 1914–1918" (Ph.D. dissertation, Johns Hopkins University, 1970), although the study encompasses more than that organization. Careful studies of the attempts to end the war by mediation are in progress. Ruhl J. Bartlett, *The League to Enforce Peace* (Chapel Hill: University of North Carolina Press, 1944), details the history of the culminating organization of traditional internationalism.

Conscientious objection to military service has won increasing attention with the resistance to the Vietnamese war and new court cases in the sixties. Lillian Schlissel's anthology of legal documents and statements of objectors, *Conscience in America, A Documentary History of Conscientious Objection in America, 1757–1967* (New York: E. P. Dutton & Co., Inc., 1968), is very useful pending the completion of full histories now under preparation, but the literature of earlier periods is already large. Edward Needles Wright presented *Conscientious Objection in the Civil War* (Philadelphia: University of Pennsylvania Press, 1931) effectively, and Peter Brock explored the preceding record in *Pacifism in America*. Four secondary works are particularly important for the World War I period: Norman Thomas, *The Conscientious Objector in America* (New York: B. W. Huebsch, 1923), reprinted as *Is Conscience a Crime?* (New York: Vanguard Press, 1927), represented the considered judgment of a leading defender of the objectors, whereas Walter Kellogg, *The Conscientious Objector* (New York: Boni & Liveright, 1919), was the careful evaluation of one charged with their supervision; Clarence Marsh Case viewed objectors as a sympathetic Socialist close to the scene in selected chapters of *Non-Violent Coercion; A Study in Methods of Social Pressure* (New York: The Century Co., 1923), whereas Paul Comly French recounted their records as an interested spokesman a generation later in *We Won't Murder, Being the Story of Men Who Followed Their Conscientious Scruples and Helped Give Life to Democracy* (New York: Hastings House, 1940). The official accounts of objectors and of provisions for them include: U.S. Department of War, *Statement Concerning the Treatment of Conscientious Objectors in the Army* (Washington, D.C.: Government Printing Office, 1919), U.S. House of Representatives, *Hearings . . . The Bill Authorizing the President to Increase Temporarily the Military Establishment of the United States, April 7, 14, and 17, 1917* (Washington, D.C.: Government Printing Office, 1918), and U.S. Selective Service System, *Conscientious Objection*, Special Monograph No. 11, 2 vols. (Washington, D.C.: Government Printing Office, 1950).

James Weinstein, *The Decline of Socialism in America, 1912–1925* (New York: Monthly Review Press, 1967), suggests the broad range of positions held by Socialists in World War I, and demonstrates the divisive effect of the issues and the crushing blows of public opinion upon the party. It should be supplemented by Merle Fainsod, *International Socialism and the World War* (New York: Octagon Books, Inc., 1966), in order to put the American story in its broadest perspective, and by Nathan Fine, *Farmer and Labor Parties in the United States, 1828–1928* (New York: Rand School of Social Science, 1928), which contains the complete text of the majority and minority St. Louis resolutions on the war, April, 1917. Other secondary works useful for data about Socialists and the war include the biographies of Norman Thomas, and Ray Ginger, *The Bending Cross; A Biography of Eugene Victor Debs* (New Brunswick: Rutgers University Press, 1949); Debs, although not an absolute pacifist, was an important symbol of resistance to wartime authoritarianism. David Shannon, *The Socialist Party of America* (New York: Macmillan Co., 1955), and especially Theodore Draper, *The Roots of American Communism* (New York: Viking Press, 1957), set the crisis over the emergence of communism within the Socialist Party in its wartime context. Shannon's study, together with Daniel Bell, *The End of Ideology* (Glencoe, Ill.: Free Press, 1960), Ralph Lord Roy, *Communism and the Churches* (New York: Harcourt, Brace & Co., 1960), and Irving Howe and Lewis Coser, *The American Communist Party* (New York: Frederick A. Praeger, 1957), describe the subsequent struggle over violence and militant strategy among Socialists and between them and Communists in the thirties. This concept is important for an understanding of how the debates over the road to Socialist power relate to attitudes toward war. James P. Cannon, *The History of American Trotskyism: Report of a Participant* (New York: Pioneer Publishers, 1944), is a useful introduction to the movement which was the context of A. J. Muste's radical activity in the early thirties.

Biographies offer the richest introduction to the antiwar movement in World War I. Of the many studies of Jane Addams, James Weber Linn, *Jane Addams; a Biography* (New York: D. Appleton-Century Co., 1937), is useful regarding her peace activity, and John C. Farrell, *Beloved Lady; A History of Jane Addams' Ideas on Reform and Peace* (Baltimore: Johns Hopkins Press, 1967), is especially perceptive. Jane Addams and Randolph Bourne are discussed in Christopher

361

Lasch, *The New Radicalism in America, 1889–1963; The Intellectual as a Social Type* (New York: Alfred A. Knopf, 1965), but their ideas and commitments are largely and unfortunately explained away in the course of attending to their personalities. Louis Filler, *Randolph Bourne* (Washington, D.C.: American Council on Public Affairs, 1943), should be supplemented by the introductions to Lillian Schlissel, ed., *The World of Randolph Bourne*, and Carl Resek, ed., *War and the Intellectuals*, and by Bourne's autobiographical writings. Mercedes M. Randall, *Improper Bostonian: Emily Greene Balch* (New York: Twayne Publishers, Inc., 1964), is sensitive and particularly good for the World War I period. Michael Wreszin, *Oswald Garrison Villard, Pacifist at War* (Bloomington, Ind.: Indiana University Press, 1965), is stronger than D. Joy Humes, *Oswald Garrison Villard, Liberal of the 1920's* (Syracuse: Syracuse University Press, 1960); for all his militancy on civil rights, Villard shied away from radical causes and came to lie outside the mainstream of liberal pacifism.

Other important studies of pacifists are Robert L. Duffus, *Lillian Wald, Neighbor and Crusader* (New York: Macmillan Co., 1938), Carl Herman Voss, *Rabbi and Minister; The Friendship of Stephen S. Wise and John Haynes Holmes* (New York: World Publishing Co., 1964), Murray B. Seidler, *Norman Thomas: Respectable Rebel* (Ithaca: Cornell University Press, 1961), and Harry Fleischman, *Norman Thomas, A Biography* (1964), David Hinshaw, *Rufus Jones, Master Quaker* (New York: G. P. Putnam's Sons, 1951), and the brief study by John Howard Melish, *Paul Jones: Minister of Reconciliation* (New York: Fellowship of Reconciliation, 1942). The only biography of A. J. Muste, *Peace Agitator* (New York: Macmillan Co., 1963), by Nat Hentoff, is oriented to a popular audience. It is undocumented, but the early chapters are based largely on Muste's autobiographical fragments. A thorough, intellectual biography of Muste is in preparation.

The record of the peace churches during World War I has been developed at length. The Society of Friends is treated in Margaret E. Hirst, *The Quakers in Peace and War: An Account of Their Peace Principles and Practice* (New York: George H. Doran Co., 1923), Lester Jones, *Quakers in Action: Recent Humanitarian and Reform Activities of the American Quakers* (New York: Macmillan Co., 1929), and is put into historical perspective in Rufus M. Jones, *The Later Periods of Quakerism*, Vol. II (London, England: Macmillan Co., Ltd., 1921). The work of the Service Committee is described in Marie Hoxie Jones, *Swords into Plowshares: An Account of the American Friends Service Committee, 1917–1937* (New York: Macmillan

Co., 1937), and Rufus Jones, *A Service of Love in War Time; American Friends Relief Work in Europe, 1917–1919* (New York: Macmillan Co., 1920), and it is traced from an English point of view in Anna Ruth Fry, *A Quaker Adventure: The Story of Nine Years' Relief and Reconstruction* (London, England: Nisbet & Co., Ltd., 1926).

The wartime experience of other peace churches is traced carefully in Rufus D. Bowman, *The Church of the Brethren and War, 1788–1941* (Elgin, Ill.: Brethren Publishing House, 1944), John Horsch, *The Principle of Nonresistance As Held by the Mennonite Church: A Historical Survey* (1927), and in Jonas S. Hartzler, *Mennonites in the World War, or Nonresistance Under Test* (Scottdale, Pa.: Mennonite Publishing House, 1922), a work that was official in the sense that the author was assisted by a church committee. The Mennonite story is carried forward in Guy Franklin Hershberger, *War, Peace, and Nonresistance* (Scottdale, Pa.: Herald Press, 1944, 1953), and *The Mennonite Church in the Second World War* (Scottdale, Pa.: Mennonite Publishing House, 1951).

Some indication of the wartime contributions of Christian churches can be gleaned from Margaret Renton, ed., *War-Time Agencies of the Churches: Directory and Handbook* (New York: General War-Time Commission of Churches, 1919), and especially from Ray H. Abrams, *Preachers Present Arms* (New York: Round Table Press, 1933). Four useful unpublished studies which trace denominational trends arising from World War I experience are James M. DeViney, "The Attitudes of the Methodist Episcopal Church Toward War from 1919 to 1927" (M.A. thesis, Northwestern University, 1928), Emma Elizabeth Haas, "The Attitude of Churches in the World War and Present European War" (M.A. thesis, University of Chicago, 1942), Doniver Lund, "The Peace Movement Among the Major American Protestant Churches, 1919–1939" (Ph.D. dissertation, University of Nebraska, 1955), and William Swanson Witte, "Quaker Pacifism in the United States, 1919–1942" (Ph.D. dissertation, Columbia University, 1954). A broader and more analytical study is Hans H. Brunner, "Coercive Power: A Study in American Protestant Ethics Between the Opening of the Twentieth Century and the Second World War" (Th.D. thesis, Union Theological Seminary, 1947). These studies rely heavily upon the published statements of church bodies instead of tracing through manuscripts the sequence of events which led to official pronouncements or agencies with special points of view. They document the shift in religion which led Walter Van Kirk to claim in 1934 that *Religion Renounces War* (New York: Willett, Clark & Co.). Charles Macfarland, *Pioneers for*

Peace Through Religion (New York: Fleming H. Revell Co., 1946), traced the work of religious leaders in traditional approaches to internationalism. Robert Moats Miller, *American Protestantism and Social Issues, 1919–1939* (Chapel Hill: University of North Carolina Press, 1958), showed convincingly that churchmen were as sensitive to the problem of war as to any other, and Donald B. Meyer, *The Protestant Search for Political Realism, 1919–1941* (Berkeley: University of California Press, 1960), interpreted that ethical concern in the light of a persistent impulse to approach social conflict realistically, and he found it epitomized in the increasingly nonpacifist writings of Reinhold Niebuhr.

The Interwar Period

Pacifist organizations have been described in relation to the whole peace movement in Selig Adler, *The Isolationist Impulse: Its Twentieth Century Reaction* (New York: Abelard-Schuman, 1957), Robert Osgood, *Ideals and Self-Interest in America's Foreign Relations* (Chicago: University of Chicago Press, 1957), Robert Ferrell, "The Peace Movement," in Alexander DeConde, ed., *Isolation and Security* (Durham: Duke University Press, 1957), and Merle Curti, *Peace or War.* Adler's account is somewhat simplistic and not sympathetic regarding the pacifists; it ignores the fact that many of them campaigned for the League, even if with misgivings, and does not take them seriously. It tends to equate internationalism itself with support of international organization—the League—, as do some other works written in the early years of the United Nations. This limitation mars the otherwise useful study of "Internationalism in American Thought, 1919–1929," by Lyman Burbank (Ph.D. dissertation, New York University, 1950).

Robert Osgood discerned the ambivalence in pacifists' reactions to the rise of totalitarianism, but he regarded their thought as "a kind of inverted idealism" which had no political analysis worth studying. Osgood never was simplistic, but he did not study pacifists in detail or in number. Ferrell and Curti were more sympathetic to pacifists, and studied them in greater detail and in the light of the peace movement. Curti wrote before the neutrality debate reached its climax; and so he stressed the organizational role, the moral qualities, and the economic interpretations of liberal pacifists rather than their political analysis. Ferrell wrote after World War II, but his emphasis is much like Curti's. Neither scholar evaluated pacifists in the light of their domestic concerns.

364

Donald B. Meyer, *The Protestant Search for Political Realism,* does evaluate the social concerns of liberal pacifists, but without taking their opinions on foreign policy for much more than a pseudomoral argument. Meyer's primary interest is in the search for a meaningful social ethics, and he handles this story with considerable deftness, but his own sympathies lie with Reinhold Niebuhr whose judgment of the political irrelevance of pacifism he accepts without political analysis. John K. Nelson, *The Peace Prophets; American Pacifist Thought, 1919–1941* (Chapel Hill: University of North Carolina Press, 1967), appears to share that bias, although he makes a concerted effort to narrate the development of pacifists' ideas and to assess their achievements. His account makes effective use of published sources but suffers from a lack of contact with manuscript records; it remains an outsider's story. Vernon Howard Holloway, "American Pacifism Between Two Wars, 1919–1941: An Analysis of Pacifist Groups and Doctrines in the United States," is a careful and rewarding analysis of the various positions taken by pacifists between the wars, but its format, tending to categorize them according to their points of view, somewhat obscures the development and historical context of their understanding. Gene Sharp, "Non-violence: A Sociological Study" (M.A. thesis, Ohio State University, 1951), employs even more restrictive categories than Holloway's study and suffers more, from a historical point of view, although it is a necessary precursor of Sharp's currently more sophisticated analysis of the sociology and strategy of nonviolence.

There have been several analyses of the organizations comprising the peace movement between the wars. The most important studies are: Elton Atwater, *Organized Efforts in the United States Toward Peace* (Washington, D.C.: Digest Press, 1936), and "Organizing American Public Opinion for Peace," *Public Opinion Quarterly,* I (Apr., 1937), 112–21; *Report of the Commission of the Coordination of Efforts for Peace* (Oberlin, Ohio: Commission of the Coordination of Efforts for Peace, 1933); and John Masland, "The Peace Groups Join Battle," *Public Opinion Quarterly,* IV (Dec., 1940), 64–73. Four other studies were published by the National Council for Prevention of War: *Organizations in the United States that Promote Better International Understanding and World Peace* (1927); Frederick Libby, *The American Peace Movement* (1930); Florence Brewer Boeckel, *Between War and Peace; A Handbook for Peace Workers* (1928); and Boeckel, *The Turn Toward Peace* (1930). Charles L. DeBenedetti, "American Internationalism in the 1920's: Shotwell and the Outlawrists" (Ph.D.

dissertation, University of Illinois, 1968), is a fine example of a historical approach which finds in the peace movement a fundamental debate over the meaning of internationalism itself.

The disarmament campaigns of the twenties are described in C. Leonard Hoag, *Preface to Preparedness, The Washington Disarmament Conference and Public Opinion* (Washington, D.C.: American Council on Public Affairs, 1941), and Arthur A. Ekirch, Jr., *The Civilian and the Military* (New York: Oxford University Press, 1956), but these books should be read in conjunction with Harold and Margaret Sprout, *Toward a New Order of Sea Power; American Naval Policy and the World Scene, 1918–1922* (Princeton: Princeton University Press, 1940), and Armin Rappaport, *The Navy League of the United States* (Detroit: Wayne University Press, 1962). Both of the latter authors write from a naval point of view, although Rappaport's is thinly disguised, and they agree upon the influence of the peace movement in retarding the growth of what they regard as an adequate navy. Ekirch carries the story of antimilitarism through the interwar period, and includes the campaigns against R.O.T.C., for which he draws upon the excellent M.A. thesis of Doris Galant Rodin, "The Opposition to the Establishment of Military Training in Civil Schools and Colleges in the United States, 1914–1940" (American University, 1949). The disarmament campaign shaded into the munitions inquiry, symbolized by the Nye Committee hearings, which have been described admirably in John E. Wiltz, *In Search of Peace; The Senate Munitions Inquiry, 1934–36* (Baton Rouge: Louisiana State University Press, 1963). A number of books popularized by pacifists but not written by them helped to make the public suspicious of munitions makers and bankers. They included: Seymour Waldman, *Death and Profits; A Study of the War Policies Commission* (New York: Brewer, Warren & Putnam, 1932), George Seldes, *Iron, Blood and Profits; An Exposure of the World-Wide Munitions Racket* (New York: Harper & Bros., 1934), Helmuth C. Englebrecht, *"One Hell of a Business"* (New York: Robert M. McBride & Co., 1934), and Englebrecht and F. C. Hannighen, *Merchants of Death; A Study of the International Armament Industry* (New York: Dodd, Mead & Co., 1934). A history of the Committee Against Militarism in Education is in preparation.

The neutrality controversy has been the subject of many books, of which William Langer and Everett Gleason, *The Challenge to Isolation: The World Crisis of 1937–1940 and American Foreign Policy* (New York: Harper & Bros., 1952), and Donald F. Drummond, *The Passing of American Neutrality, 1937–1941* (Ann Arbor: University of Michigan Press, 1955), are useful introductions. The Langer and Gleason book is oriented to the interaction of American policy with world diplomacy. Four works are especially helpful for studying the peace movement in relation to neutrality policy. Robert A. Divine's *The Illusion of Neutrality* (Chicago: University of Chicago Press, 1962), is more intensive but less clear in its definition of terms than his *The Reluctant Belligerent; American Entry Into World War II* (New York: John Wiley & Sons, 1965). Both books focus upon the State Department in relation to the foreign relations committees of the Congress and to the administration, and they narrate a frustrating search for policy. Manfred Jonas, *Isolationism in America, 1935–1941* (Ithaca: Cornell University Press, 1966), develops the positions and activities of the isolationist bloc in Congress in such a way as to illumine the tenets of isolationism itself. Allan Kuusisto, "The Influence of the National Council for Prevention of War on United States Foreign Policy, 1935–1939" (Ph.D. dissertation, Harvard University, 1950), is helpful, therefore, because it approaches the controversy carefully in terms of peace-movement lobbying. It should be used together with an M.A. thesis, Gary Lynn Nall, "The Ludlow War Referendum" (University of Texas, 1959).

Similarly, Justus D. Doenecke, "American Public Opinion and the Manchurian Crisis, 1931–33" (Ph.D. dissertation, Princeton University, 1966), documents the reaction of various wings of the peace movement to the first overt threat to world order in the thirties. Allen Guttmann, *Wound in the Heart; America and the Spanish Civil War* (New York: Free Press of Glencoe, 1962), sensitively portrays the reactions of various groups of Americans to the eruption of violence and the collapse of an apparently progressive government. Guttmann treats the specific crisis as an instance of the failure of the liberal imagination, a thesis with which the peace movement of the sixties might have wrestled; but in doing so he oversimplifies the political and economic concerns of liberal pacifists. Both the insights and the shortcomings of his book derive from his essentially literary analysis.

The neutrality controversy was essentially a contest for public opinion, and in this regard several opinion studies are useful: Gardner Murphy and Rensis Likert, *Public Opinion and the Individual; A Psychological Study of Student Attitudes on Public Questions, with a Retest Five Years Later* (New York: Harper & Bros., 1938), should be read in conjunction with James Wechsler's more descriptive *Revolt on the Campus* (New York: Covici-Friede, 1935), and with Joseph P. Lash and James Wechsler's polemic *War Our Heritage* (New York:

International Pubs., 1936); see, also, Hadley Cantril and Mildred Strunk, eds., *Public Opinion: 1935–1946* (Princeton: Princeton University Press, 1951), Harold Lavine and James Wechsler, *War Propaganda and the United States* (New Haven: Yale University Press, 1940), and Harold Tobin and Percy W. Bidwell, *Mobilizing Civilian America* (New York: Council on Foreign Relations, 1940). Wayne S. Cole, *America First; The Battle Against Intervention, 1940–1941* (Madison: University of Wisconsin Press, 1953), and Mark Lincoln Chadwin, *The Hawks of World War II* (Chapel Hill: University of North Carolina Press, 1968), are sound studies of the contending sides in the last year before declaration of war. The history of the prior organization of sentiment for collective security is developed in Roland N. Stromberg, *Collective Security and American Foreign Policy: From the League of Nations to Nato* (New York: Praeger, 1963).

There is no adequate account of the lobbying involved in securing and operating the Civilian Public Service program. The opening of the Paul Comly French papers in 1970 should stimulate such a study. Mulford Q. Sibley and Philip E. Jacob, *Conscription of Conscience; The American State and the Conscientious Objector, 1940–1947* (New York: Doubleday & Co., 1952), is the definitive study of the period, although recent writing on political and selective objection to war justifies a reexamination of the records of objectors and of the C.P.S. administration in order to evaluate the extent and sources of radical positions which appear to have fed into the cold war peace movement. Lawrence Wittner, *Rebels Against War,* interprets the war period in this way. He includes chapters on the peace movement during World War II which, although accurate and balanced, are far from the comprehensive treatment merited by pacifist activities of that time.

There are abundant sources for further studies of pacifism and the peace movement in recent American history, and it is clear that they must take into account developments within organizations as well as public events and statements. But several problems are inherent in any such studies. It is difficult to distinguish between the achievements of individual pacifists and the contribution of pacifism to their efforts. It is difficult to distinguish the assumptions which were fairly constant in pacifism from those ideas which changed. It is hard to identify the cause and effect relationships in the development both of pacifism and of foreign policy. The State Department was very cautious in the thirties, and its officers attributed its caution to the pressure of public opinion mobilized by the peace movement, for example; but it is possible that both the State Department and the public wavered in the face of alternatives whose consequences faded into the future, that both administration leaders and peace advocates were divided by similar memories of World War I. This difficulty of identifying outside influences on official policy is exacerbated by the fact that there is no comprehensive history of traditional internationalism with its varying points of view and organizations, and with its points of informal contact in government between the wars. It is not responsible to evaluate the historic influences of the peace movement as a whole until such a study is available.

This book has been addressed to a more modest task. A historian of social ideas knows that they are the product of both experience and reflection. He does not claim to evaluate the motives of men, but he must attempt to chart the assumptions from which they act and write. He can follow ruling ideas or values in time and see them change as they are brought through differing contexts into new relationships with each other and with the world of action. One such idea has been the notion of pacifism.

Notes

INTRODUCTION

Notes to pages 3–8

1. Muste, "Fragment of Autobiography," 1939, in the A. J. Muste papers, Swarthmore College Peace Collection (SCPC), Swarthmore, Penna.; Muste to Kirby Page, Sept. 2, 1936, in the Kirby Page papers, Southern California School of Theology, Claremont; and Muste, "Return to Pacifism," *Christian Century,* LIII (Dec. 2, 1936), 1603. Nat Hentoff repeats this account by quoting Muste in his informal biography, *Peace Agitator: The Story of A. J. Muste* (New York: Macmillan Co., 1963), pp. 97–98, although he does not document quotations.

2. "Memoir of Frances Witherspoon and Tracy Mygatt, The Oral History Collection of Columbia University," p. 8. Miss Witherspoon and Miss Mygatt were organizers of the Bureau of Legal Aid formed to help conscientious objectors in New York.

3. Julia Grace Wales to Clark F. Huhn, Nov. 28, 1917, Julia Grace Wales papers, Wisconsin Historical Society, Madison. Miss Wales was the author of a famous proposal for a conference of neutral mediation in World War I, and was active in the Woman's Peace Party.

4. The definitive study of religious pacifism in America is Peter Brock, *Pacifism in the United States; From the Colonial Era to the First World War* (Princeton: Princeton University Press, 1968). See also Roland Bainton, *Christian Attitudes Toward War and Peace; A Historical Survey and Critical Re-evaluation* (Nashville: Abingdon Press, 1960).

5. Allen, *The Fight for Peace* (New York: Macmillan Co., 1930), p. 16.

6. Rufus M. Jones, *The Later Periods of Quakerism,* 2 vols. (London: Macmillan & Co., 1921), I, 375–76, and II, 556. In the nineteenth century a powerful evangelical movement led many American

Friends to accept the scriptures as final authority and to identify their own doctrines with the Bible. Some became intolerant of other interpretations. This attitude resulted in part in the splintering of the society. After about 1880 it slowly returned to its original basis of life and worship, although the organizational divisions persisted. The end of the century brought a reaction against evangelicalism, a more liberal and critical interpretation of the Bible, and reemphasis on inward experience.

7. Quoted from *The Advocate of Peace,* LXXVIII (Oct., 1916), 287–88, and LXXIX (May, 1917), 160, respectively, in Ray H. Abrams, *Preachers Present Arms* (New York: Round Table Press, 1933), p. 162.

8. Quoted from *The Advocate of Peace,* LXXIX (May, 1917), 138, in Merle Curti, *Peace or War; The American Struggle, 1636–1936* (New York: W. W. Norton & Co., 1936), pp. 254–55.

9. Quoted in Devere Allen, *The Fight for Peace,* pp. 507–508.

10. *Ibid.*; Curti, *Peace or War,* p. 229; Carnegie Endowment for International Peace, *Year Book,* 1918 (Washington, D. C.: Carnegie Endowment), pp. 37–38.

11. Addams, *Peace and Bread in Time of War* (New York: King's Crown Press, 1945 [1st ed., 1922]), p. 62.

CHAPTER I

1. From an unpublished fragment of autobiography written about 1945, in the Muste papers, SCPC.

2. Lochner, *Pacifism and the Great War,* a brochure reprinted from the *Northwestern Christian Advocate* (Dec. 23, and 30, 1917), pp. 12, 7.

3. Fanny Garrison Villard, *A Real Peace Society,* printed copy of an address, distributed by the Women's Peace Society (W.P.S.), in the Women's Peace Society papers, SCPC. Mrs. Villard had in mind a society of absolutely pacifist women, which did not emerge until after the war.

4. Addams, *Peace and Bread,* p. 7.

5. Marie Louise Degen, *The History of the Woman's Peace Party,* the Johns Hopkins University Series in Historical and Political Science, series LVII: 3 (Baltimore: Johns Hopkins Press, 1939), p. 40.

6. For the complete text of the platform and preamble, and for the detailed "Program of the Party," see *ibid.,* pp. 40–42, 44–46.

7. Degen, *Woman's Peace Party,* pp. 127–50; Addams, *Peace and*

Bread, pp. 28–46, and see the discussion of sources in the bibliographical notes of this book.

8. The number of persons meeting at Garden City on Nov. 11 and 12 cited in the text is based on a study of the F.O.R. and Gilbert Beaver papers, SCPC, and the John Nevin Sayre papers, Nyack, New York; estimates ranged up to one hundred persons.

9. "The Fellowship of Reconciliation: Its Origin and Development," *Newsletter,* June, 1920, F.O.R. papers, box 29, SCPC. Richard Roberts, the second secretary of the British F.O.R., was minister of the Presbyterian church at Crouch Hill until 1915, and the next year he came to the United States, where he was minister of the Church of Pilgrims in Brooklyn. Subsequently, he was minister in two of Canada's major churches, and in 1934 he was moderator of the United Church of Canada. Leyton Richards was minister of the Borden Downs Congregational Church, near Manchester, England, and in 1923 he was minister of the Carr's Lane Church, Birmingham, England.

10. "The Observer," *Christian Work* (Nov. 27, 1915) a clipping in the F.O.R. papers, box 26. Lynch suggested that 40 members signed up at the Garden City conference, which is the smallest number I have found. At any rate, by Nov. 24, 1915, there were 75 members whose names are listed in *Forty Years for Peace: A History of the Fellowship of Reconciliation, 1914–1954* (New York: Fellowship of Reconciliation, 1954), p. 15. See also the "Minutes of the Garden City Conference on the Fellowship of Reconciliation," Beaver papers.

11. *The Fellowship of Reconciliation,* a statement of purpose (New York: Fellowship of Reconciliation, *ca.* 1916), and other items in the F.O.R. papers, boxes 1 and 29, and in the Beaver and Sayre papers.

12. Degen, *Woman's Peace Party,* pp. 40–41.

13. "New York's Parade of Preparedness," *Survey,* XXXVI (May 20, 1916), 197–98.

14. "Shall We Arm For Peace?" *Survey,* XXXV (Dec. 11, 1915), 299.

15. Robert L. Duffus, *Lillian Wald, Neighbor and Crusader* (New York: Macmillan Co., 1938), p. 151. The Anti-Preparedness Committee was formalized Nov. 29, 1915, adopted its name Jan. 3, 1916, and changed to the American Union Against Militarism for the spring tour on Apr. 3 or 4.

16. Borah's opinion was recorded in Charles Hallinan to the executive committee of the A.U.A.M., Apr. 17, 1918, A.U.A.M. papers, SCPC. The activities of the organization are fully documented in its papers.

17. "Swinging Around the Circle Against Militarism," *Survey,* XXXVI (Apr. 22, 1916), 95.

18. *Survey,* XXXVI (Apr. 1, 1916), 37. Fuller was a witty Englishman who had edited *Freeman,* helped Norman Thomas edit the *World Tomorrow,* and who married Crystal Eastman.

19. "Shall We Have War With Mexico," June 26, 1916, a reprint of the advertisement, A.U.A.M. papers. Captain Morey's account agreed in the main with a report secured from the Provisional Governor of Chihuahua, Col. Francisco L. Trevino, for the A.U.A.M. (also dated June 26), except that each side accused the other of firing first. Minutes, June 26 and 28, 1916, A.U.A.M. papers; see also David Starr Jordan, *The Days of a Man,* 2 vols. (New York: World Book Co., 1922), II, 690–703; Arthur A. Link, *Woodrow Wilson and the Progressive Era: 1910–1917* (New York: Harper & Row, 1954), pp. 136–44; and Lillian D. Wald, *Windows on Henry Street* (Boston: Little, Brown & Co., 1934), pp. 291–98.

20. Crystal Eastman, *American Union Against Militarism: Suggestions for 1916–17,* Oct., 1916, A.U.A.M. papers.

21. Addams, *Peace and Bread,* p. 57.

22. Minutes of Feb. 10, 1917, A.U.A.M. papers.

23. Lella Secor (Florence), in Julian Bell, ed., *We Did Not Fight: 1914–1918 Experiences of War Resisters* (London: Cobden-Sanderson, 1935), p. 120. Her memories are inaccurate in some details and make her and Miss Shelley appear to be the center of the antiwar movement, which they were not; but in this case her memory seems to be an accurate representation of her impressions at the time.

24. Minutes of the executive committee, Feb. 10, 14, 20, 27, and Mar. 5, 1917, A.U.A.M. papers. The referendum is described in a memorandum of Miss Wald's statement to the President which is, together with texts of the other statements, in the minutes of Feb. 27.

25. Curti, *Peace or War,* pp. 253–54.

26. Jordan to Bryan, Apr. 1, 1917, William Jennings Bryan papers, box 31, Library of Congress. Jordan had chosen the commission experts himself; Lochner served as secretary. Lochner to Jordan, Mar. 8, and Jordan to Jessie (his wife), Mar. 16, 1917, David Starr Jordan Peace Correspondence, Hoover Institution on War, Revolution, and Peace.

27. Jordan, *Days of a Man,* II, 735. These brave words covered the bitter sense of disappointment with which he acquiesced in the democratic process. "Here lies Woodrow Wilson," he wrote his wife, "who

looked toward Heaven while his steps took hold in Hell . . . . I regard the outlook as full of danger to the nation . . . from within." Jordan to Jessie, Apr. 6, 1917, Jordan Peace Correspondence. There was nothing to do but withdraw and write his autobiography, he had written the previous day.

28. *Bulletin* of the People's Council of America, I:2 (Aug. 16, 1917), People's Council of America for Peace and Democracy papers, SCPC. Regarding the council's organization, see especially Rebecca Shelley, "The People's Council for Democracy and Peace," n.d. [*ca.* May, 1917], and minutes of the organizing committee, June 13 and 21, 1917, in the council's papers; Louis Lochner to Emily Balch, May 9, 1917, in the Balch papers, box 1, SCPC; Oswald Villard to Roger Baldwin, Apr. 12, 1917, and Baldwin to Lella Secor, Apr. 11, 1917, A.U.A.M. papers; and Lochner, "Plans for Forming a People's Council," a 16-page memorandum, Louis Lochner papers, box 52, State Historical Society of Wisconsin.

29. Minutes of organizing committee of the People's Council of America, July–Aug.; "Resolutions of the First American Conference for Democracy and Terms of Peace," New York, May 30–31, 1917, and "Call" to the Second American Conference for Democracy and Terms of Peace, Chicago, July 7–8, 1917; *Bulletin*, I: 1 and 2 (Aug. 7 and 16, 1917), People's Council of America papers. Regarding the conference in Washington, see also "Report of Meeting" Aug. 9, 1917, in the Lochner papers, box 52.

30. "The People's Council Convention," an unsigned descriptive memorandum [Sept.], 1917, People's Council of America papers; see also Morris Hillquit's account in *Loose Leaves from a Busy Life* (New York: Macmillan Co., 1934), pp. 170–79.

31. Lillian Wald to Crystal Eastman, Aug. 28, 1917, A.U.A.M. papers.

32. Miss Wald had tendered her resignation (with Paul Kellogg) June 5 on the issue of the relationship of the Civil Liberties Bureau and the A.U.A.M., but it was not accepted; she renewed it on Aug. 28, but in deference to the majority decision to try out the People's Council she did not press her resignation until Oct. (after the two organizations had been severed). Minutes of the executive committee, June 5, Aug. 20 and 30, Sept. 28, and Oct. 9, 1917, and attached correspondence and memoranda, A.U.A.M. papers.

33. Crystal Eastman to Oswald Villard, Nov. 16, 1917. Miss Eastman was executive secretary of the reorganized American Union, which

stressed internationalism. Amos Pinchot was chairman, and the executive board was representative of the American Union of the previous spring.

34. Charles Hallinan to the executive committee, Apr. 17, 1918, A.U.A.M. papers.

35. Letter to the House Committee on Military Affairs, Jan. 16, 1917, F.O.R. papers, SCPC.

36. This profile is based upon a sampling of ninety-one leaders of the major peace groups founded between 1914 and 1917 for whom biographical information was available.

37. Jones, *A Service of Love in War Time; American Friends Relief Work in Europe, 1917–1919* (New York: Macmillan Co., 1920), p. 105.

38. Thomas, "What Kind of Peace?" editorial in *New World*, I (Feb., 1918), 26.

39. Max Eastman, *Love and Revolution; My Journey through an Epoch* (New York: Random House, 1964), p. 14.

40. Thomas, "Some Objections Considered," in Thomas, ed., *The Conquest of War: Some Studies in a Search for a Christian World Order* (New York: Fellowship Press, 1917), p. 42.

41. Addams, *Peace and Bread*, p. 4.

42. Evan to Norman Thomas, Dec. 30, 1915, Norman Thomas papers, box 139, New York Public Library (NYPL).

43. *The Fellowship of Reconciliation: Some General Considerations* (n.p., *ca.* 1915), p. 2.

44. *Ibid.*

45. Baldwin, "Statement in Court," Oct. 30, 1918, enclosed in a letter from Norman Thomas to Henry W. L. Dana, Cambridge, Mass., Oct. 31, 1918. Henry Wadsworth Longfellow Dana papers, box 1, SCPC. This statement was printed as *The Individual and the State: The Problem as Presented by the Sentencing of Roger N. Baldwin* (New York: n.p., 1918).

46. Thomas, *The Conscientious Objector in America* (New York: B. W. Huebsch, 1923), p. 29.

47. The theme of war threatening progressive gains pervades anti-preparedness literature. Typical are the following: "Around the Circle Against Militarism," *Survey*, XXXVI (Apr. 22, 1916), 95; John Haynes Holmes, "War and the Social Movement," *ibid.*, XXXII (Sept. 26, 1914), 629–30; and Oswald G. Villard, "Shall We Arm for Peace?" *ibid.*, XXXV (Dec. 11, 1915), 299.

48. Minutes of the executive committee, Feb. 27, 1917, A.U.A.M. papers.

49. Crystal Eastman to members of the executive committee, June 14, 1917, A.U.A.M. papers. Newton D. Baker, mayor of Cleveland (1912–16), was appointed secretary of war on Mar. 7, 1916; Frederick Keppell, dean of the College of Columbia University, became third assistant secretary of war (he subsequently was vice-chairman of the Red Cross, 1919–20, and president of the Carnegie Corporation of New York, 1923–41); Walter Lippmann, liberal commentator for the *New Republic*, was assistant to the Secretary of War, June–Oct., 1917; and progressive newspaper editor George Creel became chairman of the Committee on Public Information, Apr. 14, 1917.

50. Evans to Crystal Eastman, Sept. 28, 1917, and Norman Thomas to Crystal Eastman, Sept. 27, 1917, A.U.A.M. papers.

51. Eastman, *Love and Revolution*, p. 45.

52. "The People's Council Convention," an unsigned descriptive memorandum [Sept., 1917], People's Council of America papers.

53. "Resolutions of the First American Conference for Democracy and Terms of Peace," May 30–31, New York City, organizing committee, People's Council of America papers.

54. Bourne, "The War and the Intellectuals," Carl Resek, ed., *War and the Intellectuals; Essays by Randolph S. Bourne, 1915–1919* (New York: Harper & Row, 1964), pp. 7–8 ff. Regarding the *New Republic* group see Charles Forcey, *Crossroads of Liberalism* (New York: Oxford University Press, 1961), chaps. 7, 8; and Christopher Lasch, *The New Radicalism in America, 1889–1963, The Intellectual as a Social Type* (New York: Alfred A. Knopf, 1965), chap. 6.

55. Page to "Dear Ones," Oct. 20, 1917, Page to Howard E. Sweet, Feb. 3, 1918, and especially the manuscript of "The Sword or the Cross," Page papers; Evan to Norman Thomas, Nov. 5, 1916, Norman Thomas papers.

56. Bourne, "War and the Intellectuals," p. 10.

57. Holmes, *The International Mind* (New York: Church of the Messiah, 1916), p. 7.

58. Allen, *A War-Time Credo*, a flyer reprinted from *The Oberlin College Literary Magazine* (Feb., 1917), Devere Allen papers, SCPC.

59. Butler, *The International Mind* (New York: Charles Scribner's Sons, 1912), and see by comparison his confidential Green Cover Report, "International Mind Alcoves," 1942, in the Carnegie Endowment Archives, Columbia University.

60. Holmes, *The International Mind*, p. 12.

61. Quoted in Theodore Draper, *The Roots of American Communism* (New York: The Viking Press, 1957), p. 93.

62. Eastman, "The Uninteresting War," *Masses*, VI (Sept., 1915), 5–8; Russell, *Justice in War Time*, quoted in Holmes, *The International Mind*, p. 13.

63. Addams, *Peace and Bread*, p. 151.

64. *Ibid.*, pp. 149–50.

65. Evan to Norman Thomas, n.d. [1917], Norman Thomas papers.

66. *The Fellowship of Reconciliation*, a statement of purpose (New York: Fellowship of Reconciliation, *ca.* 1916), and other items in the F.O.R. papers, boxes 1 and 29, SCPC.

67. Addams, *Peace and Bread*, p. 127.

68. Hughan to Thomas, Mar. 24, 1917, Norman Thomas papers.

69. Letter "To Members of the Fellowship," Apr. 23, 1917, F.O.R. papers, box 22.

70. *World Tomorrow* was adopted as an appropriate name beginning with Vol. I:6 (June, 1918), after it was discovered that the original title, *New World*, belonged to a Roman Catholic weekly publication of Chicago with considerable circulation. Minutes of the Fellowship council, Apr. 26, 1918, F.O.R. papers, box 1. A new subtitle, "A Journal Looking Toward a Christian World," replaced the original, "A Monthly Journal of Christian Thought and Practice."

The original officers of the Fellowship Press, in addition to Norman Thomas, were: Gilbert A. Beaver, chairman of the editorial board (he was also chairman of the F.O.R.); Richard Roberts, editor-in-chief; and Walter G. Fuller, editorial secretary. Also on the board were Edward W. Evans, Harold Hatch, John Haynes Holmes, Rufus Jones, Oswald G. Villard, and Harry Ward. After Norman Thomas became full-time managing editor, Bishop Paul Jones was elected secretary of the F.O.R. in 1919.

71. John Nevin Sayre, *The Story of the FOR: 1918–1935* (New York: Fellowship of Reconciliation, 1935), p. 6, and notes to the author; see also Donald Johnson, *The Challenge to American Freedoms; World War I and the Rise of the American Civil Liberties Union* (Lexington: University of Kentucky Press, 1963), pp. 79–81. The *Nation*, which also had been held up, was released at the same time as the *World Tomorrow*.

72. David Shannon, *The Socialist Party of America* (New York: Macmillan Co., 1936), p. 191.

CHAPTER II

1. Moore, "In Distrust of Merits," *Collected Poems* (New York: Macmillan Co., 1944), pp. 135–37.

2. Typed MS, unsigned [probably by Rufus Jones, *ca.* 1917], a draft of a statement on behalf of the Fellowship, in the F.O.R. papers, box 22.

3. Holmes, "War and the Social Movement," p. 630.

4. "The Conscientious Objectors," *Christian Century*, XXXVI (July 3, 1919), 6–7. The article referred to unnamed "Radical Christians" who were objectors.

5. Kenneth Irving Brown, ed., *Character "Bad": The Story of a Conscientious Objector as Told in the Letters of Harold Studley Gray* (New York: Harper & Bros., 1934), p. 3. This book is based on a collection of Gray's letters which Brown edited with comments (and which Gray approved).

6. Page to "Dear Ones," Aug. 7, 1916. See also Page to Sherwood Eddy, Aug. 24, 1916, Page papers.

7. Brown, *Character "Bad,"* p. 16.

8. Page to "Dear Ones," May 19, 1917; Page to "My Dear Friends," Aug. 8, 1917, Page papers.

9. Page to "Folks," May 30, 1917, Page papers.

10. Page, *National Defense; A Study of the Origins, Results and Prevention of War* (New York: Farrar & Rinehart, 1931).

11. Shailer Mathews to Page, Jan. 20, 1917, and July 25, 1918, Page papers.

12. Page to Howard E. Sweet, Feb. 3, 1918, Page papers. Apparently several versions of the paper were circulated among Page's friends, of which one titled "The Sword or the Cross" and dated about Oct., 1917, exists among his papers.

13. Page to Howard E. Sweet, Feb. 3, 1918, Page papers.

14. *Ibid.*

15. Brown, *Character "Bad,"* p. 46.

16. *Ibid.*, p. 51.

17. *Ibid.*, p. 75.

18. Gray to Page, July 14, 1918, Page papers.

19. Page, "The Problem of the Slum," an unpublished term paper, 1915, Page papers.

20. Page to Alma (his wife), Mar. 27, 1916, Page papers.

21. Page to Rex [Kindred?], Dec. 7, 1917. See also correspon-

dence with Herbert Martin, professor of philosophy at Drake University between Aug. 11, 1917, and Nov. 8, 1919, Page papers.

22. Eddy, *Eighty Adventurous Years, An Autobiography* (New York: Harper & Bros., 1955), pp. 117–18. See also Eddy, *A Pilgrimage of Ideas, or, the Re-education of Sherwood Eddy* (New York: Farrar & Rinehart, 1934), pp. 225, 239–40.

23. Eddy to Page, July 12, 1920. See also correspondence of Feb. 20 and 23, and Aug. 19, 1920, Page papers.

24. Eddy to Page, July 12, 1920, Page papers.

25. Page to Alma, Mar. 29, 1920, Page papers.

26. Muste, typed lectures for a course on the Church and Social Action, which he gave at New Brunswick Seminary in 1944, p. 11, Muste papers, box 3, SCPC.

27. *The Fellowship of Reconciliation: Some General Considerations*, p. 2. The national council of the F.O.R. even created a subcommittee to write "a simple and compelling statement of the ultimate requirement of a Christian social order." Minutes of the F.O.R., Nov. 7, 1918, F.O.R. papers, box 1.

28. Rufus Jones, *A Service of Love*, pp. 8–9, 49f. See also pp. 66–67 for the view of Henry Scattergood addressing the Reconstruction Unit in Paris.

29. *Ibid.*, p. 7.

30. Anna Ruth Fry, *A Quaker Adventure: The Story of Nine Years' Relief and Reconstruction* (London: Nisbet & Co., Ltd., 1926), pp. xxx–xxxi. According to Fry, 1,070 English and 780 American workers were engaged in relief work, not including 270 in the London warehouse, the Ambulance Unit, or the Emergency Committee aiding enemy aliens. *Ibid.*, p. xvi. Lester Jones reported as many as 347 Americans in France at one time. *Quakers in Action*, p. 155.

31. *Ibid.*, pp. 23–165; Fry, *A Quaker Adventure*; and Rufus Jones, *A Service of Love*, 60–75, and 126–265.

32. Lester Jones, *Quakers in Action*, p. 69.

33. *Ibid.*, p. 86.

34. Russell, *The History of Quakerism* (New York: Macmillan Co., 1942), pp. 510, 517, 529.

35. Rufus D. Bowman, *The Church of the Brethren and War, 1788–1941* (Elgin, Ill.: Brethren Publishing House, 1944), pp. 171–78, 231–32.

36. Rufus Jones, *A Service of Love*, pp. 55–57.

37. Baldwin apparently offered from St. Louis to go to New York and work for the A.U.A.M.; his offer was accepted by the executive com-

mittee. "Minutes of Meeting of March 27th," 1917, A.U.A.M., Thomas papers. The prison story was related to the author by John Nevin Sayre (1966).

38. "Signs of the Times," *World Tomorrow,* I (Oct., 1918), 237.

39. "Radicalism and Liberty," *New World,* I (Mar., 1918), 64.

40. "Signs of the Times," *World Tomorrow,* I, 237.

41. *News Sheet* of the F.O.R. (May, 1917), p. 3, F.O.R. papers, box 29.

42. Regarding civil liberties and C.O.'s, see the bibliographical notes. The conversation between Sayre and Wilson is reconstructed in "Notes of Nevin Sayre on Interview with President Wilson about Treatment of Conscientious Objectors in Federal Penitentiary at Fort Leavenworth, Kansas" (*ca.* 1961, based on memory and manuscripts) and in Norman Thomas to Gilbert Beaver, Dec. 3, 1918, Beaver papers. Official acknowledgment of many complaints is recorded in Frederick P. Keppel (third assistant secretary of war) to Jessie W. Hughan (*ca.* 1918), Hughan papers, SCPC, and in Abrams, *Preachers Present Arms,* pp. 149–50. John Lovejoy Elliott was a social worker in New York.

43. Minutes of the executive committee, Sept. 21, 1917, People's Council of America papers. The best published accounts of the council are Horace C. Peterson and Gilbert C. Fite, *Opponents of War, 1917–1918* (Madison: University of Wisconsin Press, 1957), pp. 74–78, and Frank L. Grubbs, Jr., *The Struggle for Labor Loyalty: Gompers, the A. F. of L. and the Pacifists, 1917–1920* (Durham: Duke University Press, 1968).

44. Lochner to members of the executive and general committees, Nov. 21, 1918, People's Council of America papers.

45. *"Is My Name Written There?" Testimony of Archibald Stevenson, before the Overman Committee* (New York: American Union Against Militarism, 1919), A.U.A.M. papers.

46. *World Tomorrow,* XI, No. 4 (Apr., 1928), p. 162.

47. People's Council *Bulletin,* I (Aug. 7, 1917), 2–3.

48. Bourne, "The State," in Resek, ed., *War and the Intellectuals,* pp. 84, 89. Bourne's analysis of the relationship of the state and war is most succinctly put in this essay.

49. Bourne, "Twilight of the Idols," *Untimely Papers,* ed. by James Oppenheim (New York: B. W. Huebsch, 1919), p. 139.

50. Bourne, "Below the Battle," *Untimely Papers,* p. 60.

51. Norman Thomas to Mrs. Anne C. Brush, Sept. 24, 1918, Thomas papers.

52. Norman Thomas to Alexander Trachtenberg, Oct. 18, 1918,

and Thomas to Morris Hillquit, Oct. 2, 1917, Thomas papers.

53. Eastman, *Love and Revolution*, p. 26.

54. Henry May, *The End of American Innocence; A Study of The First Years of Our Own Time, 1912–1917* (New York: Alfred A. Knopf, 1959), p. 368. Clarence M. Case observed that Socialist conscientious objectors became more extreme in their views, having experienced "coercion" by the state about which they had previously but theorized. Case, *Non-Violent Coercion; A Study in Methods of Social Pressure* (New York: The Century Co., 1923), pp. 277–78.

55. Vida Scudder, *On Journey* (New York: E. P. Dutton & Co., Inc., 1937), p. 285. For the parallel view of the F.O.R., see especially *The Fellowship of Reconciliation*, a statement of purpose, and *The Fellowship of Reconciliation: Some General Considerations*, F.O.R. papers.

56. Addams, *Peace and Bread,* p. 62.

57. Max Eastman, *Love and Revolution*, p. 62.

58. Evan to Norman Thomas, Nov. 5, 1915, Thomas papers, box 139.

59. Evan to Norman Thomas, Mar. 2, 1917, Thomas papers, box 139.

60. *Ibid.*

61. Holmes, *The Spiritual Conditions of an Enduring Peace* (New York: Church of the Messiah, 1918–19), p. 10.

62. Holmes, *New Wars for Old* (New York: Dodd, Mead & Co., 1916).

63. Holmes, and Scott Nearing, *Can the Church Be Radical?* (New York: The Hanford Press, 1922).

CHAPTER III

1. Quoted from Public Law No .12, 65th Cong., 1st sess. (Washington, D.C.: Government Printing Office, 1917), in Selective Service System, *Conscientious Objection*, Special Monograph No. 11, 2 vols. (Washington, D.C.: Government Printing Office, 1950), I, 49.

2. Since there were 2,810,296 inducted men in World War I, the objectors represented about 0.0014 per cent of those drafted. *Statement Concerning the Treatment of Conscientious Objectors in the Army* (Washington, D.C.: Government Printing Office, 1919), pp. 9, 24–25; Selective Service System, *Conscientious Objection*, I, 60.

3. Norman Thomas, *Conscientious Objector in America*, pp. 81, 85–86. According to Thomas, 64,693 claims were made for noncombatant classification; 56,830 were recognized by local boards. Of these,

29,679 were rated Class I and physically fit, and 20,873 were inducted, of whom 3,989 continued to claim exemption in camp.

Failure to register was punishable by imprisonment for a maximum of one year after trial before a federal judge. The prisoner was then registered and subject to draft. Occasionally, sentences were shortened so that a man might be inducted sooner. Thomas cited several Socialists in Minneapolis who were illegally inducted into service while they were yet in jail. Upon their refusal to serve, they were court-martialed and sentenced to long prison terms.

4. *Ibid.*, p. 15.

5. *Statement Concerning Treatment of Conscientious Objectors*, p. 25; Selective Service System, *Conscientious Objection*, I, 60.

6. Walter Guest Kellogg, *The Conscientious Objector* (New York: Boni and Liveright, 1919), app. V, pp. 129 f.

7. Quoted from Public Law No. 12, 65th Cong., 1st sess. in Selective Service System, *Conscientious Objection*, I, 49. This act, the Selective Service Law of May 18, 1917, was modeled on SECTION 17, Act of Feb. 24, 1864 (13 Stat., pp. 6. 9), providing exemption on payment of fine or noncombatant duty for members of religious denominations opposed to bearing arms. "Hearings on the Selective Service Act before the House Committee on Military Affairs," 65th Cong., 1st sess., Apr. 14 and 27, 1917 (Washington, D.C.: Government Printing Office, 1917), p. 82.

8. *Statement Concerning the Treatment of Conscientious Objectors*, p. 18.

9. Public Law No. 85, 64th Cong., 1st sess. (Washington, D.C.: Government Printing Office, 1916), in Selective Service System, *Conscientious Objection*, I, 50.

10. Woodrow Wilson to Nevin Sayre, May 1, 1917, Sayre papers. Quaker historian Rufus Jones and lawyer Edward W. Evans favored asking the government to consider the nondenominational Fellowship of Reconciliation "as a religious organization within the meaning of the exemption clause of the Conscription Law." Edward Evans to Norman Thomas, June 22, 1917. Norman Thomas concluded from a poll of about two hundred clergymen that few respondents would support a campaign to liberalize the religious provision of the law. Norman Thomas to Frederick Lynch, Aug. 3, 1917, Thomas papers.

11. *Statement Concerning Treatment of Conscientious Objectors*, p. 17; Selective Service System, *Conscientious Objection*, I, 54; and Kellogg, *Conscientious Objector*, pp. 86–88.

12. Selective Service System, *Conscientious Objection*, I, 54–55,

59; *Statement Concerning Treatment of Conscientious Objectors*, pp. 17–23; Paul Comly French, *We Won't Murder, Being the Story of Men Who Followed Their Conscientious Scruples and Helped Give Life to Democracy* (New York: Hastings House, 1940), pp. 21–24.

During the war the civilian commissioner for the furlough system, R. C. McCrea, received the suggestion that several churchmen might be given the use of several thousand acres of land in the Pima Indian Reservation, Ariz., to which several hundred C.O.'s might be furloughed. Money made above expenses could go toward reconstruction work. McCrea approved the plan. Although it was abandoned as the German retreat began, it was a forerunner of the system of Civilian Public Service camps operated during World War II. Jonas S. Hartzler, *Mennonites in the World War, or, Nonresistance Under Test* (Scottdale, Pa.: Mennonite Publishing House, 1922), p. 109.

13. According to Kellogg, 122 C.O.'s were judged to be insincere and assignable to military duty. *Conscientious Objector*, app. II, p. 128. Farm furloughs were given more often than were industrial ones. In 1919, Frederick Keppel reported that 390 C.O.'s had been assigned to noncombatant service but he did not report that 15 had been assigned to hospital work. *Statement Concerning Treatment of Conscientious Objectors*, p. 24.

14. Rufus Jones, *A Service of Love*, p. 114.

15. Benét, *John Brown's Body*, in *Selected Works of Stephen Vincent Benét, Volume One: Poetry* (New York: Farrar & Rinehart, Inc., 1942), pp. 210–11.

16. Addams, *Peace and Bread*, pp. 122 f.

17. Norman Thomas, *Conscientious Objector in America*, pp. 4 f.

18. Quoted from a report to the Secretary of War, Dec. 20, 1917, in Hartzler, *Mennonites in the World War*, p. 100.

19. Mark A. May (Division of Psychology, Surgeon General's Office, u.s.a.), "The Psychological Examinations of Conscientious Objectors," *American Journal of Psychology*, XXXI (Apr., 1920), 154–61; Thomas, *Conscientious Objector in America*, p. 48; Harold J. Tobin and Percy W. Bidwell, *Mobilizing Civilian America* (New York: Council on Foreign Relations, 1940), p. 107.

20. May, "Psychological Examinations of Conscientious Objectors," pp. 160–61.

21. An important example of usage based on the grounds of opposition is Thomas, *Conscientious Objector in America*, p. 4; usage based on selective instance of objection is in Clarence Marsh Case, *Non-Violent Coercion; A Study in Methods of Social Pressure* (New York:

The Century Co., 1923), p. 119. Because the term "non-religious" as used by the government meant nonsectarian, the terms "radical" or "philosophical" objectors are used in this study to designate those who were not religiously oriented.

22. Morris Hillquit, introduction to Alexander Trachtenberg, *The American Socialists and the War* (New York: Rand School of Social Science, 1917), p. 3.

23. Addams, *Peace and Bread*, p. 122. For detailed and moving descriptions of the prosecution and prison treatment of political objectors, see Peterson and Fite, *Opponents of War*.

24. Kellogg, *Conscientious Objector*, pp. 71–72.

25. Baldwin, "Statement in Court," Oct. 30, 1918, enclosed in a letter from Norman Thomas to Henry W. L. Dana, Oct. 31, 1918, Dana papers.

26. Letter of Feb. 8, 1921, quoted in Case, *Non-Violent Coercion*, p. 261. Case was then an associate professor of sociology and anthropology at the University of Iowa. He later became professor of sociology at the University of Southern California.

27. Kellogg, *Conscientious Objector*, p. 73.

28. Thomas, *Conscientious Objector in America*, p. 29.

29. Evan to Norman Thomas, May 16, 1917, Thomas papers, box 139.

30. Evan to Norman Thomas, Feb. 2, 1917, Thomas papers, box 139. Evan Thomas found the German's moral intolerance indicated in the fact that "no English book was read so much in the camp as the life of Oliver Cromwell."

31. Letter from Roger N. Baldwin to Case, quoted in *Non-Violent Coercion*, p. 278.

32. Quoted in Thomas, *Conscientious Objector in America*, pp. 25–26.

33. Kellogg, *Conscientious Objector*, p. 53; Herbert H. Stroup, *The Jehovah's Witnesses* (New York: Columbia University Press, 1945), pp. 16–17.

34. Addams, *Peace and Bread*, p. 126; see also p. 125. This incident is discussed also in Thomas, *Conscientious Objector in America*, pp. 197–200, where some details are different; Miss Addams related the story substantially as in the text above from a personal knowledge of the wife. Case, *Non-Violent Coercion*, pp. 243–45, and Ernest L. Meyer, *"HEY! YELLOWBACKS!" The War Diary of a Conscientious Objector* (New York: John Day Co., 1930), pp. 138–39, appear to have taken their accounts from Thomas. Hartzler's version in *Mennonites*

in the World War, pp. 145–47, agrees with Thomas's, although apparently written independently.

35. Harold Gray to Kirby Page, June 17, 1918, Page papers.

36. Meyer, *"HEY! YELLOWBACKS!"* pp. 136–37.

37. *Ibid.*, 163.

38. Kellogg, *Conscientious Objector*, p. 38; see also pp. 34–41, 66–74, 81, 93–95. Kellogg, however, expressed great admiration for Quakers, whom he thought were both intelligent and sincerely religious (p. 43). There may have been some correlation between his admiration and the large proportion of Quakers who accepted alternative service.

39. Quoted in Case, *Non-Violent Coercion*, p. 267. Case wrote that this conviction, though based upon the examples and teachings of Christ, rested primarily upon a humanitarian basis: respect for life. I cannot separate the humanitarian and religious motives so neatly in the minds of these C.O.'s for whom Jesus *taught* respect for life. To separate them is to make the mistake of the War Department, which called them idealists and treated their religious convictions as sentimental opinions simply because they were not doctrinally derived. This study follows the usage of Mark May, who uses the term "religious-idealists" to describe this class of C.O.'s.

40. "Friends and War: A New Statement of the Quaker Position, Adopted by the Conference of All Friends, 1920," quoted in *ibid.*, p. 138. There emerged three distinct groups of Quakers with respect to participation in war: those who renounced pacifist tradition altogether; those who remained opposed to war in general, but regarded World War I as an exception; and those who opposed all war. Among the latter were Quaker C.O.'s, some of whom accepted alternate military service, and others who were absolutely opposed to warfare in any form.

41. Kirby Page to Harold Gray, July 16, 1918, Page papers.

42. The hunger strike is described in detail in Brown, *Character "Bad,"* pp. 125–61, and in Evan to Norman Thomas, July 29 through Sept. 1, 1918, Norman Thomas papers, box 139.

43. Letter from Lunde, Thomas, Moore, and Gray to Newton D. Baker, Aug. 21, 1918; Evan Thomas to Norman Thomas, Aug. 23, 1918, in the Thomas papers, box 139; Gray to Kirby Page, June 17, 1918, in the Page papers; interviews by the author with Harold Gray in Saline, Mich., Aug. 29, 1963, and Evan Thomas in Philadelphia, July 29, 1964.

44. Gray, quoted in Brown, *Character "Bad,"* p. 160.

45. Norman to Ralph Thomas, Jan. 10, 1919. Thomas papers, box 139. This technique of ordering C.O.'s to police regular army grounds was often used as a basis for court martial, although the Secretary of War had directed that C.O.'s were obligated only to keep themselves and their immediate surroundings in good condition.

Gray was released Sept. 5, 1919; Evan Thomas was discharged from the army Jan. 14, 1919.

46. Gray, quoted in Brown, *Character "Bad,"* p. 197.

47. Evan to Norman Thomas, June 8, 1918, Thomas papers, box 139.

48. The quoted questions are taken from Tom Gardner, "Manpower Unchanneled," the selections used by Alice Lynd to pose the issues facing contemporary C.O.'s in her *We Won't Go: Personal Accounts of War Objectors* (Boston: Beacon Press, 1968), p. 4.

49. Meyer, *"HEY! YELLOWBACKS!"* p. 209

50. Norman Thomas, *War's Heretics; A Plea for the Conscientious Objector* (New York: Civil Liberties Bureau of the American Union Against Militarism, 1917), p. 10.

51. Meyer, *"HEY! YELLOWBACKS!"* p. 83.

CHAPTER IV

1. Boeckel, *The Turn Toward Peace* (New York: Friendship Press, 1930), p. ix.

2. Morrison to Page, Jan. 12 and Nov. 5, 1920, Page papers. See also the letter of May 26, 1920, for Morrison's views when the *Christian Century* agreed to publish the book with a $600 subsidy from Page.

3. Page to Gray, July 1, 1919, Page papers.

4. Jane Addams, *Peace and Bread*, p. 187.

5. *Ibid.*, p. 179.

6. Holmes, *The Price of Peace: Are We Willing to Pay It?* (New York: Church of the Messiah, 1916), p. 7.

7. Thomas, *Conscientious Objector in America*, p. 261.

8. Scudder, *On Journey*, p. 299.

9. Chamberlain, *Farewell to Reform: Being a History of the Rise, Life and Decay of the Progressive Mind in America* (New York: Liveright, Inc., 1932), p. 304.

10. Boeckel, *The Turn Toward Peace*, p. ix.

11. Page to Sherwood Eddy, May 19, 1919, Page papers.

12. Bussey and Tims, *Women's International League for Peace and Freedom*, p. 78.

13. *Peace Year Book, 1938* (London: National Peace Council, 1938 [covers the year, 1937]), pp. 167–222.

14. *Report of the Commission on the Coordination of Efforts for Peace* (Oberlin, Ohio: The Commission on the Coordination of Efforts for Peace, 1933), pp. vi, 3–18.

15. Ashton Jones to Kirby Page, June 2, 1935, Page papers. Jones somehow got his trailer and pursued his grail, particularly in the South.

16. Van Kirk, *Religion Renounces War* (Chicago: Willett, Clark & Co., 1934), and *The Churches and World Peace, International Conciliation*, No. 304 (Nov., 1934).

17. John Masland, "The 'Peace' Groups Join Battle," *Public Opinion Quarterly*, IV (Dec., 1940), 664–73; and Allan A. Kuusisto, "The Influence of the National Council for Prevention of War on United States Foreign Policy, 1935–1939" (Ph.D. dissertation, Harvard University, 1950).

18. Kuusisto, pp. 24–25; and Atwater, *Organized Efforts in the United States Toward Peace* (Washington, D.C.: Digest Press, American University, 1936), and "Organizing American Public Opinion for Peace," *Public Opinion Quarterly,* I (Apr., 1937), pp. 112–21.

19. Denys P. Meyers, dir., *Origin and Conclusion of the Paris Pact: The Renunciation of War as an Instrument of National Policy* (Boston: World Peace Foundation, 1929), inside front cover.

20. Butler, Report of "Division of Intercourse and Education," in Amy Jones, comp., *Carnegie Endowment for International Peace: Organization and Work, International Conciliation* series, No. 200 (July, 1924), p. 215.

21. Boeckel, *Between War and Peace; A Handbook for Peace Workers* (New York: Macmillan Co., 1928), p. 4.

22. Curti, *Peace or War*, pp. 281–82.

23. "Can the Peace Forces of the World Unite?" *World Tomorrow*, VII (Jan., 1924), 3.

24. The diaries of Frederick J. Libby, entries for Apr. 17–19, 28, and May 1, and 3, 1925, in the possession of Mrs. Libby.

25. "Advocates of World Court and Outlawry of War Reach Important Agreement," a press release for July 15, 1925, and Page to Eugene E. Barnett (of the National Committee of the Y.M.C.A., Shanghai, China), n.d.[1925], Page papers; S. E. Nicholson (associate secretary of the World Alliance) to Arthur Watkins, June 29, 1925, and James S. McDonald to Mrs. Raymond Morgan, June 23, 1925, and other items, N.C.P.W. papers, box 75, SCPC.

An excellent account of the origins and significance of the Harmony Plan is Charles DeBenedetti, "American Internationalism in the 1920's: Shotwell and the Outlawrists" (Ph.D. dissertation, University of Illinois, 1968), based especially upon the papers of Salmon Levinson, Raymond Robbins, Newton Baker, and William Borah.

26. Levinson to Page, Nov. 5, 1925, Page to Libby and to James T. Shotwell, Sept. 18, 1925, Page papers.

27. Women's World Court Committee Annual Report, Nov. 30, 1925, and Laura P. Morgan to Libby, Oct. 27, 1925, N.C.P.W. papers, box 75; Morgan to Katherine Gerwick (Education and Research Division, National Board, Y.M.C.A.), Nov. 5, 1925, Page papers.

28. Levinson to Page, Dec. 31, 1925, Page papers.

29. DeBenedetti, "American Internationalism," p. 218.

30. Holmes to Page, Dec. 16, 1925; Levinson to Page, Dec. 31, 1925, Page papers.

31. Page, "War as an Institution: A Review of [Charles C. Morrison] 'The Outlawry of War,'" *World Tomorrow*, X (Nov., 1927), 447–49.

32. Masland, "The 'Peace' Groups Join Battle," p. 665.

33. Libby diaries, May 26, and June 6, 1938.

34. Allen, "The Peace Movement Moves Left," *Annals of the American Academy of Political and Social Science*, CLXXV (Sept., 1934), 150–55; Masland, "Pressure Groups and American Foreign Policy," *Public Opinion Quarterly*, VI (spring, 1942), 115–22.

35. *Statement of Principles Essential to the Maintenance of Peace*, a flyer (National Peace Conference, 1935).

CHAPTER V

1. Benét, "1936," *Selected Works of Stephen Vincent Benét, Vol. One: Poetry* (New York: Farrar & Rinehart, Inc., 1942), pp. 454–55.

2. Eby, *War* (New Haven: Yale University Press, 1936), introduction [n.p.]; Benét, "1936," 1. 15.

3. Page to Fred B. Smith, Sept. 23, 1922; Page, unpublished autobiography, "My Cup Runneth Over," pp. 155–56, Page papers.

4. Barnes, *Genesis of the World War: An Introduction to the Problem of War Guilt* (New York: Alfred A. Knopf, 1926), p. xiii. Sidney Fay, *The Origins of the World War*, 2 vols. (New York: Macmillan Co., 1928); Bernadotte Schmitt, *The Coming of the War: 1914*, 2 vols. (New York: Charles Scribner's Sons, 1930); C. Hartley Grattan, *Why We Fought* (New York: The Vanguard Press, 1929); and Walter

Millis, *The Road to War* (New York: Houghton Mifflin, 1935). See Warren I. Cohen's excellent analysis of *The American Revisionists* (Chicago: University of Chicago Press, 1967).

5. Shotwell, *On the Rim of the Abyss* (New York: Macmillan Co., 1936), p. 51.

6. Schmitt to Kirby Page, Oct. 24, 1930, Page papers.

7. *National Defense*, pp. 90–117. The historians are listed by name. To the question of whether Germany was *solely* responsible for the war the responses were: yes, 3; no, 95; in doubt, 1; no answer, 1. To the question of whether Germany was *more* responsible than other powers the responses were: yes, 32; no, 56; in doubt, 11; no answer, 1.

8. *War; Its Causes, Consequences and Cure*, by Page, and *The Abolition of War*, by Page and Eddy, were intended to be companion pieces for popular study (New York: George H. Doran Co., 1923 and 1924, respectively). The second book consisted of a testimonial by Eddy and a series of questions and answers by Page.

9. McCrea, "It's Up to the Churches," *World Tomorrow*, VII (Feb., 1924), 61–62. Gulick's endorsement was given in a letter to ministers of Nov. 6, 1923, and the number of copies distributed was recorded in Page to Harold Gray, Jan. 11, 1924, Page papers.

Warren Cohen found a wide range of estimates of the sales of the Millis book in *The American Revisionists*, pp. 154–55n. According to Houghton Mifflin Company (Feb. 24, 1969) a total of about 70,000 copies were distributed, including a Book-of-the-Month Club edition of 48,814. Sales of the publisher's edition the first year were 14,631 copies.

10. Introduction to Kirby Page, *War; Its Causes, Consequences and Cure* (New York: George H. Doran Co., 1923), p. vii.

11. Robert Moats Miller, *American Protestantism and Social Issues, 1919–1939* (Chapel Hill: University of North Carolina Press, 1958), p. 331; see especially pp. 317–50.

12. Page to Fred B. Smith, Sept. 23, 1922; Page, "My Cup Runneth Over," pp. 155–56, Page papers.

13. Page to Charles C. Morrison, May 29, 1920, and see Harry Emerson Fosdick to Page, Oct. 25, 1922, Page papers.

14. "Religious Pacifism in the News," *World Tomorrow*, XII (June 14, 1934), 291.

15. A. T. DeGroot, *Christianity Is Pacifism: The Story of Pacifism Among Disciples of Christ* (Indianapolis: Department of Social Education and Action, United Christian Missionary Society, n.d. [*ca.* 1935]). Harold Fey had been professor of sociology at Union Theolog-

ical Seminary in Manila, Philippine Islands; he was editor of *World Call,* the Disciples' missionary magazine, and subsequently was editor of the F.O.R.'s *Fellowship* magazine and of the *Christian Century.*

The view that pacifism represented allegiance to or repudiation of Jesus was expressed in nearly every pamphlet of the Fellowship and innumerable articles by pacifists. They were careful to add, however, that patriots should not be condemned as unchristian if they felt it their duty to fight. They distinguished between war as a method and the motives of men, which they did not pretend to judge.

16. An early leader was Bishop Francis J. McConnell. In 1924 numerous conferences of the church passed antiwar resolutions and the Committee on the State of the Church reported out a virtually pacifist pronouncement which was modified, however, by the General Conference. The next major step by General Conference came in 1932 when it requested that Methodist objectors be granted the same exemption to draft and military training as that accorded to Friends. See E. Franklin Carwithan, "The Attitudes of the Methodist Episcopal Church toward Peace and War" (S.T.D. thesis, Temple University School of Theology, 1944), and James Marion DeVinney, "The Attitudes of the Methodist Episcopal Church toward War from 1919 to 1927" (M.A. thesis, Northwestern University, 1928).

17. Van Kirk, *Religion Renounces War* (Chicago: Willett, Clark & Co., 1934), p. 6.

18. A 1936 poll taken in 310 Disciples of Christ churches yielded 16,304 ballots returned, of which there were promising to bears arms or support *any* U.S. war, 2,270 yes, 10,455 no, 1,322 undecided; and promising *not* to support *any* U.S. war, 3,069 yes, 6,875 no, and 3,191 undecided. DeGroot, *Christianity Is Pacifism.* Robert M. Miller reported other polls of religious bodies including a 1936 poll of Northern Baptists in which 26.62 per cent indicated they would refuse service in any case, and a poll of 12,854 Protestant and Jewish religious leaders in which 56 per cent would not sanction any war. *American Protestantism and Social Issues,* pp. 338–39.

19. "America's First Peace Plebiscite," *Social Action,* I (Dec. 26, 1935), 12–14, and see "The Peace Plebiscite Edition," *ibid.* (Sept. 15, 1935). Among those who sought to advance the Council for Social Action were pacifists Theodore Green (New Britain, Conn.), Allan Knight Chalmers (Broadway Tabernacle, New York City), and Albert B. Coe (minister in Oak Park, Ill.).

20. Kirby Page, "Nineteen Thousand Clergymen on War and Peace," *World Tomorrow,* XIV (May, 1931), 138–54.

21. Kirby Page, "20,870 Clergymen on War and Economic Injustice," *ibid.*, XVII (May 10, 1934), 222–56.

22. Page, "Nineteen Thousand Clergymen," p. 138.

23. Walter Muelder put it bluntly: "On questions of international relations and more specifically on peace policy, the leadership of Methodism was probably much more pacifist than the general membership . . . . many leaders of that period recall that the general sentiment in the pews differed sharply from that expressed in the pulpit on questions of war, military preparedness, and conscientious objection." *Methodism and Society in the Twentieth Century*, Vol. II of *Methodism and Society*, edited by the Board of Social and Economic Relations of the Methodist Church (Nashville: Abingdon Press, 1961), p. 148.

24. "The Impact of the War on Religion in America," *American Journal of Sociology*, XLVIII (Nov., 1942), 354. Ray Abrams reached the same opinion after a survey of religious opinion in "The Churches and the Clergy in World War II," *Annals of the American Academy of Political and Social Sciences,* CCLVI (Mar., 1948), 110–19.

25. Page, *War*, p. 181, and *If War Is Sin* (New York: Fellowship of Reconciliation, n.d. [*ca.* 1935]), p. 4.

26. DeGroot, *Christianity Is Pacifism.*

27. Guy Franklin Hershberger, *The Mennonite Church in the Second World War* (Scottdale, Pa.: Mennonite Publishing House, 1951), pp. 4–10. See also Harold S. Bender, "Peace Problems Committee," *The Mennonite Encyclopedia*, IV, 130–31.

The General Conference Mennonite Church also appointed a Peace Committee in 1926 which worked closely with the Mennonite Central Committee, formed in 1920, to coordinate relief work, resettlement programs, and eventually Civilian Public Service camps.

28. Vernon Howard Holloway, "American Pacifism Between Two Wars, 1919–1941: An Analysis of Pacifist Groups and Doctrines in the United States" (Ph.D. dissertation, Yale University, 1949), pp. 393–94 and *passim.*

29. Hershberger, "Pacifism," *Mennonite Encyclopedia*, IV, 105.

30. The theology of liberal pacifism is not given systematically in any American book published before World War II that is known to me. It is an organization of assumptions and assertions found throughout pacifist literature, and is developed at greater length in chap. 6 and 7 of my "Pacifism and American Life: 1914 to 1941" (Ph.D. dissertation, Vanderbilt University, 1965).

31. Adolf Harnack, although not a pacifist, documented the rejection of militarism by the early church, *Milita Christi: Die Christliche*

Religion und der Soldatenstand in den ersten drei Jahrunderten (Tubingen, Germany: T. C. B. Mohr, 1905). Cecil John Cadoux, *The Early Church and the World*, an expansion of his *Early Christian Attitude to War: A Contribution to the History of Christian Ethics* (London: Headley Bros. Publ. Ltd., 1919), remains the standard English work in the field. G. J. Heering's *The Fall of Christianity* (London: George Allen & Unwin, 1931 [the Dutch publication, 1938]) has been much used by subsequent writers. See Roland H. Bainton, "The Early Church and War," in Rufus Jones, ed., *The Church, the Gospel and War* (New York: Harper & Bros., 1948), pp. 75–92, and Rufus Jones, *Christian Attitudes Toward War and Peace: A Historical Survey and Critical Re-evaluation* (Nashville: Abingdon Press, 1960); and Kirby Page, *Jesus or Christianity: A Study in Contrasts* (New York: Doubleday, Doran & Co., Inc., 1929), pp. 53–222, among many others.

32. Ernest Freemont Tittle, "What Will the Church Do with Jesus?" *World Tomorrow*, XIV (Mar., 1931), 75–77.

33. Holmes, "Can Pacifists Resort to Force?" *World Tomorrow*, VII (Apr., 1925), 101. William I. Hull documented the pacifist indictment of war throughout history in *The War-Method and the Peace-Method: An Historical Contrast* (New York: Fleming H. Revell Co., 1929).

34. Page, *War*, p. 181.

35. *The Obligations of Catholics to Promote Peace: A Report of the Ethics Committee* (Washington, D.C.: Catholic Association for International Peace, 1940), p. 11. Catholics taking this position opposed American intervention but pledged themselves to fight if war seemed justifiable. James M. Gillis, the editor of *Catholic World*, thus vigorously campaigned for the America First program of neutrality but called Harry Emerson Fosdick's renunciation of war wild talk. He equated other pacifists with communists. "Pacifism and Common Sense," *Catholic World*, CXXXIX (July, 1934), 385–89, and "Apologia," *ibid.*, CLV (May, 1942), 129–39.

36. Two significant works denying that modern war can be just were Franziskus Stratmann, *The Church and War, A Catholic Study* (New York: O.P.P.J. Kennedy & Sons, 1931), and John K. Ryan, *Modern War and Basic Ethics* (Washington, D.C.: Catholic University of America, 1933).

37. "Catholic Students Are Against War," *Christian Century*, LVI (Nov. 22, 1939), 1428.

38. Fenwick, *A Primer of Peace* (Washington, D.C.: Catholic Association for International Peace, 1937), p. 51.

39. "Catholic Students Are Against War," p. 1428.

40. Simonds, *Can America Stay at Home?* (New York: Harper & Bros., 1932), p. 11.

41. Holmes, *The Spiritual Conditions of an Enduring Peace* (New York: Church of the Messiah, 1918–19), pp. 7 ff.

42. Page, *War*, pp. 62–63, 111.

43. Thomas, *The Challenge of War: An Economic Interpretation* (New York: League for Industrial Democracy, 1924), pp. 9–10. The responsibility of nationalism for war was a popular theme of peace literature. See, for example, Georges DeMartial, *Patriotism and Responsibility for the War* (New York: B. W. Huebsch, Inc., 1920).

44. The phrase is Devere Allen's in a "Sermon" delivered in Dec., 1916, Devere Allen papers.

45. *Eleventh Annual Report: June 1st, 1927 to May 31, 1928* (Philadelphia: American Friends Service Committee, 1928), pp. 13–15.

46. *Annual Report—1940, ibid.*, pp. 30–32, and, also, annual reports from 1930 to 1940.

47. *Fourteenth Annual Report, 1930–31, ibid.*, 1931, p. 15.

48. *Ibid.*, p. 12; and see Clarence Pickett, *For More Than Bread, An Autobiographical Account of Twenty-two Years' Work with the American Friends Service Committee* (Boston: Little, Brown & Co., 1953), pp. 338–98.

49. *Annual Report—1940*, pp. 29–30.

50. *1941 Annual Report* (Philadelphia: American Friends Service Committee, 1942), p. 28.

51. *Fourteenth Annual Report, 1930–31*, p. 14; *Annual Report, June 1, 1931, to Dec. 31, 1932* (Philadelphia: American Friends Service Committee, 1933), p. 3; *Annual Report, 1933, ibid.*, 1934, pp. 10–11.

52. Allen, *The Fight for Peace*, p. ix.

53. (New York: Doubleday, Doran & Co., Inc., 1929).

54. "Confidential Memorandum" from Allen, circulated among the staff of the *Nation* in 1932, Allen papers.

55. *Ibid.*

56. Files of Worldover Press and extensive correspondence in the Allen papers.

Chapter VI

1. Slogan used in the Disarmament parade of Nov. 12, 1921, in New York City, flyer in the Women's Peace Society papers, SCPC.

2. U.S., Senate Joint Resolution 100, *Congressional Record*, 69th

Cong., 1st sess., 1926, LXVII, 8021; S. J. Res. 1, 70th Cong., 1st sess., 1927–28, LXIX, 351; S. J. Res. 45, 71st Cong., 1st sess., 1929, LXXI, 1830 (for copy of the resolution, see p. 2748); S. J. Res. 3, 72nd Cong., 1st sess., 1931–32, LXXV, 206; S. J. Res. 24, 73rd Cong., 1st sess., 1933, LXXVII, 504; S. J. Res. 6, 74th Cong., 1st sess., 1935, LXXIX, 104; S. J. Res. 9, 75th Cong., 1st sess., 1937, LXXXI, 71. See also *Memorandum in Favor of the Proposed Amendment Making War Legally Impossible for the United States* (New York: Women's Peace Union, 1930).

3. U.S., House Joint Resolutions 89 and 159, *Congressional Record,* 74th Cong., 1st sess., 1935, LXXIX, 430, 1625; H.R.J. Res. 20 and 199, 75th Cong., 1st sess., 1937, LXXXI, 37, 947.

4. H.R.J. Res. 356, *ibid.,* 67th Cong., 2nd sess., 1922, LXII, 9360; H.R.J. Res. 423 and 540, 67th Cong., 4th sess., 1923, LXIV, 1866, 3817.

5. H.R.J. Res. 134 and 266, 68th Cong., 1st sess., 1924, LXV, 830, 8827, 8851; H.R.J. Res. 152, 69th Cong., 1st sess., 1925–26, LXVII, 3413; H.R.J. Res. 19, 70th Cong., 1st sess., 1927, LXIX, 98, 323; H.R.J. Res. 378, 70th Cong., 2nd sess., 1928, LXX, 1518; H.R.J. Res. 112, 71st Cong., 1st sess., 1929, LXXI, 3019; H.R.J. Res. 499, 71st Cong., 3rd sess., 1931, LXXIV, 4628; H.R.J. Res. 103, 72nd Cong., 1st sess., 1932, LXXV, 173 (copy of the resolution, p. 2286); H.R.J. Res. 217, 73rd Cong., 2nd sess., 1934, LXXVIII, 168 (copy of resolution, pp. 3522–23); H.R.J. Res. 108, 74th Cong., 1st sess., 1935, LXXIX, 627; H.R.J. Res. 33, 63, and 238, 75th Cong., 1st sess., 1937, LXXXI, 38, 39, 1451; H.R.J. Res. 498 and 502, 75th Cong., 2nd sess., 1937, LXXXII, 20, 102; H.R.J. Res. 553, 565, and 576, 75th Cong., 3rd sess., 1938, LXXXIII, 134, 566, 1186.

S.J. Res. 8 and 48, 68th Cong., 1st sess., 1923–24, LXV, 89, 354; S.J. Res. 102, 69th Cong., 1st sess., 1925–26, LXVII, 8342; S.J. Res. 104, 73rd Cong., 2nd sess., 1934, LXXVIII, 6898; S.J. Res. 7, 74th Cong., 1st sess., 1935, LXXIX, 1041; S.J. Res. 10, 75th Cong., 1st sess., 1937, LXXXI, 71; S.J. Res. 218, 221, and 223, 75th Cong., 2nd sess., 1937, LXXXII, 24, 61; S.J. Res. 270, 75th Cong., 3rd sess., 1938, LXXXIII, 2410.

6. Lippman, "Mr. Ludlow Prepares for War," U.S., *Congressional Record, Appendix,* 75th Cong., 2nd sess., 1937, LXXXII, 561–62.

7. Allen to Page, Mar. 25, 1926, Allen papers.

8. The bill was introduced on Jan. 25, 1935. U.S., *Congressional Record,* 74th Cong., 1st sess., Dec., 1935, LXXIX, 963. See George E. Bevans to Kirby Page, Dec. 19, 1934, Page papers. Subsequently, it

was reintroduced by Senator Neely in 1937 and 1939, revived in the Senate by Alexander Wiley of Wisconsin in 1943 and Louis Ludlow in 1945, and was advocated by Karl Mundt of North Dakota in 1945. Everett Dirksen of Illinois introduced a bill for a peace division in the Department of State when he was a representative in 1947. At least 85 bills were introduced in Congress to create a peace department between 1955 and 1968. See Frederick L. Schuman, *Why a Department of Peace?* (Beverly Hills, Calif.: Another Mother for Peace, 1969), p. 14, and Legislative Reference Service of the Library of Congress, *The Historical Development of Past Legislation to Establish a U.S. Department of Peace, with Reasons and Statements in Support of the Proposal: Report Prepared According to the Instructions of the Hon. Spark Matsunaga* (Washington, D.C.: Government Printing Office, 1968).

9. *The Colonial Gazette,* VII (Los Angeles: Fairfax High School, May 17, 1929).

10. Unsigned letter, probably written by Amos Pinchot, to the members of the executive committee, Feb. 10, 1919, A.U.A.M. papers.

11. Charles Hallinan to "Dear Friend," Aug. 16, 1919, A.U.A.M. papers. By this time, Oswald G. Villard had been elected chairman again; Agnes B. Leach, treasurer; and A. A. Berle, James Maurer, and Zona Gale had returned to their places on the executive committee.

12. C. Leonard Hoag, *Preface to Preparedness, The Washington Conference and Public Opinion* (Washington, D.C.: American Council on Public Affairs, 1941), p. 11.

13. *Ibid.*; Armin Rappaport, *The Navy League of the United States* (Detroit: Wayne State University Press, 1962), pp. 93–95.

14. Frederick J. Libby, *To End War: The Story of the National Council for Prevention of War* (New York: Fellowship Press, 1969), p. 10. The N.C.P.W. was governed by a council made up of 1 representative for each participating organization (there were 43 in Jan., 1922) plus 30 to 34 delegates-at-large drawn from among leaders in the peace movement. The policy-making arm of the council was an executive board, elected by an annual convention. This board was supposed to be checked by a provision in the bylaws that no legislative measure (as opposed to educational work) could be supported by the council unless it was endorsed by all responsible delegates. Its affiliates encouraged the council to adopt policies of its own, however, so that it became a distinct organization with policies of its own.

15. *Ibid.,* p. 13.

16. Minutes, Jan. 20, 1922, A.U.A.M. papers.

17. Rappaport, *The Navy League*, pp. 107–108.

18. Untitled flyer describing the disarmament parade of Nov. 12, 1921, in New York City, Women's Peace Society papers, SCPC.

19. Dewey, "Introduction," to Roswell P. Barnes, *Militarizing Our Youth: The Significance of the Reserve Officers' Training Corps in our Schools and Colleges* (New York: Committee on Militarism in Education, 1927), p. 3; Elizabeth Dilling, *The Red Network; a "Who's Who" and Handbook of Radicalism for Patriots* (Chicago: the author, 1934), p. 65.

20. Minutes of Feb. 5, 1932, F.O.R. papers.

21. Roswell P. Barnes, *Militarizing Our Youth,* pp. 41–45. The schools are enumerated also in *Congressional Record, 71st* Cong., 3rd sess., 1931, LXXIV, 2263–67.

22. Lane, *Military Training in Schools and Colleges* (n.p. [Fellowship of Reconciliation, 1925]). The Lane pamphlet was endorsed by distinguished citizens, including John Dewey and Senator William Borah.

23. C.M.E. papers, boxes 2, 3, 12, 50, and 103, SCPC. Nevin Sayre may be said to be the founder of the committee which initially was formed to conduct an eight-month campaign to follow up the Lane pamphlet with E. Raymond Wilson in charge. By June, 1926, Roswell Barnes had agreed to take active charge of the committee in the fall. C.M.E. papers, above, and minutes of the F.O.R., Apr. 15 and Oct. 1, 1925, and June 5, 1926, F.O.R. papers.

24. The work of the C.M.E. (and attitudes toward R.O.T.C.) is documented in detail state by state in the C.M.E. papers, boxes 58–85, and was reported in its periodicals (*News Letter,* beginning Mar. 6, 1937, and *Breaking the War Habit,* beginning Apr. 15, 1937) and pamphlets. The origin of military training in schools and arguments against it are studied in Doris Galant Rodin, "The Opposition to the Establishment of Military Training in Civil Schools and Colleges in the United States, 1914–1940," (M.A. thesis, American University, 1949).

25. The Ohio State University case is documented in C.M.E. papers, boxes 77–79, and was widely reported.

26. Indeed, a careful attitudinal survey of students in the R.O.T.C. found cadets in advanced courses favoring an elective program by a ratio of 2:1, cadets in the basic courses by 3:1, and noncadets in two control groups by 14:1. Herbert W. Rogers, "Some Attitudes of Students in the R.O.T.C.," *Journal of Educational Psychology,* XXVI (Apr., 1935), 301. Innumerable local polls indicated widespread student preference for optional courses.

27. Quoted in Barnes, *Militarizing Our Youth*, pp. 5 and 12, from

The R.O.T.C. Manual, 2nd Year Advanced, (7th ed.; Baltimore: Johns Hopkins Press, 1925), IV, 207, 294, and 255, respectively, and James A. Moss and John W. Lang, *Manual of Military Training* (4th rev. ed.; Menasha, Wis.: George Banta Publ. Co., 1923), I, 1.

28. Barnes, *Militarizing Our Youth,* p. 13. The value and efficiency of training popularized for R.O.T.C. use would be questioned for half a century in military circles, too.

29. *Ibid.,* pp. 13–21; George A. Coe, *The War Department as Educator* (New York: Committee on Militarism in Education, 1930); and most C.M.E. literature.

30. Tucker P. Smith, *So This Is War! A Study of Popularized Military Training* (New York: Committee on Militarism in Education, n.d.), p. 25.

31. Ross A. Collins, "Our Military Institution Builds the Military Mind," reprinted from the *Congressional Record,* 71st Cong., 3rd sess., 1931, LXXIV. Collins was a member of the Subcommittee on Appropriations.

32. Two hundred and ninety *U.S. Reports,* 597 (1933). The case of Ennes H. Coale is covered in C.M.E. papers, box 67. See also Arthur A. Ekirch, *The Civilian and the Military* (New York: Oxford University Press, 1956), pp. 229–30 and references.

33. Two hundred and ninety-three *U.S. Reports* 245 (1933). The case of Albert Hamilton and Alonzo Reynolds is covered together with other cases in California in the C.M.E. papers, box 58.

34. Two hundred and seventy-nine *U.S. Reports* 644 (1929), and 283 *U.S. Reports* 605 (1931). Justices Oliver Wendell Holmes and Louis Brandeis dissented in the Schwimmer case, and they were joined by Chief Justice Charles Evans Hughes and Justice Harlan F. Stone in the Macintosh case.

35. 74th Cong., 1st sess., S–3309, and HR–8950, *Congressional Record,* 74th Cong., 2nd sess., pp. 4956–57; minutes of the executive board, Dec. 20, 1934, C.M.E. papers, box 3. The campaign for the Nye-Kvale bills is thoroughly documented in boxes 90–94.

36. Agnes A. Sharp, "Girl Scout Uniforms too 'Militaristic,' " *World Tomorrow,* XI (Jan., 1928), 17; *The Campaign Against Militarism in Education* (New York: Committee on Militarism in Education, 1931).

37. The incident is recounted and the chart is reproduced in Libby, *To End War,* pp. 44–46. See also Elizabeth McCausland, "The Blue Menace" (compilation of articles originally printed in the *Springfield Republican,* Mar. 18–27, 1928), in "Attacks," SCPC.

38. Congressman Maury Maverick circulated in 1935 an incrim-

inating memorandum supposedly sent by the naval intelligence section under the official Post Office frank of the Office of the Chief of Naval Operations. According to the New York *Times,* Roosevelt had a conference with representatives of religious organizations and then instructed the military to make no comments about civilian organizations (Dec. 7, p. 1). Complaints continued to come, and Maverick wrote the President on Mar. 28, 1936, about an article in the San Antonio *Light* (Mar. 28, 1936), a Hearst paper, which ascribed new charges to U.S. "agents." Roosevelt ordered the investigation in response to this letter. Maverick to Kirby Page with enclosure, July 29, 1935, Page papers; and Franklin D. Roosevelt (FDR) papers, OF 18–X, 263 and 394, box 1, Franklin D. Roosevelt Library, Hyde Park, New York.

39. Franklin Roosevelt to Col. Henry L. Roosevelt, Feb. 2, 1934, FDR papers, OF 394, box 1. The tone of this instruction perhaps explains why the innumerable petitions and letters from individuals in the peace movement were answered politely by the President's staff.

40. Sayre's full correspondence with the War Department on this incident is printed in the C.M.E. *News Letter* No. 5 (Feb. 5, 1927), Sayre papers, Nyaak, New York.

41. Barnes, *Militarizing Our Youth,* p. 16; Columbus *Dispatch,* Feb. 16, 1927. Copies of the Scabbard and Blade *Special Situation Bulletin,* published in 1926, are filed under "Attacks," box 7, SCPC.

42. Thomas F. Meehan to chapter officers and friends, Feb. 5, 1932, State Department Records, National Archives, 811.20/220.

43. Dilling, *The Red Network,* p. 61. This book was still a source of stereotyped guilt by association in the sixties.

Page was often invited to a city for Christian evangelism by the Y.M.C.A. and even school boards. Occasionally, the American Legion would raise a ruckus which would result in a previously unscheduled meeting on war and much publicity for the pacifist position. That Page enjoyed these situations is apparent from his correspondence.

44. Minutes of Oct. 4 and Nov. 4, 1926, and Feb. 15 and Mar. 23, 1929, F.O.R. papers, box 1.

45. Ralph Lord Roy, *Communism and the Churches* (New York: Harcourt, Brace & Co., 1960), p. 86.

46. Dorothy Detzer, *Appointment on the Hill* (New York: Henry Holt & Co., 1948), p. 97, and see pp. 86–99.

47. "Will the Peace Movement Move?" A statement of the Pacifist Action Committee, probably written by Devere Allen (n.d. [1930]), Allen papers.

48. "Tentative Budget," W.I.L.P.F. papers, box 20, SCPC.
49. "Report of Mabel Vernon, Disarmament Campaign Director, April 1931 to March 1932," and folder, "Disarmament Committee, minutes and reports, 1929–35," W.I.L.P.F. papers, box 20.
50. Emma Wold, "National Committee on Disarmament . . . Report of the Secretary," June 5, 1933, and see the detailed description of "Speaking and Organizing Trip Through North West April 17–Je. 17, 1932" by Amy Woods, W.I.L.P.F. papers, box 20.
51. Libby, *To End War,* p. 81.
52. Memoranda, especially May 23 and Oct. 16, 1933, FDR papers, OF 394, box 1.
53. Emma Wold, "Report of the Secretary," June 5, 1933, W.I.L.P.F. papers, box 20.
54. Minutes of the Emergency Peace Committee, Apr. 13, 1931, Sayre papers.
55. The name was adopted Sept. 29, 1931. Twenty-eight organizations were represented on Apr. 13, 1931, when procedures for the council were adopted. Minutes and list of those present, Interorganization Council on Disarmament (I.C.D.) papers, SCPC.
56. Minutes of the executive committee, May 27, 1932, including the "So-Called 'Right Wing Platform' " and the "So-Called 'Left Wing Platform,' " and minutes of the council meetings for Apr. 11, May 2 and 9, and Oct. 19, 1932, I.C.D. papers.
57. The First Sub-Committee of the Temporary Mixed Commission of the League of Nations, *Report A.81.C.321* (Geneva, Sept. 15, 1921).
58. *The Secret International: Armament Firms at Work* (London: Union of Democratic Control, 1932); *Patriotism Ltd: An Exposure of the War Machine* (London: Union of Democratic Control, 1933); and see the book-length treatment by Fenner Brockway, prominent Labour party member and active in the No Conscription Fellowship, *The Bloody Traffic* (London: Victor Gollancz Ltd., 1933).
59. Quoted on the title page of Helmuth C. Englebrecht, *"One Hell of a Business"* (New York: Robert M. McBride & Co., 1934). The context of Jonas's letter was the conclusion of the war between Paraguay and Bolivia with the prospect of decreased business there. Libby, *To End War,* p. 104.
60. Waldman, *Death and Profits; A Study of the War Policies Commission* (New York: Brewer, Warren & Putnam, 1932); and see remarks of Senator Arthur Vandenberg of Apr. 12, 1934, *Congressional Record,* 73rd Cong., 2nd sess., 1934, LXXVIII, 6477.

400

61. *Congressional Record,* 74th Cong., 1st sess., 1935, LXXIX, 10131–43; Detzer, *Appointment on the Hill,* p. 151. A careful history of the munitions investigation has been written by John E. Wiltz, *In Search of Peace: The Senate Munitions Inquiry, 1934–36* (Baton Rouge: Louisiana State University Press, 1963).

62. Stone, "The Munitions Industry: An Analysis of the Senate Investigation, September 4–21, 1934," *Foreign Policy Reports,* X (Dec. 5, 1934), 251.

63. Seldes, *Iron, Blood, and Profits; An Exposure of the World-Wide Munitions Racket* (New York: Harper & Bros., 1934), p. 326.

64. Englebrecht and Haneghen, *Merchants of Death; A Study of the International Armament Industry* (New York: Dodd, Mead & Co., 1934). Nye acknowledged his debt to the book, which he had seen prior to public release, in *Congressional Record,* 73rd Cong., 2nd sess., 1934, LXXVIII, 6458. Englebrecht published a complete summary of the committee hearings, *"One Hell of a Business,"* (New York: Robert M. McBride & Co., 1934).

65. Wiltz, *In Search of Peace,* p. 23.

66. "Congregational Peace Plebiscite," *Social Action,* I, 22, 26.

67. Libby, *To End War,* p. 28.

68. Flyer, n.d. [1932?], w.p.s. papers.

69. Tyler, *Youth Fights War!* (Chicago: Young People's Socialist League, n.d. [*ca.* 1936]), pp. 4–5.

CHAPTER VII

1. "President Hoover's Opportunity," in the symposium, "Present Day Causes of International Friction and Their Elimination," *The Annals of the American Academy of Political and Social Science,* CXLIV (July, 1929), 146–47.

2. Beard, *The Devil Theory of War* (New York: The Vanguard Press, 1936).

3. Shotwell, *On the Rim of the Abyss,* p. 210.

4. *Study Outline based on "The Causes of War"* (New York: Macmillan Co., 1932), p. 9. This guide was a supplement to *The Causes of War* (New York: Macmillan Co., 1932), which, in turn, was the product of a series of conferences of representatives of world religion conducted between 1928 and 1931 by the World Conference for International Peace Through Religion, with which the Church Peace Union was affiliated.

5. Beatrice P. Lamb, *Economic Causes of War and the Hope for the Future* (New York: National League of Women Voters, 1932).

This was one of the best of many similar booklets, and it had the virtue of an explicit definition of economic causes: "those points of friction which arise between governments as a result of their efforts to support the economic interests of their citizens through governmental action," p. 6.

6. *The Autobiography of James T. Shotwell* (New York: Bobbs-Merrill Co. Inc., 1961), p. 307.

7. *No-Foreign-War Crusade: A Handbook of Ways and Means By Which Individuals and Groups May Help To Keep the United States Out of War and Promote World Peace* (Philadelphia: Emergency Peace Campaign, n.d. [1937]), p. 17.

8. *Ibid.*

9. Bliven and Angell, *What Causes War?* (New York: Foreign Policy Association, 1932), p. 18.

10. Norman Thomas, *The Challenge of War: An Economic Interpretation* (New York: League for Industrial Democracy, 1924), p. 12. See also Devere Allen, *Will Socialism End the Evil of War?* (Girard, Kan.: Haldeman-Julius Co., 1931), p. 32; Scott Nearing, *War: Organized Destruction and Mass Murder by Civilized Nations* (New York: Vanguard Press, 1931); Henry Noel Brailsford, *Property or Peace* (London: Victor Gollancz Ltd., 1934); Edmund B. Chaffee, *The Protestant Churches and the Industrial Crisis* (New York: Macmillan Co., 1933), pp. 78–80; J. A. Boord, *Christianity and War: Can They Co-exist?* (Burlington, Iowa: Lutheran Literary Board, Inc., 1938), pp. 200–10; and Ernest F. Tittle, *Christians in an Unchristian Society* (New York: Association Press, 1939), p. 57, for a few examples of this theme.

11. Thomas, *The Challenge of War,* p. 12.

12. "The Nemesis of Secret Diplomacy," *New World,* I (Mar., 1918), 49–52.

13. Page, *Must We Go to War?* (New York: Farrar & Rinehart, Inc., 1937), p. 91. Page's views on economic matters, as on other things, represented wide reading rather than his own systematic analysis.

14. Niebuhr, "The Use of Force," in Devere Allen, ed., *Pacifism in the Modern World* (New York: Doubleday, Doran & Co., 1929), p. 16.

15. Page, *Individualism and Socialism; An Ethical Survey of Economic and Political Forces* (New York: Farrar & Rinehart, 1933), p. 196; "The Future of the Fellowship," *World Tomorrow,* XVII (Jan. 4, 1934), 9–11; J. B. Matthews, "Pacifists Prefer Thomas," *ibid.,* XV (Oct. 26, 1932), 402.

16. Chaffee, *Protestant Churches,* pp. 62–63.

17. See, for example, *The Church and Industrial Reconstruction* (New York: Association Press, 1920), issued by the Committee on War and the Religious Outlook appointed by joint action of the Federal Council of Churches and the General War-Time Commission of the Churches. The report was written mainly by Samuel McCrea Cavert, secretary of the committee. It was a summary of religious objections to the industrial order and of the optimistic hope that it might be Christianized by winning men to the social gospel.

18. Thomas, *What is Industrial Democracy?* (New York: League for Industrial Democracy, 1925), and *As I See It* (New York: Macmillan, 1932); Reinhold Niebuhr, "Political Action and Social Change," in Kirby Page, ed., *A New Economic Order* (New York: Harcourt, Brace & Co., 1930), pp. 301–12; and see also Paul Hutchinson, *World Revolution and Religion* (New York: Abingdon Press, 1931), and John C. Bennett, *Christianity and Class Conflict* (New York: Fellowship of Reconciliation, n.d. [*ca.* 1932]).

19. Thomas, *As I See It,* p. 57; Page, *Must We Go to War?* p. 215.

20. Quoted from Henry T. Brown, member of the Social Order Committee of the Philadelphia Yearly Meeting of Friends, in 1917, in Lester Jones, *Quakers in Action,* p. 168.

21. The 1924 Socialist campaign to elect La Follette was more than a gesture, of course; it was part of a determined effort to create a third party in alliance with organized labor. It failed, weakened the party still further, and added to labor's inertia. It was an exception that confirmed the generally quiescent role of the party until at least 1929.

22. *The Fellowship of Reconciliation: Fellowship Service—Individual and Group* (New York: Fellowship Press, n.d. [*ca.* 1915–20]), p. 9.

23. Sayre, *Across International and Industrial Frontiers* (New York: Fellowship Press, 1935); minutes of the F.O.R., Apr. 9, 1921, and Dec. 3, 1928, F.O.R. papers, boxes 1 and 2.

24. Records, memoranda, and publications of Brookwood College are found in the Muste papers, SCPC, and in a collection of Brookwood Labor School, Tamiment Institute, New York City. See also minutes of the F.O.R., June 21, 1921, F.O.R. papers, box 1, and Sarah Cleghorn, *Threescore: The Autobiography of Sarah N. Cleghorn* (New York: Harrison Smith & Robert Haas, 1936), pp. 226–46.

25. James Dombrowski to Page, Aug. 14, 1933; Myles Horton to Page, Aug. 22, 1933; Page to Dombrowski, Apr. 6, 1934; and Page to "Dear Friends of World Tomorrow," June 1, 1933, Page papers. Page resigned as treasurer in Apr., 1934. A study of the folk school is

H. Glyn Thomas, "The Highlander Folk School: The Depression Years," *Tennessee Historical Quarterly,* XXIII (Dec., 1964), 358–71.

26. *The Fellowship for a Christian Social Order* (no publ., n.d. [*ca.* 1923]), a statement of purpose.

27. Page and Eddy formed an organizing committee of about 25 men and women on May 31, 1921, which then convened about 125 persons to launch the F.C.S.O. in November. Eddy was elected chairman, and Page became secretary. Page, "My Cup Runneth Over," p. 155; and Page to "Dear Friends," Oct. 7 and Nov. 12, 1921, Page papers. *News Letter* (Mar., 1922), F.O.R. papers, box 29.

28. Page to Rex Cole, June 12, 1922, Page papers.

29. Taylor to Page, June 16, 1924, Page papers.

30. (New York: Association Press, 1922).

31. "The United States Steel Corporation," *Atlantic Monthly,* CXXIX (May, 1922), 585–94. Robert E. Lewis reported that newspapers had credited the article with having led to President Harding's conference with officers of the great steel companies in May. "The Point of View," *Red Triangle* (Cleveland), XXXVI (July 31, 1922), 2. At that meeting the President asked Elbert H. Gary, president of the American Iron and Steel Institute, to appoint a committee to investigate reduction of the twelve-hour working day in the industry. One year later the industry voted its approval of the committee's report against reduction, and President Harding voiced his regret.

32. Page to Eddy, Aug. 11, 1925, Page papers. Details of the Nash case are found in Matthew Josephson, *Sidney Hillman: Statesman of American Labor* (New York: Doubleday & Co., Inc., 1952), pp. 289–300. Josephson's bias against Nash colors his interpretation. He mistakenly asserts that the Olivet conference was called by the Federal Council of Churches, and he gives no indication that Nash considered unionization before Nov. 23, 1925, although the conditions of unionizing had been discussed by the middle of August. See also Donald Meyer, *The Protestant Search for Political Realism* (Berkeley: University of California Press, 1961), pp. 65–66.

33. *Ibid.,* p. 50.

34. Muste, "Fragment of an Autobiography," Muste papers. See the minutes of the F.O.R., *World Tomorrow,* and *Christian Century* throughout the period; Robert Moats Miller, *American Protestantism and Social Issues, 1919–1939* (Chapel Hill: University of North Carolina Press, 1958), pp. 250–87.

35. Minutes of the F.O.R., Jan. 5 and Mar. 8, 1928, F.O.R. papers, box 1.

36. Allen to Oswald Garrison Villard (from France), Mar. 18, 1931, Allen papers, SCPC.

37. Minutes of the F.O.R., Mar. 10 and 22, 1922, and the *News Letter* (May, 1922), in F.O.R. papers, boxes 1 and 29.

38. Minutes of the F.O.R., Jan. 6 and Nov. 3, 1923, F.O.R. papers, box 1.

39. *Statement of Purpose* of the Fellowship of Youth for Peace, and minutes of the F.O.R., May 2, 1925, F.O.R. papers, box 1.

40. Minutes of the F.O.R., Apr. 15 and Sept. 12, 1926, F.O.R. papers, box 1.

41. Johnson, "Memorandum on the Statement of Purpose of the Fellowship of Reconciliation, January 24, 1928," circulated with a letter by Amy Blanche Greene, in minutes of the F.O.R., 1929, F.O.R. papers, box 1.

42. Paul Jones explicitly stated that he was not resigning because of any conflict in the council; he felt, rather, that the organization needed new leadership and that he needed a change himself. Minutes of the F.O.R., Mar. 23, 1929, F.O.R. papers, box 1.

43. Minutes of the F.O.R., Mar. 17, Apr. 26, 1929; "Meeting of a Special Committee invited by the chairman of the Council-Meeting to confer with Paul Jones," Mar. 30, 1929; "Meeting of the Council," May 25, 1929, F.O.R. papers, box 1.

44. "Meeting of the Council," May 25, 1929; "Meeting of the Executive Committee," minutes of the F.O.R., May 23, 1929, F.O.R. papers, box 1.

45. Minutes of the F.O.R., Sept. 14, 1929, F.O.R. papers, box 1.

46. A letter of Jan. 18, 1930, circularized to the members of the council, and containing "Suggestions by Walter Ludwig"; Joseph B. Matthews, "On the 'Religious Basis' "; "Extracts from Letters of Charles Thomson"; and Amy Blanche Greene, "Memorandum on Paul Jones' Challenge to the F.O.R."; all of which favored change; F.O.R. papers, box 1. See also Devere Allen to Kirby Page, Feb. 7 [1930], Page papers. When the executive committee considered employing J. B. Matthews as a secretary, he gave it the impression that "he strongly feels the necessity of retaining a definite relation to the personality of Jesus as a standard of reference." Minutes of the F.O.R., May 15, 1929, F.O.R. papers, box 1. Matthews took the opposite position in 1933–34 when he also opposed the rejection of violence in the class struggle; his actions and opinions precipitated a split in the organization that year.

47. Sayre to "Fellowship Council and Secretaries," June 2, 1930;

"Suggestions of J. N. Sayre," circularized to council members in a letter of Jan. 18, 1930, F.O.R. papers, box 1.

48. Minutes of the F.O.R., June 6, 1930, F.O.R. papers, box 1. The subcommittee consisted of Nevin Sayre, J. B. Matthews, Kirby Page, Jessie Hughan, and A. J. Muste. Minutes of the F.O.R., Sept. 5, 1930; *The Fellowship of Reconciliation: Statement of Purpose* (New York: Fellowship of Reconciliation, 1930), F.O.R. papers, box 1.

49. Enclosed in Sayre to Page, July 31, 1931, Page papers.

50. Johnson to Mr. and Mrs. [Reinhold] Niebuhr, July 1, 1931; Sayre to Page, July 31, Aug. 3 and 20, 1931, Page papers.

51. Johnson to Page, Aug. 27, 1931, Page papers. Johnson had been released from jail by Sept. 15; the next year he began to organize unemployed workers in Ohio, an effort which culminated in the Ohio Unemployed League in Feb., 1933.

52. Sayre, *Across International and Industrial Frontiers,* p. 12. Minutes of the F.O.R., July 3 and 18, 1930, and June 6, 1931; and "Report of Charles C. Webber" in the minutes of the national council of the F.O.R., 1930–33, F.O.R. papers, box 1.

53. "Annual Report of Howard Kester," minutes of the national council of the F.O.R., Oct. 14–15, 1933, F.O.R. papers, box 1.

54. Frances Perry to Page, Nov. 6 and 9, 1934, Page papers.

55. *Ibid.,* Nov. 9.

CHAPTER VIII

1. Allen to "Irene," June 18, 1932, Allen papers.

2. Minutes of the F.O.R., Dec. 19, 1931, Apr. 15 and May 31, 1932, F.O.R. papers, box 1.

3. "Statement by J. B. Matthews," minutes of the F.O.R., Mar. 3, 1933, F.O.R. papers, box 2.

4. Minutes of the F.O.R., Mar. 3, 1933. These minutes contain statements of the position of most members of the council. Sayre's position is developed also in his "Annual Report" for 1933 in the minutes of the Fall Conference and Council, Oct. 13–15, 1933, F.O.R. papers, box 2.

5. This attitude is evident throughout the minutes of Mar. 3, 1933; it was explicitly formulated by Elizabeth Gilman in "Concerning the F.O.R.," *World Tomorrow,* XVI (Dec. 21, 1933), 694–95. The attack on those who took an absolute pacifist position in the council is developed in Francis A. Henson, "A Dialectical Marxist Interpretation," *ibid.,* XVII (Jan. 4, 1934), 8; Bradford Young, "Reconciliation or

Justice?" *ibid.* (Jan. 18, 1934), 42; and J. B. Matthews, "An Open Letter to Kirby Page from J. B. Matthews," *ibid.*, pp. 40–41.

6. "Statement by J. B. Matthews," minutes of the F.O.R., Mar. 3, 1933. See also his discussion in the minutes for June 3, 1933; his "Annual Report" in the minutes of the Fall Conference and Council, Oct. 13–15, 1933; and his "The Cross and the Sword," *Christian Century,* L (Dec. 6, 1933), 1540–42.

7. See, for example, Arthur M. Schlesinger, Jr., *The Politics of Upheaval* (Boston: Houghton Mifflin Co., 1960), pp. 15–207; Reinhold Niebuhr, "Catastrophe or Social Control?" *Harper's,* CLXV (June, 1932), 114–18; and George Soule, "Are We Going to Have a Revolution?" *ibid.*, CLXV (Aug., 1932), 277–86. Some historians caution that the assertion of impending revolution was a test of factional loyalty among Socialists. See especially Murray Seidler, *Norman Thomas: Respectable Rebel* (Ithaca: Cornell University Press, 1961), pp. 128–29, and Daniel Bell, "The Background and Development of Marxian Socialism in the United States," in Donald Egbert and Stow Persons, *Socialism and American Life,* 2 vols. (Princeton: Princeton University Press, 1952), I, 374–82.

8. Minutes of the F.O.R., Mar. 3, 1933, F.O.R. papers, box 2.

9. Chaffee, "Pacifism at the Crossroads," *Christian Century,* L (Nov. 15, 1933), 1439–41; minutes of the Fall Conference and Council, Oct. 13–15, 1933.

10. An additional 158 replies were received after Dec. 16, but they made no change in the results. The total questionnaires sent was 6,395. Matthews's claim in Jan., 1934, that there were 8,500 members of the F.O.R. undoubtedly was too high.

11. Minutes of the F.O.R., Dec. 16, 1933, F.O.R. papers, box 2.

12. Minutes of the F.O.R., Dec. 16 and 29, 1933, and Jan. 10 and Feb. 20, 1934, F.O.R. papers, box 2; *News Letter,* Jan. and July, 1934. Kester was retained until Mar. when he became secretary of a new Committee on Racial and Industrial Justice. Reinhold Niebuhr resigned from the council, but not, at that time, from the F.O.R.

13. Minutes of the F.O.R., Oct. 12 and 25, 1934, and subsequent minutes, F.O.R. papers, box 2; Kirby Page, "How Can We Face the Crisis?" *Christian Century,* LII (Apr. 17, 1935), 513.

14. Seidler, *Norman Thomas,* p. 107. For descriptions of the factionalism in the Socialist Party see also pp. 104–70, and David Shannon, *The Socialist Party of America* (New York: Macmillan Co., 1955), pp. 211–18, and 235–46.

15. Senior, "Win or Perish," *Eighteenth National Convention of the Socialist Party of America* (Chicago: Socialist Party of America, 1934), p. 10.

16. *Declaration of Principles of the Socialist Party of the U.S.A.* (Chicago: Socialist Party of the U.S.A., 1934). The declaration is available in full in Devere Allen, "Why the Declaration Must Pass," *World Tomorrow,* XVII (June 28, 1924), 323–24.

17. Allen, "Why the Declaration Must Pass," *World Tomorrow,* XVII, 325.

18. Norman Thomas, "What Happened at Detroit," *World Tomorrow,* XVII, 321. Thus, Joseph Sharts, an old Socialist leader from Dayton, Ohio, left the party because it had been, as he said, "captured by religious pacifists." Quoted in Allen to John Haynes Holmes, Nov. 15, 1934, Allen papers.

19. *Declaration of Principles of the Socialist Party of the U.S.A.*

20. Seidler, *Norman Thomas,* p. 144. Holmes sometimes reacted to situations suddenly, and reflected upon them later. This statement does not represent his best judgment of the case, but it was his immediate impression.

21. Thomas, "What Happened at Detroit," *World Tomorrow,* XVII, 321.

22. Allen, "Why the Declaration Must Pass," *World Tomorrow,* XVII, 326.

23. Seidler, *Norman Thomas,* p. 150.

24. Irving Brown, "A Program of 'Militant' Centrism," *Revolutionary Socialist Review,* I (Nov., 1934), 12; *An Appeal to the Membership of the Socialist Party* (New York: Revolutionary Policy Committee, 1934).

25. Thomas, "What Happened at Detroit," *World Tomorrow,* XVII, 321.

26. Brown, "A Program of 'Militant' Centrism," *Revolutionary Socialist Review,* I, 14. Allen expressly criticized the committee for being dogmatic. The leaders of the R.P.C. stringently criticized the *Declaration,* but urged its members to vote for it on the grounds of "organization control," meaning that they preferred "militant pacifism" to the "sterile legalism" of the old guard. *Vote 'Yes' . . . on the 'Declaration of Principles'* (New York: Revolutionary Policy Committee, 1934), p. 2. Such was factionalism among the Socialists.

27. Gregg to John Nevin Sayre, Feb. 23, 1933, Sayre papers.

28. Niebuhr to Page, Feb. 13, 1932, Page papers. Gandhi's autobiography was published serially in *Unity,* beginning in 1926.

408

29. Minutes of the F.O.R., Mar. 19, Apr. 17, and June 6, 1930, and Mar. 19, 1932, F.O.R. papers, box 1. The league was an American counterpart of the British Friends of India's Freedom.

30. Detzer to Page, Nov. 18, 1930, Page papers. Richard Gregg thought Page's *Mahatma Gandhi and His Significance* (New York: Eddy and Page, 1930) the best brief presentation then available.

31. (Philadelphia: J. B. Lippincott Co., 1934). A revised and condensed version was published in 1944 by the F.O.R., and had a second printing in 1951; a second revised edition was published in 1959.

32. (Triplicane, Madras, India: S. Ganesan, 1929).

33. Gregg, *The Power of Non-Violence,* pp. 41–78.

34. *Ibid.,* pp. 51, 80. Gregg drew heavily on a wide range of American, English, and French psychologists for his analysis of bodily changes with emotion, cruelty, and the power of suggestion. He was eclectic in his use of psychological literature, and he did not hesitate to cite representatives of such differing schools as behaviorism (John B. Watson), hormic psychology (William McDougall), dynamic and functional psychology (John Dewey), Freudian psychology (E. B. Holt), and William James, who defies classification.

35. *Ibid.,* p. 51.

36. *Ibid.,* pp. 45–46, 129–54.

37. Niebuhr, *Moral Man and Immoral Society: A Study in Ethics and Politics* (New York: Charles Scribner's Sons, 1932), p. 141.

38. Gregg, *The Power of Non-Violence,* p. 54.

39. Niebuhr, *Moral Man and Immoral Society,* p. 163.

40. *Ibid.,* p. 248.

41. Gregg, *The Power of Non-Violence,* p. 51.

42. *Ibid.,* p. 53.

43. *Ibid.,* p. 80.

44. *Ibid.,* p. 125.

45. *Ibid.,* pp. 128, 226–94.

46. Martin Oppenheimer and George Lakey, *A Manual for Direct Action* (Philadelphia: Friends Peace Committee, 1964), p. 123. Among the handbooks Gregg wrote are *Training for Peace: A Program for Peace Workers* (Philadelphia: J. B. Lippincott Co., 1937), and *A Discipline for Non-Violence* (Wallingford, Pa.: Pendle Hill, n.d.).

47. Gregg, *The Power of Non-Violence,* p. 206. See also pp. 117, 127, and Gregg, *Gandhiji's Satyagraha or Non-Violent Resistance* (Triplicane, Madras, India: S. Ganesan, 1930), p. xiii.

48. See Harold Fey's reviews of Aldous Huxley, *Ends and Means,* "Ends and Means," *Fellowship,* IV (Feb., 1938), 2. Joan Bondurant

describes Gandhi's view of means as "ends becoming" in *Conquest of Violence: The Gandhian Philosophy of Conflict* (Princeton: Princeton University Press, 1958), an analysis of *Satyagraha* in terms of western political philosophy. See, however, Gene Sharp, "A Review of Joan V. Bondurant, Conquest of Violence: The Gandhian Philosophy of Conflict," *Journal of Conflict Resolution,* III (1959), 401–10.

49. Gregg, *The Power of Non-Violence,* pp. 237–39.

50. *Ibid.,* p. 133. This view is more explicitly presented in the 1959 edition of the book, p. 176.

51. Huxley, *Ends and Means; An Enquiry Into the Nature of Ideals and Into the Methods Employed for Their Realization* (New York: Harper & Bros., 1937), p. 112.

52. Shridharani, *War Without Violence: A Study of Gandhi's Method and Its Accomplishments* (New York: Harcourt Brace & Co., 1939).

53. "Realistic Reconciliation," *Fellowship,* I (Dec., 1935), 5. Fey was then the executive secretary of the F.O.R.

54. "The Local Council on Religion in Economics"; minutes of the F.O.R., Apr. 13 and June 24, 1935, F.O.R. papers, boxes 2, 26. Nelson's pamphlet, *Can Guns Settle Strikes? A Study of Violent Aspects of the 1934 Textile Strike in Three Southern States* (New York: Fellowship of Reconciliation, n.d. [1935]), dealt with strikes in North and South Carolina and especially in Georgia.

55. Minutes of the F.O.R., Mar. 19 and June 8, 1939, F.O.R. papers, box 2; Harold Fey, "Sharecroppers Organize," *Fellowship,* I (Apr., 1935), 405; Claud Williams, "Prison Memoir," *ibid.,* II (Jan., 1936), 3–4.

56. "The Sit-Down Technique, Statement Adopted by F.O.R Council," *ibid.,* III (May, 1937), 6. See also Muste, "New Era in Labor," *ibid.* (Apr., 1937), pp. 5–6; and "Does Union Organization Constitute 'Labor Dictatorship?', Statement of F.O.R. Executive Committee," *ibid.,* (Jan., 1937), p. 14.

57. Allen, "The New White Man," in Allen, ed., *Pacifism in the Modern World,* pp. 51–63.

58. Minutes of the F.O.R., Mar. 14, 1931, F.O.R. papers, box 1. Ira DeA. Reid was director of the Department of Research and Investigations of the National Urban League.

59. Minutes of the F.O.R., Mar. 11 and Sept. 7, 1941, F.O.R. papers, box 2.

60. This account is drawn primarily from George M. Houser, *Erasing the Color Line* (New York: Fellowship Publications, 1951), pp.

31–34; a letter from Lee Stern to Hari and Grace Sharma, Cleveland, Ohio, July 18, 1964, courtesy of Mr. Stern; and on an interview with Lee Stern at Nyack, New York, July 21, 1964.

61. Minutes of the F.O.R., Apr. 11, 1942, F.O.R. papers, box 2. The Farmer memoranda of Feb. 19 and Mar. 9, 1942, are conveniently reprinted with the minutes of the F.O.R. council meeting of Apr. 11 in Francis L. Broderick and August Meier, eds., *Negro Protest Thought in the Twentieth Century* (Indianapolis: Bobbs-Merrill Co., Inc., 1965), pp. 211–21.

62. Reports of youth field workers James Farmer, George Houser, and Bayard Rustin, minutes of the F.O.R., Nov. 28, 1941, F.O.R. papers, box 2. See also "Non-Violence vs. Jim Crow—II," *Fellowship*, VIII (Oct., 1942), 171, and "Non-Violence Works Again," *ibid.* (May, 1942), p. 84.

63. George Houser, *Core, A Brief History* (New York: Congress of Racial Equality, 1949), p. 5. For accounts of CORE's early work, see also Houser, *Erasing the Color Line*, pp. 22–27, 37–38.

64. "The Fellowship of Reconciliation: Memo on CORE and Relation to F.O.R." (unsigned carbon copy), July 21, 1944, CORE papers, SCPC.

65. James Farmer, "The Race Logic of Pacifism," *Fellowship*, VIII (Feb., 1942), 24–25; Bayard Rustin, "The Negro and Non-Violence," *ibid.*, (Oct., 1942), pp. 166–67.

66. "Randolph Urges Negroes to Try Non-Violence," *ibid.*, IX (Feb., 1943), 35; Herbert Garfinkel, *When Negroes March: The March on Washington Movement in the Organizational Politics of FEPC* (Glencoe, Ill.: The Free Press, 1959), pp. 133–37 and notes.

67. Broderick and Meier, *Negro Protest Thought*, p. 210.

CHAPTER IX

1. "Child of an Aching Heart," *World Tomorrow*, XV (Apr., 1932), 112.

2. Eddy to Page, Oct. 31, 1931, Page papers.

3. Kagawa, "Make Not Japan a Second Germany," *World Tomorrow*, XV (Apr., 1932), 112.

4. "Japanese Militarists Strike," *ibid.*, XIV (Nov., 1931), 340; Devere Allen, "Pacifism in the World Crisis," *ibid.* (Dec., 1931), 392–94; "China Will Yet Win," *ibid.*, XV (Jan., 1932), 5–6. The sentiment that Japan could not withstand world opinion, possible economic sanctions, and Chinese resistance was widespread in the peace movement during the winter of 1931–32.

5. "A Far Eastern Policy," *ibid.* (Mar., 1932), p. 91.

6. Justus Doenecke, "American Public Opinion and the Manchurian Crisis, 1931–33" (Ph.D. dissertation, Princeton University, 1966), p. 48.

7. McDonald, address before the Seventh Congress of the Committee on the Cause and Cure of War, quoted in *ibid.*, p. 94.

8. Minutes of the Emergency Peace Committee, Sept. 29, 1931, Emergency Peace Committee papers, SCPC, and minutes of the Interorganization Council, Sept. 29, 1931, I.C.D. papers. The delegation met with the Secretary of State on Oct. 6. The organization previously had favored but not adopted a statement criticizing the administration for lack of boldness.

9. Minutes of Nov. 9, 1931, I.C.D. papers; Resolution of Nov. 9, 1931, Sayre papers, Nyack, New York. The F.O.R. concurred in it, minutes of Nov. 13, 1931, F.O.R. papers, box 1.

10. Libby, N.C.P.W. *Bulletin*, X (Dec., 1931), 1–3, 10.

11. Page, "Is Coercion Ever Justifiable?" *World Tomorrow*, XV (June, 1932), 134.

12. Minutes of the F.O.R., Nov. 13, 1931, and Feb. 14, 1932, F.O.R. papers, box 1.

13. Emergency Peace Committee to Hon. Henry Stimson, Mar. 1, 1934, Sayre papers.

14. Minutes of the Board of Directors, American Friends Service Committee, Dec. 7, 1932, A.F.S.C. papers (Haverford College Library), quoted in Justus Doenecke, "The Debate Over Coercion: The Dilemma of America's Pacifists and the Manchurian Crisis" (unpublished paper, New College, Sarasota, Fla.), p. 13.

15. Doenecke, "The Debate Over Coercion," pp. 14–15.

16. Minutes of the Interorganization Council, Oct. 14, 1931, I.C.D. papers.

17. Sayre to Theodore Walser, May 4, 1932, Sayre papers; minutes of the Interorganization Council, Feb. 8, 1932, I.C.D. papers. Despite his reservations, Sayre presented the Emergency Peace Committee program to President Hoover in March.

18. Page to Egbert Hayes (of the Chinese Y.M.C.A.), Feb. 15, 1932, Page papers.

19. Sayre to Walser, May 4, 1932, Sayre papers.

20. Eddy to Page, Dec. 8, 1931, Page papers.

21. Quoted in Doenecke, "American Public Opinion and the Manchurian Crisis," p. 84.

22. Morrison, "The Shattered Fabric of World Peace," *Christian Century*, LIV (Sept. 15, 1939), 1128–29.

23. Walser to Sayre, Jan. 6, 1932, Sayre papers.

24. Walser to Sayre, Apr. 2, 1932, Sayre papers.

25. Walser to Sayre, Jan. 3, 1933. See also especially correspondence of Apr. 2 and 9, May 2, and June 29, 1932, and the "Friends of Peace Bulletin No. 4," Mar. 25, 1932 (published by Japanese pacifists), Sayre papers.

26. Résumé of correspondence with Ray Stannard Baker in regard to his gift copy of the *Life and Letters of Woodrow Wilson*, Nov. 1, 1935; Cordell Hull to Roosevelt, Oct. 13, 1935, FDR papers, OF 1561.

27. Shotwell to Newton Baker, Feb. 7, 1929, Newton Baker papers, box 208, Library of Congress.

28. Robert A. Divine, *The Illusion of Neutrality* (Chicago: University of Chicago Press, 1962), pp. 13–41. Divine traces the neutrality controversy in careful and fascinating detail.

29. *International Disarmament Notes* (of the N.C.P.W.), May 19, 1933. The Foreign Relations Committee had no sooner reported the amended resolution than Libby phoned the State Department to say that he was surprised it "should consent to such an undermining" of Norman Davis's position. Memorandum, May 27, 1933, 811.113/311 State Department Files, National Archives, Record Group 59.

30. Libby diary, May 30, 1933.

31. *Ibid.*, June 5 and 12, 1933.

32. Moore to Roosevelt, Aug. 27, 1934, FDR papers, OF 1561. See also Charles Warren, "A Memorandum on Some Problems in the Maintenance and Enforcement of the Neutrality of the United States," Aug., 1934, 811.04418/28 State Department Files.

Moore's shift was dramatic and perhaps indicative of the crossfire of advice the State Department was getting. He told Undersecretary of State William Phillips on Dec. 20, 1933, that he favored mandatory legislation because although he trusted Roosevelt, "what some future President might do is unpredictable." 811.113/377 State Department Files. But in 1935 he warned the President that such legislation was "an invasion of the . . . power of the Executive to conduct the foreign relations of the United States." Moore to Roosevelt, Aug. 29 (and the longer memorandum of Aug. 28), 1935, FDR. papers, OF 1561.

33. Memorandum No. 6 for the Attorney General from William Phillips, Dec. 8, 1934, 811.04418/8, State Department Files.

34. E. C. Kalbfus to Secretary of the Navy Claude Swanson, Dec.

22, 1934, and Swanson to Cordell Hull, Dec. 15, 1934, 811.04418/9 and –/14, State Department Files.

35. Norman Davis to Sumner Welles, Mar. 27, 1935, Norman Davis papers, box 63, Library of Congress.

36. Roosevelt to Col. Edward M. House, Sept. 17, 1935, FDR papers, PPF 22. Roosevelt was considerably more sympathetic in conversation and correspondence with the sponsors of those "wild-eyed measures."

37. Joseph Green memorandum of a meeting with the Nye committee in executive session at Hull's request, Apr. 12, 1935, 811.04418/44, State Department Files.

38. The estimated attendance is Libby's, as recorded in his diary, May 27, 1935.

39. Libby diary, Aug. 20 and 22, 1935. For details of neutrality in this session of Congress see especially Allan Kuusisto, "The National Council for Prevention of War," pp. 140–49; Divine, *Illusion of Neutrality*, pp. 92–117, and the files of the N.C.P.W.

40. Department of State, *Peace and War: United States Foreign Policy, 1931–1941* (Washington, D.C.: Government Printing Office, 1943), pp. 266–71.

41. Allen to Charles Kimball, vice-president of the League of Nations Association, Oct. 20 and 30, 1937, Allen papers.

42. Arthur L. Swift, Jr., "U-Table on Sanctions," *Fellowship*, I (Nov., 1935), 8; "Can Sanctions Bring Peace?" *ibid.*, pp. 3–4.

43. Page, *Must We Go to War?* (New York: Farrar & Rinehart, 1937), p. 100, and see pp. 101–10; Thomas, *Socialism on the Defensive* (New York: Harper & Bros., 1938), p. 186; Allen, "Intrigue in Abyssinia," *World Events*, II (Mar. 15, 1935), 1, and "British Stakes in Ethiopia," *ibid.*, III (Dec. 15, 1935), 1.

44. Daniel Hogg, "Dynamite under Europe," *Fellowship*, III (Jan., 1937), 11.

45. H. Runham Brown, "If I Were in Spain," *ibid.*, II (Dec., 1936), 9–10. See also his *Spain: A Challenge to Pacifism* (London: Finsbury Press, 1936), a pamphlet distributed in the United States by the War Resisters League.

46. "Tradedy [*sic*] of Spain," typewritten copy of an editorial (n.d. [1938]), Muste papers.

47. Thomas, "Memorandum on the Spanish Situation in the Socialist Party" (n.d. [1937]), Thomas papers, box 24.

48. Devere Allen, "Aid to the 'Enemy,' " *World Events*, V (Feb. 15, 1938), 1, and "Is It Peace?" *ibid.* (May 15, 1938), p. 1.

49. Norman Thomas to Mrs. Horace A. Eaton, Jan. 21, 1937, Thomas papers, box 24.

50. Minutes of the National Action Committee, N.E.C., Socialist Party, Dec. 23 and 31, 1936, Thomas papers, box 138.

The Debs Column was threatened for a time with indictment under SECTIONS 21 and 22 of Title 18, *U.S. Penal Code*, which made it illegal to enlist or hire someone to enlist in the service of a foreign state at war. The State Department did not prosecute, although it publicized the *Code* and withheld passports for Spain.

The Socialist Party and Norman Thomas papers contain innumerable examples of the manipulation of the Spanish issue for factional purposes, especially by the radical Left and Communists who made it the "crucial testing ground" (as one Communist circular put it) for Marxist allegiance and popular front work. For this reason the national executive committee was very circumspect in handling the issue.

51. "We Will Not Fight in Spain: Statement of Executive Committee [of the] Fellowship of Reconciliation on Socialist Recruiting for Spanish War," *Fellowship*, III (Jan., 1937), 10.

52. Holmes to Norman Thomas, Jan. 7, 1937, Thomas papers, box 24.

53. "Norman Thomas Replies," *Fellowship*, III (Feb., 1937), 13, and see "Memorandum on the Spanish Situation," Thomas papers, box 24.

54. Thomas, "Memorandum to Devere Allen and Max Delson," Jan. 5, 1937, and see Thomas to Roy Burt, Feb. 3, 1937, Thomas papers, box 24.

55. Thomas to the Hon. Sam McReynolds, Feb. 20, 1937, Thomas papers.

56. Roosevelt to Hull, June 29, 1937, FDR papers, OF 1561, and see Roosevelt to the Secretary of the Treasury, May 22, 1937.

57. Hull, *The Memoirs of Cordell Hull,* 2 vols. (New York: Macmillan Co., 1948), I, 512.

58. Roosevelt to Norman Thomas, Dec. 25, 1937, Thomas papers, box 26.

59. At the height of the controversy, in Jan., 1937, Thomas wrote repeatedly that he had not for some years been a religious pacifist in the sense that he was during the World War, but was "still deeply opposed to war." See Thomas to Miss Phoebe D. Lovell, Jan. 6 and to Mrs. Horace A. Eaton, Jan. 21, 1937, Thomas papers, box 24. As late as November he assured Ray Newton that volunteering for Spanish service did not violate the pacifist pledge, since service could be taken

in medical work, and that he had not veered from his basic antiwar conviction. Thomas to Newton, Nov. 16, 1937 (copy), Allen papers.

Allen Guttmann overdramatizes the important Spanish crisis in writing that pacifists "excepting always the Friends," abandoned "the cry of 'peace,'" in order to support the Republic. Guttmann, *The Wound in the Heart; America and the Spanish Civil War* (New York: The Free Press of Glencoe, 1962), p. 114. The shift from pacifism was neither as sudden nor as complete as this statement suggests.

60. Allen, "Spain Will Make Good," *World Tomorrow*, XIV (June, 1931), 184–86; *News Letter*, July, 1931.

61. Brittain, "Pacifism After Munich," *Fellowship*, IV (Nov., 1938), 3–4. See also Henri Rosser (a prominent French pacifist), "An Island of Freedom," *ibid.*, (Apr., 1937), pp. 12–13.

62. Detzer, "Dirge for Collective Security," *Fellowship*, IV (Nov., 1938), 6–7.

63. A pamphlet signed by twenty-three prominent pacifists and distributed jointly through the F.O.R., N.C.P.W., A.F.S.C. Peace Section, W.R.L., and W.I.L.P.F., n.d. [*ca.* 1943], p. 3.

64. "War in Europe: A Statement by the 1939 National Conference of the Fellowship of Reconciliation," *Fellowship*, V (Oct., 1939), 3. The same view is found in representative publications from other pacifist groups.

65. Richard Gregg and Ernest F. Tittle, "How Can Hitler Be Stopped?" *ibid.*, p. 6.

66. "Statement #1," a typewritten MS by Collins apparently considered for publication, n.d. [*ca.* 1938], Page papers.

67. Kolnai, "Must Democracy Use Force? Pacifism Means Suicide," *Nation*, CXLVIII (Jan. 21, 1939), 87–88.

68. Page to Sherwood Eddy, Sept. 4, 1939, Page papers.

69. Holmes, "The Hitler Horror," *Unity* (Apr. 3, 1933), quoted in Kenneth Jackson Smith, "John Haynes Holmes: Opponent of War" (B.D. thesis, Meadville Theological School, 1949), p. 112. Sentiments such as these abound in pacifist literature and correspondence.

70. "Germany and Democracy," *World Tomorrow*, XIII (Sept., 1930), 355; "The Germany Elections and War Guild," *ibid.* (Oct., 1930), p. 390; "Which Way Germany?" *ibid.* (Nov., 1930), p. 437; and "The Germany Political Situation," *ibid.*, XIV (Jan., 1931), 4–5.

71. "Can France Be Saved?" *ibid.* (Sept., 1931), p. 280.

72. "Hitler and the Middle Classes," *ibid.*, XVI (Feb. 15, 1933), 147. For a similar view see Norman Thomas, *Socialism on the Defensive* (New York: Harper & Brothers, 1938), pp. 70–104.

73. "July 1, 1932?" *World Tomorrow*, XIV (Aug., 1931), 243; "Repudiation in Place of Cancellation," *ibid.*, XV (Feb., 1932), 37.

74. "Hitler's Foreign Policy," *ibid.* (July, 1933), p. 438; "Germany Defies the Victors," *ibid.* (Oct. 26, 1933), p. 529.

75. Thomas, *Socialism on the Defensive*, pp. 20–21, 70–102.

76. Page, *Must We Go To War?* pp. 29–30.

77. *Ibid.*, pp. 58–64, 75–94; Thomas, *Socialism on the Defensive*, pp. 178–79.

78. Thomas, *Socialism on the Defensive*, pp. 11–12, 187; Page, *Must We Go To War?* p. 25.

79. "The 'C.O.' After Twenty Years," *Fellowship*, IV (Dec., 1938), 6. This very idea, and the fear that war would result from it, led Evan Thomas to take a leading role in the War Resisters League and in the counseling of objectors as the Second World War approached.

80. Hull wrote that "the most moving and impelling influence supporting dictators' ambitions is unemployment and distress among the masses . . . . it is a general rule that the largest single cause of riots, revolutions, and wars of aggression is a people in severe economic distress." *Memoirs*, I, 235.

81. Dulles wrote his approval of Page's *Must We Go To War?*: "I think your analysis of the international situation as the cause of war is penetrating and sound, as also most of your suggestions with reference to what can be done about it." He disagreed with Page's analysis of internal economic and social problems, and with his absolute pacifism. Dulles to Page, Jan. 17, 1938, Page papers.

Dulles's own *War, Peace and Change* (New York: Harper & Brothers, 1939) reflected this concurrence of views; and it, in turn, made a significant impression on Frederick Libby, who contacted Dulles and obtained his support and counsel on several N.C.P.W. projects.

82. Norman Thomas and Bertram D. Wolfe, *Keep America Out of War: A Program* (New York: Frederick A. Stokes Co., 1939), pp. 4, 19.

83. Sayre to Mrs. Margaret Bradford Malone, n.d. [*ca.* 1937–39], Muste papers.

84. Lavine and Wechsler, *War Propaganda and the United States* (New Haven: Yale University Press, for the Institute of Propaganda Analysis, 1940), p. 92.

85. Villard, "Retrospect," *Nation*, CXLVI (Apr. 2, 1938), 388.

86. "A Call to American Pacifists," *Fellowship*, V (Nov., 1939), 20.

87. Edward Weeks, "The Editor Speaking," *Atlantic Monthly*, CLXIV (Nov., 1939), n.p.

88. Villard, "Valedictory," *Nation*, CL (Jan. 29, 1940), 782. Villard had contributed his first article to the *Nation* in 1894.

89. Minutes of the F.O.R., Sept. 12, 1939, F.O.R. papers, box 2; "War in Europe," *Fellowship*, V (Oct., 1939), 4.

CHAPTER X

1. Quoted in "Moves for Peace," New York *Times*, Dec. 14, 1930.

2. John W. Masland, "The 'Peace' Groups Join Battle," *Public Opinion Quarterly*, IV (Dec., 1940), 665.

3. There were at the August 27–29 World Congress 2,196 delegates from 27 countries (plus 1,800 visitors), but mainly from France and Germany. Most were workers. The Russian delegation was barred by the Dutch government but, nevertheless, there were present 830 Communists, 281 Social Democrats, 24 Left Socialists, 1,041 "without party allegiance," and "10 of the Communist Opposition." An anticapitalist bias flavored the whole manifesto of the congress. *The World Congress Against War* (New York: American Committee for Struggle Against War, 1932), p. 4.

4. *Ibid.*, p. 19.

5. Allen, *World Tomorrow*, XVI (Oct. 12, 1933), 571.

6. Minutes of the F.O.R., Dec. 29, 1933, F.O.R. papers, box 2.

7. Ward to Page, Mar. 9, 1933, Page papers. For accounts of the American League Against War and Fascism in relation to other left-wing peace groups, see Ralph Lord Roy, *Communism and the Churches* (New York: Harcourt, Brace & Co., 1960), pp. 84–97; and Irving Howe and Lewis Coser, *The American Communist Party: A Critical History* (New York: Frederick A. Praeger, 1962), pp. 348–55.

8. Minutes of the F.O.R., Feb. 9, 1935, F.O.R. papers, box 2. See especially Page, "Why I Am Not a Communist," *Christian Century* (Aug. 21, 1935), pp. 1057–59; and correspondence with and about Ward for 1934–35, Page papers.

9. Minutes of the F.O.R., Jan. 18 and Feb. 9, 1935, F.O.R. papers, box 2; and *Ere the Community Is Burned* (New York: Fellowship of Reconciliation, n.d.), a folder dissociating communism from socialism.

10. Allen to the League Against War and Fascism, Feb. 20, 1934, Allen papers.

11. Minutes of the national executive committee (N.E.C.), Socialist Party of America (S.P.A.), Jan. 12–13, 1936, Thomas papers. Allen was chairman of the committee, at first. The League Against Fascism was set up by the national executive committee of the Socialist Party

as the American Section of the international Matteoti Fund organized by the Labor and Socialist International Federation of Trade Unions. Its purpose was to aid the labor movement in countries which lacked democracy, especially in Poland, Italy, and Germany. American members included men who were as opposed to communism as to fascism: Devere Allen, Norman Thomas, Kirby Page, Morris Hillquit, Clarence Senior, and others. *League Against Fascism* (a flyer signed by Daniel W. Hoan, July, 1933).

12. Edwin C. Johnson, "Students Refuse to Fight Foreign Wars," *Fellowship*, I (Mar., 1935), 5. An earlier poll of students in sixty-five schools was taken by the National Student Federation, the Intercollegiate Disarmament Council, and the Brown University newspaper; it purported to show that of 22,000 students, 8,000 were absolute pacifists and another 7,000 would not fight overseas. This poll was probably stimulated by the Oxford Pledge movement in England, and was designed to add to the antiwar movement in the United States. Frank Olmstead, *The Significance of the College Peace Poll* (New York: War Resisters League, 1933). See Gardner Murphy and Rensis Likert, *Public Opinion and the Individual; A Psychological Study of Student Attitudes on Public Questions, with a Retest Five Years Later* (New York: Harper & Bros., 1938), pp. 214, 254–55.

13. Mulford Q. Sibley and Philip E. Jacob, *Conscription of Conscience; The American State and the Conscientious Objector, 1940–1947* (Ithaca, New York: Cornell University Press, 1952), p. 84.

14. James Wechsler, *Revolt on the Campus* (New York: Covici-Friede, 1935), pp. 121–22, 141–42.

15. In addition, the Student Christian Movement and the National Student Federation of America were unofficially represented in planning for the strike. Joseph P. Lash, *The Campus Strikes Against War* (New York: Student League for Industrial Democracy, n.d. [1935]). Lash was then national secretary of the Student League. See also Vernon Howard Holloway, "American Pacifism Between Two Wars, 1919–1941" (Ph.D. dissertation, Yale University, 1949), pp. 308–309.

16. Letter of Apr. 2, 1936, in the papers of the Socialist Party of America, Y.P.S.L. files, Perkins Library, Duke University. The Chicago program is outlined in "Plan of Action for Anti-ROTC Protests," 1935, S.P.A. papers, Y.P.S.L. files; and Page's experiences are recorded in Page to Monroe Sweetland, Apr. 12, 1935, and other correspondence, Page papers.

17. John H. Clarke to James Shotwell, Feb. 4, 1930, James T. Shot-

well papers, League of Nations Association file (Correspondence and Office Records), Columbia University. John Clarke was a former Supreme Court Justice and a founder of the League of Nations Non-Partisan Association.

18. Eichelberger-Shotwell correspondence of Nov. 1 and 2, 1932, Shotwell papers, League of Nations Association file. The implication follows more from the context of the correspondence than from its content.

19. Reports of the general secretary to the trustees of the World Peace Foundation, Feb. 6, May 15, Aug. 26, and Dec. 9, 1933, and Feb. 12 and Mar. 28, 1934, in the Newton D. Baker papers, box 241, Library of Congress.

20. Report of the general secretary to the trustees of the World Peace Foundation, Feb. 13, 1935, Baker papers, box 241.

21. Baker to Butler, Mar. 27, 1935 (at the request of the trustees of the World Peace Foundation), Baker papers, box 242.

22. Robert Divine, *Second Chance; The Triumph of Internationalism in America During World War II* (New York: Atheneum, 1967), pp. 22–23. Those who accepted Butler's invitation to dinner were Henry A. Atkinson, George Blakeslee, Raymond L. Buel, Professor of Law Ada Comstock, Norman Davis, Col. Edward M. House, Thomas P. Lamont, Roland S. Morris, Sen. James P. Pope, Hon. James R. Sheffield, Maurice S. Sherman (editor of the Hartford *Courant*), James Shotwell, Gov. John G. Winant, and of course Newton Baker. Butler to Baker, Apr. 1, 1935, Baker papers, box 242.

23. Morris was a Philadelphia lawyer. Baker, John Clarke, and Blakeslee were also involved in the consultations of the committee, and the primary draft was Baker's. See Baker's correspondence with them from Apr. 20–May 11, 1935, Baker papers, box 242.

24. George Blakeslee to Baker, May 1, 1935, Baker papers, box 242. Blakeslee was the president of the World Peace Foundation.

25. Pope to Baker, May 3, 1935, Baker papers, box 242.

26. Pope to Baker, May 21; but see also his comments on June 8, 1935, Baker papers, box 242.

27. Shotwell to Baker, Oct. 15, 1935 (author's italics), Baker papers, box 242.

28. Shotwell to Baker, Oct. 22, 1935, Baker papers, box 242. Van Kirk and Baker concluded their negotiations on the position by Nov. 15. Baker to Butler, Nov. 15, 1935, Carnegie Endowment Archives, IV A141:70057–70072, Columbia University.

29. Henry S. Haskell to Butler, with attachment, Nov. 19, 1935, Carnegie Endowment Archives, IV A141.

30. Haskell to Butler, Nov. 19, 1935, Carnegie Endowment Archives, IV A141; plan of organization adopted Dec. 18, 1935, *National Peace Conference* (New York: National Peace Conference, n.d. [1936]), p. 5.

31. "Buck Hills Falls," notes of the organizing conference by Miriam and E. Raymond Wilson, Dec. 4, 1936, E.P.C. papers, box 1, SCPC.

32. E. Raymond Wilson to Kirby Page, Oct. 21, 1935; Owen Geer to Ernest Freemont Tittle, Oct. 16, 1935, and Ray Newton correspondence, E.P.C. papers, box 1, SCPC.

33. Minutes of the F.O.R., Oct. 13, 1935, F.O.R. papers, box 2.

34. Memorandum of meeting of department heads. Mar. 3, 1936, E.P.C. papers, box 2.

35. Minutes of the executive committee of the E.P.C., Mar. 3, 1936, E.P.C. papers, box 2.

36. "Condensed report of the conference, Cambridge, Mass.," Dec. 30, 1935, E.P.C. papers, box 4.

37. Memorandum of a meeting of representatives of the E.P.C. and N.P.C., n.d. [*ca.* Mar. 1, 1936], Kirby Page papers.

38. *No-Foreign-War Crusade* (Philadelphia: Emergency Peace Campaign, n.d. [1937]), pp. 6, 7, 34.

39. According to the New York *Times*, Apr. 22, 1936, he was taken off the liner by a Coast Guard cutter. Lansbury remembered it as "an ancient-looking steam tug loaded with all kinds of gear." Lansbury, *My Pilgrimage for Peace* (New York: Henry Holt & Co., 1938), p. 41. In fairness to his American hosts, it should be noted that they offered to take him to Washington by air, but he declined, "being a feeble kind of person where height is concerned."

40. The sketch of activities and the figures cited for the campaign are based upon a "Brief Summary of Activities, April 18 to September 19, 1936"; "Reports of Departments," Sept., 1936; "Brief Statistical Survey," June, 1937; and departmental files in the E.P.C. papers, especially boxes 1–4.

41. *Manifesto of the Veterans of Future Wars* (n.p., n.d. [1936]), a flyer in the Sayre papers.

42. *Evening Public Ledger* (Princeton, N. J.), Apr. 18, 1936.

43. *Ibid.*

44. *Evening Ledger* (Philadelphia), Mar. 19, 1936.

45. Minutes of the council, Feb. 18, 1936, E.P.C. papers, box 2.

46. New York *Times*, Apr. 22 and 23, 1936; Joseph P. Lash, "The Student Strike," *Fellowship*, II (May, 1936), 5–6; and "General Clippings," in a scrapbook, E.P.C. papers, box 1.

47. Two important interviews were with the People's Mandate to End War (a woman's peace coalition sponsored by W.I.L.P.F. leaders with Carrie C. Catt as honorary chairman) on Mar. 12, 1936, and with a delegation from the National Peace Conference (Walter Van Kirk, James Shotwell, Josephine Schain, Dorothy Detzer, Estelle Sternberger, William Stone, John Nevin Sayre, and Stanley High) on Mar. 13, 1936. FDR papers, OF 394, box 1; and notes on the "Conference with the President," Sayre papers.

48. "Condensed Report of the Conference, Cambridge, Mass.," Dec. 30, 1935, E.P.C. papers, box 4.

49. Van Kirk to Newton Baker, June 16, 1936, Baker papers, box 74. Copies of the flyer are in E.P.C. papers, box 4.

50. Dorothy Detzer to Ludwell Denny, June 16, 1936, W.I.L.P.F. papers. Denny was a newspaperman with the Indianapolis *Times*. Miss Detzer's letters to him were confidential, and after World War II the two were married. She described this account as "almost verbatim."

51. Fred Atkins Moore, "Preliminary Report on 1936 Fall Meetings," in the minutes of the council, Nov. 12, 1936, E.P.C. papers, box 2. This increase represented relatively stronger local initiative and less national organizing.

52. Minutes of the council, Oct. 13, 1936, E.P.C. papers, box 2.

53. Minutes of a meeting to consider neutrality legislation with the trustees of the World Peace Foundation and several State Department officers, Mar. 6, 1937, in the Baker papers, box 242. Herbert Feis was economic adviser to the department.

Pacifists supported bills by Jerry Voorhis of California (an F.O.R. member) and Herman Koppelmann of Connecticut, H.R. 1491 and H.R. 3875, which went beyond even the resolution sponsored by the isolationist bloc of the Nye committee, S.J. Res. 60.

54. *No-Foreign-War Crusade* (Philadelphia: Emergency Peace Campaign, n.d. [1937]).

55. Moore to Roosevelt, Mar. 4, 1937, FDR papers, OF 1561.

56. Emergency Peace Campaign *Legislative Letter*, May 7, 1937, p. 2.

57. Fey to Page, Aug. 29, 1936, Page papers.

58. Minutes of the F.O.R., Nov. 17, 1936, F.O.R. papers, box 2.

59. Sayre to Newton, Dec. 29, 1936, E.P.C. papers, box 20.

60. Newton to Sayre, Jan. 4, 1936, E.P.C. papers, box 20.

61. Eddy to Kirby Page, Oct. 30, 1936, Page papers.

62. Eugene Staley to Harry E. Fosdick (chairman of the E.P.C.), May 21, 1936, and Staley to Page, Oct. 16, 1937, Page papers. Staley was an economist at the University of Chicago.

63. Joseph Myers to Kirby Page, July 13, 1936, Page papers.

64. Byrd to Clarence E. Pickett (copy of a letter), Dec. 4, 1936, Page papers, and minutes of the council, Jan. 9, 1937, E.P.C. papers, box 4.

65. Eichelberger to Ray Newton, Oct. 15, 1936, E.P.C. papers, box 11. Eichelberger specifically exempted Newton "and a few in the E.P.C." from this charge.

66. Libby diary, Jan. 11, 1937.

67. Van Kirk to Newton Baker, Mar. 19, 1937, Baker papers, box 174.

68. "Is a Coalition of Peace Agencies Possible and Desirable?" n.d. [Mar. 28, 1937], Page papers. Previous drafts and a blueprint of the organization can be found in the Page and E.P.C. papers.

69. Minutes of the committee on reorganization of the N.P.C., May 12 and 13, 1937, E.P.C. papers, box 18.

70. H.R.J. Res. 20 and 199, *Congressional Record*, 75th Cong., 1st sess., 1937, LXXXI, 37 and 947.

71. The resolution was reduced to acknowledging that within the conference "there is a difference of opinion regarding the immediate invocation of the Neutrality Act." "National Peace Conference Declaration on the Far Eastern Situation," n.d. [Sept. 7, 1937], Sayre papers; Libby diary, Aug. 30 and Sept. 7 and 8, 1937.

72. Dorothy Detzer, "Neutrality at the Special Sessions," *Fellowship*, III (Nov., 1937), 3–4.

73. Probably the speech reflected Roosevelt's lack of a clear direction, the conflicting advice coming to him, and his sense of the imperative need for some kind of action, as Dorothy Borg concluded from her analytical "Notes on Roosevelt's 'Quarantine' Speech," *Political Science Quarterly*, LXXII (Sept., 1957), 405–33.

74. Eichelberger to Roosevelt, Oct. 9, 1937, FDR papers, PPF 3833. Eichelberger asked for an appointment to discuss what support he might give, but he was put off.

75. Minutes of the Board of Trustees, World Peace Foundation, Oct. 16, 1937, Baker papers, box 242; James T. Shotwell, memoran-

dum of Oct. 13, 1937, of talk with Eichelberger, Shotwell papers, League of Nations Records. Villard to Roosevelt, Oct. 19, 1937 (résumé), FDR papers, OF 1561.

76. Kuusisto, "The Influence of the National Council," pp. 189–211; Divine, *Illusion of Neutrality,* pp. 219–20. Ludlow, *Hell or Heaven* (Boston: Stratford Co., 1937).

77. This account is based on Kuusisto, "The Influence of the National Council," p. 195; Libby diary, Dec. 13 and 14, 1937; and the recollections of Francis Case in his letter to Jesse MacKnight, Sept. 2, 1938, N.C.P.W. papers, box 82.

78. The supporting committee was formed on Dec. 28, 1937, and the sponsors represented a more conservative group than was characteristic of pacifist front groups.

79. Hull, *Memoirs,* II, 564.

80. Moore to James Shotwell, Dec. 6, 1937, Shotwell papers, League of Nations Records. Moore's tone was doubtless influenced by the fact that he had recently been involved in an automobile accident, but other State Department officers had confided similar feelings to the Carnegie group of peace advocates.

81. Charles W. Yose to Secretary Hull, Dec. 1, 1937, a memorandum of a phone conversation, seen by Walton Moore and noted by Hull (Dec. 11), 711.00/748 State Department Files.

82. The "Statement" is included in Michael Francis Doyle to Roosevelt, Dec. 29, 1937, FDR papers, PPF 1771.

83. Kuusisto, "The Influence of the National Council," pp. 201–203, 212–18; Divine, *Illusion of Neutrality,* p. 220; Dorothy Detzer, "Dress Rehearsal for War," *Fellowship,* IV (Feb., 1938), 6. The fullest account of the Ludlow Amendment controversy is Garry Lynn Nall, *The Ludlow War Referendum* (M.A. thesis, University of Texas, 1959).

84. Detailed notes of a luncheon discussion with Stanley K. Hornbeck, political adviser, Department of State, in minutes of the Board of Trustees, World Peace Foundation, Oct. 16, 1937, Baker papers, box 242. The notes purport to be an accurate, but not literal, account of Hornbeck's comments.

85. Congressman James M. Mead to Mrs. Sophie M. Townsend, Feb. 14, 1938, N.C.P.W. papers, box 82. Libby previously had recorded his surprise that Ludlow was trying to avoid active support of his own measure, diary, Dec. 29, 1937.

86. Shotwell to Mrs. Emmons Blaine, Jan. 4, 1938, Shotwell papers, League of Nations Records.

87. Minutes of the Board of Trustees, World Peace Foundation, Mar. 6, 1937, Baker papers, box 242.

CHAPTER XI

1. These lines of poetry were recalled by Winston Churchill from his boyhood days when he was in the midst of his fight for air power in 1935. *The Gathering Storm* (Cambridge: Houghton Mifflin Co., 1948), p. 123.

2. Libby diary, Jan. 17, 1938; "Keep America Out of War Committee: An Outline of its Origin, Program, and Plan," n.d. [1938], Page papers.

3. Libby diary, Jan. 19 and 22, 1938. The story, broadened by rumor, acquired great currency in the isolationist camp, and prompted Secretary Hull to deny, among other things, that the United States contemplated the use of its navy with that of another nation. Hull, *Memoirs*, II, 573–74. Nonetheless, on New Year's Day a naval emissary from Roosevelt arrived in London to begin joint staff conversations against the background of full discussions of Anglo-American collaboration against the Japanese. Anthony Eden, *Facing the Dictators; The Memoirs of Anthony Eden, Earl of Avon* (Boston: Houghton Mifflin Co., 1962), pp. 617–20.

4. Minutes of the national action committee, Jan. 8, 22, and 29, 1938, s.p.a. papers, national office files, 1938; Libby diary, Jan. 26, 1938.

5. Thomas, "Collective Security Means War," Jan. 2, 1938, s.p.a., national office files, 1938.

6. Minutes of the Keep America Out of War Committee, Feb. 7, 1938, Norman Thomas papers, box 27; "Program of Action" and "Proposed 6 Months Budget March-August, 1938," a.f.s.c. Archives, e.p.c. file; Libby diary, Feb. 16, 18, and 25, Mar. 6, 1938.

7. Minutes of the f.o.r., Feb. 19, 1938, and Thomas to n.c.p.w., *et al.*, Feb. 15, 1938, f.o.r. papers, boxes 2, 22.

8. *Report of the Committee of Experts to the Conference on World Economic Cooperation* (New York: National Peace Conference, 1938), p. 6. The number of delegates is given in the "Address of Welcome" of John Nevin Sayre, Mar. 24, 1938, Sayre papers.

9. *Report of the Committee of Experts*, p. 23.

10. New York *Times*, Mar. 25, 1938.

11. *Ibid.*, Feb. 6, 1936. Previous international conferences were the Genoa Conference, Apr. 10–May 19, 1922, called to consider Russian relations and world economic problems; the International Economic

Conference at Geneva, May 4–23, 1927; and the International Economic Conference, June 12–July 27, 1933, at London.

12. New York *Times*, Apr. 23, 1936.

13. *Ibid.*, Apr. 26, 1936.

14. Sayre, "Lansbury Visits Rulers," *Fellowship,* II (Nov., 1936), 3.

15. Lansbury to Roosevelt, May 26, 1936, FDR papers, OF 394, box 1; and Lansbury, *My Pilgrimage for Peace,* pp. 61–63.

16. The joint statement was forwarded immediately by Ambassador William E. Dodd to Hull. It occasioned great interest because the State Department had been sounding out various nations that spring regarding a conference on economic cooperation and arms limitation with previously ambivalent to negative responses from the Germans. Hitler had declined an invitation to the League Commission on Accession to Raw Materials to discuss programs for erasing restrictions. New York *Times,* Feb. 23, 1937; U.S. Department of State, *Foreign Relations,* 1937, Vol. I (Washington, D.C.: Government Printing Office, 1954), 638–51; Hull, *Memoirs,* I, 549. Regarding Lansbury's visits, see his *My Pilgrimage for Peace*; Nevin Sayre, "Hitler Says 'Yes' to Lansbury," *Fellowship,* III (Apr. 25, 1937), and "World Conference or World War?" *ibid.*, (May, 1937), pp. 3, 8–9; New York *Times,* July 10, Dec. 9, 11, 17, and 26, 1937; and Lansbury, *Peace Through Economic Co-operation* (London: Embassies of Reconciliation, n.d. [an address delivered in Vienna, Dec. 17, 1937]).

17. New York *Times,* Jan. 28, 1938, includes the text of the report. Regarding the origins and course of the investigation, see *Foreign Relations,* 1937, Vol. I, 80, 652–53, 671–96, 712, 834–37.

18. Percy W. Bartlett, *The Economic Approach to Peace with a Summary of the Van Zeeland Report* (London: Embassies of Reconciliation), p. 11. Eichelberger discussed the project with Roosevelt.

19. The fullest description of his thinking is Hull's extensive memorandum of conversation with Prime Minister Mackenzie King of Canada on Mar. 5, 1937, in *Foreign Relations,* 1937, I, 641–48, but see also his *Memoirs,* I, 518–30. Hull's description of a group of nations "proclaiming a broad, concrete basic program to restore international order" and well-being from which dictatorships might refrain at their own loss reads like a prescription for the subsequent European Recovery Program.

20. *Foreign Relations,* 1937, I, 665–70; William L. Langer and S. Everett Gleason, *The Challenge to Isolation: 1937–1940* (New York: Harper & Bros., 1952), pp. 19–23. The Welles memorandum

was dated Oct. 6, 1937, and is linked to the President's Chicago speech in the State Department serial file.

21. Hull, *Memoirs*, I, 546–49.

22. Langer and Gleason, *Challenge to Isolation*, pp. 23–32. Langer and Gleason do not suggest the context of these negotiations, such as the Lansbury initiative, the Van Zeeland report, or the American-British peace movement for a world economic conference, See Arnold A. Offner, *American Appeasement: United States Foreign Policy and Germany, 1933–1938* (Cambridge: Harvard University Press, 1969), pp. 217–25, for a careful analysis of the negotiations.

23. Eden, *Facing the Dictators*, chap. 12, especially pp. 625–27.

24. Shotwell to various friends, Aug., 1938, Shotwell papers, box 53; Eichelberger to Roosevelt, Aug. 31, 1938, FDR papers, PPF 3833.

25. Sayre, "Confidential Memorandum on Conference with President Roosevelt," Sept. 12, 1938; "Notes of J. N. Sayre on Interview . . . December 28, 1938"; and "Statement Read to President . . . December 28, 1938," Sayre papers.

26. Churchill, *The Second World War: The Gathering Storm* (Boston: Houghton Mifflin Co., 1948), p. 265.

27. *Washington Information Service,* I (June 1, 1938), 2, and see also the discussion of the Van Zeeland report, *ibid.* (Feb. 2, 1938), pp. 3–4.

28. *Report of the Committee of Experts*, pp. 23–24. The committee added that no revision should be undertaken without the cooperation of the majority of economically important countries, and that the United States should "not aid in the consolidation of military conquest by permitting capital to be supplied from this country for the development of territories taken by force . . . ."

29. New York *Times*, Mar. 24, 1938. See also *ibid.*, Mar. 25, 26, and 27; Libby diary, Mar. 23–26, 1938; and John Nevin Sayre, "Address of Welcome."

30. Eichelberger, memorandum "To the Special Committee [for reorganization] of the National Peace Conference," May 7, 1937, E.P.C. papers, N.P.C.

31. May 28–30, 1938, Page papers.

32. Al Hamilton to Roy Burt, Apr. 7, 1938, and minutes of the national action committee, Apr. 7 and 21–23, S.P.A. papers, Y.P.S.L. and national office files, 1938; Libby diary, Jan.–Apr., 1938.

33. Thomas to Ray Newton, Nov. 16, 1937 (copy), Allen papers; "Student Pacifists Organize," *Fellowship*, III (Dec., 1937), 8.

34. Press release, Apr. 28, 1938, S.P.A. papers, Y.P.S.L. files, 1938.

35. Charlotte Bentley, "World Youth Prepares for War," *Fellowship*, IV (Sept., 1938), 2.

36. Libby diary, Dec. 8–9, 1938, and Jan. 17, 1939.

37. Report to the national executive committee, Apr. 14–16, 1939, S.P.A. papers, national office files, 1939. The Youth Committee Against War was formed in May, 1938, to succeed the Youth Committee for the Oxford Pledge.

38. Libby, *Fighting for Peace*, p. 229.

39. Minutes of the F.O.R., Apr. 13, 1935, F.O.R. papers, box 2.

40. "Preparing to Meet a War Situation," memorandum in the minutes of the F.O.R., *ibid.*

41. "Pacifist Preparedness," *Fellowship*, III (Feb., 1937), 8.

42. Minutes of the Pendle Hill conference on the "Community Organization of Pacifists," Jan. 22–23, 1937, F.O.R. papers, box 22. About thirty representatives of the F.O.R., W.I.L.P.F., Friends, W.R.L., and E.P.C. were present.

43. "Pacifist Preparedness," *Fellowship*, III, 5.

44. *Ibid.*, p. 7.

45. *Ibid.*, p. 6.

46. *Christian Pacifist Conferences* (n.p., n.d. [1939–40]); minutes of the F.O.R., Apr. 10–12, and Sept. 22, 1939, F.O.R. papers, box 2. Minutes of the F.O.R., May 13, June 10 and 23, 1941, F.O.R. papers, box 2.

47. In denominations where there was no body of pacifists affiliated with the F.O.R., other provisions were made for conscientious objectors. Congregationalists enlisted pacifists through their Council for Social Action, for instance. In 1935 the Presbyterian Department of Social Education circulated a pledge not to support the nation in any foreign wars. Four years later there were at least twelve teams of pacifist Presbyterian students. The Methodist Peace Fellowship, led by its general secretary, Charles Boss, and aided by the National Council of Methodist Youth, the Epworth League, and Wesley Foundations, reported that it had enlisted "several thousand" pacifists and organized many teams. Several Protestant churches petitioned the government to respect the rights of their C.O.'s. At least seventeen of them designated church officials to furnish information about the law and to register the objectors among their numbers. For a survey of denominational positions see French, *We Won't Murder: Being the Story of Men Who Followed Their Conscientious Scruples and Helped Give Life to Democracy*, pp. 135–52.

48. "Affirmation of Christian Pacifist Faith," *Fellowship*, V (Mar., 1939), 6.

49. Muste, *The Fellowship of Reconciliation* (New York: Fellowship of Reconciliation, n.d. [*ca.* 1945]), Muste papers, box 2.

50. Muste, "Will the Pacifist Issue Split the Church?" (typewritten summary of a sermon given at the Presbyterian Labor Temple, Jan. 22, 1939); Muste, "Unity in Crisis" (typewritten summary of a sermon given at the First Presbyterian Church of Brooklyn, July 27, 1941), Muste papers, box 1.

51. Johnson, *The Social Gospel Re-examined* (New York: Harper & Bros., 1940), p. 202.

52. *A Call to Our Fellow Christians* (New York: Department of International Justice and Goodwill, Federal Council of Churches of Christ in America, 1939).

53. "A Plan of War-Time Procedure," *Fellowship*, II (Apr., 1936), 7. The members of the Brethren committee were Rufus D. Bowman, chairman, Ross D. Murphy, secretary, and Dan West.

54. "Pacifists Visit President," *Fellowship*, III (Mar., 1937), 14.

55. Minutes of the Peace Section, Dec. 27, 1939, A.F.S.C. Archives, Peace Section. The message given to President Roosevelt Jan. 10, 1940, is quoted in full in Sibley and Jacob, *Conscription of Conscience*, pp. 83–84.

56. Paul Comly French, *We Won't Murder*, pp. 117. According to French, this wording was created in 1926 by a Joint Army and Navy Selective Service Committee (pp. 112–16).

57. Sibley and Jacob, *Conscription of Conscience*, p. 47. Regarding the British act, see pp. 2–7. See also p. 141; and A. J. Muste to Hon. James Wadsworth, Aug. 16, 1940, Muste papers.

58. SECTION 5(g) of the act of 1940 pertains to conscientious objection, and is printed in full in Sibley and Jacob, *Conscription of Conscience*, p. 487.

59. *Ibid.*, 68–69. Officers of the Selective Service differed in their interpretation of the religious provision. The first director, Clarence A. Dykstra, stated that "any and all influences which have contributed to the consistent endeavor to live the good life may be classed as 'religious training.' Belief signifies sincere conviction. Religious belief signifies sincere conviction as to the supreme worth of that to which one gives his supreme allegiance." Colonel Hershey, who succeeded Dykstra, issued his own definition of religious training and belief as that "which contemplates recognition of some sources of all existence, which, what-

ever the type of conception, is Divine because it is the source of all things." Some court decisions apparently contradicted Hershey's interpretation, but they did not change the official position. In 1965 the Supreme Court defined religious belief in a broadly ethical sense similar to that of Dykstra, in United States v. Seeger, 380 U.S. 163 (1965).

60. *Conscription of Conscience.*

61. Luke E. Ebersole, *Church Lobbying in the Nation's Capital* (New York: Macmillan Co., 1951), p. 63.

62. Sibley and Jacob, *Conscription of Conscience,* p. 117. The government opened projects of its own beginning on July 1, 1943, in order to satisfy men who objected to religious-sponsored camps. These men were not paid for their work, however, as the original proposal had suggested. For the story of the government camps see pp. 112–17, 242–56.

63. Minutes of the F.O.R., Dec. 23, 1940, F.O.R. papers, box 2.

64. Minutes of the F.O.R., Oct. 22, 1940, *ibid.*

65. Evan Thomas to A. J. Muste, Nov. 5, 1940, Muste papers.

66. Gregg to A. J. Muste, Aug. 18, 1940, *ibid.*

67. "C.P.S.C.," *Fellowship,* VII (Aug., 1941), 144.

68. Sibley and Jacob, *Conscription of Conscience,* p. 111.

69. Olmsted, "The International Executive Meeting of the W.I.L.," *Fellowship,* IV (Nov., 1938), p. 8.

70. Sayre, "Some I Can Save," *ibid.,* p. 4.

CHAPTER XII

1. Sign carried during picketing of a William Allen White address urging more aid to Britain, reported in the *Anti-War News Service* (of the Keep America Out of War Congress), Nov. 22, 1940. Socialist Party of America (S.P.A.) papers, Duke University.

2. Niebuhr, "Leaves from the Notebook of a War-bound American," *Christian Century,* LVI (Oct. 25, 1939), 1298–99.

3. *Christianity and Power Politics* (New York: Charles Scribner's Sons, 1940), p. 33.

4. "If America Is Drawn into the War," *Christian Century,* LVII (Dec. 18, 1940), 1578.

5. Lavine and Wechsler, *War Propaganda and United States Foreign Policy* (New Haven: Yale University Press, 1940), 91; "A Christian Choice of Evils," *Christian Century,* LVIII (Jan. 1, 1941), 13.

6. Eddy to Page, Oct. 31, 1939, Page papers; "A Tragic Dilemma," *Christian Century,* LVII (Mar. 27, 1940), 406–407. Magnes was president of Hebrew University, Jerusalem.

7. Roosevelt to Libby, Sept. 12, 1939, FDR papers, OF 1561, PPF 87. The speeches to which Libby and others objected were made to the V.F.W. in Boston on Aug. 28, 1939, by Louis Johnson, assistant secretary of war, and Hugh Wilson, former ambassador to Germany. The President's letter was drafted by the Secretary of State in response to a request of Aug. 31.

8. Libby diary, Sept. 1–Nov. 3, 1939; N.C.P.W. papers, office files for 1939; Divine, *Illusion of Neutrality,* pp. 298–300.

9. "National Peace Conference, September, 1939–September, 1940," report of the executive secretary, Arthur D. Reeve, Jr. (Walter Van Kirk resigned in 1940 to take up more active duties with the Federal Council of Churches), Sayre papers.

10. Minutes of the F.O.R., Sept. 12, 1939, F.O.R. papers, box 2; "War in Europe," *Fellowship,* V (Oct., 1939), 4.

11. Hull, *Memoirs,* I, 710–12; *Foreign Relations,* 1939.

12. "War in Europe," *Fellowship,* V (Oct., 1939), 4.

13. John Nevin Sayre, first draft (not used) of statement to Cordell Hull with National Peace Conference delegation, Jan. 20, 1940, Sayre papers.

14. Sayre to Hull, Feb. 6, 1940 (but see also his letters of Nov. 28 and Dec. 7, 1939); Hull to Sayre, personally acknowledging the letter, Feb. 12, 1940, Sayre papers. Sayre wrote repeatedly to Roosevelt along these lines from his various roles as leader in the N.P.C., F.O.R., and K.A.O.W.C. Catchpool, an English Quaker, had been imprisoned for three years as a conscientious objector in World War I. He and his wife engaged in relief work in Germany where they remained until 1936.

15. Allen to Norman Thomas, collect night letter from England, n.d. [spring, 1940], and general correspondence, Allen letters. Allen mentioned especially Gunnar Anderssen speaking for President August Lindberg of the Swedish Federation of Labor, and also important labor leaders in Belgium.

16. Hull, *Memoirs,* II, 1626–27; Robert Divine. *Second Chance; The Triumph of Internationalism in America During World War II,* pp. 31–34.

17. Hull, *Memoirs,* II, 1628; and see I, 737–40, II, 1625–28.

18. Langer and Gleason, *The Challenge to Isolation: The World Crisis of 1937–1940 and American Foreign Policy* (New York: Harper & Bros., 1952), p. 354.

19. Arthur D. Reeve, Jr., "Conference with Secretary Hull—Na-

tional Peace Conference Delegation, January 30, 1940," typewritten recollections, Sayre papers. The delegation included, besides Sayre and Reeve, Florence B. Boeckel, J. E. Sproul, and Richard Wood.

20. Quoted in Robert Divine, *Second Chance; The Triumph of Internationalism in America During World War II*, p. 33.

21. Thomas, "Mediation, the War and the Administration," statement for the national executive committee of the Socialist Party, Feb. 10–12, 1940, s.p.a. papers, office files, 1940.

22. Minutes of the national action committee of Youth Against War Committee, Mar. 14, 1940, in s.p.a. papers, Youth Committee Against War files.

23. Mark Lincoln Chadwin, *The Hawks of World War II* (Chapel Hill: University of North Carolina Press, 1968). Among those whom Chadwin cites as being most influential in the Group were: Francis P. Miller, organization director for the Council on Foreign Relations; Henry P. Van Dusen, close friend of Reinhold Niebuhr at Union Theological Seminary; and Lewis W. Douglas, head of the Mutual Life Insurance Company and member of the executive committee of the William Allen White committee.

24. Arthur G. McDowell, "Revise 'Defense' Policy," June, 1940, s.p.a. papers, War, Peace, and Totalitarianism file, box A; "Resolution on War," Socialist Party national convention, Apr. 6–8, 1940, s.p.a. papers, national office files, 1940.

25. Minutes of the national executive committee, especially June 17, Aug. 14, and Sept. 11, 1940, s.p.a. papers, national office files, 1940.

26. "The Yanks Are Not Coming," a song printed in *Bulletin No. 1* (Feb., 1940) of The Yanks Are Not Coming Committee. The song was written by Mike Quin, columnist for *People's World,* a West Coast Communist paper. The pamphlet of the same name was issued in an edition of 200,000 copies, and was followed by stickers, buttons, petitions, and committees organized out of the "KAOW Committee" of District No. 2 of the Maritime Federation of the Pacific. The k.a.o.w.c. expressly rejected this unauthorized use of its name by an organization which it believed to be Communist controlled. Minutes of the k.a.o.w.c., Jan. 4, 1940; s.p.a. papers, War, Peace, and Totalitarianism files.

27. Minutes of the k.a.o.w.c., Feb. 5, 1940.

28. *Ibid.*, Jan. 4, 1940.

29. Wayne Cole, *America First; The Battle Against Intervention, 1940–1941* (Madison: University of Wisconsin Press, 1953), pp. 15–16.

30. Thomas to Louis Gottesman, Nov. 26, 1941, Thomas papers, box 40.

31. *Ibid.*

32. Senate Concurrent Resolution 7 was introduced on Mar. 27 by Senators Nye, Wheeler, Capper, La Follette, Bennett C. Clark, and Hendrik Shipstead. Available A.F.C. funds were reported to the K.A.O.W.C. on Mar. 31, although according to Wayne Cole the A.F.C. executive committee did not commit itself to the campaign until June 23. Minutes of the K.A.O.W.C., Mar. 31, 1941; *America First*, pp. 57–58.

33. Minutes of the K.A.O.W.C., Feb. 5, 1940, and Mar. 3, 1941.

34. Minutes of the F.O.R., Jan. 28, 1941, F.O.R. papers, box 2. The minutes of Feb. 11 and Mar. 11, 1941, and A. J. Muste to Alice Dodge, Jan. 31, 1941, Norman Thomas papers, box 30, suggest that the F.O.R. also was concerned about the tendency of the K.A.O.W.C. to become a competing membership organization.

35. Minutes of the K.A.O.W.C., Aug. 5, 1941. Libby was still co-operating fully, of course, although he did not attend committee meetings often.

36. Minutes of the K.A.O.W.C., Mar. 3, 1941.

37. Ickes to "Missy," May 13, 1941, FDR papers, PSF Interior: Ickes, 1940–45. Aviator and popular idol, Charles A. Lindbergh campaigned aggressively for the America First Committee.

38. Résumé of correspondence concerning a letter from Edward K. Carr, Dec. 19, 1940, FDR papers, OF 394, box 4.

39. Chadwin, *Hawks of World War II*, chap. 7.

40. Meyer, *The Protestant Search for Political Realism*, pp. 361, 387–88; but see the whole of chap. 18 for a careful analysis of Niebuhr's theological development in relation to the war question.

41. "Ministers Covenant," *Fellowship*, VII (July, 1941), 121, and press releases and bulletins of the Ministers No War Committee and related groups, Jan. 28, June 16, and Oct. 13, 1941, Sayre papers.

42. Cole, *America First*, p. 154.

43. Minutes of the K.A.O.W.C., Sept. 30, 1941.

44. Thomas to Wheeler, Nov. 21, 1941, Thomas papers, box 40.

45. Minutes of the K.A.O.W.C. and supplement, Dec. 16, 1941.

46. Thomas to Devere Allen, Dec. 11, 1941, Thomas papers, box 40.

47. *Our Position in Wartime* (New York: War Resisters League, Dec. 19, 1941), p. 2.

48. Emily Balch to Clara Ragaz, June 18, 1942, quoted in Mercedes M. Randall, *Emily Greene Balch,* p. 349.

49. Randall, p. 356. Mrs. Randall's sensitive portrayal of Emily Balch's anguish invites comparison with Jane Addams's recollections in *Peace and Bread.*

50. "The Course Before Us: Statement of F.O.R. Executive Committee, December 10, 1941," *Fellowship,* VIII (Jan., 1942), 2.

51. "An Important Announcement for the W.I.L.P.F. and F.O.R.," *Fellowship,* IV (Dec., 1938), 2; A. J. Muste, "The Lakeside Conference and After," *ibid.,* VII (Oct., 1941), 172; "Heard at the National Conference," *ibid.,* VII (Oct., 1942), 172; "Statistics" (1954), F.O.R. papers, box 4; "The Fellowship of Reconciliation," *Fellowship,* IV (Feb., 1938), 16; "Financial Report of 1941," *ibid.,* VII (Feb., 1942), 31; minutes of the F.O.R., Jan. 8, 1946, and "Membership Statistics" (1954), F.O.R. papers, boxes 3 and 4; Lawrence Wittner, *Rebels Against War,* p. 54. Active membership was variously defined, mainly as dues-paying members as opposed to persons receiving *Fellowship* magazine.

Conclusion

1. John Ciardi, "The Size of Song," *Person to Person* (New Brunswick: Rutgers University Press, 1964), p. 3.

2. Bennett, *When Christians Make Political Decisions* (New York: Association Press, 1964), p. 76; interview with John Bennett, at Union Theological Seminary, July 23, 1964.

3. Page to "Dear Friend," Jan. 1, 1942, Page papers.

4. Thomas, "Ends and Means," *Fellowship,* VIII (Sept., 1942), 151.

5. Muste to Nevin Sayre, Sept. 17, 1936, Sayre papers.

6. For comparison see Alfred Hassler, "The Fellowship's Statement of Purpose, 1930–1965," *Fellowship,* XXXI (Sept., 1965), 18–19.

7. Muste, *Non-Violence in an Aggressive World,* p. 4.

8. *Ibid.,* pp. 4–5.

9. Thomas, "Pacifism and Absolutism," *Fellowship,* VII (Apr., 1941), 52.

10. *Our Position in Wartime.*

11. Thomas, "Ends and Means," *Fellowship,* VIII (Sept., 1942), 150. For expressions of Muste's view see especially *Non-Violence in an Aggressive World,* and *The World Task of Pacifism* (Wallingford, Pa.: Pendle Hill Pamphlets, 1941).

12. Shridharani, *War Without Violence,* p. 270.

13. *Ibid.,* pp. 270–71.

14. *Ibid.,* p. 94.

15. Holmes, *Out of Darkness* (New York: Harper & Bros., 1942).

16. Muste, *Non-Violence in an Aggressive World,* pp. 74–75.

17. John H. Hallowell, *Main Currents in Modern Political Thought* (New York: Henry Holt & Co., 1950), p. 110.

18. Bondurant, *Conquest of Violence,* pp. 223–24.

19. Muste, "Pacifism Enters a New Phase,' *Fellowship,* XXVI (July 1, 1960), 21–25, 34.

20. Jackson Mac Low, tribute in "A. J. Muste," special supplement of WIN magazine (n.d. [Feb., 1967]).

21. Muste, "Pacifism Enters a New Phase," p. 25.

Acknowledgments

In the course of this study I have been helped by more people than I can mention here. I am indebted to the Danforth Foundation, the Clement and Grace Biddle Foundation, and the Board of College Education and Church Vocations of the Lutheran Church in America for various grants which made possible much of the research and revision. Wittenberg University and the Mershon Center for Education in National Security jointly made available time and assistance for the final writing. My research owes much to the conscientious help of librarians at the Joint University Libraries (Nashville), Wittenberg University, Ohio State University, Duke University, Southern California School of Theology, the F.D.R. Library at Hyde Park, the New York Public Library, and especially friends at the Swarthmore College Peace Collection.

Mrs. Alma Page encouraged me to open and organize the papers of her husband, Kirby Page, and shared, too, something of her life. Mrs. Marie H. Allen helped me to organize the papers of her husband, Devere Allen, and interpreted the collection to me. Mr. John Nevin Sayre has been a generous critic, friend, and source of encouragement. My wife and I treasure the friendships this work has brought, of which these are special examples.

For their care in reading various parts and versions of the manuscript I wish to thank Dr. Henry Lee Swint and Dr. Lyman Burbank of Vanderbilt University, Mr. John Nevin Sayre of the Fellowship of Reconciliation, Dr. Merle Curti of the University of Wisconsin, Dr. Kenneth Boulding of the University of Colorado, Dr. Martin Dubin of Illinois Northern University, Mr. Harold Gray, a conscientious objector during World War I, and Jean Kuenn of the Ohio State University Press. Whatever errors remain are, of course, my own responsibility.

I should acknowledge two published articles which are based on portions of this book. "Pacifists and Their Publics: the Politics of a

437

Peace Movement," *Midwest Journal of Political Science*, XIII (May, 1969), 298–312, drew heavily upon chapter four, and "World War I and the Liberal Pacifist in the United States," *American Historical Review*, LVI (Dec., 1970), 1920–37, extended the analysis in the first two chapters. I am grateful to the editors of these journals and also to those of presses which by their declinations encouraged me to rethink and rewrite all aspects of this story.

The line drawings appearing on the half-title page, on the back of the title page for Parts 3 and 4, and as the tailpiece are used through the courtesy of Iowa State University Press and are from its 1951 publication *Pulitzer Prize Cartoons: The Men and Their Masterpieces*, by Dick Spencer III. The drawing appearing on the reverse of the title page for Part 1 is an adaptation of the *Harper's Weekly* cover for September 18, 1915; and that used on the reverse of the title page for Part 2 is taken from *No-Foreign-War Crusade* (Philadelphia: Emergency Peace Campaign, 1937), p. 22.

It seems appropriate, too, to acknowledge the influence of my parents and five teachers especially: Dr. Allen T. Price of Oak Park High School (Illinois) and Wittenberg University, Dr. F. Garvin Davenport and Dr. Samuel M. Thompson of Monmouth College (Illinois), Dr. Henry Lee Swint of Vanderbilt University, and my colleague, Dr. Robert G. Hartje of Wittenberg. My greatest debt is to my wife, Mary, who participated in many stages of this study and whose unfailing love has endured my preoccupation, frustration, and occasional periods of separation.

Index

Addams, Jane, 11, 16–18, 22–23, 36, 38–39, 54, 62, 74, 81, 93, 95, 203
Allen, Devere, 36, 107, 146, 162, 191, 212, 214, 257–59, 332, 335–36; biographical facts, 138–41; international thought, 227, 238–40, 247–48, 316; on religious basis of pacifism, 7, 181–82, 185, 331; Socialist Party, role in, 43, 173, 195, 199–202, 207, 408 n. 26; Spanish Civil War, view of, 241–45; mentioned, 31, 40, 55, 137, 207, 211, 267, 279
America First Committee, 321–22, 325
American Boycott Association, 226
American Civil Liberties Union, 187, 326. *See also* National Civil Liberties Bureau
American Committee for the Struggle Against War, 257. *See also* American League Against War and Fascism
American Friends Service Committee, 29–30, 97, 110, 114, 136–38, 162 n, 267, 281, 322, 326; provisions for conscientious objectors, 50–51, 55, 70, 72, 305–309; relief work, 51–54, 253; social work, 177–78 n, 215
American League Against War and Fascism, 107, 257–61, 296
American League for Peace and Democracy, 296. *See also* American League Against War and Fascism
American Neutral Conference Committee, 25–26
American Peace Society, 9–10
American School Citizenship League (formerly American School Peace League), 10, 96
American Union Against Militarism, 34, 56, 61, 146, 150, 396 n. 11; founding in antipreparedness campaign,

American Union (*cont.*)
21–24; Mexican policy, 24; response to threat of intervention, 25–27; wartime role, division over, 28–29. *See also* National Civil Liberties Bureau
American Union for a Democratic Peace, 29
Angell, Norman, 164, 171
Antipreparedness campaigns. *See* American Union Against Militarism, founding; arms limitation; munitions inquiry
Anti-Preparedness Committee, 22–23, 373 n. 15. *See also* American Union Against Militarism
Arms limitation, 21–24, 146–51, 159–64, 295, 297
Atkinson, Henry A., 125, 284 n

Babbitt, James, 51
Bainton, Roland H., 51, 52 n
Baker, Newton, 34, 58, 68, 70–72, 146, 169, 262–67, 377 n. 49, 420 n. 23
Balch, Emily Greene, 18, 26–27, 34, 94–95, 227, 287, 326–27
Baldwin, Roger N., 177, 186, 193, 203, 331–32; American Union Against Militarism, 26–27, 29, 33, 380 n. 37; conscientious objection, views on, 77–79, 83; National Civil Liberties Bureau, 56–57
Barbusse, Henri, 257
Barnes, Harry Elmer, 122–23
Barnes, Rosewell, 153, 267 n
Bartlett, Percy, 290 n, 316
Beaver, Gilbert A., 20
Benét, Stephen Vincent (quoted), 73, 121
Benezet, Anthony, 7–8
Bennett, John C. (quoted), 330

439

441

445

For Peace and Justice was set on the Linotype in ten point Times Roman with two points of spacing between the lines. The book was designed by Jim Billingsley, composed and printed by Heritage Printers, Inc., Charlotte, North Carolina, and bound by the Nicholstone Book Bindery, Inc., Nashville, Tennessee. The paper on which the book is printed is designed for an effective life of at least three hundred years.

THE UNIVERSITY OF TENNESSEE PRESS